Small Group
Communication

Small Group Communication
Theory and Practice
Third Edition

Ernest G. Bormann
University of Minnesota

1817

Harper & Row, Publishers, New York

Grand Rapids, Philadelphia, St. Louis, San Francisco,
London, Singapore, Sydney, Tokyo

Sponsoring Editor: Barbara Cinquegrani
Project Editor: Susan Goldfarb
Art Direction: Heather Ziegler
Text Design Adaptation: Heather Ziegler
Cover Coordinator: Mary Archondes
Cover Design: Mary Archondes/Wanda Lubelska
Cover Illustration: Thomas Thorspecken
Production: Willie Lane

Small Group Communication: Theory and Practice, *Third Edition*
Originally published as *Discussion and Group Methods: Theory and Practice.*

Copyright © 1990 by Harper & Row, Publishers, Inc.

Library of Congress Cataloging-in-Publication Data

Bormann, Ernest G.
    Small group communication : theory and practice / Ernest G.
Bormann. — 3rd ed.
        p. cm.
    Rev. ed. of: Discussion and group methods. 2nd ed. 1975.
    Includes bibliographies and indexes.
    ISBN 0-06-040869-3
    1. Communication in small goups. 2. Small groups. I. Bormann,
Ernest G. Discussion and group methods. II. Title.
HM133.B58   1990   89-1976
302.3′4 — dc19   CIP

89 90 91 92 9 8 7 6 5 4 3 2 1

Contents

Preface

The first course in small group communication has assumed a central place in the study of communication. *Small Group Communication*, Third Edition, was written to meet the needs of undergraduate students in this first course. It reflects the growing new vitality and substance of the subject.

The philosophy underlying this book gives equal weight to solid content and early and continued practice in participating in group meetings. A beginning student might think of group discussion as a simple matter, but attempts to work with groups under guidance soon reveal the complexities of group communication. This book is designed to be used in conjunction with a series of exercises and projects in small group communication.

Small Group Communication presents both theory and practice on the assumption that good theories are practical. A major goal of the book is to provide students with the necessary education about small group communication to enable them to work with groups, primarily as participants. To that end, practical applications are stressed. However, sound explanations are not slighted, because another goal of the book is to satisfy the native curiosity of students who wish to know more about the processes that underlie small group communication.

This edition of *Small Group Communication* benefits from the insights, criticisms, and suggestions of many instructors who have used the text in small group communication classes in a variety of different institutional settings. In making this revision, I have tried to meet their needs and wishes. The book also benefits from research developed in the years since the previous edition was published. The text reflects over 30 years of reading and synthesizing research results in social psychology, industrial and educational psychology, psychiatry, and sociology. It draws upon the time-tested best of small group research in these fields. However, the book relies most heavily on the increasingly valuable research in speech communication. As with the two previous editions, much of the new material in this edition is based on the program of research in small group communication at the University of Minnesota. This book thus provides the most comprehensive report available on this entire program of research.

The material in this edition has been reorganized. The text now begins with the basic principles of group discussion and progresses logically into an examination of the dynamics of small group communication. This theoretical grounding makes the book equally adaptable in courses that emphasize problem solving and decision making, courses that emphasize group processes, and courses that present a balanced treatment of both. A new Chapter 5 deals with fantasy sharing and group acculturation. The material in Chapter 6, "The Social Climate of Groups," has been broadened to include a comprehensive treatment of group conflict. The portion of the book dealing with the task dimension has been expanded to include new material on creativity in small group work, with an emphasis on the relationship of sharing fantasies to creativity; it incorporates new developments in research on decision-making patterns and practices. The chapter on leadership has been expanded to include recent research relating to women and leadership.

For the material in this book I am indebted to the research of many scholars in many different disciplines, as the references listed at the end of each chapter indicate. My colleagues at the University of Minnesota have been particularly supportive of my efforts to teach and do research in the area, and I am grateful for the comments and suggestions of those who reviewed the manuscript: Suzanne Hagen, University of Wisconsin; Joel Litvin, Bridgewater State College; Larry Nadler, Miami University; Miriam McMullen Pastrick, St. John's University; and Mary Ann Renz, University of Northern Iowa. Most especially I want to thank my many students over the years in the sequence of courses in small group communication at Minnesota.

ERNEST G. BORMANN

Small Group
Communication

Chapter
1

The Nature and Development of Group Discussion and Small Group Communication

*I*n a highly organized urban society such as ours, everyone works in groups for at least several hours each day. In addition to being part of a family group and a group at work, many of us sit in on committee meetings, participate in discussion groups, or attend business conferences. We often watch televised discussions or listen to radio programs in which important public affairs topics are discussed. We may take part in conferences offering small group meetings to increase our understanding, knowledge, and skills. The field of study relating to how to communicate in such groups is called small group communication.

SMALL GROUP COMMUNICATION

The term *small group communication* refers to the theory and practice relating to one or more meetings of a small group of people who communicate face-to-face in order to fulfill common purposes and achieve group goals. This book is designed to provide you with an understanding of how such groups work and with practical guides to help you in participating effectively in group meetings.

The Nature of Small Groups   *at least 3 people*

Extensive studies by social scientists indicate that the small group is an identifiable social entity. The introduction of a third person into a social field changes the nature of the communication. A small group is, therefore, composed of at least three people. Authorities do differ about specifying a number as the upper limit of a small group. Nonetheless, the communication networks and interpersonal relationships that develop when a few people meet change markedly when the size of the group is increased. The qualitative changes in group dynamics that result from increasing membership serve to identify the small group.

When the size becomes so unwieldy that a group begins to change character, it is no longer small. One important way that groups change with size is in their patterns of communication. (Patterns in small group communication are sometimes referred to as *communication networks*.) In groups of 5 or fewer, all participants generally speak to one another. Even those who speak very little talk to all the others. In groups of 7 or more, the talk centralizes more and more around a few people, and group interaction falls off. The quiet members often cease to talk to any but the top people in the group.

Forston's study of the deliberations of 12-person juries found that 5 to 7 members often hold the discussion while the others watch and listen. In permanent work groups larger than 11, people tend to form smaller groups (known as *cliques*) within the larger one. Often these cliques are formalized in terms of an executive committee or subcommittees. When groups grow still larger, they find it difficult to conduct business in a free and easy way. In larger groups, some standard procedure such as that provided by parliamentary rules is often necessary in order to ensure orderly turn taking and proper discussion of questions.

The optimum size for a small decision-making group is 5 or 7 people. A group of 10 or more is often unwieldy. Groups with fewer than 5 members complain that they are too small, their viewpoints too narrow, and their resources too limited. Groups composed of an even number of people tend to have more trouble coming to agreement and establishing roles and status, and they tend to be less efficient than groups containing 5 or 7 people.

An aggregation does not become a small group until the people have communicated and formed an impression of one another. When the group members go to work and get to know one another, they divide up, coordinate, and structure their working procedures. They also develop liking and status relationships which link them to one another. They develop a sense of group identity, and group membership may become part of their personal self-image. They come to have a sense of group cohesiveness and history. They develop a group culture. These communicative features characterize small groups and distinguish them from aggregations and large groups.

The Nature of Communication in Small Groups

A group does its work and maintains social relationships by means of verbal and nonverbal *communication*. In ordinary language, the word *communication* is often used interchangeably with words like *discussion* or *conversation* to refer to talk about almost anything — the weather, foreign policy in the Middle East, student morals, football, sex, religion. However, in the context of small group communication it refers to something more specific: serious and systematic talk about a clearly specified topic. People engaged in group meetings have a common purpose and are striving for common goals. They focus on making decisions and solving problems. The primary purpose of much of the talk in a meeting is to establish the group's task and the relationships among the members. Communication in the small group setting requires an understanding of how to communicate in general and of the dynamics of the small group in particular. To that end, it is important to understand the meaning and use of the theories relating to small group communication.

DEFINITIONS OF THEORY IN COMMUNICATION

People often use the term *theory* rather loosely. Sometimes students complain that a textbook is too theoretical and dull. They often think of theory in a negative way as consisting of any abstract discourse or comment removed from practice, as in the expression "That is all well and good in theory but it would never work in practice." In this sense, a theory refers to meaningless abstractions that do not have a practical payoff, to pointless, dull, and jargon-filled analyses.

Theory will be defined quite differently in this book. According to legend, Kurt Lewin, a leader in the social scientific study of groups, maintained that nothing is as practical as a good theory. Although theoretical explanations are careful and precise, they are not impractical. You may have to work a bit harder to read about and understand theories than to scan jazzed-up, entertaining lists of recipes designed to provide easy answers to group problems. But in the long run the effort to understand good theories will pay off. Recipes seldom work, whereas good theories form the basis for an education that enables students to make wise and practical decisions about small group communication.

People also use the term *theory* to indicate a hunch or untested idea or opinion, as in the expression "I have a theory that groups are more reliably creative than individuals." Such a comment tends to confuse tested ideas with untested ones. In this book, the term *hypothesis* will be used for hunches and untested ideas that serve for further study and research. The term *theory* will be reserved for explanations that have been verified by research or practices that have been tested by experience.

Scholars in the social sciences and humanities often use the term *theory* to mean two distinctly different things. The first kind of theory, *theory$_1$*, consists of a collection of rules and principles tested by experience in group work that guides practice. Theory$_1$ stresses prescriptions about what a good group meeting is like (an ideal model). Theory$_1$ also contains how-to-do-it advice on communicating effectively at meetings.

Meetings resemble one another (have a recurring form) because the participants understand theory$_1$ and work together to create a good meeting patterned after the ideal model. Theory$_1$ is also the source of practical advice in the form of rules of thumb that experienced people have found helpful in dealing with nut-and-bolts problems that crop up when working with groups. Theory$_1$ also contains a justification for the communication to which it relates (philosophical rationale). Finally, theory$_1$ provides the understanding needed to evaluate communication.

Scholars also use the term in a second way: *Theory$_2$* refers to social scientific statements that explain in general how the world works. To qualify as part of theory$_2$, such statements have to be supported by careful and systematic research. Hypotheses or hunches are important for research, but until they are tested and supported they cannot be part of theory$_2$. Theory$_1$ tells you how to work productively in a group and prescribes ways to communicate successfully. Theory$_2$ tells you how groups develop and why the dynamics of the group are as they are.

Of course, using the word *theory* in so many different ways may cause confusion and misunderstandings in any discussion of small group communication. Professionals in small group communication have been particularly plagued by using the term to mean both theory$_1$ and theory$_2$. Certainly students can be easily confused when they are asked to read research reports and textbooks which contain both kinds of theories. Practical advice on how to participate in groups is part of theory$_1$. Important research studies in the field are usually designed to further the development of theory$_2$. It is important to understand the differences among the four ways that theory is used in general conversation as well as in technical explanations. But most important to your becoming a better communicator in small group situations is an understanding of the differences between theory$_1$ and theory$_2$.

A good way to sort out the differences and avoid confusion is to distinguish between theory$_1$ as a special communication theory and theory$_2$ as a general communication theory. *Special theories* are specific to a certain time and culture and function. They contain information about how to do it. These are the theories in textbooks and handbooks that explain the nuts and bolts of selecting people for committees and groups, planning, conducting, and participating in meetings, and utilizing the results of decisions. Special theories explain how to make good decisions, how to solve problems, how to create cohesive groups, and how to achieve leadership.

Special theories are developed out of practice and tested by their usefulness. They change with changing conditions over time, as well as from cultural group to cultural group. People may choose to follow or to break the rules and norms of a given special theory. However, unless they do choose to follow the rules and norms and try to have a good meeting according to the ideal form, the communication event will not take place.

Small group communication is, therefore, a joint social venture that requires the willing cooperation of the participants in trying to work together to create a group meeting along the lines prescribed by the special theory.

Special theories relate only to the communication practices of a community restricted in time and culture. *General theories* of communication, on the other hand, are analogous to the theories of the natural sciences that account for broad classes of events. General theories apply to events in the past and the present as well as to what might happen in the future. They cut across the different special theories that govern group meetings in different times and cultures. An example of a statement that is part of a general theory is the well-supported generalization that when groups of people work and communicate together they begin to act and speak in similar ways. The technical term for such standard ways of doing things is a *norm*.

Norm emergence is part of a general theory that, like the law of gravity, applies to all groups. The difference between a generalization such as the law of gravity and the rules of special theories is the difference between having to accept something as being that way (necessity) and being able to do it or not (choice). It is pointless for people to say, "In this meeting we won't obey the law of gravity." They may try to get their members to fly by jumping unaided out of a second-story window, but the law of gravity will still cause them to fall to the earth.

Rules, however, are joint agreements that the participants may choose to follow or not. Thus, although the rules in a meeting may state that all members will take part and no member will dominate the discussion, some people may choose not to participate and others may choose to dominate the discussion. In short, rules can be broken: It is a question of mind over regulations. General laws *cannot* be broken: It is *not* a question of mind over matter. Caesar and his advisers, discussing whether they should cross the Rubicon in Roman times, felt norming pressures. Groups as different as Australian aborigines and North American city dwellers experience similar norming dynamics today, as would groups of interplanetary space travelers in the future.

General communication theories are tested against empirical data and are verified when observations of communication events confirm the theory's generalizations. The summaries that interpret and apply research findings in the remainder of this book are usually presented to support general theories. These summaries are based on examining and synthesizing thousands of research reports over the last 30 years. This research literature stresses studies conducted in speech communication but also includes studies in social psychology, sociology, psychology, education, and business management. The references at the end of each chapter include the most recent of these research reports bearing on the general theories discussed in the text.

SPECIAL THEORIES EXPLAINED

Joint ventures require that the participants act according to some agreed-upon model of how to work together. The people who take part in such ventures need to know the plan of action or the proper script to follow.

People enjoy joint ventures and willingly cooperate in creating and participating in them. Joint ventures include such cooperative activities as group game playing, musical performances, and dancing, as well as communicating. In order to create a joint venture, all participants must agree to play the game or the music, to dance, or to communicate according to the rules, conventions, and ideals of the special theory that applies.

Figure 1 depicts the major features of special theories. These consist of (1) a philosophical rationale, (2) an ideal model of the communication event, and (3) practical advice (rules of thumb) on how best to communicate in order to achieve the ideal model.

A *philosophical rationale* is a justification for communicating in the recommended way. It includes statements of the purpose, function, and correctness of the communication. An *ideal model* is a prescription of the recommended communication processes. The ideal group meeting may be depicted in graphic form or it may be illustrated by an ideal event or by a general verbal description of a good meeting. *Practical advice* consists of rules of thumb on how to communicate. These practical tips are the

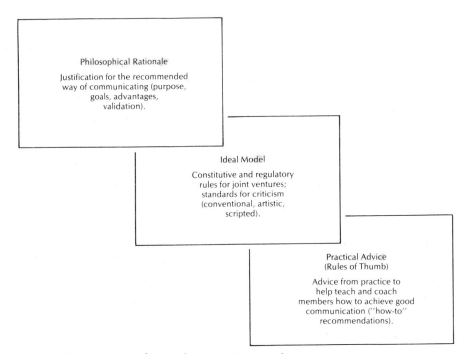

Figure 1 Components of special communication theories.

province of the teacher and coach, who often have individuals practice communicating and then evaluate their strengths and weaknesses. Following the evaluation, the coach or teacher may suggest another try at the basics under study and will give pointers on improvement. The rules of thumb discussed in this text are summarized as practical advice at the end of each chapter.

Small group meetings should be joint ventures in which all parties understand the special theory and choose to try to have a good meeting according to its recommendations. In a sense, people may say to one another, verbally or nonverbally, "Shall we communicate in a business meeting?" in much the same way that they might ask, "Shall we play a game of touch football?" or "Shall we dance a waltz?"

The dancers might decide to waltz or square dance; the game players might decide to play football or basketball; the communicators might decide to take part in a sensitivity group, a business meeting, or a creative meeting. If some of the players think the game is checkers while others think it is backgammon, chaos will result. If some members think that the meeting is called to make an important job-related decision and others think it is called for group therapy, confusion is likely to result.

Because they are joint ventures, small group meetings are conventional, artistic, and more or less staged. The conventional nature of joint ventures means that there is no necessity to follow the rules. The artistic component refers to the fact that some members will be more talented than others in working to create the ideal model. Their style will be pleasing and enjoyable to the group. A particular meeting may also exhibit an esthetic dimension if it approximates the ideal. Part of the critical judgment about a participant or a meeting, therefore, might be based on how pleasing and enjoyable the critic found the communication.

Finally, joint ventures are all staged to some degree. Often they require a special place for their performance, such as a dance studio, a chess club, or the boardroom of a company. Joint ventures may be so completely staged that they approach the scripted nature of a theater production. For example, the chair of a meeting may go quickly through an agenda, point by point, with members making only a few comments as they rubber-stamp conclusions that were reached in earlier meetings. At the other extreme, some joint ventures are so unstaged and unscripted that members improvise throughout, so that the outcome of the meeting cannot be anticipated.

An important component of any special communication theory is a description (model) of an ideal meeting. The model provides a pattern to be followed or an example to be emulated by the participants. The model implies or spells out the rules to be followed if a member wants to participate in the meeting. A hypothetical example of rules that could serve to create a small group communication form might include the following:

• To have the meeting, we need at least 4 people but no more than 13.

- Members must sit in a circle.
- One member, called the starter, begins each round by commenting on one of the previously selected "topics for the rounds" for one minute or less.
- After the starter completes a comment, members to the starter's left comment in turn until all have spoken, at which point the round is complete.
- A session consists of two halves, with a 15-minute break at halftime.
- Each half consists of 8 rounds.

The above are the *constitutive* (how-to-create) rules. When people put special communication theories into practice, they usually break some of the how-to-create meeting rules. The rule breaking may be a result of lack of skill or it may be a conscious choice made to gain personal or team advantage. When a given constitutive rule is broken often, people who participate in joint ventures may draft a second type of rule: a "can do" or "can't do" regulation designed to ensure that the constitutive rules are followed. The regulation may provide that the rule breaker is to be penalized in some fashion. Suppose that in the small group meetings created by the above rules some members talk for more than a minute when it is their turn. A regulatory rule might be drafted to the effect that an official timer will clock each member and anyone who speaks for more than a minute will forfeit his or her turn to speak in the next round.

Most people understand the special small group communication theories in our culture, so they can participate in meetings without being at a complete loss as to what is going on. Still, many are confused and unsure about some kinds of meetings and decide not to participate rather than do something embarrassing. This book provides the special communication theories useful for task-oriented (decision-making and problem-solving) groups. The reader who understands these theories will be able to participate effectively in small group meetings.

GENERAL SMALL GROUP COMMUNICATION THEORIES

In examining the general theories of small group communication, it is useful to distinguish between a viewpoint or set of assumptions about how groups work and the actual theories themselves. For example, a useful and common position toward group work is the systems viewpoint. Viewing groups as systems assumes that their communication is dynamic and interrelated, and that the sum of all the communication is somehow greater than any given comment. However, several students of small group communication might share a systems viewpoint but come up with different specific theories about the kinds of systems that characterize group communication.

The main general theories that are important to the special theory of small group communication are developed in the remainder of this book. Three formulations are illustrative.

The first general theory provides an account of cohesiveness. This *exchange theory* is general in the sense that the explanation of cohesiveness is asserted to hold for all groups within the scope of the theory. It is based on the construct of *a communicating human being*. The communicating human being is assumed to be similar to all humans everywhere; thus, the behavior of the constructed individual can be generalized. The theory is similar in structure to theories of economics that are based on the construct of *an economic human being*. If one assumes that the economic human being will buy cheap and sell high, a number of laws can be generalized on that basis. The law of supply and demand, for example, is deduced from the mass behavior of economic human beings who do the logical thing.

The communicating human being is one who communicates to gain rewards and avoid costs. If one assumes that the communicating human being will seek approval and reward, a number of principles relating to how groups can be rewarding and attractive to the members can be deduced.

Of course, exchange theories are helpful only insofar as the basic construct turns out to be enacted by large numbers of people. If people, in fact, buy high and sell low, then economic predictions will not be borne out. Indeed, sometimes people do pay more for things because of where they buy them or because of a label or other status symbol. The same holds true for an exchange theory of small group communication. If people communicate in ways which seek out the costs and shun the rewards as defined in the theory, then the theory will not hold.

A second general theory is *symbolic convergence*. It deals with how individuals in a collection communicate and share fantasies until they generate a unique culture and become an identifiable group. Symbolic convergence is analogous to theories in biology and botany that explain how certain species of plants and animals come into being, flourish, and are sustained or become extinct. Theories of this form are general in that they explain observable facts but do not allow for prediction (in contrast to certain theories in chemistry and physics).

A third general theory is that of *emergence*. The emergence theory accounts for the dynamic processes by which roles, leadership, and decisions emerge from group communication.

THE SPECIAL THEORY OF GROUP DISCUSSION

An early and popular form of communication in our culture is group discussion. In small group communication, as in art, there is an interdependent relationship among theory, practice, and criticism. Each special theory begins with practice. Some people start up novel joint ventures in small group communication, and because the practice is interesting, others desire to take part. In this way, the communication grows.

People who practice the new communication often talk about their experiences. They discuss what was good or bad about a given session. Practice soon brings the rudiments of a special theory which allows people to criticize meetings. Without the beginnings of a special theory, particularly the ideal model, there cannot be a common ground for criticism. With practice and criticism comes elaboration of the special theory. The special theory provides the information needed to coach newcomers so they can effectively take part in meetings. Thus, the special theory shapes practice and is the basis for criticism; in turn, it is shaped by criticism and practice.

The following explanation traces the beginnings of group discussion and sketches the development of the special theory. The mature theory is explained in terms of its philosophical rationale, and the ideal model, and the explanation concludes with a comment about rules of thumb.

Background for Group Discussion

Courses in group discussion are largely a development of the last 60 years. In the 1930s, faculty members in communication or speech communication (then called speech) departments offered highly popular courses in public speaking and debate, but they did not offer courses in group communication. However, societal forces were encouraging the practice of group meetings outside the college and university setting.

Adult education programs were using the discussion group as an educational tool as early as 1920. Church groups and YMCA groups met regularly to discuss religious questions. Agricultural groups discussed farming matters and public policy. The increasing use of discussion groups by proponents of the Progressive movement's proposals for educational reform was accompanied by the appearance of handbooks on how to conduct and participate in meetings. The practice began to spread and the special theory began to emerge. In 1928, for example, the Adult Education Association published Harrison Elliott's *The Process of Group Thinking,* one of the first books to spell out the new special theory.

An important technological development that influenced the teachers of public speaking and debate was the start of public radio broadcasts in the 1920s and 1930s. Radio was not only an important source of entertainment; it was also used for political and economic persuasion. Public affairs broadcasts became commonplace. As programmers grew to realize the intimate, informal qualities of radio, they sought to create an illusion of spontaneity and informal conversation in their shows. Soon some of the early public speeches and lectures were replaced by round-table discussions of public issues or question-and-answer panel programs. Network discussion programs such as the "Chicago Roundtable of the Air" and the "Northwestern Reviewing Stand" set the style for many programs on local stations.

Some teachers of speech studied the discussion format, read what they could find about the subject, held informal talks among themselves about what was going on, and tried to gain expertise in the emerging way of communicating in groups. As discussion groups proliferated in the nonacademic world, teachers of public speaking and debate were often asked to give talks, offer workshops, or write articles on the subject.

Teachers of speech were used to teaching students to speak and debate before audiences; they thought of discussion as a way to make decisions in a democracy. Many referred to the new form of communication as *public discussion*. Some began to introduce a unit on discussion in their courses in public speaking and debate. Soon they were writing articles and books on the subject, a sure sign that a special theory of communication was emerging. In 1928, the same year that Elliott wrote his book, A. Craig Baird, a speech teacher at the University of Iowa, published *Public Discussion and Debate*. Another early textbook by Henry Lee Ewbank and J. Jeffrey Auer of the University of Wisconsin was entitled *Discussion and Debate*.

Features of the Special Theory of Group Discussion

The first major feature of the special theory is the philosophical rationale. As noted earlier, discussion was initially regarded as a technique for making decisions in a democracy. Indeed, an early textbook by Laura Crowell (1963) was entitled *Discussion: Method of Democracy*. Discussion informed citizens in a democracy of basic problems and enabled them to hear all sides of a controversy. The first courses in discussion contained considerable material on public discussion as a decision-making tool in public policy.

The early courses stressed public discussion as the best way to mold public opinion and make decisions. In this context, the term *discussion* had a considerably broader meaning than the preparation and presentation of discussion-type programs before audiences, although the practical sections of early handbooks often stressed the latter.

Discussion was contrasted with other techniques for social control. It was compared favorably with the use of decrees and orders backed by the threat of force in totalitarian societies. It was contrasted with the manipulation of public opinion by mass persuasion, and it was asserted that discussion encouraged the citizen to participate in public decisions.

In addition to citing its virtues for democratic decision making, early writers in the field stressed the relation between public discussion and freedom of speech. They used the classical formulations of John Stuart Mill in his essay *On Liberty*. According to Mill, all opinions and arguments should be allowed a fair hearing; if all points of view are presented, the people will distinguish truth from error. He asserted that repressing unpopular ideas is unwise, because they may contain truth. If the public is searching for truth, the majority must not shut off any possible avenue to knowledge. However, Mill continued, even if the unpopular ideas are false, they should be given a hearing, because the old, familiar truths lose their vitality unless they are periodically challenged and defended. He contended that the continued challenge of the orthodox is sound practice, since the defense of orthodoxy revitalizes the truths it contains.

The defense of public discussion as the main technique of social control rested on certain assumptions that are part of the justification of representative democracy. The first assumption is that citizens can vote wisely if they are given an opportunity. By means of public discussion, they are given a chance to hear all sides of important public questions. Although some citizens will not act wisely, in the long run the majority of informed citizens will make wiser decisions than the most enlightened of despots. Paraphrasing Lincoln, you can fool some of the people some of the time, but you can't fool all of the people all of the time.

On occasion, students in classes in discussion will express a different attitude. They will try to avoid discussing a complex public question, such as some aspect of American foreign policy, because the topic is confusing, or because they feel they cannot become well enough informed to consider the matter. If the experts in the State Department do not understand or cannot solve the problem, how can they be expected to do so? Perhaps the complexities of the modern world make the above basic assumption of democracy untenable, but students should be aware of the implications of rejecting it. If citizens cannot make broad policy decisions and support their convictions at the polls, then they must put their trust in experts. Even if experts begin to make all important decisions, public opinion must still support them. This stand implies a political situation in which an elite group of decision makers rules the country and then uses experts in mass persuasion to manipulate or (in the words of Edward Bernays, a leading public relations counsel) "to engineer" public opinion.

A second assumption grows naturally from the first: that the individual citizen has an innate worth and dignity. The individual is important in his or her own right and is not a cog in the machine of the state or a means to a more ultimate end which is the state. Therefore, citizens have a right to participate in determining their own destinies. They should not be manipulated and treated as though their selfhood and individuality are unimportant. They must be consulted about decisions that affect their welfare. Even though they may choose unwisely, they have the right — in Jefferson's words, an "inalienable right" — to make certain decisions. The authorities may feel that the citizen should not smoke cigarettes or read pornography or spend $15,000 for an automobile, but according to this assumption, the citizen should have the right to make such decisions. They must, therefore, be given a mechanism by which they can obtain information and make judgments about public policy as well as about their personal affairs. Thus, public opinion is not a commodity to be brought into line with public policy, but rather a sign to be considered in determining public policy.

The use of public discussion as a technique of social control also assumes that, although people frequently commit irrational acts, they also act rationally, basing some decisions on facts. Further, it assumes that such rational decisions are the best decisions that people make. The conclusion then follows that training in public discussion, with heavy emphasis on discovering the facts and drawing sound inferences from them, is also training for democratic citizenship.

For the intellectuals at the turn of the century, the ultimate tool of reason was the scientific method. Therefore, they thought that, with training in public discussion which incorporated the main features of the scientific method, citizens should be able to solve those problems of human relations they had hitherto never successfully solved. As the engineer solved the problem of protecting people from heat and cold, so the application of the scientific method to human relations would solve the problems of juvenile delinquency, marriage and divorce, labor—management relations, race relations, and war and peace. Early training in public discussion sought to accomplish this miracle by inculcating the scientific attitude and the scientific pattern of inquiry.

In the early years of the twentieth century, the intellectuals had an image of the scientist in the laboratory as a person who was open-minded and objective. If the experiments turned out in an unexpected way scientists did not ignore the new results, but were willing to reject old theories in favor of new and better ones. They weighed facts objectively. They purged themselves of all emotional prejudices, interests, and biases. They erected elaborate safeguards to ensure their objectivity. In addition, scientists were curious. They wanted to know and would go where the facts led them. They were not committed to a position that they defended to the death. Lawyers as advocates had a much different attitude; they had a duty to defend their clients to the best of their ability no matter what the facts. The scientists, on the other hand, had no duty but to the truth; they tested all evidence rigorously, and when they found evidence that withstood this rigorous testing, they accepted it and accommodated their theories to it.

Of course, the scientists working in their laboratories seldom resembled this idealized portrait, but the writers of early handbooks in public discussion adopted the idealization of the scientist as the model for the participant in public discussion. They urged students to adopt the scientific attitude, to be open-minded, to welcome differences of opinion and challenges to their own thinking, to remain objective and uninvolved when evaluating ideas and facts. They stressed the notion that public discussion was the application of the process of inquiry. The discussion group was to seek the best solution to the problem under consideration on the basis of facts; the group, like the scientist, was to follow reality to the best solution. This adaptation of the scientific approach to the discussion of social and political problems was called the *discussional attitude.*

The second major component of the special theory is the ideal model for a good discussion. In the early courses in public discussion, this model reflected the late-nineteenth-century tendency to apply the scientific method to human affairs. Early writers suggested that the proper way to use public discussion to solve problems was to adopt the objective, empirical attitude of the scientist and the techniques of scientific inquiry. The philosophy and logic of the philosopher John Dewey provided the details of a scientific process of inquiry appropriate for public discussion. Dewey was a pragmatist, thoroughly imbued with the basic assumptions of democracy, and one of the foremost advocates of education for the realities of life. Although he was trained as an idealistic philosopher and was a student of Hegel, he was heavily influenced by scientific methodology. He published a book in 1910, *How We Think*. The book was largely philosophical and speculative, but it did contain, in prescriptive form, an analysis of *reflective thinking*. Reflective thinking is a somewhat generalized model of scientific and rational thinking.

Dewey's analysis of logic and reflective thinking was particularly well suited to the problems of teachers of public address who were searching for theoretical foundations for public discussion. They incorporated Dewey's notion of reflective thinking into the group context, recommending that the group should use in its search for truth precisely the form of thinking recommended by Dewey in *How We Think*. Dewey suggested that reflective thinking followed a pattern that began with a problem or a felt difficulty. The individual tries to make an indeterminate situation determinate. When a person locates the source of the difficulty, the mind leaps forward to suggest possible ways to resolve the problem. At this juncture, rather than blindly trying solution after solution as one would do through trial and error, a person deliberates and reflects on the solutions available and, weighing the advantages and disadvantages of each, selects the best. If the difficulty is removed, the solution has been sound, and the individual is again in a state of equilibrium with the environment. If not, the person examines the remaining solutions and tries again.

Dewey's analysis of reflective thinking was translated into the *discussional pattern* or the *steps in the discussional process*. These steps varied in number and formation, but most of them contained the hard core of Dewey's pattern in the form of (1) analyzing the problem, (2) listing the possible solutions, (3) weighing the alternative solutions, (4) selecting the best solution, and (5) taking steps to implement the solution. Quite often two additional steps were added to this core: the definition of terms and the establishment of group goals.

The basic form of group discussion courses solidified along these lines during the decades immediately preceding World War II. By the 1940s, a great number of such courses had been developed and were offered for credit by departments of speech.

The human relations dimension of the ideal model for the special theory of group discussion was encompassed in the concept of the discussional attitude. This attitude was a reflection of the scientific approach to the reasonable process of inquiry and to reflective thinking. The discussant was supposed to be open-minded and, in contrast to the debater, willing to go where the facts led. A discussant could have a tentative position on the question at issue, but a good participant did not have an emotional investment in his or her own ideas. In addition, a good discussant did not allow emotional responses to affect his or her reasoning and ability to follow the steps of the discussional process.

In terms of the dynamics of group development, the special theory of group discussion set out two types of roles: the role of moderator and the role of participant. People fulfilling either role were expected to adopt the discussional attitude and strive to achieve the steps in the discussional process.

The moderator handled most of the administrative details of planning and organizing the discussion program. In addition, the moderator led the meeting by introducing participants, handling audience questions or comments, and making sure that participants took turns. The moderator's task was to guide the group through the steps of the discussional process and to handle special communication problems (such as the too talkative or too silent) in order to achieve the ideal model of group discussion.

The role of the participant was to be well informed about the topic in question, to participate fully, and to integrate his or her participation into the overall flow of the discussion. Participants were to be properly objective and cooperative in their discussion and to express their ideas in clear language with good speaking voice, articulation, and use of gestures.

Over the years, practitioners of the group discussion special theory developed a number of formats that could be used for different purposes and in different contexts. They also developed a substantial number of rules of thumb to use in coaching people on how to become more effective discussants.

However, the special theory gave relatively short shrift to the human relations aspect of group process. It became apparent that, given the dynamics of group process, individuals found it difficult to follow the steps of the discussional process while hard at work evaluating a given problem. With the growing interest in task-oriented group work in committees, task forces, and organizational work groups, the courses in small group communication began to deemphasize public discussions. New emphasis was given to the more private, continuing task-oriented groups that had common problems to solve and decisions to make.

THE SPECIAL THEORY OF SMALL GROUP COMMUNICATION

As the research into small groups and communication grew, it became apparent that continuing task-oriented groups were more complicated than envisioned in the special theory of group discussion. The human relations features of group interaction were clearly important, and as understanding of this fact grew so did changes in the study and teaching of group dynamics.

Group techniques used in psychiatry and psychological counseling —

including sensitivity groups and encounter training—began to influence the teachers of group discussion. Over time, they began to develop a new special theory of how to work productively in small task-oriented groups. The term *small group communication* came to be used for the new special theory.

The following explanation of small group communication traces the beginnings of the practice and sketches the development of the special theory. The mature theory is explained in terms of its philosophical rationale and the ideal model. The discussion concludes with a comment about the rules of thumb.

Background of Small Group Communication

The same historical forces that brought about the public discussion courses in speech departments were operating to bring the small group to the attention of social scientists—including sociologists, anthropologists, and psychologists. They began discovering the importance of the small group for a number of their concerns.

Industrial psychologists studying worker morale and productivity found that one of the important factors in industrial psychology was the nature of workers' immediate social group and how they related to it. Sociologists began to study the group in the hopes of discovering in miniature the social mechanisms that controlled larger institutions and organizations that were more difficult to study. As their study continued, however, they found the small group worthy of study in its own right. Psychologists, on the other hand, studied the small group because they hoped to find out more about individual psychology.

Social scientists did not begin large-scale research programs on small groups until World War II. Students of politics and business administration, on the other hand, had long been interested in the phenomenon of leadership and had developed theories explaining the phenomenon, although they had not often used the research method of the behavioral sciences. Since the time of organized warfare, the military had developed programs to train "leaders." World War II gave the study of small groups considerable impetus because of the need for military leaders and industrial managers. Interestingly enough, the German army, even before World War II, was using the technique of leaderless group discussion to aid in selecting officer candidates.

The war put a great premium not only on leadership but also on morale and productivity. Both government and private industry mobilized many social scientists to research such diverse matters as whether a persuasive speech or a group discussion would influence more consumers to buy visceral meats and how stress situations affected the performance of bomber crews.

The work during these years revealed the practical importance of the relationships among group interactions, morale, and productivity. The trend toward small group research is indicated by the number of books and articles reporting research in group dynamics and small groups. A. Paul Hare's *Handbook of Small Group Research*, published in 1962, contains a bibliography of 1385 items. Hare reports that his search of the literature reveals that the number of items dealing with social interaction in small groups grew from about 5 in the decade from 1890 to 1899, to 112 from 1920 to 1929, to 210 from 1930 to 1939; and to an annual output of over 150 items per year by 1950. Today the body of research literature relating to small groups has grown to voluminous proportions.

The *Psychological Abstracts* first indexed research articles under the term *group dynamics* in 1945. The reference was to work by the Gestalt psychologist Kurt Lewin. Lewin developed the notion of a dynamic social field and a topological psychology. Under Lewin's direction, the Research Center for Group Dynamics was set up at the Massachusetts Institute of Technology in 1945; through his influence, a similar center was established at the University of Michigan. At this center, Dorwin Cartwright and Alvin Zander edited a collection of research articles entitled *Group Dynamics: Research and Theory* in 1953 and brought out revised collections of articles in 1960 and 1968. The work of the Michigan laboratory, as well as some of the early work of Lewin and his associates, was inventive, thorough, and impressive. Particularly useful was the portion of their work that related to investigations of group process under controlled conditions. A number of teachers, consultants, and counselors from a wide variety of fields who were interested in the practical application of group techniques also used the term *group dynamics*. Some of these new apostles of group dynamics were zealous; critics felt they were on the way to intellectual faddism. As early as 1950, Robert Gunderson made this charge about the work of the National Training Laboratory of Group Development at Bethel, Maine, in an article entitled "Group Dynamics—Hope or Hoax?" He was answered by Herbert Kelman, in an article entitled "Group Dynamics—Neither Hope nor Hoax."

Partly to offset the odium attached to the term *group dynamics* by some zealots, the term *small group* gradually gained preferred status. It appeared in the *Psychological Abstracts* for the first time in 1950, under the indexed work of Bales and Deutsch. Since 1950, *small group* has become the most popular label for serious research into the social dimension of group interaction. Much of the work in this area has been basic research which has contributed to the development of general theories of small group communication. Some of it has been poorly designed, and the results have been trivial. Yet a sound analysis of group process is gradually emerging from the mass of research.

Immediate Source of Development

The general prestige of science and rationalism was challenged in the 1960s by the rise of a romantic impulse, which some observers characterized as the alternative culture or counterculture. The movement challenged the morality of scientific research, charging it with being a tool of militarism, capitalism, and colonialism. The impulse further challenged the validity of the scientific method by glorifying immediate experience and mystical consciousness raising. The movement created alternatives to behaviorism in human psychology—such as humanistic psychology and the human potential movement.

The romantic tradition's impulse was reflected in its glorification of deep feeling and mysticism, its denial of rationalism, and its emphasis on authenticity, openness, sincerity, and the stripping away of manners, cultural artifacts, and social "masks." The core of the movement rested solidly on group methods for its technique and on a value system that denigrated individualism and celebrated groupness. The goals of the new romanticism were communal. Participants sought community and group mystical experiences. The group techniques varied from relatively mild sensitivity sessions borrowed from the group dynamics tradition, to intensive marathon groups meeting continuously for several days, to group drug-taking sessions, to nude encounter groups, to people living in communes and practicing group marriages.

Other group techniques included such nonverbal exercises as trust walks, in which a blindfolded person allowed another to lead him or her about, and psychodramatic exercises in which members of the group would flail one another with pillows, lift a member in the air, search another's eyes, and seek to communicate without words. Under the pressure for conformity to norms established by such techniques, members often grew emotional: Some would cry, others would grow angry. Tension was released with laughter, and some of the intense experiences reached the level of communion characteristic of religious mysticism. Many who did not achieve religious experiences, nonetheless, felt part of a close and warm group in which they could risk disclosure of their innermost hopes and fears.

The group values inherent in the communication style of the movement included being cooperative rather than competitive and being open and honest rather than manipulative, secret, or reserved. The conventional manners that typified some segments of the society were rejected as "games people play"; the alternative value system suggested that such game playing was dehumanizing, but the immersion in a rewarding, deeply personal, and intense group experience would free a person and release the human potential in the group's members.

Emergence of Small Group Communication

Instructors of group discussion courses in departments of speech and communication did not ignore the new developments relating to empirical research in other disciplines. Many scholars in speech and communication were impressed by and caught up in the impulse toward humanistic psychology and the human potential movement. By the late 1950s, several textbooks in discussion used the language and concepts of group dynamics and small group research for the development of some of their materials, particularly those relating to role development and role playing. Although the impact of humanistic psychology and the human potential movement was, perhaps, greatest in the area of interpersonal communication, it also came to influence small group communication by the 1970s.

Contemporary theory and practice of small group communication thus combine the results of empirical research in small groups and some of the values and practices of the human potential movement. Courses in small group communication usually continue the tradition of training students in skills relating to decision making and problem solving, and often include adapting group methods to conflict resolution, building trust, establishing cohesiveness, and developing a positive social climate in the small task-oriented group. The result is a course in applied small group communication that is relevant to many of the basic needs of contemporary society and that promises to be of increasing significance in the future.

Features of the Special Theory of Small Group Communication

The philosophical rationale for small group communication shifted the focus of group work from citizenship, freedom of speech, and public discussion to the importance of task-oriented groups in organizations of all kinds.

As early as 1953, Rensis Likert and his associates at the Institute for Social Research at the University of Michigan made extensive studies into "what makes organizations tick." Likert discovered that managers tended to emphasize the supervision of individuals. In so doing, they overlooked the important leadership methods involved in managing informal and formal small groups in the unit. Likert and his associates suggested that, in addition to working with individuals, supervisors think of the unit as a team and develop teamwork and group loyalty.

In the 1960s, John Kenneth Galbraith's popular book *The New Industrial State* presented a comprehensive and thoroughgoing depiction of the small task-oriented group as the key to the technology of industrial economies such as those of Western Europe, North America, and Japan.

Galbraith viewed the small group as a corporate invention to replace individual genius, which he portrayed as rare and unreliable. He saw the modern corporation as a pyramid of committees. The lower-level committees discussed corporate matters, made suggestions for decisions or solutions, and forwarded their findings upward. The committees at the next higher level repeated the process, and so the work continued until the recommendations reached the highest-level committees for final action.

Committee meetings in the corporate context could bring together a

small group of people, all narrowly but thoroughly trained in their particular specializations, and provide a context in which they could communicate with one another face to face with a maximum of give-and-take. By
means of such small group communication, for example, a lawyer, several
engineers, a marketing expert, and a certified public accountant (CPA)
could focus their individual skills and professional educations on a large
project. The organization used small task-oriented group meetings to
make decisions, solve problems, and implement large projects that individuals could not manage on their own.

By the 1960s, according to Galbraith, the real power in society had
passed to the managerial class, which had the knowledge and ability to
meet with a small group of people around a table and arrive at understanding and decisions.

In the 1970s, Alvin Toffler's best-seller *Future Shock* not only assumed
the importance of small group communication as outlined by other
scholars but also depicted a future in which organizations would no longer
be organized into divisions with lines of authority but would form temporary work groups (task forces) to deal with projects and tasks. Toffler
predicted that people who worked productively in organizations would
have to absorb the social shocks inherent in starting up totally new (zero-
history) groups to deal with significant problems over substantial periods
of time.

Engineers who were applying scientific theory to practical problems
of communication gave the special theory of small group communication
some of its philosophical rationale in the years following World War II.
Norbert Wiener, a pioneer in the field of transferring information from
people to machine, from machine to machine, and from machine to people, focused attention on *feedback* as one of the most important features of
interaction.

Wiener used the term *cybernetics* to refer to the way people set goals
and control behavior to achieve those goals, and to the way machines can
come to perform the same function. Feedback was an important part of
the process. It came to refer to the principle of a receiver of information
furnishing data to an automatic control device so errors could be cor-
rected and performance controlled. The principle of feedback is illustrated in simple terms by the thermostat. The homeowner selects a temperature level as a goal and sets the control to that temperature. The
thermostat contains a sensing mechanism that measures the actual temperature level. When the actual level departs from the desired level (the
goal), the thermostat sends a message which either turns on the furnace to
bring the heat level up to the setting or cuts off the furnace to allow the
temperature to cool back down to the desired point.

Early influential figures in the development of small group communication were taken with the world view that saw a tendency to disorganization in human communication. They used the word *entropy* to refer to
the process. They thought of information as fighting against the natural

tendency toward disorganization. In their view, the creation and transmission of messages required energy and was sustained only by effort and skill. Left alone, organization would decay under the natural tendencies to uncertainty. However, energy was also a value to be expended carefully and to be saved.

Norbert Wiener described communication as a cooperative game between speaker and listener against the forces of confusion. In his view, people talking to one another in a competitive setting, such as a legal trial or a bargaining session, are not always willing to join together to fight entropy. Indeed, such settings encourage bluff, simulated temper tantrums, misleading nonverbal communication, and other strategies that can increase confusion rather than decrease it.

The new special communication theory saw an ideal in which fidelity of communication was maximized. *Fidelity* refers to how much of the message is sent without distortion from the source to the receiver. *Noise* (a technical use of the term) in the channels cuts down on fidelity; one way to overcome such noise is to repeat elements of the message. Such repetition is called *redundancy*. However, repeating messages is costly in terms of time and energy, so the theory came to include efficiency and low cost as well as accuracy as part of the ideal. In the ideal situation, the communicators cooperate to carry on a joint enterprise against confusion, an enterprise in which noise is minimized and the redundancy level is adjusted to achieve the desired degree of fidelity with no unnecessary repetitions.

Figure 2 depicts the emphasis on high-fidelity transmission of information characteristic of the special theory of small group communication. The model can be traced to an early schema developed by Shannon and Weaver in a book called *The Mathematical Theory of Communication*. It was subsequently modified by Schramm and further adapted by Berlo.

The schema begins with a message *source*. In the case of small group communication, the source is an individual making a comment verbally or nonverbally to the others in the group. The source has information in mind to communicate and so encodes a *message*, the second element in the schema. The message translates the information into a form that can be sent through one or more *channels*, the third element. Through those

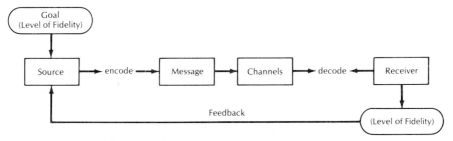

Figure 2 Diagram of schema for high-fidelity transmission of information.

channels a *receiver*, the fourth element, can perceive and decode the message. The goal is to have the receivers (others in the group) decode the message in the same fashion as the source encoded it so they understand the information accurately. To ensure such accuracy, the receivers provide the source with feedback to see if the information has been properly decoded. If not, the source sends further messages, adding redundancy, to achieve the goal of understanding.

This logical and structured model of information transmission was useful in the development of a special theory of small group communication, but it did not take into account the general theories governing group dynamics. The general theories portray groups as social systems capable of emotional responses, role specializations and conflicts, norm development, cohesiveness, group culture, and other features that add an important socioemotional dimension to groups.

Another set of developments in the field of group communication focused on the socioemotional dimension of groups. While Lewin and his associates were applying social scientific perspectives in the study of groups, they also sought ways to apply their findings to everyday problems. Followers of Lewin began to design workshops to train people to participate more effectively in groups. A training laboratory at Bethel, Maine, set up workshops in small group dynamics designed to help people communicate more effectively in groups. The trainers called their approach *sensitivity training*, and the groups that achieved the goal of educating participants about group process were referred to as *training groups*, or *T-groups*.

Other influences were at work in the disciplines of clinical psychology and psychiatry, where group techniques were used to help people with personal psychological problems. The late 1960s saw the rise of humanistic psychology, the human potential movement, and interpersonal communication. The impulse for emphasizing socioemotional features of human interaction found its outlet in group training sessions. These resembled T-groups in some respects but placed less emphasis on scientific findings and more on humanistic psychology. The training was done in *encounter groups*.

The ideals of both the sensitivity group and the encounter group include the notion that people who really communicate have learned to cease playing games with one another. They treat others as authentic human beings and not as things or machines to be manipulated. Good communicators do not wear masks that make them less human and shield them from contact with others. In a good group, all members are able to open up and disclose their feelings. Self-disclosure is risky, and people begin communicating about themselves with fear and trembling; but once risked, self-disclosure opens up others and they in turn disclose. The climate of the group meeting is warmed by such disclosing communication, and as people take more and more risks and are accepted for themselves, trust evolves. Thus, the need to wear masks or play roles or games is dissipated.

In the warm and trusting climate of a good meeting, people can express their innermost feelings, discuss their hopes and fears, and discover their authentic selves, all without worrying about being accepted or rejected. As the climate builds to ever more intimate and significant communication, important relationships evolve among the participants. The American philosopher George Herbert Mead's notion that a person's self-image is built up through communication with others emphasizes a strong and positive self-image as a key to effective communication. Honest feedback to the speaker is expressed in terms of feelings. The frank acceptance of the feedback by the speaker, followed by a sincere attempt to change, is basic to the sensitizing of the participants and to the dynamics of groups. Feedback in the sense of reacting and evaluating is, of course, different from providing a message source with a reading of how a receiver decoded the information in a message. Both meanings are widely used, and care should be taken to use the word in its appropriate context.

The new perspective stressed heightened awareness, a careful and sharper tuning of the senses, and the importance of nonverbal communication. Greater attention was paid to the geography of group arrangements. Important questions were raised: Are different seating arrangements important in group interaction? Do gestures and vocal intonations influence group process? What is the relationship in face-to-face interaction between verbal and nonverbal comments?

The new interest in sensitivity and encounter groups and interpersonal communication provided a focus and information that were useful to the emerging special theory of small group communication. Particularly important was the emphasis on creating and sustaining good socioemotional climates and contexts for group meetings.

The ideal model of the special theory of small group communication takes as a given that certain dynamics (explained by general theories) inevitably apply when small groups of people work cooperatively to perform tasks. The ideals of how to form, conduct, and use small group communication should be realistic in terms of the nature of group process.

A good task-oriented group meeting is one in which the potential for feedback as an aid to understanding is both spontaneous and continuous. Thus, high-fidelity transmission of information, efficient use of time and energy, and an ideal ratio of noise to redundancy are essential to a good task-oriented small group meeting. A good group must allow for and encourage participants alternately to assume the role functions of source and receiver (speaker and listener).

Two key features of small group dynamics encourage people to play the cooperative game against confusion. First, a clearly stated common objective encourages members to work cooperatively to achieve it. Second, people tend to identify with a group in which they participate; they achieve a feeling of belonging and of attraction to a group, a phenomenon called *cohesiveness.* Cohesiveness thus becomes a vital concept for good group meetings. A common goal and group cohesiveness combine to encourage a helpful, unselfish climate in a group meeting. A person who willingly becomes a good listener must be unselfish enough to appear uninformed, careful enough to decode messages clearly, and willing enough to risk loss of status to ensure group success. Every member must give clear and frequent feedback.

The general theories of group development must also be accommodated to achieve a cohesive and productive meeting. These include the general drive for groups to develop norms and for individuals to specialize in their tasks. Such specialization is called *role emergence.* When people specialize in a role for a group, they also assume a certain standing or status in it.

When group roles are not stabilized, members often strive for status or power and are reluctant to play the part of a listener. They may become competitive and engage in display activities designed to show others their competence and interest. If the roles are stabilized, high-status members often get the floor more easily and talk more than low-status members. Status arrangements can make it difficult to achieve the goal of high-fidelity transmission of information. In addition, low-status members may feel they are being treated as less than human and find themselves alienated from the group.

A pivotal role that emerges in task-oriented groups is that of leader. Chapter 9 deals with leadership in detail. Suffice to note here that the psychiatric study of groups reveals that leadership is a powerful symbol and can become the battleground for internal conflicts or the basis for group flight taking. Questions of power and authority and gender lead to irrational and immature behavior that make group productivity and cohesiveness difficult. Good groups need to go through a shakedown cruise, or period of internal adjustment, in order to mature and become an effective task-oriented social system.

Group members share fantasies which create a common subculture for the participants. The group's culture can be a coping one which creates the symbolic basis for good information transmission, for good socioemotional discussions, and for successful testing of ideas and mobilizing of resources. The group's culture can also become a noncoping one which cripples the participants' efforts to work successfully. The ideal group consistently displays a coping group culture.

Finally, the good group successfully negotiates the shakedown cruise, experiences a successful emergence of roles and leadership, and continuously keeps its socioemotional climate healthy while focusing on the task dimension. That is, even though task is a high-priority item, it is not the only concern of the group. Hard work without social interaction tears the social fabric, and such rents must be mended or they will disrupt the task efforts.

In the following chapters the special and general theories of group work important to understanding and participating in meetings are explained in depth. Chapters 2 and 3 describe the special theory of group discussion and apply it to the kinds of meetings for which it remains most useful—namely, one-time meetings often held in public settings. Chapters 4 to 11 explain the special theory of small group communication and integrate it with the general theories of communication that impinge upon it. These chapters apply the special and general theories to the kinds of meetings for which they are most useful—namely, those that meet over time, often in private, for important tasks. These groups are typically part of larger social systems (such as organizations) and their work relates to all aspects of the larger culture.

SUMMARY

Small group communication refers to the body of information dealing with one or more meetings of a small group of people who communicate face to face to fulfill a common purpose and achieve a group goal. The small group is an identifiable social system. Five is an excellent number for a small task-oriented group. An aggregation does not become a small group until the participants have communicated enough to form a structure and an impression of one another.

People often use the term *theory* to mean impractical abstractions, hunches, or hypothetical information. This book views theories as useful explanations, providing practical information (*special communication theories*) and social scientific formulations (*general communication theories*). Special theories are joint ventures in which participants willingly cooperate in creating good group meetings. Special theories consist of a philosophical rationale, an ideal model, and practical advice.

Three important general theories are the exchange theory of cohesiveness, the symbolic convergence theory of group acculturation, and the emergent theory of roles, leadership, and decision making.

The special theory of group discussion emerged in the early decades of the twentieth century, when people outside the academic world began to participate in small group meetings. The philosophical rationale of group discussion stressed citizenship, the application of scientific thinking to human relations problems, and the importance of freedom of speech to encourage the discussion of public questions. Under this rationale, the ideal group discussion was one in which the participants used an openminded, objective attitude to apply the principles of reflective thinking to the steps of the discussional process.

The special theory of small group communication emerged with practices in task-oriented groups in organizational contexts after World War II. Social scientific research into the dynamics of groups indicated that special theories could not function unless they were tailored to the parameters of what is possible in terms of general theories. The increasing use of sensitivity and encounter groups and the growing understanding of the socioemotional dimension of group work combined to create elements of the special theory that stressed norms, roles, leadership, group culture, and nonverbal communication.

The philosophical rationale included the concept of high-fidelity transmission of information, with an eye to conserving energy and time. The rationale also stressed an understanding of the emotional dimensions of group work and the influence of general theories on both the task and socioemotional features of task-oriented groups.

☞ Rules of Thumb

Practical Advice on How to Be a Good Group Member

Drawn from Chapter 1

- ☞ A good size for a small task-oriented group is 5 or 7 participants. (Even-numbered groups have a harder time reaching agreement.)
- ☞ In a small task-oriented group, communication should be aimed at a clearly specified topic related to a common goal.
- ☞ Theories are not necessarily dull and meaningless abstractions that have no practical payoff.
- ☞ In the long run, good theories are more practical than lists of recipes for how to communicate in a specific situation.
- ☞ Be sure to distinguish special theories from general theories whenever you read or hear about small group communication.
- ☞ When you agree to take part in a joint venture, be sure you know the rules and goals that will guide the communication.
- ☞ After agreeing to take part in a joint venture, do not knowingly break the rules.
- ☞ When agreeing to take part in a joint venture, learn the extent to which it is staged and scripted.
- ☞ When studying general theories, be sure to distinguish between viewpoints or perspectives about the kinds of theories and the actual theories themselves.
- ☞ To be a good manager, you must supervise groups as well as individuals.
- ☞ To work productively in today's corporate setting, you must learn to absorb the social shocks inherent in moving from work group to work group.
- ☞ To achieve a meeting of the minds in a group, you must learn to play the role of receiver and provide feedback to the speaker.
- ☞ Be willing to take part with the other members in your group in the joint effort against confusion.
- ☞ Develop a feeling for how much repetition is needed to transmit information clearly in a group.
- ☞ Treat people as authentic human beings and not as things or machines to be manipulated.

☞ A good socioemotional climate is as important to group success as is good task-oriented communication.

☞ Do not confuse the two meanings of *feedback* used in message and relationship communication.

☞ A clearly stated goal encourages group members to work cooperatively to achieve it.

☞ To willingly become a good listener, you must be unselfish enough to ask questions that reveal ignorance or confusion.

☞ Secrecy, bluff, and the hiding of feelings go counter to developing group cohesiveness and achieving group goals.

☞ Encourage role emergence to ensure a good task group.

☞ Expect your group to go through a shakedown period of insecurity and frustration for the members before maturing into an effective group.

QUESTIONS FOR STUDY

1. How would you define small group communication?
2. What are some typical meanings of the term *theory*?
3. What is the nature of special communication theories? Of general communication theories?
4. What is a joint venture?
5. What are the main elements of the special theory of group discussion?
6. How valid is John Stuart Mill's defense of free speech for today's citizen in an urban corporate culture? Explain.
7. What is the nature of the discussional attitude?
8. How does the idea that good communication should consist of high-fidelity transmission of information compare and contrast with the idea that good communication should be authentic and real and honest?
9. How does the treatment of human relations in group discussion compare and contrast with its treatment in small group communication?
10. What are the three major general theories to be covered in detail in later chapters of this book?

EXERCISES

1. Analyze a recent free-speech debate that took place on your campus or another campus and that was reported in the press. Write a 300-word case study of the controversy suitable for class discussion.
2. Examine some of the early textbooks on group discussion (see the reading list that follows) and make a comparison of the ways in which they treat John Dewey's steps of "reflective thinking."
3. Select a textbook or handbook on small group communication and write a two-

or three-page paper analyzing the ideal model or models of good group meetings prescribed in the book.

4. Observe a group meeting and try to infer what special theory is guiding the participants. Briefly describe the extent to which the members are participating in a joint venture to create a good meeting according to that theory.

5. Organize a meeting along the lines of the constitutive rules set up on pp. 7–8 in this chapter. Hold a discussion afterward about the nature of special theories.

REFERENCES AND SUGGESTED READINGS

For Forston's study of 12-person groups, see:

Forston, Robert. "The Decision-Making Process in the American Civil Jury: A Comparative Methodological Investigation." Ph.D. dissertation, University of Minnesota, 1968.

For a more detailed analysis of special and general communication theories, see:

Bormann, Ernest G. *Communication Theory.* Prospect Heights, IL: Waveland Press, 1989.

For an exchange theory account of groups, see:

Thibaut, John W., and Harold H. Kelly. *The Social Psychology of Groups.* New York: Wiley, 1959.

For an exchange theory of interpersonal communication, see:

Stephen, Timothy D. "A Symbolic Exchange Framework for the Development of Intimate Relationships," *Human Relations,* **37** (1984), 393–408.

For some early books on discussion method growing out of the adult education movement, see:

Elliott, Harrison S. *The Process of Group Thinking.* New York: Association Press, 1928.

Fansler, Thomas. *Discussion Methods for Adult Groups.* New York: American Association for Adult Education, 1934.

For some early books on group discussion written by speech communication professors, see:

Baird, A. Craig. *Public Discussion and Debate.* Boston: Ginn, 1928.

Ewbank, Henry Lee, and J. Jeffrey Auer. *Discussion and Debate,* 2nd ed. New York: Appleton-Century-Crofts, 1952.

For a book stressing discussion and democracy, see:

Crowell, Laura. *Discussion: Method of Democracy.* Glenview, IL: Scott, Foresman, 1963.

For the source of Mill's freedom of speech argument, see:

Mill, John Stuart. *On Liberty.* London: Longmans, Green, 1867.

For the source of the application of the scientific method to group discussion, see:

Dewey, John. *How We Think.* Boston: Heath, 1910.

Dewey, John. *Logic: The Theory of Inquiry.* New York: Holt, Rinehart and Winston, 1938.

Several bibliographies of research on small groups list some of the early research literature upon which the general theories in this book are based. They include:

Collins, Barry E., and Harold Guetzkow. *A Social Psychology of Group Processes for Decision Making.* New York: Wiley, 1964.

Hare, A. Paul. *Handbook of Small Group Research.* New York: Free Press, 1962.

McGrath, Joseph E., and Irwin Altman. *Small Group Research: A Synthesis and Critique of the Field.* New York: Holt, Rinehart and Winston, 1966.

The research articles on group dynamics were collected in:

Cartwright, Dorwin, and Alvin Zander, eds. *Group Dynamics: Research and Theory.* New York: Harper & Row, 1953 (rev. 3rd ed., 1968).

The articles raising the issue of the validity of group dynamics are:

Gunderson, Robert G. "Group Dynamics — Hope or Hoax?" *Quarterly Journal of Speech,* 36 (1950), 34–38.

Kelman, Herbert C. "Group Dynamics — Neither Hope nor Hoax," *Quarterly Journal of Speech,* 36 (1950), 371–377.

For Likert's notions about groups in management, see:

Likert, Rensis. *New Patterns in Management.* New York: McGraw-Hill, 1961.

For Galbraith's and Toffler's analyses of the importance of groups, see:

Galbraith, John Kenneth. *The New Industrial State.* Boston: Houghton Mifflin, 1967.

Toffler, Alvin. *Future Shock.* New York: Random House, 1970.

The sources for the ideal model of communication relating to high-fidelity transmission of information include:

Berlo, David K. *The Process of Communication: An Introduction to Theory and Practice.* New York: Holt, Rinehart and Winston, 1960.

Schramm, Wilbur. "How Communication Works." In Wilbur Schramm, ed., *The Process and Effects of Mass Communication.* Urbana, IL: University of Illinois Press, 1954, pp. 3–10.

Shannon, Claude E., and Warren Weaver. *The Mathematical Theory of Communication.* Urbana, IL: University of Illinois Press, 1949.

For an early discussion of the concepts of entropy and feedback, see:

Wiener, Norbert. *The Human Use of Human Beings: Cybernetics and Society.* Boston: Houghton Mifflin, 1954.

For a discussion of training groups, see:

Batchelder, Richard L., and James M. Hardy. *Using Sensitivity Training and the Laboratory Method.* New York: Association Press, 1968.

Bradford, Leland P., Jack R. Bigg, and Kenneth D. Benne. *T-Groups Theory and Laboratory Method: Innovation in Reeducation.* New York: Wiley, 1964.

Golembiewski, Robert T., and Arthur Blumberg, eds. *Sensitivity Training and the Laboratory Approach.* Itasca, IL: Peacock, 1970.

For a popular survey and introduction to the romantic impulse as expressed in group practices, see the articles in:

"The Group Phenomenon" (various authors), *Psychology Today,* December 1967, pp. 16–41.

For a popular book in the romantic tradition, see:

Reich, Charles A. *The Greening of America.* New York: Random House, 1970.

For encounter groups, see:

Burton, Arthur, ed. *Encounter: The Theory and Practice of Encounter Groups.* San Francisco: Jossey-Bass, 1969.

Shultz, William C. *Joy: Expanding Human Awareness.* New York: Grove, 1967.

For Mead's analysis of the social emergence of mind and self, see:

Mead, George H. *Mind, Self, and Society: From the Standpoint of a Social Behaviorist.* Chicago: University of Chicago Press, 1934.

Chapter
2

Problem-Solving
Group Discussion

*D*espite the shifting emphasis on the types and nature of task-oriented small groups, the special theory of group discussion does have a continuing role in the study and practice of group work today. Most of us work with one-time meetings. We may attend a conference and find ourselves in a small group meeting as part of the deliberations. We may take part in a radio or television discussion. We may attend a campus meeting for a discussion on public policy. We may be asked to meet with a committee that does its work in one session. Because we still work in so many one-time meetings, these communication events remain important, and their special requirements make group discussion theory a practical and pertinent field of study.

This chapter presents the special theory of discussion adapted to contemporary needs, with an emphasis on a good all-purpose agenda for one-time problem-solving groups. The agenda is based on the steps of the discussional process.

THE NATURE OF THE ONE-TIME MEETING

The Latin term *ad hoc* means "for this special purpose." An ad hoc meeting is one set up for a special purpose for which the participants have not met before and are not likely to meet again. Some of the members may have participated with one another in other ad hoc meetings, and some may be acquainted from social contacts or other business meetings; but the composition of an ad hoc meeting is unique and temporary.

An ad hoc or one-time meeting differs from an ad hoc committee. Some organizations, such as universities, may form an ad hoc committee for a special purpose of such significance that the committee may meet a number of times and continue for a period of weeks or even months. In an organization, an ad hoc committee differs from the standing (permanent) committees. Some organizations also create project teams to work on a given task. A computer company, for instance, may set up a special project team to develop a new information-processing system. In contrast, the planners of a one-time meeting anticipate achieving their purpose in a single session.

Since the people in a one-time meeting have not met before, they form a zero-history group. The fact that the group has no history means that the members have no experience on which to base future expectations of roles, norms, goals, or culture. In short, both the social field and the task objectives are unstructured and ambiguous.

The leaderless group discussion may also be a zero-history group; but, in contrast to the one-time meeting, it has a *future*. A group's future plays an important part in the dynamics of even the first session and results in the process described in Chapters 4 through 10.

Continuing groups test potential leaders and other influential members, develop norms and other features of their group culture carefully, take nothing at face value, and check reputations, formal status, and assigned structure before accepting them. Much is at stake; hence, the members search and evaluate the social realities of the group with more rigor in the first session of the ongoing group than they do in the one-time meeting.

One of the most important tendencies in the one-time meeting, on the other hand, is to accept leadership. The members are likely to accept and appreciate guidance from the moderator whether she or he is self-appointed or has been assigned by some organizational unit to lead the meeting. The group needs to get to work quickly without the leadership contention and role testing which characterize groups with a future. Members realize that they have little time and tend to accept arbitrarily stipulated goals and procedures with little challenge.

The members of a one-time meeting tend to take shortcuts to structure the group into a "pecking order," so they can get on with the business at hand. They are willing to risk substantial mistakes because of the shortage of time and because they often perceive the task as less important than the assignments characteristic of longer-term groups. They tend to use organizational status, professional standing, and community reputation as ways of assigning leadership and influence. Thus, if seven people attend an ad hoc meeting and one is known to be the dean of the college, another the student body president, and a third the editor of the student newspaper, that information will help structure a hierarchy of influence and importance. Once the discussion is under way, quick stereotypes are formed to find a role for those members who do not have societal positions or community reputations to help assign them slots in the group.

Members of one-time meetings also tend to accept a stereotyped picture of how a meeting ought to be run. The zero-history group that will meet for many sessions will work out its own roles, norms, and culture according to the dynamics described in Chapters 4 through 10. Time limitations, however, force the members of the one-time meeting to use some other tactic. The culture of a given society or region will tend to develop a general stereotype of how a one-time meeting should be organized and conducted. In North America, the culturally accepted notion of how a group discussion should proceed includes the assigned role functions of moderator, leader, or chair and, often, of a secretary or recorder.

The moderator, leader, or chair is expected to tend to the administrative details of setting up the meeting place. In addition, the chair typically plans the agenda, sends out preliminary information, and schedules the meeting. During the course of the session, the assigned chair is expected to "lead" the discussion. Much of the following advice on how to plan, moderate, and participate in one-time meetings reflects the cultural expectations for such sessions in the United States.

Of course, the notion of how a good one-time meeting should proceed varies from what actually takes place in a typical meeting. All participants do not willingly follow the assigned moderator, even when they know they should. They are, however, much more likely to do so in a one-time meeting than in a group with a longer life. Even in a short meeting, role differentiation does take place. A few people talk more than others despite the best efforts of the moderator. Some people are silent. Some are friendly, humorous, and likable. Others are well organized and insightful and contribute to the success of the group's work. The general cultural expectation that discussion is composed of one leader and a group of indistinguishable "participants" soon evaporates under the natural dynamics of group pressure.

Generally, one-time meetings are held in three contexts: (1) a group of people who have come together in private to discuss a topic; (2) a group of people who have come together to discuss a topic for an audience that observes the discussion live or on television or hears it on radio; and (3) a group of people who have come together for a conference or workshop in which they listen to lectures and audiovisual presentations such as films, and who alternate these sessions with short meetings with other participants.

The one-time meeting is an important and widespread communication situation. The student of small group communication is well advised to learn how to participate in ad hoc meetings both because of their intrinsic importance and because the communication skills useful in such sessions transfer to the more complicated task force and business meetings in which the dynamics of role emergence and norm development come into play. The fundamentals of communication learned and practiced in the one-time meeting, when combined with an understanding of small group communication theory, have valuable applications to other, more important group settings.

OVERVIEW OF PROBLEM-SOLVING GROUP DISCUSSION

Chapter 1 described John Dewey's analysis of reflective thinking and the ways that early theorists in group discussion adapted his analysis to the steps in the discussional process. Although subsequent experience and research have indicated that long-term groups find it difficult to follow a logical, step-by-step procedure in their problem solving, the agenda remains a good one for the one-time meeting. It provides a basis for carefully thinking through the purpose of the meeting, for preparing prior to the session, and for establishing a useful starting agenda for the deliberations. Most participants will have some understanding of a problem-solving approach and will accept the agenda as the basis for their brief joint enterprise.

The steps in the discussional process can be described as follows:

Step 1: Defining the key terms of the discussion question.

Step 2: Clarifying the group's goals for the discussion.

Step 3: Analyzing the discussion problem.

Step 4: Listing possible solutions.

Step 5: Analyzing the solutions pro and con.

Step 6: Selecting the best solution.

Of course, to remain true to the spirit of Dewey's reflective thinking process, the solution should be tested after it is chosen. However, years of experience in using the steps for problem-solving discussions have made it clear that many one-time meetings cannot test the solution. To be sure, if you meet once as a committee to plan a party for a departmental club, you will have both the resources and authority to implement your decision. When a group meets with the express goal of putting a solution into effect, the members can add a final step to the agenda:

Step 7: Try out the best solution.

Of course, before the discussional process can be set in motion, one-time groups must clearly formulate a topic and gather the information needed to begin deliberations.

SELECTING THE TOPIC

Discussions are often organized around general themes or topics. Selection of a topic should be influenced by an analysis of the participants, and of the audience that will view the program if the discussion is presented to the public. Will attendance be compulsory? Will the audience be well informed? What attitudes and interests will the audience represent?

To some extent, the purpose of the discussion determines the suitable topics. Often, the occasion will help formulate the purpose. Some occasions are created in order to achieve the purposes of the planners; other occasions call forth the program, and the purposes must be adapted to it.

The general theme of a program should usually be phrased to arouse interest and promote attendance. The working topic for the discussion, however, should be a question, and a clear and definite one. A very generalized theme such as "Taxation" or a vaguely worded question such as "What about racism in professional sports?" will succeed in identifying the subject area but do little to limit or structure the discussion.

Specific and limited discussion questions regarding taxation might be: What policy should the city council adopt toward property taxes? What stand should the federal government take on progressive income taxes? A good question limits the topic to enable adequate discussion in the time allotted, yet allows for some range of inquiry into alternative solutions. A good question also facilitates the purposes of the program.

Questions of Fact

A factual question furthers the aim of informing the participants. Examples of factual questions are: Is communism growing in influence in Central America? To what extent is drinking related to automobile accidents? Has there been a decrease in premarital sexual relations on the part of American teenagers?

Questions of Value

A group may wish to prod members of the audience to examine its value systems. For example: Is euthanasia justified? Should couples applying for a marriage license be required to take an AIDS test? Should abortions be limited by law? Questions of value are best adapted to audiences composed of people who are still unsure of their position. The group can expect considerable differences of opinion in a discussion of value, and these differences will often end in the ultimate argument of "Should!" versus "Shouldn't!"

Questions of Conjecture

Sometimes groups phrase questions in terms of conjecture about future events. Examples are: Can the United States avoid another major depression? Is atomic war inevitable? Can Germany be reunified? Such questions are often used as attention-getting devices. They can be helpful to participants who are drafting speeches designed to get people to listen to the discussion, but they aren't useful for seriously exploring a problem.

Questions of Policy

An excellent question is one that asks for a clear statement of policy. A question of policy focuses on the issue "What should we do?" It directs the group's attention to a problem and asks for the best solution. Examples are: What should Tri Zeta's rush program be for the next quarter? How should the student body respond to the CIA's visiting the campus for job interviews? What should the federal government's policy be toward a space defense initiative?

GATHERING INFORMATION

Once the group has selected a topic, participants need to gather information in preparation for the actual discussion. Most students of discussion have had previous training in seeking information, using the library, preparing bibliographies, and taking notes. However, a summary of these techniques as they relate to the general features of information gathering, with an emphasis on those items important to preparing information for the group, is in order.

Sources of Information

Personal Experience One of the major sources of information will be the discussant's background and experience. The student should not rely on spur-of-the-moment inspiration, but should write down the information to discover the gaps to be filled.

On occasion, participants can round out their background by direct observation of the conditions under discussion. If the group's topic deals with new teaching techniques, they might visit classes taught by closed-circuit television or observe teaching machines in use. They should record their observations by taking notes during or immediately after the field trip.

Interviews Another excellent source of information is the interview. Students may find eyewitnesses to question about events, or they may interview authorities on a subject. Authorities may testify concerning both facts and opinions. If the group plans to interview a large sample of people, participants may want to draw up a list of questions to ask each person. If only a few people are being interviewed in depth, group members will want to conduct an open-ended interview, which enables the authority to introduce directions they may not have considered. The interview should be planned to elicit as much of the desired information and opinion as possible. If several participants are interviewing, a common set of questions is important. The results of the interviews can be more easily compared if all respondents are asked the same questions. Too often, students begin an interview with a vague statement that they would like to know about communism in Central America. If the interviewed authority asks what specific information the students want, they cannot provide an answer. Interviewing is a complex and difficult task. If the group members are to use many interviews, they should study research methods dealing with interviewing techniques.

An accurate record of the interview should be kept, using a tape recorder if possible. If the interviewers plan to quote people directly, they must record all statements verbatim and should inform people that their actual words will be used. Such statements should be carefully and clearly written at the time of the interview.

Electronic Media   Many current events are reported on radio and television. Often our earliest information comes from the electronic media. Radio and television also present in-depth analyses of public affairs through investigative reports, interviews, and documentaries. The addition of sound and pictures adds a valuable dimension to such information. As with direct interviews, it is important to make as accurate a record as possible from media reports.

Libraries and Archives   A final and important source of information consists of written documents, records, manuscripts, letters, diaries, books, journals, magazines, and newspapers. Students of discussion find the library their richest source of information. The ability to use the library effectively is part of the equipment of an educated person. One wit observed that he could become the world's *second* greatest authority on any subject in three weeks, given the resources of a good library.

Bibliography

In a general sense, bibliography refers to the study of writings and publications. This study includes the history, identification, description, and evaluation of published works. More specifically, the term often means a list of writings dealing with a particular subject, writings that have been read in the original by the lister. Such a bibliography may be annotated; that is, it may contain short descriptions and evaluations about the items. The term *bibliography* will be used here to refer to the discovery, evaluation, and systematic listing of writings that the student has consulted on a particular subject.

Collecting Bibliography   Most librarians now use computers to search for and retrieve information. Since many libraries are computerized, group members can collect items for study by making computer searches of indexes to books, government documents, periodicals, and newspapers.

The group should work up a list of key words before its members begin an extensive search for materials. Of course, during the investigation, new key words will be discovered, but puzzling about key words as a group early in the investigation will cut down the drudgery of preparing a bibliography.

The next step is to find bibliographies already written on the subject. Three good general works of this sort are: (1) *A World Bibliography of Bibliographies and of Bibliographical Catalogues, Calendars, Abstracts, Digests, Indexes, and the Like;* (2) *Bibliographical Index: A Cumulative Bibliography of Bibliographies;* (3) *Bulletin of Bibliography and Magazine Notes.*

Most questions suitable for public discussion have been the subject of books and dissertations. Bibliographies at the end of such works can enlarge the group's bibliography.

Often, background information can be quickly gathered by examining reference books and encyclopedias. Library researchers should become familiar with such works as *Guide to Reference Books, Fundamental Reference Sources,* and *Reference Books: A Brief Guide for Students and Other Users of the Library.*

After bibliographic records have been made for sources that look promising, researchers should become familiar with the major indexes to contemporary magazines and journals. These include the *Readers' Guide to Periodical Literature, Applied Science & Technology Index, Business Periodicals Index, The Education Index,* and *Social Science and Humanities Index.*

Since 1851, *The New York Times* has been indexed in *The New York Times Index.* Many libraries have a file of recent issues of *The New York Times,* and discussants can quickly locate the news stories relating to their work. To check a local paper's version of a story, they can review the files for the local paper on the days surrounding the date of the story in *The New York Times.*

Students preparing for discussion should not overlook the publications of local and state governments as well as the United States Government Printing Office. An important index to local publications is the *Monthly Checklist of State Publications.* Because government publications are so diverse and voluminous, many libraries have a separate Government Document Section with librarians available to help find sources. The *Congressional Record* is carefully indexed and contains information on most questions of public policy. A good general index to federal government publications is the *Monthly Catalog of United States Government Publications.*

Bibliographic Information   When researchers find an item that seems pertinent and useful, they should make out a bibliographic notation. The group should decide on the form of bibliographic notation that every member will use. If they keep a common bibliographic file, all members should use the same bibliographical form.

The bibliographic notation should include the name of the author, compiler, or editor; the exact title as it appears on the title page of the book; the place of publication; the name of the publisher; the number of the edition if it is a revised edition; the number of volumes; the date of publication; and pertinent page numbers in an edited volume or periodical.

In addition to the essential information about a book or article in the file, the participant should add a brief annotation concerning its value. Discussants often cite authorities such as Henry Kissinger and James Reston, but when asked for further information, they can report only that the expert has had experience in the government or that he is a newspaper reporter. Thus the information on file for an important book or article should also include a brief note about the author's background, training, position, and bias. Some of this information is available on the book jacket or in the preface. Participants can often learn more about the author from such reference works as *Who's Who in America* and *A Dictionary of Current Biography*. Book reviews in *Book Review Digest, Saturday Review,* and *The New York Times Book Review* can be helpful.

When it comes to magazines, it is good to learn their reputation for accuracy and the slant of their interpretations. Research that is confined to *U.S. News & World Report* will provide a much different impression of Central American affairs than that confined to *Ramparts* magazine. Magazines as diverse as *Reader's Digest, National Review, The Nation, Time, Newsweek, The Atlantic Monthly, Harper's Magazine, The New Republic,* and *The Progressive* may slant the news in their unsigned stories. They also tend to print signed articles that support their editorial positions. Students should appraise the magazines in their bibliography so that their reading is not confined to sources with a similar bias. People tend to seek out reading materials with attitudes similar to their own. If discussants want the soundest information available, however, they must examine magazines and newspapers that represent a broad spectrum of opinion.

Investigators can keep records of their findings in data bases if they have access to a personal computer. If not, they can use the more traditional card index of an annotated bibliography.

Here is a sample of a brief record of useful information:

Fisher, B. A., and R. K. Stutman. "An Assessment of Group Trajectories: Analyzing Developmental Breakpoints," *Communication Quarterly,* **35** (1987), 105–124.
B. A. Fisher was a professor in the Department of Communication at the University of Utah. R. K. Stutman is an assistant professor in the Department of Speech Communication at the University of Illinois-Urbana.

This article is useful for its further investigation of the nature of breakpoints in the trajectories of group development as originally outlined in Poole's Multiple Sequence Model of group development. It examines group interaction and comes to five tentative conclusions:

1. Trajectories of group development require frequent maintenance through statements that route group work on the way.
2. Trajectories are typically introduced and maintained by prospective routing statements.

3. Group development often follows a trial-and-error pattern which functions to affirm the existence of a developmental trajectory.
4. Agenda-setting statements can lead to breakpoints if properly timed.
5. Procedural statements may constitute breakpoints when associated with a substantive issue relevant to a groups task.

Keeping Records of Information

Discussants keep records of information for two primary purposes. First, they will need the records for their own use during the discussion. Their system for storing and retrieval can be very personal as long as it ensures adequate information, accurately transcribed, and in a form they can quickly find. Second, they need to keep careful, organized records so that other group members or members of the audience can use the information.

Most libraries now have the technology to facilitate recordkeeping. All students have access to fast, inexpensive copying machines. Many also have access to personal computers and the software to store information and print out what is required in short order. If necessary, students can always use handwritten or typewritten notes.

Researchers should take the same care with their notes that they take with their bibliographies. Each note must have the exact citation for the material recorded from radio or television or print. The addition of a general heading or key words will facilitate filing material and searching for it later. Again, computerized data bases are ideal for such storing and retrieval.

Most of the reports and background analyses will contain statements about factual matters, arguments based on these statements, and value judgments. If the factual matters are particularly important to the group, their original source should be located. For example, if a written report or radio or television program quotes statistical information drawn from the Bureau of Labor Statistics, the members should find the original bureau report and use it. This is particularly crucial if the statistics differ in various books and articles. Information that is commonly accepted by all commentators on a question and that is of incidental importance to the group's work can be gathered from secondary sources.

When a member finds something to record, he or she must decide whether the material should be copied verbatim or outlined or paraphrased. Many students waste time copying too much material word for word. Much information can best be preserved by outlining or summarizing. A good rule of thumb is to paraphrase or outline *unless* the student can think of a good reason for taking a direct quotation. If other members of the group are going to read the cards, the notes must be complete enough to be self-explanatory.

Although discussants need not make direct quotations very often, on some occasions they should do so. If a member plans to support or refute an argument he or she may wish to quote the argument directly. If the author is unusually authoritative, has expressed an idea in a particularly apt or interesting way, or has testified to factual matters in such a way that the language expresses important distinctions, a direct quotation may be preferable.

When recording direct quotations, students must use the exact wording, spelling, and punctuation of the original. If they find an error, they should insert the Latin word *sic,* underlined, in brackets following the error. *Sic* means "thus," and when other members of the group refer to the note later, they will know that the mistake was in the article and not in the copying. Omitted material is replaced by ellipses (. . .). Underlining indicates italics.

Notes should always reflect the general spirit and tenor of the original material. Quoting out of context often distorts the position of the authority. Indeed, one form of dishonesty is to quote out of context purposely to distort the position of the witness. If necessary, the student can add explanatory material in brackets within a direct quotation to ensure that when others examine the note they will not distort the quotation by mistake.

Group members must judge the relevance, importance, and soundness of the material they read in order to take good notes. Each bit of information recorded in a note must be tested, and only the information that passes the appropriate tests should be recorded.

THE STEPS IN THE DISCUSSIONAL PROCESS

Armed with a clearly defined topic, thorough research, and a body of relevant and solid information, group members can now initiate the steps in the discussional process.

Defining the Key Terms of the Discussion Question

Group members assemble to begin their deliberations on the chosen theme. If a working topic has not yet been well formulated, the group should draft a suitable question. The process of definition is important in the formulation of the question and equally important as the group conducts its business.

The members of the group need to come to a common understanding of what the question means. Sometimes this can be done quickly: A few minutes of consideration will reveal a general agreement about the meaning of key terms. On other occasions the group may need to take a bit longer to clarify the most useful ways to use important terms in its discussion.

Reasoning often depends on moving from one term to another, and upon the assumptions implied by definitions. Discussants who examine the manner in which important terms are used can often settle misunderstandings or reveal weaknesses in reasoning. As the discussion continues through the additional steps, the discussants may find themselves confused or in conflict; they are then well advised to clarify definitions of key terms.

Definitions may be made in three ways. First, a term may be defined arbitrarily. A given word can be made to mean different things in different groups. A group may agree to use *lobbyist* or *communist* or *nonconformist* in a clearly specified and stipulated way. Discussants should decide what particular definition will prove most useful to the group and should not be overly concerned about whether that is the "dictionary" meaning of the word. To be sure, unusual and bizarre definitions of common words will be troublesome because old language habits carry over, and the immediate response may be the more usual meaning of the term. For this reason, insofar as possible terms should be used as they are defined in everyday discourse, with arbitrary restrictions and clarifications as needed.

Second, a definition can be made by describing the facts. Descriptive definitions relate not to the meaning of words but to the facts indicated by them. A group member discussing Central America might define communism as a political force in countries that are militantly and aggressively colonizing other countries in the name of world revolution. What the member asserts is not that the word *communism* should be defined arbitrarily to mean such political forces or even whether such militant aggressive forces exist in Central America, but rather that there are, in fact, a number of countries that are militantly and aggressively colonizing other countries for world communism. This definition should be checked, of course, as any other statement of fact would be. What countries is the member referring to? What evidence is there that they are colonizing other countries? If one member of the group uses the term arbitrarily while another is talking about actual countries and the facts involved, they may come to misunderstanding and conflict.

Third, definitions can be made by presenting opinions. For example, a group member may define the *discussional attitude* as an open-minded cooperative approach in which the discussant does not become an advocate. In using this definition, the group member is prescribing a course of action or expressing a value judgment. The definition is not a stipulation assuming certain facts. Obviously, the definition is not descriptive, since some discussants do not have this attitude. If the member means that this is the attitude the group *ought* to have, the definition can be challenged. Another member might say that the preferred attitude is one of competition and commitment.

Clarifying the Group's Goals

After the group has defined the important terms in the question, the next item on the agenda is to clarify the goals that the group hopes to achieve as a result of the meeting. What should a good solution accomplish?

If the problem were being solved by an individual, the person would presumably have a clear goal or goals to guide personal reflective thinking. Since a number of people are involved in the deliberations, however, the members may have conflicting or vague goals. Some discussion to come to agreement on this matter will facilitate subsequent deliberations.

Often the analysis of goals will be brief and group members can come to quick agreement about their objectives. The goals should be recorded and kept available for further consideration as the meeting continues. If the group is not in agreement about goals, it should not proceed in its deliberations. Rather, it should continue to thrash the matter out to save confusion and difficulty in later steps. The goals are of particular help when the group evaluates the various solutions that have been proposed to deal with the problem.

Analyzing the Discussion Problem

In analyzing a problem, the group should begin with several questions: Is something wrong? Is there a problem? Is a change necessary? If the group discovers that things are going well and little is to be gained from change, it should answer the questions negatively. Most one-time discussions deal with topics that result from a feeling that something is certainly wrong. Thus begins a detailed examination of the key question: What are the facts that constitute the problem?

Understanding the Facts   The student will find that some of the information collected is held to be true by all observers and authorities. For example, the wording of the income tax laws of a given state can be found in the legal code, and once the wording is known to the group that fact need not be investigated further. The question of how the wording has, in fact, been interpreted is more open to dispute. Many statements of fact become the subject of dispute. Some observers and authorities maintain that in the last taxable year company X trucked large quantities of its merchandise across the state line just before the tax assessment time. Others maintain this statement is false. If the truthfulness of an important statement of fact is disputed, a question that isolates the disputed point should be asked. For example: Did company X truck large quantities of merchandise across the state line last year? Such a question points up the factual controversies unique to the particular topic.

Describing the Problem   When discussants have resolved the factual controversies, they should begin to fit the statements together. The result will be a coherent description that serves as an answer to the question: What are the facts that constitute the problem? Examples of such statements might be: The state debt as of the last fiscal year was $256,562,000; state mental institutions have four psychiatrists on their staff; the governor's committee to study mental health facilities observed rats in the kitchens of all mental hospitals; the rate of recovery and discharge at all state hospitals for the last ten years has averaged 30 percent.

Explaining the Problem   When the problem has been described, the method of explaining the facts should be determined. Usually the group assumes that these facts can be accounted for in terms of (1) prior facts and (2) human motives. The commonsense label for this complex of forces is *causes*. Thus, the question can be phrased: What causes the problem?

Causal analysis is difficult because commonsense definitions of *cause* are often ambiguous and confused. Discussants must define the various uses of the term to make successful communication possible.

Consider the relatively simple case of a patient who is not feeling well. The doctor can easily describe the symptoms in factual terms: The patient has a temperature of 103 degrees, has difficulty in breathing, and coughs frequently. The doctor can also describe blood count, blood pressure, and pulse rate. She must make a *diagnosis* in order to *account* for the patient's symptoms. The doctor might account for the symptoms on the basis of a bacterial infection in the lungs and say the patient is suffering from pneumonia. If she treats the bacterial infection with penicillin and her diagnosis is correct, the temperature will be lowered, and the other symptoms will disappear. In this instance, the doctor might say that the pneumonia was *caused* by an infection and that the infection was *caused* by bacteria. Such a causal analysis is adequate for her purposes.

A more complex case might be the factual statements relating to the tax situation of a given state. The governor discovers that the kitchens at the state hospitals are infested with rats. The governor tells the superintendent to clean the kitchens and exterminate the rats. The superintendent says he cannot afford to hire exterminators, but if given more money, he would be delighted to clean up the hospital buildings. The governor says that more money is not available because the state is heavily in debt. The superintendent asks why the state is in debt, and the governor answers that the tax structure does not collect enough money to provide the services authorized by the legislature. When asked about revising the tax structure, the governor replies that the legislators are not willing to change the tax base or to raise the tax rates. When asked about their unwillingness, the legislators reply that they will not be reelected if they raise taxes. They indicate that the voters are unaware of conditions in the state hospitals and therefore are willing to pay more taxes to correct them. If this is so, the best solution is to inform the public about the problem in the state hospitals. If people do not want taxes to be raised so that the conditions can be improved because they do not care about the rats in the kitchens and want to keep their money for themselves, a campaign should be started to appeal to their consciences.

The analysis might proceed in another way. If the superintendent says that he does not have enough people or money for the job, the governor might reply that the budget is much larger this year, so that the superintendent can hire more staff; however, further investigation may reveal inefficient administration. In this case, firing the superintendent may be a wise solution. Clearly, an investigating group must account for the facts in a realistic way in order to take wise action.

When a group has determined the underlying causes, it can then develop an effective policy of action to eliminate a problem. Discovering underlying causes of public policy is very difficult, however. The symptom – diagnosis – treatment – cure pattern works almost every time in situations governed by the laws of the natural sciences. If an automobile stops running, the cause may be a lack of gas. The treatment is to add fuel, which makes the car start. If the car still does not work, however, the driver seeks further causes, assuming that several things are wrong. The driver may discover that the carburetor is stuck and the motor flooded. When all the causes for the stopped car are taken care of, the car *inevitably will run.*

A *causal analysis* is one that isolates and organizes the relevant factors or variables relating to a problem in such a way that the problem is explained or accounted for, and dealing with the factors *invariably* results in a solution. A group will usually be successful in solving problems for which causes in this sense of the term can be isolated.

Often problems cannot be subjected to a causal analysis of the type just defined. Sometimes diagnosis of a problem serves to isolate factors that are not invariably associated with the symptoms. If the car is out of gas, the motor invariably stops; but if bacteria are present in the human system, body temperature is not invariably elevated.

Consider the problem of bright students who flunk out of college. Do they lack interest in their work, and if so, why? Perhaps they are emotionally disturbed, lack a clear purpose in life, or are rebelling against their parents, who pressure them to get a degree. Perhaps they lack funds. All these factors may be involved, but a bright student who is emotionally disturbed, has no clear purpose in life, is under great parental pressure to succeed, and lacks funds may still graduate with honors.

When group members explain such situations, they move into the difficult region of probabilities. The failure of the student can be explained by asserting that under such conditions and given these motivations, the results were highly likely or probable. One meaning of the term *probability* is synonymous with the assumption of pure chance — that is, that the events have no discernible pattern and each event happens purely by chance. Using probability in this sense, a statistician can ask, "What is the probability that a coin will turn up heads, or that the next throw of a pair of dice will total 6?" When the assumptions of chance do account for the numbers selected by a roulette wheel or the hands dealt in a poker game, the wise gambler makes decisions on the basis of probabilities in this mathematical sense of the term.

The traditional use of the term *probability* in the study of discussion relates to discovering highly likely patterns in events even if they are not as clearly discerned and invariable as patterns described by the laws of science. If a man has frequently cheated to make money, even at the expense of his health and family, will he be likely to react to a new opportunity to make a large amount of money in the same way? In light of previous observations of this man, a group may project his behavior into the future and assume that he will continue to act as he has in the past.

Since probabilities do not always come true, and the ability to predict what will happen in the future is vital to the decision making of a group, the student of group discussion must understand the basis for reasonable prediction. Often experts disagree about the nature of the causes, probabilities, or human purposes that account for the facts. The discussant should isolate these points of disagreement with questions: To what extent are conditions in the state hospitals the result of inadequate funds or of poor administration? Why are more funds not provided? Is the governor's political ambition a factor? Questions that point up specific controversies relating to a given inquiry are most useful.

The next phase of a discussion group's deliberations is characterized by opinion and evaluation. The group turns to the opening question: How do we evaluate the problem? To answer this question, all members must agree on certain statements of value and their arrangement in some order of priority. How does this question compare with other problems of a similar nature? Is the support of state hospitals to be placed ahead of the support of state universities?

Assume that a student and his parents discuss a common problem facing the family group: the student's falling grade average. A few statements of fact describe the problem. The grade in chemistry is F, in psychology D, in English C, and in German D. Accounting for the problem takes a bit more time. The family group agrees that the grades cannot be explained by a lack of ability. High school grades, passing grades for the fall semester at the university, and high test scores on the entrance examinations all discount this explanation. At first, the parents feel the student has not been working hard enough, but the student persuades them that he has been working very hard: He has carried 16 credits and has been working 30 hours a week at a downtown department store. Finally the family group decides that the problem results from trying to do too many things. The parents perceive that their son is more interested in his car (which he holds down a job to maintain) than in his degree. The parents judge the problem to be severe and large. The student feels that one term on probation will not jeopardize his college career. He wants to continue for a time and see how things work out. His parents discuss the issue from a set of value statements that places top priority on gaining the degree and rather low priority on keeping the car. The student, on the other hand, places considerable value on the university diploma, but would sacrifice the degree if necessary to keep the car.

Listing Possible Solutions

The next major question in the analysis of a problem is: What are the representative solutions suggested to solve the problem? At this point in the discussion, the group members are searching for plans and programs that people trying to deal with the problem have put forward as answers. The group members should simply list the solutions in enough detail so all members understand the proposals. The group should next develop additional solutions that seem effective to the members. These should be added to the list. At this stage in the deliberations, some freewheeling creativity is in order.

Analyzing the Solutions Pro and Con

In this phase of the problem-solving meeting, the group members should take up their list of possible solutions and reflect about the strengths and weaknesses of each. The group should use the goals developed in step 2 to guide its evaluation of the recommendations.

The group members might begin with questions of practicality. How practical is the proposed solution? Is it economically feasible? Can it be developed and put into operation in time? Do we have the knowledge, material, and other human resources needed to implement the solution?

The group should next turn to questions of beneficiality. Will the proposed solution be beneficial? Will it deal with the problem as analyzed in step 3? Will it treat surface symptoms or get at root causes? Will it achieve the goals the group established in step 2?

Finally, the group should consider questions of desirability. Will the proposed solution be detrimental? Will it bring undesirable results not anticipated by its proponents? Will it create new problems that will have to be dealt with in turn?

Selecting the Best Solution

After thoroughly examining the proposed solutions and weighing them pro and con, the group members should select the solution which seems best upon careful analysis. This solution may be one currently under consideration by society or one suggested by the meeting participants. Finally, the members might decide to improve their decision by adding to or subtracting from a solution on their list or by merging several solutions or portions of several solutions.

The selection stage is the point where the group must strive for productive disagreement. In a one-time meeting it is easy to take flight from disagreement and conflict, both of which are socially unpleasant; but a good meeting needs to have a communicative climate in which such thrashing out of alternatives is possible.

The steps in the discussional process as explained above were the core of the ideal meeting in the early days of group discussion. This ideal — the problem-solving meeting — still has validity today. Many group meetings are of that nature or can use such an approach to their deliberations to good effect. With the passage of time, however, the scope of the teaching about one-time discussion groups has expanded to include meetings designed for purposes other than problem solving. In the remainder of this chapter the broadened view of the uses of one-time meetings will guide the analysis.

ADDITIONAL USES OF ONE-TIME MEETINGS

Using Meetings to Inform

People developing or planning a short course, symposium, seminar, or retreat might well consider one or more of the many additional forms of discussion in order to give participants information. Public discussion encourages audience participation, thus ensuring that the available time is used to answer questions the audience wants and needs to have answered. In addition, when experts are free to challenge one another, information will not be accepted simply because it comes from an authority.

The business meeting is often a briefing session, designed in part to guard against the charge that important people within the organization have not been informed or consulted.

Using Meetings to Stimulate Interest

Participants often use the public discussion program to stimulate interest in important questions. If experts present relevant information about an important problem and discuss representative solutions, even though they do not reach a solution, listeners become more aware of the problem and may begin to investigate it.

Discussion is prevalent in educational settings. The short course, symposium, seminar, or retreat seldom sustains itself entirely with a series of lectures. Most conference planners try to pack a great amount of material into a short time. Conferees, however, will seldom tolerate eight to ten hours a day of concentrated lectures, no matter how dynamic, entertaining, and informative the lecturers may be. One way to change pace is to alternate lectures with discussions. An audience has a tendency to sit back and relax when an instructor begins to lecture. The instructor may hold their interest, but the audience is not actively involved in the learning process. When the program of the conference moves from a lecture to a discussion, the participants are under considerable social pressure to take part; thus, participation fosters interest.

Using Meetings to Stimulate Creativity

Discussion programs are sometimes used to stimulate creativity and new ideas. The dramatic form of such discussion is the one developed and popularized by the advertising executive Alex Osborn under the label *brainstorming*. Osborn used the informality and spontaneity that characterizes discussion programs to stimulate people to dream up "wild" ideas and solutions to specified problems.

An interesting variation of brainstorming is the *nominal group*. Investigators comparing the brainstorming group to generate ideas with the efforts of the same subjects working individually discovered that people sitting together and working silently generated more ideas than they did when participating in a brainstorming session. Conference planners applied the research discovery to encourage creativity by using the nominal-group technique. The participants are divided into groups and given a period of time in which to think up ideas and write them down while sitting with the others. After a period of listing ideas in the nominal group, the members begin to communicate and form an interacting group. They select a recorder, and each member reads his or her list. The recorder puts the list of ideas on a blackboard or flip chart, combining similar ideas, until all suggestions are before the group. The members then begin to evaluate the list critically, culling out the unsatisfactory ideas until a solution emerges.

TYPES OF DISCUSSION FORMATS

Planners of discussion programs can choose from a wide variety of formats. There is so much diversity that considering all the details or even most of the modifications is pointless. Students who plan a discussion program may want to introduce some novelty in the format by modifying current practice. However, some general features of discussion programs cut across the many different specific formats.

Forum Discussions

If there is a special time set aside during the program for audience participation, the program is a *forum discussion*. If the discussion program is presented on radio and television, the audience may ask questions by letter or telephone. Regardless of the form of the discussion proper, the producers may aim for audience participation if one of their purposes is to involve the audience and thus stimulate their interest. A forum period is sometimes not used because of time limitations or the explosive nature of the subject and the occasion.

Panel Discussions

In the *panel discussion*, a small group of discussants talk, much as in a conversation, about the topic. Informality is the keynote, and the members of the group can interrupt one another. A *moderator* may be assigned the role of cutting off verbose members and encouraging quiet ones. The panel discussion is often organized around an outline of topics or questions, and the participants extemporize their comments much as a speaker might outline and deliver a speech extemporaneously. The panel using an outline can adapt to the audience situation and to the unfolding discussion. If participants get "going" and depart to some extent from the planned outline, the group may prefer to continue on a tangent for a time because it is rewarding. In like manner, if a topic is covered more quickly than expected, the group may modify its time allotment. This freedom to maneuver is one of the virtues of the panel discussion. It allows a panel of experienced public discussants to present a lively, extemporaneous program that gives the illusion of being a spontaneous working session and at the same time offer an organized program that covers the topic concisely and efficiently. The good panel discussion program appears to be a natural and spontaneous conference. The illusion is the result of careful planning and considerable artistry on the part of the participants.

The flexibility of structure can also be a liability. The participants must keep a balance between improvisations and planning. They may assume that there is no need for preparation since the panel discussion is informal and consists of just "kicking the topic around." The result is that they may flounder about and fail to cover the topic. This is a distinct danger in classroom panel discussions. Students should not be misled by the deceptively simple format of the panel. On the other hand, a group must also guard against the other extreme: If planned too carefully, the program may proceed with dispatch and be well organized, but seem like a "canned" performance.

The panel discussion is well adapted to public discussion programs on radio and television. Radio is preeminently an informal and intimate medium. The radio panel discussion is one of the most popular formats and is widely used for public affairs broadcasting and political campaigning. The panel discussion also exploits the visual potentialities of television. The television camera can convey the facial gestures that highlight verbal intonations as the individual participants speak. The extemporaneous nature of the panel discussion projects a naturalness that allows viewers to get a clear impression of the personalities of the participants.

The panel discussion is also well suited to presenting programs to relatively small audiences in informal surroundings. The 40-seat classroom that is filled to capacity is a good setting.

Symposium Discussions

Another widespread form of public discussion is the *symposium discussion*. In the symposium, a group of experts divides up the topic. Each is allotted a certain amount of uninterrupted time in which to make a brief statement. After the prepared speeches, the experts may participate in a panel discussion, they may question one another, another group of interrogators may question them, or the audience may be invited to participate.

The symposium is less spontaneous and more formal than the panel discussion; however, audience participation and questions and answers from other participants may add a measure of spontaneity. It does have the advantage of not requiring extensive planning. Care must be taken that the symposium does not become simply a program of speeches. There must be an attempt at give-and-take. Symposiums also require participation by all discussants. Panel discussions are sometimes dominated by the more extroverted, voluble members, with the result that some positions are not represented adequately.

The symposium is suited to programs presented from a stage to a relatively large audience in an auditorium. It is also useful when the occasion calls for more formality and for greater emphasis on the authoritative nature of the participants than can be furnished by a variation of the panel discussion.

Interrogations

Broadcasters have popularized another version of the discussion program — a format that, essentially, involves the questioning of experts. In the dialogues of Plato, Socrates plays a game in which one party to the dialogue agrees to answer all the other person's questions. In this fashion, the questioner is given a chance to test the adequacy of the other person's ideas. The oral examining committee that questions a graduate student operates in a similar way. The questioning is probing and is designed to catch inconsistencies or inadequacies of thinking. Questions can also be used to elicit further information or to gain greater understanding. Many radio and television programs have had formats in which an expert or a group of experts answers the questions posed by another group of people. According to the rules, the questioners are not to make statements and speeches, and the experts are not to ask questions. Such television programs as *Meet the Press* and *Face the Nation* are examples.

Interrogation is a popular technique in broadcasting, for it often results in conflict, and conflict is inherently interesting. The audience likes a dogfight, and if the questioner can pin down the expert or make the expert angry, the program is likely to be more interesting. Conflict also allows the members of the audience to identify with one or more of the personalities involved. Programs of this sort are dramatic and have much appeal. Interrogation formats that force participants into conflict are often used because public affairs programs must compete with entertainment programs for audiences. As a result, the number of interrogation formats that exemplify the spirit of inquiry is very small.

A prevalent use of interrogation is as a modification of another form of public discussion. For example, at some point in a panel discussion the audience is invited to ask questions, or the members of a symposium discussion are given a chance to question one another. The interrogation period is useful in testing ideas and gaining audience involvement and participation. And it is perhaps most worthwhile as a device to ensure that information is understood. Questions from the audience indicate what is grasped and what is not.

Students planning a discussion program for an audience will find that asking questions for information and clarification will be the least troublesome and most useful type of inquiry. Questioning to test ideas requires considerable skill in the art of interrogation. Too often, the questioner who tries to test the authority ends by making speeches in the form of questions.

Conferences

Conferences in which a large number of people actively participate, as compared to the small group program, are also usually organized around a central theme, although they may continue for several days or even a week or longer. Conferences that use discussion as a main procedural tool may have groups meeting in private, or the groups may meet in a large room.

Conference sessions tend to be intensive, and many participants are not accustomed to working in such a setting. Conference planners must bear in mind the importance of holding the audience's attention. In addition to a wide range of audiovisual devices such as films, filmstrips, tape recordings, and flannelboard presentations, they often use special techniques to stimulate participation.

Combining and Modifying Forms of Discussion

Freshness of format is achieved through combining and modifying the basic forms of discussion to serve the needs of a specific program or conference. A panel discussion might be combined with a forum period, making a panel–forum discussion. A symposium discussion can also be combined with a forum period. The symposium may be followed by a panel discussion by the members of the symposium, and this, in turn, may be followed by an audience forum. The program might begin with an opening set of statements by the participants (symposium), followed by an interrogation period to test ideas and to examine the experts, and finally by a closing set of statements (another symposium). Or the program might begin with a panel and end with a closing summary by each member. A symposium presentation could be followed by a forum period including everyone in the audience. A conference could begin with a lecture, followed by an interrogation session, followed by a symposium composed of a spokesperson from each of the discussion groups, followed by a forum under the direction of the lecturer.

Obviously, the possibilities for innovation and modification are numerous; and when students plan a discussion program, they should ask themselves which forms in what combinations will help them best to achieve their objectives for the given program or conference.

SUMMARY

The one-time meeting is a communication event composed of a group of people drawn together for a purpose that is to be achieved in one meeting. The composition of the group is unique to the occasion.

Because of its transitory nature, the one-time meeting accepts prescribed structures and uses stereotyping devices to provide procedures for doing its work.

One-time meetings include the private discussion, the public discussion, and the conference or workshop.

Discussion is often organized around a general theme. Even so, a good meeting requires a working topic formulated as a question to limit and structure the program. The questions may be ones of fact, of value, of conjecture, or of policy.

Group members gain most of their information from personal experience, interviews, the electronic media, and library materials. The first step in gathering material is to develop bibliographic information. Once group members find useful items, they should begin recording information in computer data bases or on note cards.

The first step in the discussional process is to define key terms. Definitions can be made in three ways: (1) the definitional form can be arbitrary within the confines of usage, (2) the definitional form can be used to describe facts indicated by a term, and (3) the definitional form can be used to present opinions.

The second step in the discussional process is to clarify the group's goals and ensure that the members agree on what is to be achieved by a good solution.

The third step in the discussional process is to analyze the problem. During the third step, the discussants discover the nature and extent of the problem and an explanation for it. They decide on the severity and importance of the problem and compare it with other problems.

The fourth and fifth steps in the discussional process are to list the representative solutions and to discuss each one pro and con. Group members examine the solutions in terms of how practical and beneficial they are as well as for their potential detrimental effects.

The sixth step is to find the best solution. Group members engage in productive disagreement, thrashing out the merits of alternative solutions. Members finally eliminate the less practical and beneficial options until the best solution emerges.

One-time meetings are useful for purposes other than problem solving. One-time meetings may be used to inform participants, to stimulate interest in a topic, to encourage participants to form their own opinions, and to stimulate creativity.

The basic forms of public discussion are the forum, the panel, the symposium, and the interrogation. Forum discussions are those in which the audience is encouraged to participate; panels are organized around a topic in ways that encourage a free flow of communication; symposiums are set speeches by the participants; interrogations are periods devoted to questions and answers.

Group discussions are widely used in conferences. These often include long or short one-time meetings to discuss part of the conference agenda. Group reports are then made available to the larger group of conference participants.

☞ Rules of Thumb

Practical Advice on How to Be a Good Group Member

Drawn from Chapter 2

- ☞ When you are a member of a one-time meeting, accept assigned leadership and procedures in order to achieve stipulated goals.
- ☞ Many of the communication skills useful in the one-time meeting transfer to long-term groups.
- ☞ Be sure that your discussion group has a clearly formulated statement of its topic.
- ☞ An excellent question for a discussion is one that asks for a policy statement rather than about facts or about values.
- ☞ Examine your personal background and experience for information and organize your thinking in preparation for a discussion.
- ☞ Interviews, the electronic and print media, and libraries are all excellent sources of information in preparing for a discussion.
- ☞ When you find information that seems pertinent, you should make a bibliographic record of it.
- ☞ Appraise the sources of your information to discover their biases, and do not confine your search to sources with similar biases.
- ☞ Keep systematic records of your information in a personal computer data base or on annotated note cards.
- ☞ Locate original sources for important factual material whenever possible.
- ☞ When recording direct quotations, be sure to use the exact wording of the original.
- ☞ Take notes that reflect the general spirit and tenor of the original.
- ☞ Use the steps in the discussional process to guide your research into a discussion question.
- ☞ Think through the definitions useful in clarifying the most important key terms.
- ☞ In analyzing key definitions, keep in mind the differences among definitions that stipulate a meaning for a term, definitions that describe facts, and definitions that present an opinion.
- ☞ In the beginning of your analysis, consider possible goals for the group.
- ☞ Your analysis of the problem is an important feature of proper preparation for discussion.
- ☞ A careful listing and evaluation of possible solutions is a key to successful analysis.
- ☞ A tentative consideration of the best solution is indicated, but leave final selection to the discussion proper.

☛ One-time meetings can be used to stimulate interest in a topic or to stimulate creativity in dealing with a problem.

☛ There are a wide variety of formats for the one-time meeting, including the panel, symposium, and forum discussions and the interrogation.

QUESTIONS FOR STUDY

1. What is the difference between a one-time meeting and an ad hoc committee?
2. What are the cultural expectations for a one-time meeting in the United States?
3. How might questions of fact, value, conjecture, and policy be compared and contrasted for group discussion purposes?
4. What are some typical sources of information for group discussion and how might they be used in preparation for a meeting?
5. How might the three ways of defining terms be compared and contrasted in the first step of the discussional process?
6. How can the clarification of group goals in the second step of the discussional process aid in the subsequent discussion?
7. What are some techniques for describing and explaining the problem in the third step of the problem-solving discussional process?
8. Briefly explain the process of listing and evaluating solutions in the fourth and fifth steps of the problem-solving discussional process.
9. How might groups proceed to select the best solution in the sixth step of the discussional process?
10. What are some of the uses of one-time meetings in addition to the problem-solving discussion?

EXERCISES

1. List 20 topics that you would like to discuss in class. Include 5 questions of fact, 5 questions of value, 5 questions of conjecture, and 5 questions of policy. Take particular care to word the questions clearly and precisely.
2. With a group of your classmates, select a topic for discussion. Each member is to search the library for sources relating to the topic and prepare 20 bibliographic notations in proper form for use by the group.
3. With a group of your classmates, select a topic for discussion. Each member is to survey useful information relating to the topic and prepare 10 items of information in a form suitable for use by the group.
4. With a group of your classmates, select a question of policy to serve as the basis for a discussion. After a thorough search for information, make a careful analysis of the topic. Prepare an outline that includes (a) a description of the problem, (b) an explanation of the problem, (c) an evaluation of the importance of

the problem, and (d) a list of possible solutions with their advantages and disadvantages considered. Follow accepted outlining procedure, and note the sources for your information in the margin.

5. With a group of your classmates, prepare a problem-solving discussion. Conduct the meeting in the style of a panel discussion and go through the steps of the discussional process. Tape-record your discussion so you can evaluate it afterward.

REFERENCES AND SUGGESTED READINGS

For other descriptions of the one-time meeting, see:

Bormann, Ernest G., and Nancy C. Bormann. *Effective Small Group Communication.* 4th ed. Minneapolis, MN: Burgess, 1988.

Brilhart, John K. *Effective Group Discussion.* 6th ed. Dubuque, IA: William C. Brown, 1988.

For more on message analysis, see:

Bettinghaus, Erwin P. *Message Preparation: The Nature of Proof.* Indianapolis: Bobbs-Merrill, 1966.

Schiff, Roselyn L., et al. *Communication Strategy: A Guide to Message Preparation.* Glenview, IL: Scott, Foresman, 1981.

Chapter
3

Planning and Participating in Group Discussions

*T*he last chapter described the ideal models for group discussions, models that provide the basis for joint enterprises, with an emphasis on the good one-time problem-solving meeting. This chapter presents the rules of thumb growing out of experience with group discussions and provides recommendations on how to achieve good discussion groups.

PLANNING THE GROUP DISCUSSION

Selecting a Suitable Format for Discussion

Analysis of the purpose, the audience, and the occasion aids meeting planners in picking a format. An informal discussion designed to stimulate audience interest could take the panel, forum, or interrogation form—or a combination of them. When the purpose is to furnish information to large audiences, the group might select an adaptation of the symposium. A group producing a discussion show for radio or television will want to exploit the intimacy of these media by using innovations in the panel–interrogation format.

Selecting the Physical Setting

The planners must select a suitably sized room, arrange furniture, and attend to such matters as seeing to the public address system and being sure that the doors are open on time and that the room is clean and adequately ventilated.

Program planners will find careful attention to details of room selection and arrangement to be worthwhile. Investigations of the effect of spatial relationships on communication in small groups indicate that the physical setting and proximity of members are of considerable significance.

Individuals and groups tend to select a territory and then defend their proprietary rights to the area. Seating arrangements tend to increase or decrease the members' feelings of ease or discomfort as to where they are sitting. Individuals also have boundaries of personal space that they do not like to have invaded, and the arrangement of tables and chairs should take this fact into account. The distances that separate members will also influence the flow of communication. The members will have preferences for what they consider comfortable distances for talking with one another depending on the degree of intimacy among them and on the content of the communication.

Most important for the planners of a meeting to consider is the fact that the spatial arrangements in terms of table shape, size, and location in the room and the placement of chairs around the table will affect the flow and direction of messages. When the group is placed at a round or square table, the situation will encourage the flow of communication across the table. Members will tend to talk to others facing them rather than to the persons adjacent to them. If the table is rectangular, the members tend to perceive one end of it as the head position, and they will tend to look to the person sitting there for direction. Often the moderator of a one-time meeting will arrange to have a rectangular table in order to sit at the head and encourage the group to accept the moderating of the meeting.

A relatively bare meeting room is better than a lavishly furnished conference room. Overstuffed chairs and mahogany conference tables are comfortable, but they separate members of the group. Also, such a setting distracts the group's attention away from the meeting.

Auditoriums are not always suitable for presenting speeches or discussion programs. The wise planner will shun the large, spacious auditorium with a high stage or platform, an elaborate speaker's stand, and a complicated public address system. Experienced public speakers who wish to talk to their audiences, judge their response, and perhaps encourage their participation will often speak from *in front of the stage*, rather than from the speaker's stand up on the stage. Raised platforms and stages establish a distance between the audience and speakers that inhibits informality and spontaneity.

In general, planners should check the facilities before scheduling the program. Sometimes the best available is far from ideal, and they should then exploit the room's possibilities. For example, even if the program is held in a large auditorium with a stage, all the seats can be roped off except for a few in the front rows. The participants can then use chairs in front of the stage immediately before the audience, at its level.

The settings for after-lunch or after-dinner programs are often particularly poor. The audience may be scattered around the room, facing different directions, while tables are being cleared. One solution to this problem is to set up chairs in rows in a separate section of the dining room, to which the audience can move for the program. If this cannot be done, members of the audience may be requested, after the meal, to move their chairs around and arrange themselves in a more suitable manner.

Arranging the Participants

It is most important that the participants be able to talk easily to the audience and to each other. One good arrangement is to seat them along one side of a table, with the more active participants at each end. Another is to seat members in a semicircle with the moderator in the middle and the talkative members at the ends. Another common arrangement is to place several tables in the shape of a U, with the panel at the head table and the audience seated at the other tables. If a meal is to be served first, an audience seated around U-shaped tables is in a better position to listen and participate than an audience scattered at smaller tables throughout the room. Members of such an audience are sometimes more willing to participate, and they are all part of the same group. However, these advantages do not apply to a large group; with more than 30 people, this arrangement is unwieldy. For larger audiences, the planners should rearrange the room so that the audience sits in rows. Even if they need tables to write on, rows of tables are more conducive to audience participation than the U-shaped arrangement.

In planning a conference, the facilities for each discussion group should be carefully arranged. A table is helpful, as it furnishes a focal point for the deliberations. It allows members to lean forward and to write more easily. Everyone at the table, in a sense, is invited to participate. However, the table can become a problem. If the table is not large enough, members with a reluctance to speak up may use the lack of space as an excuse to withdraw from the discussion. If the table is rectangular, role struggles may be accentuated because early in the discussion considerable significance is attached to sitting at the "head" of the table. If the table is too large, it may serve as a mental barrier to the flow of discussion. When an oversized central table is used, conference planners are wise to place chairs away from the table and have the groups huddle together for discussion.

Preparing for Public Discussion

In the classroom, the instructor may expect all students preparing a discussion to hold planning meetings. The importance of joint planning cannot be overemphasized. The process of working together on the plan will provide clues about interactions that may develop during the program. Even a short planning period will accomplish some of the necessary social structuring of the group. The entire group should, when possible, work out the outline that will serve to organize the program.

Planners of discussion programs for community organizations may find that it is impossible to assemble all the experts for a planning session. If the program is for radio or television, a preliminary meeting might be held just prior to air time. A half-hour or hour warm-up discussion over coffee before taping or air time will break the primary tension of the members and create a livelier program from the beginning.

Preparing the Outline   The discussion program has much in common with the extemporaneous speech, and, when possible, the group should outline its performance in a similar way. First, the participants should clarify the purpose of the program. If the discussants disagree about purpose, this should be the first item on the agenda of their planning meeting. Then the group should select and arrange the material and decide how time should be apportioned, considering the importance of the items on the outline and the interests, informational background, and understanding of the audience. Here is a sample agenda for the discussion group's planning session:

1. What should be the purpose of our program?
    a) Is our primary purpose presenting information?
    b) Is our primary purpose to arouse interest in the question?
    c) Is our primary purpose to stimulate members of the audience to engage in further study and make up their own minds?
    d) Is our primary purpose to encourage creativity and new ideas?
    e) Is our primary purpose to go through the process of inquiry, seeking a solution to the problem?
2. What materials should be included in the program?
    a) What problems should we discuss?
    b) What evidence should be presented?
    c) What points of view should be included?
    d) What solutions should be considered?
    e) What devices to interest the audience should be included (examples, analogies, personal experiences, narrative materials)?
3. How should the material be arranged?
    a) Should we follow the steps of the discussional pattern (definitions, goals, problems, solutions, analysis of solutions, selection of best solution)?
    b) Should the material be organized topically?
    c) Should the material be organized chronologically?
    d) Should the material be organized spatially?
4. How should we apportion discussion time?
    a) What is the most important section? The next most important? Can some of the material be dropped? Have we forgotten anything?
    b) How much time should we allot to the most important section? To the next most important?
    c) How much time should we provide for introduction and conclusion?

Individuals may keep detailed outlines containing examples, statistics, personal experiences, or positions to be included under each major division. Just as an extemporaneous speaker may modify a speech, so the discussion group can depart from its outline because of changing conditions. The group members may find it impossible to include certain material, or they may forget to do so. Nonetheless, the program will have greater unity, clarity, and impact if the discussion group develops an outline to use as a basis for its program.

Here is a sample of an outline suitable for a 30-minute panel discussion:

[Intro.: 1 min.]	*Purpose:* To obtain audience involvement and participation in an important problem.
	Question: What policy should the United States follow to halt the spread of communism in Central America?
[Definition: 2 min.]	1. What terms need to be defined?
	a. What do we mean by communism?
	b. What do we mean by Central America?
[5 min.]	2. How widespread is communism in Central America?
[3 min.]	3. Is it likely to spread further?
[5 min.]	4. Why is communism gaining influence in Central America?
[12 min.]	5. What might our government do to stop the spread of communism in Central America?
[Conclusion: 2 min.]	

The symposium discussion is somewhat easier to plan, since each member has a definite responsibility and a certain amount of time. The group should draw an outline similar to the one for the panel discussion and then assign the major topics to individual members. Here is a sample of an outline suitable for a 30-minute symposium discussion:

[3 min.]	Introduction of topic and speakers by moderator.
	Purpose: To obtain audience involvement and participation in an important problem.
	Question: What policy should the United States follow to halt the spread of communism in Central America?
[6 min. each speaker]	*First Speaker:* The present situation.
	1. Definition of terms.
	2. Current state of communism in Central America.
	3. Evidence for future growth.
	Second Speaker: Factors encouraging the growth of communism in Central America.
	Third Speaker: Economic solutions to the problem.
	Fourth Speaker: Political and diplomatic solutions to the problem.
	[Additional minutes to allow a cushion for changing speakers]

Rehearsal of the Panel Discussion A good program stops when audience interest and involvement are high. A rehearsal of the program helps to attain this objective. Since panel discussion groups have a tendency to try to cover too much ground, a rehearsal will indicate whether the group has too much material. Of course, it will also reveal too little material on the agenda. Members of the audience should leave the program feeling that they would have *liked* more time, but not that they *needed* more time to understand the material.

A rehearsal will also enable members to be more fluent during the program. Having expressed their ideas, participants will be able to find the words to express them again more readily. The pace of the program can then increase. In general, the faster people join in with comments, the greater sense of pace and tempo the program will project; also, pauses and gropings for expression that slow the pace will be reduced.

The discussion group must be careful not to rehearse so thoroughly that the program seems "canned" or mechanical. It is a mistake to destroy the illusion that the program is a spontaneous and informal discussion, and the overrehearsed group may sound like an amateur drama in which the cast has not learned its lines.

PARTICIPATING IN A ONE-TIME MEETING

Characteristics of a Good Participant

Participants should adopt an open-minded, objective, and unbiased attitude. They should listen to all points of view and describe problems as the observation of the facts indicates they are, rather than as they wish the facts were. This ideal is often beyond reach of the participants, but it is a goal worth striving to approximate.

Good participants contribute to the program with their full ability. Their comments are short and to the point. They gear their contributions exactly to the topic and develop only one point at a time.

Participants in a one-time meeting do not have time to develop appropriate idiosyncratic group norms. Instead, certain culturally approved norms govern social interactions for strangers meeting for a brief discussion program. These norms are simply *good manners*—the regulation of conduct so that disagreements are tactfully phrased and so that all members of the panel and the audience are treated with courtesy and have an equal opportunity to participate. Breaches of good manners disturb the participants because they violate expectations. Tactless comments and impolite behavior suggest that some members of the group are not willing to abide by the generally accepted rules of behavior. The members, aware that working out a new set of standard operating procedures would require considerable time and energy, often become irritated by such behavior. For these reasons, the good discussant conforms to the expectations of tact, good manners, politeness, and courtesy. The discussant should not sacrifice relevant information or refrain from asking questions to test information for fear of embarrassing someone. Good participants manage to test information by suggesting with their language and manner that they are concerned with the *content* of what is being said, not the *person* who says it.

Characteristics of a Good Moderator

Good participants expect one person to be responsible for procedural and administrative decisions relating to the meeting, just as that person expects good manners among the discussants. The person who assumes this role is usually called a moderator, chair, or leader.

Moderators must have a commitment to the meeting and a desire to produce a good discussion. They should have enough time and energy to devote to the task. They should enjoy participating in discussions and in the give-and-take and frustrations sometimes associated with the process of inquiry. They should be good speakers. Above all, they should be knowledgeable in the skills and principles of public discussion. They must know how to use discussion groups for various purposes and be familiar with the formats most suitable to their needs. They should understand the nature of inquiry and advocacy and the advantages and disadvantages of each kind of public program.

MODERATING THE ONE-TIME MEETING

Duties of a Moderator

The moderator usually introduces the members to one another, and to the audience if it is a public meeting. Moderators also introduce the topic and conclude the session. Most important, they supervise the channels of communication and try to involve members who are not participating and to allow any person who has not spoken to have the floor before someone else has a second chance. They try to prevent one or two members from talking too much and keep an eye on the time and the agenda. They try to keep the group on the subject and on schedule. If the program is a public forum, they call on members of the audience and control the discussion, much as the chair of a parliamentary meeting does.

The moderator also has a number of less well-defined duties pertaining to the social climate of the meeting. For example, the general social tone will be set early, and the moderator is largely responsible for establishing the mood that allows people to relax and to participate.

Since the role of moderator is so complex, the question of substantive participation often arises. A case can be made for restricting the moderator to the special functions of administration and procedural control. If the panel contains an adequate representation of authorities and the moderator can serve little useful function by taking substantive part in the discussion, the meeting is better served if the moderator remains confined to the procedural role. But if the panel is small and the moderator is an authority or a person whose opinion the audience wants to hear, the moderator may serve as both a procedural organizer and a contributor. If the latter course is chosen, the moderator should announce that dual role early in the session so that the members will know what to expect.

The moderator has three basic tools to use in conducting procedural leadership during the discussion: the question, the summary statement, and the direction.

Asking Questions Many one-time meetings take place in a voluntary context and arouse expectations that democratic procedures will be used; that is, the audience assumes that all points of view will be presented, that everyone will be allowed to speak, and that majority opinion will prevail. The audience expects the moderator to be democratic and to ask people what they *want* to do rather than tell them what they *will* do. The question is one of the most important devices available to the moderator.

The moderator may phrase questions in such a way that they suggest a response of a certain kind. In one kind of phrasing, the proper response is either *yes* or *no*. For example, the moderator may ask a panel member, "Dr. Homberg, are you a member of the American Medical Association?" Such questions are useful in getting a considerable amount of factual information quickly. Several skillful questions of this sort can reveal a great deal of information. However, such questions do not encourage participation. The aggressive participant may go on to a statement. Dr. Homberg might respond, "No, I do not belong to the AMA," and then interrupt the moderator's next question to say, "Just let me explain for a minute why I do not." But a participant who is reluctant to enter the discussion may simply respond with a *no*.

Another kind of phrasing, characterized as the either–or question, suggests that *either* answer A *or* answer B is appropriate. "Do we want to explore this point further or should we move on to the next problem?" The form of the question makes it difficult to supply a third answer. An aggressive participant may respond, "Neither. I suggest we take a five-minute break." But participants are more likely to accept the implications of the question and select one of the suggested answers. The moderator can use questions of this type to suggest procedure and to structure the group's response without appearing autocratic. This sort of question is also useful in eliciting information quickly, but tends to restrict the range of responses.

A third kind of question is open-ended and seeks a wide range of responses. The moderator may ask, "Where should we begin?" or "How do you react to this suggestion?" Asked early, such a question is likely to be met with silence because it provides little suggestion as to the appropriate response. The participants must do too much of the structuring. In addition, the nervous tension present in the first minutes of a meeting often inhibits quick responses. Both of these factors can produce embarrassing silence. If the moderator senses that the panel is tense and unsure, he or she might begin with the more structured questions, moving to the open-ended type only after tensions have eased and the panel has warmed up. Open-ended questions suggest an atmosphere of respect for the group's opinion and suggestion. They emphasize the moderator's role as gatekeeper for group opinions and decisions rather than as a giver of directives. Open-ended questions are, therefore, democratic; but they can invite anarchy and confusion. Because they do little to structure the response, they may stimulate discussion far removed from the point under consideration.

On occasion, moderators may wish to participate in the discussion without seeming to do so, and they may then use assertions framed in question form to present their ideas. Sometimes these questions are characterized as leading questions, loaded questions, or argumentative questions. However, the group will find it less confusing to think of these as *propositions* asserted in the grammatical form of questions rather than as interrogations or inquiries. The following are propositions asserted in question form:

"When will the AMA cease being a reactionary force and recognize the needs of the American people for medical security?" (*Translation:* The AMA is a reactionary force that does not recognize the needs of the American people for medical security.)

"How do you explain the inconsistency in your position when you advocate freedom and in the next breath deny freedom of speech?" (*Translation:* You are inconsistent, for you both advocate freedom and deny certain individuals the right to speak.)

"Don't you think that it is simple justice to give the man in a divorce proceeding equal rights before the law in regard to the custody of the children?" (*Translation:* Men do not now have equal rights before the law in regard to the custody of children, and this is unjust.)

Generally, use of this technique is dangerous in public discussion. Moderators who use many such assertions will inject themselves into the discussion in an indirect way that often confuses both the participants and the audience. If the participants are unaware of what the moderator is doing, they become confused. They realize that something about the question prevents them from answering it as they would like to. The grammatical form of the statement tricks them into regarding it as an interrogation. If they realize what is going on, they will treat the question as an assertion and begin by answering that they do not agree with its assumptions or implications. This reaction involves the moderator as a debater. Thus, if the participant responds with violent disagreement to the assertion that the AMA is a force of reaction, the moderator is forced out of the role as moderator into a role as debater.

In such a situation, moderators can retreat and resume their normal role or accept the challenge and continue the debate either with further assertions phrased as questions (which becomes quite a tax on anyone's ingenuity) or with argumentative statements. Moderators who do this, however, can no longer assume the role of objectively and dispassionately steering the discussion. Also, if they lose the argument, they will also lose considerable status and thus be less effective. Finally, once moderators enter a debate they may monopolize the proceedings, as their role includes the control of the channels of communication. Moderators need much self-discipline to let a participant have the floor when they have a winning argument on their lips. Nonetheless, the moderator keeps this technique of propositions in question form in reserve so that when certain positions of importance are being slighted, those positions can be expressed. Sometimes a moderator will use this technique simply to enliven a program that threatens to become very dull.

A discussion program often begins by orienting the audience to the facts in the case. Fact-finding questions are generally phrased in *what* form: "What is the case at Roosevelt High School?" "What are the current income tax rates in this state?" By confining themselves to questions that ask for factual information early in the program, moderators are more likely to keep the group on topics that orient the audience. Factual information tends to be less controversial and thus is a good place to begin the discussion. The moderator may use yes–no, either–or, or open-ended questions. After the audience has been oriented, the moderator often asks questions designed to isolate factors or causes that explain the facts. These can be thought of as *why* questions: "Why did the United Nations fail to keep the peace in the Middle East?" "Why is there anti-American feeling in Central America?"

After the audience has been oriented to the *why* of the case, the program may consider possible courses of action. Questions that emphasize *how* will then be useful: "How might we overcome anti-American feeling?" "How can we deal with drug problems at Roosevelt High School?" "How can we improve our divorce laws?" As the group proceeds with the program, the moderator may periodically ask various participants to evaluate the accumulating facts and suggestions. Questions that imply the *what* form are most useful to get evaluations. The moderator may use yes–no, either–or, or open-ended questions to determine the *what*, the *why*, and the *how* of the topic. For example, the moderator may ask, "Do you think drug taking is immoral?" "Do you think we should treat narcotics addicts as criminals or as mentally ill people?" "What do you think about the way drug addiction is treated in England?"

Making Summaries   The second major device available to a moderator is the summary statement. Moderators often keep brief notes on the discussion to remind the group of what has been said, notes that may include direct quotations and condensed outlines of what has been covered. The summary statements can be brief or elaborate and may include some direct quotations in restating or outlining the proceedings. They may be expressed in terms of a familiar quotation or maxim. The moderator may say, "Well, then, we seem to be saying that we ought to do unto others as we would have them do unto us in the United Nations. Is that a fair statement of our position?"

Summaries are used primarily to organize the discussion program. Keeping both the time and the agenda in mind, the moderator can interrupt the discussion with a summary and lead the group from one topic to the next. If the group has drifted from the agenda, the moderator can bring it back by summarizing without including the digression. The moderator can also use summaries to remind the audience of the program's overall structure. By emphasizing the main topics and their relationship, the skillful moderator furnishes a pattern that enables the audience to see the relevance of the details being discussed.

The summary can serve as a diversionary tactic when difficult social situations arise. The moderator can use a summary to stop a participant who talks too much without arousing social tensions, since the group generally accepts a summary as an important procedural function. Also, the moderator can interrupt any conflicts for a summary and prevent a situation from becoming painful.

Summaries will become less effective if overused and can irritate the participants. The moderator should not interrupt useful and heated discussions to summarize points that most of the audience has in mind anyway. If, however, the moderator does not provide needed summaries, some other member may begin to do so.

Giving Directions   The third tool of the moderator is the direction. If directions are given tactfully and seem useful to the group's purposes, they are generally obeyed and facilitate the procedure. The following examples indicate the nature of such directions:

"Let's have each panel member make a very brief statement of where he or she stands on this question."

"Let's start with Roosevelt High School."

"Please raise your hands in the audience and I will give everyone a chance, but we must take one at a time."

"At this point I must stop the discussion of this topic so that we can consider some of the suggestions for improvement."

"Just a minute, Joe. You've talked on this before and some members haven't. Let's hear what they have to say."

Skillfully given directions are willingly followed and help structure a program and enable brisk, logical progress. If the moderator is alert for cues, she or he can give directions the group will follow, because it feels the need for such structure and welcomes the guidance. However, the moderator must avoid being dictatorial. If the directions seem to shut off discussion, or if the moderator does not seem to give all sides a fair hearing, the directions may not be followed; instead of facilitating the procedure, they will lead to conflict and confusion.

Leading the Discussion

Getting the Discussion Started Because a new social situation always creates some tension, the moderator faces a difficult task at the start of the meeting. Questions are among the useful techniques to get the program under way. The moderator should direct open-ended questions to the members most likely to respond with poise and fluency early in the session. Later on, the moderator may wish to cut such members off, but a talkative member is a big help at the beginning. Questions such as the following are useful in opening the discussion:

"Mary, do you think we are in serious trouble because of the size of our national debt?"

"Bill, what has been your experience in dealing with this problem?"

"Karen, what is the situation as you understand it?"

The moderator should establish early that comments should be short and to the point. He or she can do this by interrupting the first speaker and asking a direct question of another participant. The first few contributions should not sound memorized, but it can be useful to designate particular members to respond to the first two or three questions.

Keeping the Discussion on the Topic Among the most common problems facing the moderator is the natural tendency of a group to drift from topic to topic. When such tangents lead to important matters of interest, the skillful moderator recognizes their worth and lets the discussion proceed. More frequently, however, digressions are wasteful, and the moderator should end the digression by using questions, summaries, and assertions. Questions such as the following can focus the discussion once more:

"Can we tie this in with the point about broken homes?"

"Are we getting out in left field?"

"Just a moment. How does this relate to the problem of who gets the custody of the children?"

"Let's see now. I'm a bit confused. Where are we in relation to our goals for this discussion?"

To assert that the group is off the subject and suggest that it return to the topic, the moderator may say:

"We seem to be getting off the subject. Let's get back to what Bill said about the main problem."

"This is interesting, but it really doesn't help us much in regard to the question of responsibility."

"I've been listening to the last few minutes here and wondering how it ties in. We must return to the basic question that Helen mentioned earlier."

Moving the Program Along   The group often expects the moderator to apportion the time devoted to each topic. The skillful moderator looks for cues from the audience and panelists that indicate the item under discussion has been adequately treated, and then moves to the next point. The moderator also looks for a slackening of interest, drifting from the subject, and repetitions.

The participants might be able to discuss the main question for hours, but they have to apportion their time so that all important points are raised and discussed briefly. The moderator must decide how much time the discussants can profitably spend on each major division of the outline and then move them from point to point even if it means interrupting a lively and pertinent discussion. The moderator must balance the members' interest in the point under discussion with its importance in the overall discussion pattern. If the moderator breaks in at a point that leaves both discussants and audience with a feeling of frustration and incompleteness, the entire program may be damaged. On the other hand, if too much time is spent on one topic, other equally important or more important matters may be slighted. The moderator can try to foresee possible situations of this sort *before* the program begins and work out some tentative plans to handle them. Even so, the situations that develop during the discussion may require improvisation.

The most useful technique for moving the discussion to another topic is the summary, which concludes one section of the program and furnishes a transition for the next. The moderator may ask the discussants if they would like to move on, or may state that they have spent enough time on a given point and direct them to change.

Helping the Group Reach a Decision   From time to time, the group may feel the need for a consensus. The moderator can help by stepping in at such points and explaining the consensus or decision for the participants. The moderator may use such questions as the following:

"Are we in substantial agreement, then, on this point?"

"What have we done up to this point?"

"Can we all agree that the problem is concentrated in the core of the
city?"

The moderator may also assert that she or he senses agreement on
certain issues and summarize the points of agreement. The moderator
may help the group reach a majority decision by stating the issue and
asking for a vote. A small group may vote by a nodding of heads, or, if no
one disagrees, the moderator may simply assume a group decision. The
unscrupulous moderator may manipulate a discussion at these decision
points, using the evidence of silence to assert a group consensus when
none really exists. Members of one-time meetings should be alert for this
tactic and object when it is used.

Even if the group fails to reach a decision, the moderator must bring
the discussion to a satisfactory conclusion. Again, the summary is the most
useful device for this purpose. The moderator can summarize any definite
conclusions the group has reached. If the group has reached very few
conclusions, the moderator may make a "progress" report indicating how
much has been accomplished. If the group remains divided at the end of
the meeting, the moderator may ask members to summarize their individual positions in place of the moderator's own customary summary.

Handling Difficult Situations

Participants Who Monopolize the Discussion   Perhaps no problem is more
widespread and awkward for the moderator than the member who domi-
nates the discussion. A blunt approach to talkative members may embar-
rass the others. Instead, the moderator can ask yes–no questions, and
when talkative members answer, the moderator can quickly direct an
open-ended question to another participant. The following dialogue is
illustrative:

MODERATOR: [*breaking in*] Just a minute, Joe. Would you be willing to
vote for a candidate who advocated a termination of all
our foreign aid programs?

JOE: Now I didn't say . . .

MODERATOR: [*interrupting*] I just want to clear this up. Would you
vote for such a candidate?

JOE: Well, no, but . . .

MODERATOR: [*interrupting again*] Jane, I wonder how you feel about
this matter?

Sometimes, people who monopolize the discussion by speaking at an
abstract level can be stopped with a question asking for specific information and examples.

JANE: Altogether too many people are going into bankruptcy
because it is the easy way out. After all, why shouldn't
you go into bankruptcy when all you have to do is . . .

MODERATOR: [*interrupting*] Excuse me, Jane, but how many people in our state declared bankruptcy last year?

JANE: I don't have the figures right with me, but I know that there were way too many . . .

MODERATOR: [*interrupting again*] Just a moment. Does anyone have information on the rate of bankruptcy?

A summary interrupts and terminates a long-winded contribution. If the summary concludes with a direct question to a different member, the moderator can tactfully limit a talkative participant.

Moderators may have to use assertions about procedure to limit participation. They might try some of the following:

"This is an extremely important point. Let's get the reactions of the rest of the group."

"Just a minute. You have raised three or four important points. Before you go on, I would like to spend a little more time on this question of responsibility. Let's hear what some of the rest of us think about it."

"You have made some very interesting and provocative statements. I notice several other members are eager to get into the discussion."

"I'm going to ask you to stop there for a minute and hold your next comment; everyone has not yet been heard on this point. When we have heard from the others, we will come back to you."

"Let me interrupt here. We have so many people eager for the floor that I think the best way to proceed is to limit our comments to about one minute and give everyone a chance to speak once before anybody has a second turn."

Participants Who Do Not Take Part A less spectacular, but almost as difficult, situation for the moderator is the participant who will not talk. The moderator should direct questions to the reticent member by name and should use open-ended questions rather than a yes–no or either–or type of inquiry. When moderators are drawing out a reluctant participant, they should ask relatively easy questions to avoid embarrassing the reluctant member. Thus, if moderators are in doubt about the factual information available to the member, they should ask for an opinion instead. Questions such as the following are designed to draw out the reticent:

"Mary, what do you think about this proposal to limit the university's enrollment?"

"Jim, where do you stand on the moral issue involved in helping India use birth control techniques to limit population?"

"Helen, we haven't heard from you about this yet. What do you think?"

Participants Who Come Into Conflict   The moderator should not take sides in a conflict. If questioned about a personal opinion, the moderator can relay the question to the group. "That is a tough one. Can someone on the panel answer?" Or the moderator may return the question to the questioner. "Let me ask you: How would you answer the same question?" If the moderator answers questions about substantive matters, he or she will be drawn into the conflict, and becoming part of the discussion proper damages the ability to make procedural decisions.

If several participants come into conflict, the moderator should interrupt to focus attention on the group process rather than on the individuals in conflict. The moderator can remind the *group* of the areas of agreement and admit that intelligent people differ, but that different opinions should be expressed calmly and rationally. The moderator should emphasize the importance of the ideas rather than the personalities in the conflict and suggest that one of the virtues of a discussion is the opportunity it presents to understand all points of view. The moderator can also use humor (not sarcasm or irony) to relieve tensions.

SUMMARY

The planners of a group discussion should select a suitably sized room, arrange furniture, see to the public address system, and make other physical arrangements. The planners should also see that spatial arrangements (table shape, size, location, and so forth) encourage the proper flow and direction of messages. In general, planners should check audiovisual equipment and other facilities before scheduling the program.

It is most important that the participants in a public discussion be able to talk easily to the audience and to one another. This is why the facilities for each discussion group should be carefully arranged.

The discussion program has much in common with the extemporaneous speech, and the participants should have some planning sessions in which they develop an outline of their program. The outline consists of a series of questions leading to the major points to be covered and often indicates the proportion of time allotted to each major division.

A skillful participant in a discussion exhibits an inquiring attitude, contributes in a balanced way, speaks to the point with short comments, and follows the accepted norms of tact and good manners common to one-time meetings.

The duties of the moderator include introducing the program and the participants, keeping the channels of communication open, drawing out the silent member, and discouraging the talkative participant. The moderator checks the time and the agenda and holds the group to its plan and purpose. In addition to these procedural tasks, the moderator supervises the social climate of the meeting, relieving the stiffness typical of the beginning of a program and minimizing the disruptive influence of any conflicts that develop.

The moderator has three basic tools to guide the meeting: the question, the summary, and the directive. The question is most useful for the moderator adopting the democratic style of leadership. The summary helps to keep the program on the agenda. The directive is most helpful for a moderator using a more authoritarian style.

The moderator's most difficult tasks involve starting the meeting in a lively and spontaneous way, keeping the discussion on the outline, moving the discussion along, and helping the group reach a decision. At times, the moderator may need to use special tactics to handle participants who are too vocal or quiet, or those who come in conflict with one another.

     ## Rules of Thumb

Practical Advice on How to Be a Good Group Member

Drawn from Chapter 3

- ☞ Program planners should carefully select a suitably sized room, proper furniture, and other features of the physical setting.
- ☞ Participants should be arranged in such a manner that they can talk easily to the audience and to one another.
- ☞ Whenever possible, the entire group should work out the outline for the program.
- ☞ A rehearsal of the program can help ensure audience interest and involvement.
- ☞ Adopt an open-minded, objective, and unbiased attitude when planning for and participating in a discussion.
- ☞ Contribute to the discussion with brief, to-the-point comments.
- ☞ In a one-time meeting, follow the accepted norms of tact and good manners.
- ☞ If you are the assigned moderator, you are responsible for procedural and administrative decisions.
- ☞ If you are the assigned moderator, you should introduce the members to one another and to the audience.
- ☞ If you are the assigned moderator, it is wise to restrict your communication to matters of procedure and administration.
- ☞ If you are the assigned moderator, you should use democratic procedures in structuring the discussion.
- ☞ The question is one of the most important communication devices for the moderator using the democratic style.
- ☞ If you are the assigned moderator, it is a good policy not to use assertions phrased as questions (rhetorical questions).
- ☞ The summary is a useful communication device to help a moderator make transitions and suggest decisions.
- ☞ Giving directions is a useful communication device for a moderator, but directions can suggest an authoritarian style.
- ☞ The skillful moderator often uses open-ended questions to get the discussion started.

☛ The skillful moderator decides when digressions are useful or distracting and ends distractions by asking questions and making summaries.

☛ The skillful moderator looks for cues that the panelists have exhausted a topic and then moves the discussion on to the next point.

☛ The skillful moderator helps the group reach decisions.

☛ The skillful moderator directs open-ended questions to quiet members with an eye to improving participation.

☛ The skillful moderator cuts off a member who is speaking too much and allows other members to have the floor.

☛ The skillful moderator does not take sides in a conflict but helps to resolve and manage disagreements.

QUESTIONS FOR STUDY

1. What should be kept in mind when selecting a suitable format for discussion?

2. What should be kept in mind when selecting a suitable room and furniture arrangement for a discussion?

3. How can spatial arrangements for a discussion affect the flow and direction of messages?

4. What should be kept in mind when arranging the participants for a discussion? For a conference?

5. How can group members prepare and use an outline for the discussion?

6. What are the characteristics of a good participant in group discussion?

7. What are the characteristics of a good moderator?

8. What are the duties of a moderator?

9. What are the three basic tools that a moderator can use in conducting the discussion? How may they be used?

10. What are 10 important rules of thumb for leading the discussion?

EXERCISES

1. With four or five of your classmates, prepare a radio panel discussion. Appoint someone to introduce the panel and to sign off the program. Prepare an outline for a 30-minute program. Tape-record your discussion and play it for the class.

2. With five or six of your classmates, prepare a symposium discussion. Draw up an outline for a 30-minute program, and allow the remainder of the hour for an audience forum period. Present the program to your class.

3. With five or six of your classmates, prepare a television interrogation program. Plan the program for 30 minutes. Allow the remainder of the period for class evaluation.

4. Evaluate the moderator in one of the panel discussions performed in class (or a moderator who performs on radio or television). Discuss the moderator's ability

to use questions, to summarize, and to give directions. How well does the moderator handle the difficult situations?

5. Listen to the tape recording of your radio panel discussion and write a short evaluation of your participation.

REFERENCES AND SUGGESTED READINGS

For additional advice on how to conduct the one-time meeting, see:

Beebe, Steven A., and John T. Masterson. *Communicating in Small Groups: Principles and Practices.* 2nd ed. Glenview, IL: Scott, Foresman, 1986.

Brilhart, John K. *Effective Group Discussion.* 6th ed. Dubuque, IA: William C. Brown, 1988.

Cragan, John F., and David W. Wright. *Communication in Small Group Discussions: An Integrated Approach.* 2nd ed., St. Paul, MN: West, 1986.

Chapter
4

Cohesiveness and the Task-Oriented Group

*P*eople have been aware of one of the major features of groups at least since the beginnings of recorded history. Military commanders and athletic coaches long ago discovered the importance of teamwork, group loyalty, and morale. The troop or team that coordinated its activity and acted quickly as a unit was effective, and sometimes its members would be stimulated to extraordinary effort. Members of groups develop loyalty, a feeling of belonging, and a willingness to work for the good of everyone.

Cohesiveness is another term for group loyalty and esprit de corps. Cohesiveness is the ability of a group to cohere or stick together, to work for the good of all, to make the group goals one's own, to help one another, to identify with the group and wish it well.

Approaches to teamwork and cohesiveness, to individual competitiveness versus group cooperation, vary from culture to culture. North American industrial organizations have tended to stress individual rewards and individual competitiveness to achieve success. Japanese industrial organizations typically stress group rewards and group efforts. In recent years, however, the importance of teams and team building to business and industrial success has become clear. Recent interest in using quality circles or involvement teams to improve productivity and quality in the workplace highlights this trend.

A SYMPTOM OF GROUP HEALTH

The level of a group's cohesiveness depends on the extent to which each individual member has made the group's goals his or her own. If a fraternity member must get up at 6:00 A.M. to clean the bathroom, how willing is he to make this sacrifice? If a basketball player has intercepted a pass and is driving toward the basket, does she pass to a teammate for a sure goal, or does she herself shoot in the hope of increasing her own point total? Can group members sit in a meeting and listen to the group drift toward a bad decision without speaking up because they do not want to "rock the boat" or "hurt our cohesiveness"? Or are members committed enough to the group to create the social tension required to say, "Stop. This is a dumb decision and we will go down the drain if we make it"? The answers to such questions provide a partial index of the group's cohesiveness.

Cohesiveness is one dimension of small groups that applies to large organizations as well. It is an important feature of the professional organization, the business corporation, the teaching faculty of a high school, the student body of a college (school spirit), the Loyal Order of the Old Buffaloes, and Tri Zeta. This discussion will include information useful to large organizations as well as small groups.

In general, the more cohesive the group, the more uninhibited and unruly the work meetings will be. When members feel sure of themselves and their place, they can relax. They need not be continually on guard. Matters of importance are attended to. The participants are interested and involved. They disagree. Bales and his associates at Harvard studied a number of different kinds of groups and discovered the most disagreements in husband-and-wife teams. The family group is often highly cohesive, and members feel free to disagree because they know the family will not break up as a result. The PTA or Lions Club, NOW or the NAACP, or even people working together in the same office often are not as cohesive; and the personnel of such organizations do not disagree as much as do the members of a family. People are nicer and more polite in groups composed of acquaintances than in their family groups.

In addition to being polite, the members of a group with little cohesiveness seem bored and disinterested. Their conversation is desultory and punctuated by pauses, yawns, and sighs. They seem to want to finish the meeting quickly. When they disagree, they use gestures rather than words. They shake their heads, frown, or look away from the speaker.

Cohesive groups spend much time in social interplay. People make comments about family, friends, and other interests. They may take off their coats, loosen their ties, or put their feet up on the desk, and they are likely to use first names or nicknames. They make many comments about the excellence of the group. They mention its glorious past, its present achievements, and its future potential. Individuals are complimented when they do a good job. Members offer to help one another. They disagree and argue about decisions affecting the group. They show deference to high-status members.

Members of cohesive groups have come to share a social reality. They have developed a group subculture that includes a common set of heroes, villains, saints, and enemies. They have similar attitudes, values, and emotions in regard to certain key human actions. They often have "in jokes" which consist of allusions to dramatizations of their common history or of their common fantasies.

The interactions of groups with little cohesiveness are the converse of these. Such groups talk about their work rather than about social matters. Much of this talk is devoted to procedures to be followed rather than to the work itself. When they do talk of irrelevancies, they pick safe topics like the weather. They seldom coin nicknames for one another and seem uncomfortable when using first names. Members seldom disagree and rarely argue. At a point where someone in a cohesive group would say, "You're wrong!" or "I disagree!" an individual in a less cohesive group will say, "I don't understand," or "I'm confused." Members of groups with little cohesion have yet to create much of a common social reality. They have few common heroes, villains, saints, or enemies. They have few "in jokes" and are not sure that they share many common values, attitudes, or motives.

Cohesiveness is an easily misunderstood concept. Often students in small group communication classes say that they did not do as well on the task as they should have because their group was so cohesive. They go on to suggest that they did not want to thrash out task-related issues that would bring about conflict because they were afraid such conflict would hurt their cohesiveness.

In a study of high-level decision-making groups, Irving Janis comes to a similar conclusion about cohesiveness. Janis describes the bad results of "too much" cohesiveness as *groupthink*. According to Janis, groupthink is characterized by such features as pressure for consensus, which reduces critical thinking, coerces the doubtful to support the group decision, encourages members to support the leader's thinking, and pushes members to believe that they have reached a real consensus.

Groups that assume cohesiveness in their social fabric is so important that good group work needs to be sacrificed in order to be a "team player" or to indulge in "pseudo-agreement" so as to not damage the group's morale confuse the flight-taking tendency of groups with cohesiveness.

When groups are, indeed, cohesive in the sense that the term will be used in this book, the members do not fear the effects that task disagreements and conflicts might have on their social fabric. *Cohesive groups have strong enough social bonds to tolerate productive conflict over tasks*. The members of a cohesive group are so dedicated to the group's welfare that they *must* raise the thorny task issues and resolve them through productive disagreement. Indeed, Bales found that one index of cohesiveness in group meetings is the number of disagreements in the deliberations. The greater the number of disagreements, the more cohesive the group. Groups with low levels of cohesiveness do not dare to disagree because their social bonds are so weak that disagreement might blow the group apart.

What often happens is that group members find in their early interaction in a new group that the social chitchat is pleasant and rewarding. They like one another and get on well until they try to work cooperatively on a common task. Then they come into conflict, which produces tension. They rationalize the good time they have socializing as cohesiveness (a good end in itself) and take flight into small talk whenever the task discussion threatens to get too uncomfortable.

Cohesiveness and Group Evaluation

The cohesive group may seem to be simply a *good* group. However, groups should be judged on both their productivity and the soundness of their social dimension. Work groups should be judged by the quantity and quality of their work. Some find this criterion sufficient; but our democratic traditions emphasize the importance of the individual and stress that groups exist for the individual to some extent, rather than the opposite. Groups should be judged on the social satisfactions members receive from them as well as on their efficiency.

Some people question the necessity of judging a pragmatic group on social grounds. However, the social dimension of task-oriented groups can be an end in itself. Member satisfaction with the group is related to its productivity. *But for certain kinds of work, a group may not be as efficient and productive as the same people working individually.* In these cases, the main virtue in doing the job through group effort comes from the by-products of the social dimension.

Much early small group research was concerned with whether a group was more efficient than individuals. The question was relevant to the argument proponents of public discussion made to the effect that if citizens discussed all sides of a dispute, they would make the right decision. If a group could do a better job than an expert, this argument would be supported. The research results indicated that groups often made better decisions than most individuals, but that for many tasks one or two of the most talented members could do a better job alone.

One authority on organizational meetings, Norman Maier, suggests that management decisions be divided into two types: problems that require a high-quality technical decision and problems that require a high level of group acceptance. For the situations that require a high-quality solution, he recommends an individual decision be made after consultation with technical experts. For problems that require a high level of group acceptance, he suggests a group decision. Judging a group solely on the quality of its work leaves out the important dimension of group commitment to the decision.

More important, if the members of an organization believe that the individual should not be exploited by the group, the social dimension must be considered. Even in business and industrial organizations there is growing acceptance of the idea that employees must find satisfaction in their work, and that this is important over and above whatever effect morale may have on productivity and profits.

In general, a highly cohesive group will be productive and its members will be pleased and happy. People can become very upset and disturbed in a highly cohesive group, however. To fail, to lose status, or to be unable to gain a prestige position is more painful in a highly cohesive group than in a less cohesive one. An executive who belongs to an important and tightly knit business organization may dedicate his life to it. He worries less about his success or failure in a loosely knit community organization like the PTA. A college student may be more interested in her place in a highly cohesive sorority than in the loosely knit departmental club. The criterion that members be happy with the group adds another dimension to the notion of cohesiveness.

The highly cohesive group is more likely to be productive, and the overall social satisfactions of *most* members are likely to be greater than in a group that is not cohesive. Rensis Likert, a leading management consultant, and his associates at the Institute for Social Research at the University of Michigan discovered as early as the 1950s that cohesiveness was a vital concept to management. Likert discovered that "group loyalty" was related to productivity, employee morale, and communication efficiency. Highly cohesive groups have workers who cooperate and help one another. Work flows back and forth among the workers depending on the load, and members show more initiative in distributing and handling the overload in a crisis.

The highly cohesive group has a climate that maximizes feedback and therefore encourages more effective communication. Members of cohesive groups will ask for information they need because they have little fear of appearing ignorant and thereby losing status. Cohesive groups do not punish members who ask for information that is required for group success. As indicated before, they also will disagree more. Members who feel a given decision is bad will raise questions. They cannot sit quietly and watch the group make a mistake. In organizations with low cohesiveness, people often allow the group to take unwise action rather than strain the social fabric with disagreements.

Cohesiveness is not static. A highly cohesive organization will change membership, the nature of the internal structure and interactions will change, and over a period of time the group may lose cohesiveness until it dies. The fraternity that has been a top organization on campus for three or four years may degenerate until it becomes inactive. Indeed, group loyalty will fluctuate slightly from day to day.

Cohesiveness is a function of the assembly effect (group composition) plus interaction. The *assembly effect* consists of the individual characteristics of the members such as age, sex, intelligence, and psychological and social needs. Added to this factor is the element of compatibility. How do individuals who join the group mesh with one another in terms of the overall composition of the group? Are they compatible or incompatible?

Is the group homogeneous or heterogeneous with respect to such factors as dominance, intelligence, authoritarianism, and the need for structure in a social environment? All these factors relate to the assembly effect. The final factor of interaction has to do with the way the group develops, and this incorporates the message content and communication patterns that dynamically build relationships among the members and create a common social reality, a common group culture.

THE ASSEMBLY EFFECT AND COHESIVENESS

Each member brings to a new group his or her personal characteristics which influence the way the individual behaves and the way others respond to that behavior. An individual's style of communication, typical reactions to others, and skills and abilities provide the basic raw material for group interaction and are thus of considerable importance in the dynamics of the group.

The biographical characteristics of members include age, sex, physical features, intelligence, and communication ability. A good deal of research has been aimed at discovering the influence of individual characteristics on group process. Much of the research is difficult to compare because the investigators did not use similar scoring techniques to assign numbers to the various indexes and rating systems used to quantify individual characteristics. Thus, a short summary is sufficient to present the conclusions that have emerged from the research to date.

Age has an influence on member participation in groups in that social participation increases with age until the teenage years. This increase in participation is related to both formal and informal group membership as well as amount of communication. Individuals tend to increase in their conformity to group norms from a young age until about 12, and then the conformity behavior tends to decrease.

Most researchers have assumed that sex differences affect small group interaction and have often tried to control their studies to rule out the effect of gender, and a growing number of studies have been directed to specific questions relating to male–female behavior in small groups. Unfortunately, the research results that have accumulated over the years may well be a function of cultural norms about women's role in society. These norms have changed a good deal in the last two decades with the growth of the women's movement and the general change in society's norms in regard to role expectations for both sexes.

In a recent survey of research on sex differences, Shaw concluded that women are less self-assertive and less competitive in groups than men, use eye contact as a form of communication more frequently than men, and conform more to majority opinion than men do.

In recent years, students in the small group communication seminar at the University of Minnesota have made a number of case studies and written a number of seminar papers, theses, and dissertations which focused on the effect of the sexual composition of groups on group process.[1] Certainly the case studies at Minnesota do not reveal that women in general are less self-assertive or less competitive in groups than men. Quite typically, groups of five to seven members that contain three or four female members will also have at least one and often several women who are very self-assertive and competitive with males in the group. The tendency to find assertive and competitive females in groups in classes in discussion and small group communication at Minnesota has accelerated with the growing popularity of ideas relating to female equality.

The Minnesota studies also indicate that physical attractiveness and sexual interest have an effect on the communication and the interaction patterns in small groups and may affect the formation of coalitions and cliques and the emergence of group structure.

The case studies also reveal that age and sex interact in groups where there is a considerable disparity in age; that is, if a group is composed of five individuals, four in their twenties and a fifth person who is 40 or 50 years of age, the oldest person will have considerable difficulty finding a role as a peer in the group. A number of groups in the Minnesota studies had one older woman as a member, and these women often became a preoccupation of the group. Frequently, the older women were intelligent, dependable, and efficient. Women who return to the university after raising a family and being influential in the community are often capable and assertive, and they frequently have extensive experience in managing important projects. The younger members of these groups typically expressed their resentment of capable older women by saying they did not want to be "mothered." The older women, in turn, were often intensely frustrated because they felt that the group could be much more effective, and they often worked very hard to make it so, only to have their ideas and efforts rejected as being too bossy, pushy, or aggressive. Older men also have difficulty finding a role in a group of predominately young members.

The research also indicates that intelligence is correlated slightly with leadership, a bit more with activity and popularity, and the more intelligent person tends to be less conforming to group norms than the less intelligent. These correlations, while interesting, are not very strong and do not explain much about the development of group processes. Once

---

[1]The conclusions about discussion groups were drawn from a large-scale program of research conducted by the author and his associates in the small group communication seminar at the University of Minnesota. Some of the work has been reported in unpublished doctoral dissertations, master's theses, convention papers, and journal articles, but the rest of this book reports in comprehensive fashion the results of this continuing research program. Frequent references will be made to the research results of these studies. They will subsequently be referred to in the text as the Minnesota studies. See the Appendix for a more detailed description of the research program.

again, the difficulty with past research lies with the use of testing procedures to score intelligence and then trying to correlate test scores with individual behavior in a social field as complex and powerful as that found in a small group.

MEMBER NEEDS AND COHESIVENESS

Each member brings to a new group his or her dreams, desires, and needs. Although the group may modify or drastically convert the dreams and the expression of the needs, the latter do provide the energy that compels an individual to act in support of or counter to the achievement of group goals. Thus, an analysis of the way individual needs can be satisfied in a group provides a partial account of group cohesiveness.

As noted in Chapter 1, an exchange theory explains interpersonal behavior in terms of the exchange of costs and rewards on the part of the participants. Thibaut and Kelly formulated one important exchange explanation to account for the social psychology of groups.[2]

The level of group cohesiveness at any instant is a function of the forces affecting each member. There are always some centripetal forces pulling an individual into and some centrifugal forces pushing that person out of the group. The centripetal forces consist of the material and psychological rewards that the group provides. The centrifugal forces consist of the costs that the group extracts from the individual. The rewards and costs cannot be assessed in isolation. An investigator determining the pull of a group on its members must provide a context of competing or *comparison* groups for each member. For example, if one of the rewards is a salary of $25,000 per year, a person must examine the pull of this reward against the next best salary he or she could make. If the next best salary is $20,000, the monetary reward of the first group is stronger than if the next best offer is $22,500. The comparison group is always the next *best* group.

Figure 3 presents a diagram indicating how rewards and costs provide pulls and pushes on group members that affect their level of cohesiveness.

Rewards Defined

A typical dictionary definition suggests that a *reward* is a "recompense" that is "given for some service or attainment." In order to examine group attractiveness, however, the concept must be limited to those recom-

---

[2]The exchange account of cohesiveness that follows is based on the Thibaut and Kelly framework; but it has been considerably modified by the Minnesota studies and by the author's experience in teaching classes in small group communication, working in adult continuing education, and consulting for commercial, industrial, religious, and government groups.

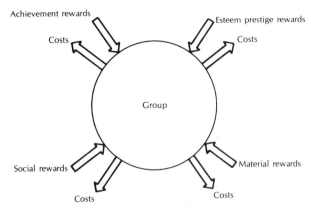

Figure 3 Diagram showing how rewards and costs provide pushes and pulls that make a group more or less cohesive.

penses that the member finds attractive. The person who is offered a reward of $5 when he is expecting $100 may reject the offer in disgust. Psychologists studying the learning behavior of rats often use the term *reinforcement*. By this they mean a reward that makes the animal learn the behavior that brings the recompense. A *reward*, then, is a material or psychological recompense provided by the group which is sufficient to reinforce individual behavior in the direction of group loyalty. Cost is the converse of this. A *cost* is a material or psychological punishment provided by the group which is sufficient to extinguish an individual's group loyalty or reinforce a person's withdrawal behavior.

In the realm of human behavior, conventional definitions such as these can lead to circular reasoning. For example, the definition of a reinforcement can result in explaining any bizarre behavior of an individual rat by saying it was reinforced to act in this way. But sometimes no explanation can be given for what served as the reinforcement or why it worked. The conventional definition of a reward could lead in the same direction. If a member often has a temper tantrum and upsets the rest of the group, that behavior can be explained by saying that the group rewards the member's temper tantrums. If the group responds to the temper tantrums in a way that observers perceive to be punishing, the explanation can still be that it was not punishing to the person who had the tantrum. What reward do people get from pounding their heads against a stone wall? The circular answer is that nobody knows, but they must get some or they would not do it.

This circle can be broken by an explanation of how a given reward works. It is not enough to say that what the group does for member A is a reward because A acts as though it is a reward. An adequate explanation provides reasons for member A's behavior. An explanation of the rewards and costs that the group furnishes its members is given by an analysis of human needs.

Material Rewards

Groups have the power to furnish their members with material rewards. In some cases this is as obvious as a $25,000 per year salary. Groups can also give an individual less obvious material rewards. Joining a certain country club may give an insurance salesperson contacts that increase sales commissions. Groups may encourage their members to do business with one another.

On the other hand, membership in a group may cost an individual money. An actress may have an opportunity to make $30,000 a year with another theater group. If she decides to stay despite the cost, she must gratify other needs. Even so, the fact that membership costs her money weakens the pull of the group. The group's dues may go up to the point where it is an extravagance for a member. Some groups may hurt certain members' business. Their association with the group may bring them notoriety and economic retaliation.

Money may serve as a means to satisfy a number of human needs. If members are physiologically deprived, they can buy food, clothing, drink, or medical care to satisfy their needs. Money can provide security and may even buy entrance into organizations that gratify social needs. For some individuals, material rewards can enhance the status within an organization, and even satisfy some self-esteem needs.

Perhaps the most obvious way in which a group can increase its cohesiveness is to increase the material rewards it furnishes its members. Raising salaries or paying bonuses will often increase the cohesiveness of the group. If the organization gives monetary rewards on the basis of group rather than individual success, the effect will be increased. An important study by Deutsch indicates that a spirit of competition *within* the group strains the bonds that hold it together. If an instructor sets up discussion groups and suggests that only one student will receive an A, that only one student will receive a B, a C, a D, and an F, the group will not develop much cohesiveness. Such a setting encourages each member to work independently. Should the instructor evaluate the discussion as a whole and give each student a common group grade, cohesiveness would be encouraged.

Competition within the group is disruptive; competition among groups often increases cooperation. One of the strong forces for developing cohesiveness in athletic teams is the fact that they are competing with other teams. For many years, particularly after World War II, forensic contests in high school and college often included competition in public discussion. Students participated in discussions and received a rating. Although the judges watched to see if a contestant was open-minded and cooperative, clever contestants soon found ways to make others in the group look bad. For example, the clever competitor waited until a knowledgeable member was rearranging note cards to ask for specific information. The member frequently became flustered and was unable to find the suitable card, and the judge would get the impression that the contestant was not as knowledgeable as first seemed.

The bitterness that developed in these discussions disturbed many forensic directors, and the practice of having competitive tournaments waned in popularity. As the individual forensic tournament waned, contests arose in which discussion teams from various schools would compete with one another. The judges evaluated the quality of each team's work, and the group won or lost as a team. Such conditions were more hospitable to the development of cohesiveness. The same principles of cooperation and competition can be applied to the distribution of monetary rewards.

On occasion, an organization will want to use individual rewards. If managers wish to stimulate ingenuity to improve or increase productivity, individual incentives may be useful. If cohesiveness is a relatively minor feature of a loosely knit group in which most of the work is done by individuals in isolation, such as a group of writers, painters, or teachers, the rewards of individual incentives might be advisable.

Social Rewards

The rewards that the group is uniquely able to provide are social in nature. The group furnishes refuge from loneliness. It provides members with friends and enemies, either within their own or within competing groups. Members gain a sense of belonging from the group. They learn to know other people and to find that they like and respect others.

Any group has, ostensibly, every reason to be highly cohesive. The group furnishes its members with many rewards, both material and psychological. Yet a group can be torn with dissension, full of backbiting, rancor, and cliques. In such a social climate, members spend their time and energy feuding among themselves. For example, the Minnesota studies of task-oriented groups of college students working together for 12 weeks on similar tasks and under comparable conditions revealed that roughly one of every four such groups was highly successful and cohesive, two were moderately so, and one was socially punishing. The major differences among these groups were the number of social rewards they furnished their members. The greater the number of social rewards, the greater the cohesiveness.

The importance of the social dimension of group work stems largely from the fact that basic social needs can be met only within a group context. To some extent, a group may satisfy an individual's security needs: People need not only a secure physical environment but also some security within their social environment. They need to know that their friends will remain friendly and that the people they trust today will be trustworthy tomorrow. Groups can provide their members with a secure social environment. = TRUST

Since groups can furnish such rewards, they can also deprive their members of these basic needs. Individuals can be rejected by the group. They may not receive affection but, rather, hostility and antagonism. The social climate of the group can be in a constant state of flux and thus deny the members a feeling of security in their social relationships.

The one dimension of groups that can be changed radically and consciously through an understanding of group methods is the social dimension, and fortunately so, since social satisfactions are important. This is true in small task-oriented discussion groups like those in discussion courses. Students can apply their knowledge about group methods to the practical problem of generating greater cohesiveness within their classroom discussion. Often they have no such freedom to structure material rewards or the other incentives to cohesiveness that are available to managers and supervisors in organizations. Of course, social rewards are also important in larger groups.

The student who wants a list of formulas with which to improve the social rewards and cohesiveness of the small group will be disappointed. The social dynamics of a group are too complex to allow for simple recipes that cover a wide variety of situations. The next few chapters examine the social functioning of groups. The student who understands the basic process will be able to make wise choices and develop creative and comprehensive plans of action designed to increase the social rewards and cohesiveness of a particular organization.

Esteem and Prestige Rewards

People strive for prestige largely because of their esteem needs, so the two concepts are closely related. However, prestige differs from esteem in one important respect. Prestige rewards can be conferred on an individual by an organization, but esteem must be earned. Since receiving prestige from an organization is often easier than earning esteem, the power of a group to confer prestige is one of its attractive features.

In a given community, similar groups will develop reputations of varying excellence. A sorority, for example, may develop a reputation of being the best sorority on campus. Any group has a spongelike ability to absorb the prestige of its members. Fraternities gain luster from members who are star athletes or leaders in student government. Of course, the group also suffers if its members have a bad reputation. It may try to protect itself by putting pressure on members not to bring disgrace on the organization.

In addition to absorbing the prestige of its members, the group develops a public image in its own right, by doing a good job. The business organization that shows a profit and gives a large dividend increases its prestige. In this regard, as in others relating to the development of cohesiveness, groups often undergo cyclical changes. Success increases the prestige. Increased prestige exerts a stronger pull on the members and creates greater cohesiveness, which in turn contributes to more success. If the cycle is broken by a change in personnel or by accident, the same cyclical development can occur in the opposite direction. Failure reduces the prestige, thus reducing the cohesiveness and contributing to future failures. Organizations often go through periods of boom and bust. A college gridiron power may have a series of national championships followed by a number of losing seasons. The saying "Nothing succeeds like success" applies to the prestige of an organization.

Another factor that contributes to prestige is a high standard of membership. Open groups have more difficulty establishing a reputation than do those that restrict their membership. Many state universities and colleges must accept any qualified high school graduate, while private schools restrict their enrollments. A parent may be proud of a daughter accepted at Wellesley or Smith or Princeton because such acceptance indicates that she and her family are "better" people.

Of course, open groups may have a good reputation because they are productive and are composed in part of important people, and an exclusive group may get a bad reputation. An exclusive prep school may restrict membership with a high tuition fee; yet, because of poor curriculum and poor instructors, and because its students are reputed to be flunk-outs from other schools, the school may have little prestige.

On rare occasions, organizations with extremely bad reputations exert a strong pull on their members because they are all outcasts. For example, an organization composed of a persecuted minority group might be highly cohesive because it is a haven from discrimination and a bulwark against society.

Not only does the group absorb the prestige that the members bring to it, but *the group's prestige is transferable to each and every member*. By being publicly associated with an elite organization, people gain status within the community. They are rewarded because some of their important esteem needs have been fulfilled. The group's prestige may improve their self-images as well as their reputations and the amount of respect they receive from chance acquaintances. Prestige conferred by an organization is often less satisfying than esteem earned by the individual, but it is much easier to achieve. All one has to do to gain these rewards is to gain membership. To *earn* esteem, however, requires work and talent.

An organization furnishes a context in which esteem rewards can be earned. In every organization, some people become important and well liked. Other members listen to the esteemed members' comments, weigh their suggestions carefully, seek and follow their advice. Such direct and personal esteem rewards are among the most powerful factors drawing a person into a group.

Prestige rewards are also provided internally by the high-status positions within an organization. They explain the increased feeling of cohe-

siveness that often accompanies election to a position of formal leadership. Often a member who is only moderately committed will, upon
election to an office, work very hard for the organization.

The members of an organization with a bad reputation experience
some deprivation of their esteem needs. The last-place team is less attractive to its members than is the championship team. The most important
deprivation of an individual's esteem needs, however, is a lack of standing
within the organization. Low-status members find the group socially
punishing. If the others fail to pay attention to them as people and ignore
their opinions and feelings, the group deprives them of esteem needs.

An organization may increase its cohesiveness by establishing a good
reputation within the community. Ultimately the group's reputation rests
on the quality of its membership and the effectiveness of its work, but
these qualities must be communicated to the public. The group should
pay some attention to public relations. A judicious use of the mass media
is advisable. Members should work out informal communication channels
so that the right people hear about the good works of the organization.
The organization may encourage and organize this grapevine systematically to ensure its success.

Organizations often attach the prestige of the group firmly to each
individual by the use of some publicly displayed, clearly identified symbol. If the group does not wish to adopt a crest or a coat of arms, the
members may get the same effect from a common mode of dress. The
members of a high school clique may all wear dirty buckskin shoes, or a
similar hairstyle, or leather jackets. The group may adopt certain slang
words that identify members to the general public. The difficulty with
informal modes of identification is that outsiders may adopt them. Thus,
the ruling clique of the high school may have to discard dirty buckskins
because everybody is wearing them.

Influential members should take the time and effort to help a member
gain esteem. Even the new recruit in the last rank can be assured by word
and deed of being an important part of the group. The group often asserts,
"No group is stronger than its weakest member [no chain is . . .] and we
are strong because everyone is a good member. Everyone is vital to the
workings of this organization." The group should support these words
with actions. One problem in dealing with the social maintenance of
groups is that insincerity and attempts to manipulate the group by correct
behavior work only for a short time. When people work together for more
than a few hours, they soon recognize the person who is insincere, and the
latter's attempt to manipulate them fails.

Individuals tend to be more strongly committed to a group if they
have had to overcome a number of barriers to gain membership. If people
must be invited to become members or must in some way prove themselves before they are selected, the prestige of the organization is likely to
be increased.

In addition, if the new member must go through a testing period before becoming a full-fledged member and if each test is more difficult than the last, the cohesiveness of those who survive will be increased. Some research by social psychologists suggests that the old practice of hazing may be more than sadism and may, indeed, increase esprit de corps for some organizations. The pledge class that goes through hell week together is often welded into a cohesive unit.

The loyalty that develops in members that "have been through hell together" helps account for low-prestige groups that are highly cohesive. Although in times of war the combat infantry is the least prestigious branch of the service, the infantry soldier who survives a number of battles often develops a feeling of commitment to the infantry and to his comrades that is one of his strongest sources of support—and one of the major reasons for infantry squads that succeed as fighting units.

Achievement Rewards

In addition to furnishing rewards that satisfy all the basic needs, groups are attractive because they offer their members opportunities for personal growth. They may provide a chance for both self-actualization and self-transcendence. The two main achievement rewards furnished by organizations are work satisfaction and the opportunity to fight for a cause.

The task-oriented group requires that each member do a certain amount of work. It may enable someone to do the kind of work he or she likes. The teacher who enjoys teaching drama and directing plays will be attracted to a high school with such a job available. This organization provides the member with an opportunity for self-actualization. A person may sacrifice some material rewards, particularly if her or his physiological and security needs are gratified, in order to gain work satisfactions.

If the organization requires members to do jobs that they dislike, it loses some of its attraction. It may require members to ring doorbells and ask for donations. Insofar as they dislike the work the group asks them to do, they will feel less committed to membership.

The desire to do a good job, to make a contribution to other people, to feel that life has meaning over and above the satisfying of subsistence needs are all met by work satisfactions that an organization can sometimes provide. If members do important and difficult tasks and see opportunities for additional training and competence, they can gratify some of their desire for self-actualization.

A number of organizations are dedicated to religious or spiritual objectives. Closely related to these are the groups organized to fight for a cause or a world view. Such groups exert a considerable pull on their membership because they provide an opportunity to transcend the self and find a larger meaning in life.

Joining an organization with a cause that the individual considers important is positive action. Members may feel that they are having a positive effect on the course of history. Such a group can help assuage guilt feelings. The Puritan religious heritage stresses that everyone is sinful and guilty and must be saved, and that once people are saved, they must work actively to save others. If they do not do so, they partake of the others' guilt. Rewards of this type often create a level of commitment that exceeds any that can be generated by rewarding the needs on the deficit ladder. History is filled with examples of individuals who chose to give their lives fighting for a cause.

A widely used rule for increasing group commitment is that a new member must be given a job. If every person has work that fulfills individual growth needs, cohesiveness will increase. Various people will, all other things being equal, enjoy some jobs more than others. Insofar as the group finds congenial work for the maximum number of members, work satisfaction will increase.

The group can provide additional rewards by appreciating the end product. The part-time potter shows his vase to friends and they admire it; the hobbyist shows off her end table. Seldom do either of them find enough satisfaction in solitary contemplation of their work. They enjoy the vase or end table much more if others are aware of the work and appreciate it. Thus, the organization that gives all members worthwhile tasks to perform and then appreciates the work when it is well done will increase cohesiveness.

Some organizations that work for causes or that are dedicated to a specific religious view cannot change their goals to increase cohesiveness. On the other hand, some organizations have ostensible spiritual purposes or stated world views, but their real purposes are different. In that case, they may be able to manipulate the "platform" or the "dogma" to make it more palatable to the membership.

Even when the goals cannot be changed, some attention to this factor can improve the cohesiveness of the group. The organization can clearly spell out its benefits and reiterate them to the membership. If the stand is unequivocal and radical, the cohesiveness of the group will be increased. The number of people drawn to the group will be smaller, but those who are attracted will be more dedicated. The group with clear goals that the members perceive as realistic is likely to be cohesive.

If the cause can be changed, the group often can draft a more attractive platform. If the political party's main purpose is to get candidates elected rather than to fight for certain programs, its platform may be abstract and ambiguous in order to avoid discouraging potential supporters. This strategy, however, will reduce the pull of the cause or spiritual satisfaction, and the group must increase other rewards to achieve high cohesiveness.

GROUP COMPOSITION AND MEMBER NEEDS

This discussion of the way groups reward or punish members has been stated in general terms. Like much of the early laboratory research on groups, it is an input–output account of group attractiveness; that is, the framework suggests that members with certain needs enter a group, interact, and emerge rewarded or punished. A complete account of group cohesiveness should include a process analysis of what happens within the group to reward or punish the members and to create a common social reality and a group identity.

The first step in such an account is to examine the assembly effect resulting from the particular composition of a given group. As noted earlier, the assembly effect is the idiosyncratic behavior of a group which stems from the particular combination of individuals that comprise it. Much of the research aimed at discovering the effects of such characteristics as age, sex, and intelligence on group process foundered because of the complexity of factors contributing to the assembly effect in groups. Groups of four or more allow for a bewildering variety of combinations and permutations of traits, which are usually too complex to explain in terms of one or two characteristics. For instance, in a group with only four members and considering only the two characteristics of age and sex, member A could be young and female, old and female, young and male, or old and male. Each of the three remaining members could be one of the four combinations. Thus, there are 16 possible combinations of the two characteristics. With five-person groups, these two characteristics furnish 32 possible combinations.

Thus, the student of small group communication should be aware of past efforts to account for group outcomes on the basis of personality, but should keep in mind that the investigators usually posed research questions that were too general and limited to too few characteristics to yield results of more than academic interest.

Investigators studying the assembly effect have often based their research on the assumption that some ideal combination of member characteristics would result in highly compatible groups. The researchers assumed that if they could isolate the key personal characteristics and scale them in some way, they could discover the most compatible combinations as indicated by evaluations of group productivity and member satisfaction. If such research discovered the factors contributing to compatible groups, then the practical results would be substantial. People who had to form task-oriented groups could then give some paper-and-pencil tests to a pool of possible group members and select individuals on the basis of the best combinations and thus ensure compatible, productive, and satisfying groups. Commonsense experience in working with groups provides some hope for the success of such projects. Experienced administrators often have the notion that certain people would work more effectively than others in committees, task forces, and work projects. The notion that, as members in the case studies at Minnesota often put it, "We just seemed to get along well together," reflects a common experience and makes the search for the factors that make for compatibility plausible.

One body of research fits in with the exchange framework of costs and rewards developed above in that it is based on the concept of need compatibility. The assumption of much of the research is that when the needs of two or more members can be mutually satisfied through interaction and communication in the group, the group will be more cohesive. The research in need compatibility is illustrated by the work of Schutz, who isolated three individual needs that he felt were important to compatible or incompatible group composition. Schutz and his associates called the approach the "fundamental interpersonal relations orientation" (FIRO). The needs consisted of *inclusion* (the need to be noticed and to have esteem and prestige), *control* (the need to dominate and have power over others), and *affection* (the need for friendship and close personal ties). Schutz developed a general account suggesting that the more compatible the needs among members of a group are the greater the group's productivity and cohesiveness will be.

Although confined to only three needs, FIRO was nonetheless an extremely complex system. Schutz expanded the approach to include three different types of compatibility; thus, he could compute compatibility indexes for each of the three types within each of the three need areas. Schutz and his associates conducted a number of studies to test the FIRO assumptions, and their findings generally supported the hypotheses. Other studies, however, failed to discover the effects of compatibility anticipated by the FIRO account. Although Schutz's approach was more sophisticated, his research questions may have been too complex to be answered by the scaling devices currently available to the small group researcher.

In addition to research into compatibility of needs, some further work dealt with compatibility of displayed role functions. A group of investigators studied the behavior of group members as anticipated from tests of personality characteristics. The investigations into member behavior have been largely confined to studies of dominance and authoritarianism. The studies tend to indicate that different combinations of dominant–submissive individuals do yield more or less compatible groups. The work on authoritarianism has not produced unequivocal results. Again, the dynamic interplay of five or more people within a small group is so complex that whatever features of behavior a pencil-and-paper test can distinguish among research subjects are often washed out among the powerful forces within the social field.

A final group of studies deals with the compatibility implied by creating homogeneous or heterogeneous groups according to some member characteristic such as intelligence, sex, or personality profile. The results of such investigations are of interest in a suggestive rather than definitive way. Generally the research suggests that groups with heterogeneous membership as to ability perform better than groups that are homogeneous, that members of groups composed of males and females conform more than all-female or all-male groups, and that groups heterogeneous as to personality profiles of members are more effective in the task area than groups with homogeneous membership.

To this point, the Minnesota studies have isolated only one member characteristic that seems related to interaction and communication within the group meetings strongly enough to be discernible. Members of natural groups in the discussion classes at Minnesota appear to vary as to their need for group structure. Some members of most groups need a defined structure which includes clearly stated goals for meetings and termination dates for larger projects. They need an agenda or a plan of action that is relatively specific and clear. They need to know what they are to do for the group and what they can anticipate others will do at certain clearly specified times. At the other end of the continuum, some members of most groups dislike structure. They feel restricted and hemmed in by an agenda. They prefer a freewheeling discussion and like to "kick ideas around." They want to enjoy the play of ideas and the discussion itself and dislike a preoccupation with time pressures and deadlines.

In the early phases of a group's development, those members who need structure are often frustrated by what they perceive to be the group's aimless wallowing around. They often suggest plans that would structure the group more clearly. They prepare agendas or, if sufficiently frustrated, grow angry and demand that the group pay attention to the passage of time and the need to get something done. On the other hand, should the group develop ways of working that are highly structured, particularly if the norms result from a dominant individual's aggressive efforts, the members who dislike structure will be frustrated. They will frequently withdraw from participation after several attempts to inject what they perceive to be exciting or important ideas are met by group communication about time pressures, deadlines, or wandering off the topic. They will often report in their journals of group experience that they dislike the group and feel it is being run by a dictator, and that the group seems eager to get something, anything, accomplished even if the work is worthless.

Homogeneity of structure needs tends to make for an easier time in getting the group under way. Group work norms emerge more easily, and members tend to be more satisfied earlier in a leaderless group discussion that is relatively homogeneous as to members' needs for structure. Homogeneity of low structure needs tends to make for a boisterous and stimulating conversation. On occasion, groups may spend an entire meeting on tangents unrelated to their task.

Heterogeneity of structure needs makes it more difficult for groups to evolve norms and roles. Quite often, members with widely varying needs for structure will develop "personality conflicts," and if several members have strong needs for structure and several others have a distaste for it, the group may divide into coalitions that work counter to one another. On the other hand, some good groups in the Minnesota studies were composed of members with high and low structure needs. These groups developed work norms that exploited the contributions that both structured and unstructured members gave to the task dimension. The structured members learned to tolerate periods of unstructured brainstorming or "mulling things over" at appropriate points in the group's grappling with a task. At those points where the group had to get the "lay of the land" and find out what various members thought of the situation or where the group needed a different angle on a problem that was proving difficult to solve, the structured people went along with the creative, free-associative, elliptical, communicative give-and-take that the unstructured members enjoyed. Often the seemingly unstructured periods of group meetings produced new perspectives and creative solutions. On the other hand, once the group made a decision, the unstructured members learned to tolerate and even appreciate the way others would swing into action to lay plans, set deadlines, and mobilize the group's resources.

Putnam has developed a scale or test for assessing a person's need for structure while working in a small task-oriented group. In addition, investigators at Minnesota used the case study procedure to identify the characteristic of the need for structure. The case study involves both participant and nonparticipant observers listening to tape recordings and watching videotapes of group meetings to identify communication associated with the characteristic of the need for structure, as well as group and individual interviews to discover participant perceptions in regard to the need for structure. Most of the groups at Minnesota that worked out ways to accommodate both high and low structure needs in members did so through group discussions of their work procedures and of the various individuals' need for structure. Often individuals discover that they desire structure in a group when they previously thought of themselves as more comfortable in an unstructured situation, and vice versa. Conceivably, the need for structure is not a consistent characteristic which an individual takes from group to group, but it may be, to some extent, a function of the group's social field. Putnam's test for comfort with high or low procedural order has proved to be a useful tool for students and participants examining the way group members respond to structure in their work.

The concept of need for group structure is most useful for those groups that have been interacting for some time and that find themselves dissatisfied with their work procedures. Often members of such groups can discuss their group process and use the concept of individual needs for structure to discover some of their difficulties. Discovering that they have a heterogeneous group as to needs for structure might account for some of their troubles, and they can then go on to try to change their procedures so that the group will be rewarding for all members.

Although individual characteristics and group composition are important to cohesiveness, in the final analysis what happens once the members meet and begin working together is of overriding concern. The communication networks and the messages that flow through them ultimately determine the attractiveness of the group for its members. The chapters on small group communication theory that follow present many of the dynamics that account for how individual needs are met or frustrated in a group. The student of small group communication will find much in the subsequent chapters that relates back to the way the unfolding communication within a small group contributes to the group's cohesiveness.

SUMMARY

The task-oriented group has two basic dimensions: social and task. The social dimension includes the way in which members perceive, relate to, and interact with one another. The task dimension consists of the communication and behavior directed toward achieving the work objectives.

The task-oriented group should be judged on both of its dimensions. First, the good group is productive. It does its work efficiently and well. Second, the good group rewards its members socially. They are committed to the group and enjoy working with the other members.

Cohesiveness is a function of both group composition and interaction. The first important factor is comprised of the individual characteristics of the members; the second involves the way the individuals mesh with one another and the way the group develops dynamically.

The level of cohesiveness at any given instant is the sum of forces affecting each member. The centripetal forces consist of the rewards the group provides; the centrifugal, of the costs it extracts. These cannot be assessed in isolation, but must be determined in the context of a comparison, which is the next best group a member could join.

Groups can provide their members with a wide range of rewards of varying attractiveness depending on how frustrated an individual's deficit needs may be. Among the important rewards that groups provide are money and other material goods; a feeling of security, of belonging, of being well liked, and of self-esteem and importance; and an opportunity to grow as a productive person. One important form of self-transcendence is to lose oneself in a group battling for a good cause.

The assembly effect is the behavior of the group which stems from the particular combination of individuals that comprise it. Most of the research into the assembly effect has been directed to discovering compatibility of needs or responses in a group.

Although individual characteristics and group composition are important, the way the members communicate with one another is of overriding concern.

☛   Rules of Thumb

Practical Advice on How to Be a Good Group Member

Drawn from Chapter 4

☛ Groups that are truly cohesive are committed enough to encourage and tolerate disagreement and conflict.

☞ Evaluate groups on both their productivity and the soundness of their social dimension.

☞ Group loyalty is related to productivity, employee morale, and communication efficiency.

☞ Past research efforts to account for group outcomes on the basis of the assembly effect have been inconclusive.

☞ If group members have differing expectations about procedural order, they should have a meeting and change their procedures to make them more comfortable for all.

☞ To build cohesiveness, set clear attainable goals and keep reminding members about them.

☞ To build cohesiveness, always talk about *our* group and what *we* hope to accomplish.

☞ To build cohesiveness, stress teamwork and the notion that success of the team is more important than individual success.

☞ To build cohesiveness, encourage the group to fulfill members' social and esteem needs.

☞ To build cohesiveness, get the group to recognize good work on the part of individual members.

☞ To build cohesiveness, ensure that the group gets common rewards that all can share equally.

☞ To build cohesiveness, if you receive individual recognition, reflect the reward back on the group.

☞ To build cohesiveness, treat members as people rather than as cogs in a machine.

☞ To build cohesiveness, raise the status of other members.

QUESTIONS FOR STUDY

1. How would you define cohesiveness?
2. How might highly cohesive groups be compared and contrasted with less cohesive groups?
3. In what way is Janis's definition of cohesiveness as related to groupthink one-sided?
4. How might the exchange theory be applied to the study of group cohesiveness?
5. How might groups provide their members with rewards?
6. How might groups exact a cost from their members?
7. What mechanisms might a group use to provide its members with achievement rewards?
8. What mechanisms might a group use to provide its members with social rewards?
9. What mechanisms might a group use to provide its members with esteem and prestige rewards?
10. What is the assembly effect? How has it been studied?

EXERCISES

1. Select a group that you have worked with in class and describe its cohesiveness. List the steps that you might take to increase the group's cohesiveness.
2. Select a nonclass group that you have worked with for some time and that in your opinion is highly cohesive. Write a short paper in which you discuss the group's reward system in relation to some comparison level or comparison group.
3. Form a group with some of your classmates and work out and implement a systematic program to develop the group's cohesiveness.

REFERENCES AND SUGGESTED READINGS

For the student who wishes to read an extensive survey of the research relating to group composition and cohesiveness, see:

Shaw, Marvin E. *Group Dynamics: The Psychology of Small Group Behavior.* 3rd ed. New York: McGraw-Hill, 1981.

Bales's method for counting disagreements and the reports of some early research using his methods are found in:

Bales, Robert F. *Interaction Process Analysis: A Method for the Study of Small Groups.* Reading, MA: Addison-Wesley, 1950.

For surveys of cohesiveness, see:

Drescher, Stuart, Gary Burlingame, and Addie Fuhriman. "Cohesion: An Odyssey in Empirical Understanding," *Small Group Behavior,* **16** (1985), 3–30.

Evans, Nancy J., and Paul A. Jarvis. "Group Cohesion: A Review and Reevaluation," *Small Group Behavior,* **11** (1980), 359–370.

For Janis's concept of cohesiveness in his formulation of groupthink, see:

Janis, Irving. *Victims of Groupthink.* 2nd ed. Boston: Houghton Mifflin, 1983.

For studies of Janis's analysis of cohesiveness and groupthink which fail to support his conclusions, see:

Callaway, Michael R., and James K. Esser. "Groupthink: Effects of Cohesiveness and Problem-Solving Procedures on Group Decision Making," *Social Behavior and Personality,* **12** (1984), 157–164.

Leana, Carrie R. "A Partial Test of Janis' Groupthink Model: Effects of Group Cohesiveness and Leader Behavior on Defective Decision Making," *Journal of Management,* **11** (1985), 5–17.

Discussions of the two types of decisions can be found in:

Maier, Norman. *Problem-Solving Discussion and Conferences: Leadership Methods and Skills.* New York: McGraw-Hill, 1963.

Likert's management theories can be found in:

Likert, Rensis. *New Patterns in Management.* New York: McGraw-Hill, 1961.

The exchange account of interpersonal relations is from:

Thibaut, John W., and Harold H. Kelly. *The Social Psychology of Groups*. New York: Wiley, 1959.

For the effect of initiation on group commitment, see:

Aronson, Elliot, and Judson Mills. "The Effect of Severity of Initiation on Liking for a Group," *Journal of Abnormal and Social Psychology*, **59** (1959), 177–181.

Gerard, Harold B., and Grover C. Mathewson. "The Effect of Severity of Initiation on Liking For a Group: A Replication," *Journal of Experimental Social Psychology*, **2** (1966), 278–287.

For a synthesis of research dealing with group composition, compatibility, and cohesiveness, see Shaw (p. 98). For earlier studies see also:

Haythorn, W. W. "Composition of Groups: A Review of the Literature," *Acta Psychologica*, **28** (1968), 97–128.

For a theoretical account of FIRO and reports of research supporting the assumptions, see:

Schutz, William G. *FIRO: A Three-Dimensional Theory of Interpersonal Behavior.* New York: Holt, Rinehart and Winston, 1958.

Schutz, William G. "On Group Composition," *Journal of Abnormal and Social Psychology*, **62** (1961), 275–281.

For a study that failed to support FIRO, see:

Altman, I., and W. W. Haythorn. "The Effects of Social Isolation and Group Composition on Performance," *Human Relations*, **20** (1967), 313–340.

For a study that partially supported FIRO, see:

Rosenfeld, Lawrence B., and Paul A. Jessen. "Compatibility and Interaction in the Small Group: Validation of Schutz's FIRO-B Using a Modified Version of Lashbrook's PROANA 5," *Western Journal of Speech Communication*, **36** (1972), 31–40.

For a study reporting the test for comfort with procedural order, see:

Putnam, Linda L. "Preference for Procedural Order in Task-Oriented Small Groups," *Communication Monographs*, **46** (1979), 193–218.

For a study examining procedural order, see:

Hirokawa, Randy Y., Richard Ice, and Jeanmarie Cook. "Preference for Procedural Order, Discussion Structure, and Group Decision Performance," *Communication Quarterly*, **36** (1988), 217–226.

For other representative studies of cohesiveness, see:

Baker, Paul Morgan. "Division of Labor: Interdependence, Isolation and Cohesion in Small Groups," *Small Group Behavior*, **12** (1981), 93–106.

Segal, Mady Wechsler. "Varieties of Interpersonal Attraction and Their Interrelationships in Natural Groups," *Social Psychology Quarterly*, **42** (1979), 253–261.

Taylor, Donald M., Janet Doria, and J. Kenneth Tyler. "Group Performance and Cohesiveness: An Attribution Analysis," *Journal of Social Psychology*, **119** (1983) 187–198.

Tziner, Aharon. "Group Cohesiveness: A Dynamic Perspective," *Social Behavior and Personality,* **10** (1982), 205–211.

———. "Differential Effects of Group Cohesiveness Types: A Clarifying Overview," *Social Behavior and Personality,* **10** (1982), 227–239.

Weinberg, Sanford B., et al. "Common Group Problems: A Field Study," *Small Group Behavior,* **12** (1981), 81–92.

Chapter
5

Fantasy Chains and Group Culture

*T*his chapter delves more deeply into the group communicative processes that contribute to cohesiveness, norms, roles, leadership, and decisions. After meeting for some time, group members often experience a sense of "groupness" that they perceive as something new. They find that when they attend group meetings they are crossing the boundaries into a new social field and that they have created a new culture which is a part of their group experience. This chapter examines the way in which communication contributes to the creation of this new consciousness and the way the new consciousness works itself out as a group culture.

Earlier chapters have drawn the distinction between special and general theories and have described in detail the special communication theories related to group discussion and small group communication. Chapter 4 presented a general theory called the exchange theory to explain the pushes and pulls that relate to individuals being drawn into or pushed away from groups. Here another general theory of communication is applied to the symbolic processes that people employ in group meetings, a theory known as *symbolic convergence.*

Whereas the exchange theory is similar in its general shape to some cost–benefit analyses in economics, the symbolic convergence theory resembles theoretical formulations in such areas as biology and geology. For example, geological observers may note that an earthquake has taken place and explain what caused it. The explanation might describe the flow of heat within the earth that causes the inevitable distorting and faulting beneath the crust of the earth's surface. Sudden fractures occur when the strain of movements within the earth becomes too great and breaks the crust, usually along lines called faults. The more or less violent breaking of the earth's surface results in quaking or tremor. The theory explains the causes of the observed phenomenon, namely, an earthquake. In similar fashion, communication observers may note that the members of a small group have come to a meeting of the minds or that they have made a shared emotional investment in a group symbol. Symbolic convergence theory then explains the causes of common consciousness on the part of the members.

Geologists can anticipate earthquakes, but they cannot predict them. In the same fashion, communication experts can describe and explain the results of group consciousness but they cannot predict when symbolic convergence will take place.

SYMBOLIC CONVERGENCE AND GROUP CULTURE

The basic communicative dynamic of the theory is the sharing of group fantasies, which brings about symbolic convergence for the participants.

Investigators in small group communication laboratories discovered the process of sharing fantasies when they investigated dramatizing messages and their effect on the group culture. Bales and his associates originally developed 12 categories to use in making a content analysis of communication in small groups. One of the categories was "Shows Tension Release," but over the years investigators changed the category to "Dramatizes." Continued work in which observers investigated the communication episodes associated with dramatizing led to the discovery of "group fantasy events."

The Minnesota studies replicated the work of Bales and his associates beginning in the early 1970s. The preliminary results of these investigations were reported in the previous edition of this book, and the results of the small group studies since that edition was published, culminating with the formulation of the symbolic convergence theory, are summarized in this edition.

Dramatizing Messages

A dramatizing message is one that contains one or more of the following: a pun or other word play, a double entendre, a figure of speech, analogy, anecdote, parable, allegory, fable, or narrative. Puns and double meanings are important for imaginative portrayals in that they provide the basis for group members to see the mirroring of meaning. *Metaphor* is sometimes used as an umbrella term for all comparisons. *Tropes* and *figures* are other rhetorical terms used for imaginative language. In symbolic convergence theory, however, figures of speech refer to short, direct or implied comparisons as well as to the important figure of personification, in which a nonhuman object or life form is portrayed as having human features and characteristics. *Analogies* are defined as longer comparisons that extend the similarities through the discourse. Metaphor analysis is, thus, only one part of dramatizing messages.

The term *myth* is sometimes used to mean large collections of narratives and sometimes to mean a narrative frame and sometimes a specific story. Narratives and stories have become important features of rhetorical study in recent years. This is true in symbolic convergence theory as well. In the building of group culture, the narrative material in dramatizing messages is most important. However, it is also important to realize that the technical term *dramatizing message* includes material often referred to in other works on communication as metaphor and myth as well as narrative and story.

A number of scholars have suggested that it is useful to view the process of a communication episode as dramatic action. Thus, even everyday behavior can be interpreted as role playing or self-monitoring and self-presentation. All the world becomes a stage and we are all actors at all times. Portraying everyday life as drama does provide some useful insights into human communication, but the analogy ought not be pushed too far. After all, a small group meeting such as a jury deliberation portrayed in a motion picture is not the same as a jury deliberation over the fate of a defendant in a court of law.

The studies of dramatizing messages, therefore, have led to the conclusion that it is useful to distinguish between the ongoing unfolding of experience and the messages that discuss events in other than the here and now.

If in the middle of a group discussion several members come into conflict, the situation would be dramatic; but because the action is unfolding in the immediate experience of the group, it would not qualify as the basis for the sharing of a group fantasy. Immediate experience is often confusing and contradictory. We may not know for sure what happened or whom to blame or praise for their actions during the event. If, however, the group members begin talking about a conflict some of them had in the past, or if they envision a future conflict, of if they dramatize a current conflict taking place somewhere else, these comments would be dramatizing messages. Such messages make sense out of our confusing experiences and provide an explanation and interpretation of what happened.

The Communicative Process of Sharing a Fantasy

As they studied these messages, the Minnesota investigators found, as did Bales and his associates, that some seemed to fall on deaf ears: The group members did not pay much attention to certain comments. Other dramatizing messages, however, caused a symbolic explosion in the form of a chain reaction. The tempo of the conversation picked up. People grew excited, interrupted one another, blushed, laughed, lost self-consciousness. The tone of the meeting, which was often quiet and tense immediately prior to the dramatizing, became animated and boisterous. In the chaining process, both verbal and nonverbal communication indicated participation in the drama. Then, as abruptly as it started, the episode was broken off by a member who changed the subject, often by pulling the group back to work. The people who shared the fantasy did so with the appropriate responses. In short, the replications at Minnesota found the same processes of apathy or chaining when group members dramatized as did other investigators.

In addition, the Minnesota studies found that not all dramatizing messages result in a group's sharing a fantasy or in a group's ignoring the message or responding with a "ho hum" attitude. Some dramatizing messages are actively rejected. Members express disapproval or groan when they should laugh, or laugh when they should feel sadness. Further study of the active rejection of dramatizing messages found that such messages also provide important evidence for the analysis of group culture by indicating the symbols, meanings, and emotions toward which the members do not converge.

Group fantasy chains are those moments of dramatization in which all or most of the members participate. You should not get the impression that the term *fantasy* as used here means that the communication is bizarre like science fiction, or unrealistic like a cartoon, or make-believe like a fairy tale. A group fantasy may and often does deal with real-life situations and people.

Figure 4 presents the nature of dramatizing messages and the possible responses of members of a group. Note that if the dramatizing message results in member participation and sharing, the result is a *group fantasy*.

In symbolic convergence, the term *fantasy* means the creative and imaginative shared interpretation of events that fulfills a group's psychological or rhetorical need to make sense of its experience and to anticipate its future. Rhetorical fantasies often deal with things that have actually happened to group members or that are reported in works of history, the news media, or the oral history and folklore of groups and communities.

Bales argues persuasively that fantasies are not usually developed entirely out of the mind. Most often, fantasies are formed in context, and the internal fantasy life of group members is full of images that are produced as a result of the "furniture" of the world. Members are likely to perceive objects of the environment in similar ways. The fantasy chain is, thus, seldom a case of mind over matter. Stressing the subjective aspects of human response to experience or the effects of individual differences is likely to miss substantial similarities. It is better to assume that the dramatizing messages that result in fantasy chains are, in Bales's words, traceable to "*some* 'original facts'."

If symbol systems stood in a one-to-one relationship with experience, then it might be argued that group communication mirrored the facts. A *sign* relationship is one in which the sign is invariably related to the experience. Thus, lightning is a sign of thunder and thunder inevitably

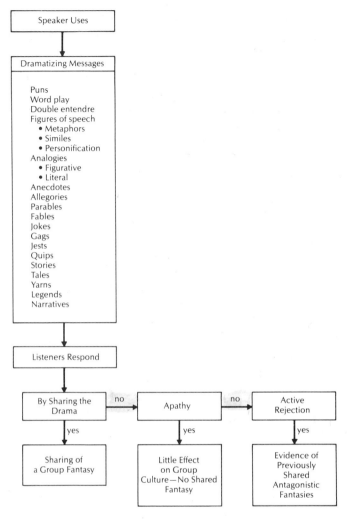

Figure 4 **The nature of dramatizing messages and the possible responses of group members.**

follows. Symbols, however, open the way for embroidering the facts. The symbol for lightning can denote the flash of light in the sky and signify the sound of thunder, but the symbol may also be placed on a military uniform to denote an elite corps or on a bottle to denote a potent kind of "white lightning." In short, objects of the real world when dramatized symbolically are, in Bales's words, "selected, re-made, smoothed out, and bent to some semblance of consistency with the existing mental world of the particular individual or group."

When group members respond emotionally to a dramatic message, they publicly proclaim some commitment to an attitude. They also have evidence that a new meaning has been shared by others for a symbol that has been singled out and made important. A fantasy chain brings the participants who share it into symbolic convergence and creates a common ground of meaning and culture that enables group members to achieve empathic communion as well as a "meeting of the minds."

A fantasy chain is symbolic because it deals with the human tendency to interpret signs, signals, current experience, and action and invest them with meaning. When we share a fantasy, we attribute events to human action and thus make sense out of what may have previously been a confusing state of affairs. We do so in common with others who share the fantasy with us. Thus, we come to symbolic convergence on the matter and we envision that part of our world in similar ways. We have created common villains and heroes and celebrated certain basic dramatic actions as laudable and pictured others as despicable. We have created some symbolic common ground and we can talk with one another about that shared interpretation with code words or brief allusions.

A number of studies into *attribution process* have documented the importance of this tendency to explain events by attributing them to motivated human action. Studies indicate, for example, that subjects attribute quite arbitrary qualities to social actions with considerable consistency, that group members attribute different motivations to fence straddling in small groups depending upon the context, and that the attribution of group success or failure affects group cohesiveness.

Convergence refers to the way in which, during certain processes of communication, two or more private symbolic worlds incline toward each other, come more closely together, or even overlap. When members placed in a new group participate in fantasy chains, their private symbolic worlds begin to overlap as a result of symbolic convergence. Having experienced symbolic convergence, they share a common group consciousness. They have the basis for communication with one another to raise the consciousness of new members, to sustain the consciousness of group members when challenged, to discuss their common concerns and experiences as group members, and to agree on how to make decisions.

The members of a new group may all have previously come to symbolic convergence in other groups so that they bring the same symbolic common ground, the same heroes and villains, with them to the group. Case studies indicate that such luck or accident is extremely rare, however; and although members often bring some commonalities with them, they usually must share new fantasies in order to build a unique group consciousness. The creation of such a common consciousness is essential to the development of a group culture and cohesiveness.

Fantasy Themes ✜

The content of the dramatizing message that sparks the fantasy chain is called a *fantasy theme*. The fantasy theme is the pun, figure, or analogy that characterizes the event, or it is a narrative that tells the story in terms of specific characters going through a particular line of action.

When someone characterizes an event with a figure of speech or dramatizes what happened, he or she must select certain people to be the focus of the story and present them in a favorable light while selecting others to be portrayed in a more negative fashion. Without protagonists (heroes) and antagonists (villains), there is little drama.

Shared fantasies are coherent accounts of past experiences or those envisioned in the future that simplify, organize, and form the social reality of the participants. The group's shared dreams of the future, no matter how apocalyptic or utopian, provide artistic and comprehensive forms for thinking about and experiencing the future. Fantasy themes always put a spin on the facts, which are thus slanted, ordered, and interpreted. By sharing different fantasy themes, members of different groups have the rhetorical means to account for and explain the same experiences or events in different ways. For example, often the classroom groups that received a grade of A to be shared by all members will participate in fantasy chains that account for and explain what happened in terms of their innate excellence and superior work, whereas the groups that received a grade of C or D might explain the results in terms of unfair teacher evaluations.

Symbolic Cues ⚓

The Minnesota studies revealed another important communication phenomenon in the workings of *symbolic cues* or triggers. The communication phenomenon of the inside joke is an example of such a trigger. The studies showed that only those who have shared the fantasy theme that the inside joke refers to will respond in an appropriate fashion.

Of course, the symbolic cue need not be an inside joke. The allusion to a previously shared fantasy may arouse tears or evoke anger, hatred, love, or affection as well as laughter and humor. The symbolic cue may be a code word, phrase, slogan, or nonverbal sign or gesture. Using symbolic cues to trigger previously shared emotions and meanings is a sure sign that participants have shared fantasies and that they have, at least, the beginnings of a group culture.

Fantasy Types ⚓

The symbolic cue is an induction which allows members to symbolize an entire fantasy chain with a brief allusion to it. Such inductions provide the basis for further clusterings of similar dramatizations. When the similar clusters deal with stories, the way is open for outside observers and group members to generalize to another communicative feature of small groups: the use of *fantasy types*. When a number of similar themes, including particulars of scene, characters, and situations, have been shared, members often move to a more abstract level of making a general description of a fantasy type that refers to all similar dramatizations.

A fantasy type is a stock scenario repeated again and again by the same or similar characters. For example, the Minnesota study of zero-history leaderless natural groups in the classroom revealed several groups in which members shared personal-experience stories about parties they had recently attended. Often these stories began to fall into a stock scenario of what the members should do on such occasions to have a good time, what they celebrated as laudable, and what they portrayed as bad. When these stories began to have a similar form, observers could classify them as forming a type.

Participants, too, make typal classifications of fantasy themes, and after they have created a group culture they tend to use the more abstract and general fantasy type in their communication. Rather than dramatizing a fantasy theme with specific characters in a specific setting, they present only the general plot line. A participant might say, "What really makes me angry is trying to find a professor to talk to during registration. You know how professors are. They're never around when you really need to talk to them. Why is it that there's never anyone in the office and the answering machine is all you get when you telephone?"

Whenever a participant casts a generalized persona—such as a teacher, a student, a worker, a bureaucrat, a banker, or a farmer—as part of an anecdote, the result is likely to be a fantasy type. Of course, if the group has shared a number of similar stories about the same character, a fantasy type might be about that individual. "Joe got in trouble again last night. He went out partying, and as usual he ended up in a hassle with the police. And you can guess the end of the story. Janet went down to the stationhouse and got him out again."

Group members can also use a fantasy type as a way of fitting their unfolding experiences into their shared consciousness. Thus, classroom participants might share a utopian fantasy portraying themselves as a cohesive and effective group of problem solvers who fail only when some outside person (such as the class instructor) frustrates them. Should they fail to make a good group grade on a class assignment, they may portray the experience as an instance of the fantasy type. ("It's our instructor's fault that we did not get an A.")

By using the fantasy type as a script to explain and evaluate new events, the members bring these events into line with the overall values and emotions of their group culture. They also sustain a key element of their consciousness: their utopian group fantasy. Since the utopian drama is often a noncoping fantasy, it tends to make the group ineffective in dealing with changing circumstances and the environment. In this way, the sharing of group fantasies can lend an emotional tone to the group experience and affect overall decision-making effectiveness.

Figure 5 charts the relationships among fantasy themes, inside cues, fantasy types, and group culture. Note that symbolic convergence pro-

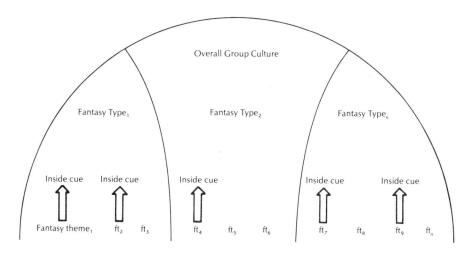

Figure 5 Relationships among fantasy themes, inside cues, fantasy types, and overall group culture.

vides an explanation for how the communication (what a member says) is responded to by the listeners in order to create cohesiveness and the common ground required for productive discussion.

Reasons for Fantasy Sharing

Why do group members share some fantasies, respond to others in a ho-hum fashion, and actively reject still others? Three promising factors explain why people share or reject fantasies: (1) the members' past hang-ups and their current baggage of personal and previously shared fantasies; (2) the common concerns that group members have because of their experiences in the group; and (3) the rhetorical skill with which participants dramatize during the group meetings.

Bales provided a psychoanalytic accounting that was heavily Freudian. However, the importance of the chaining out of dramas to the group's culture can be explained without such heavy reliance on Freudian concepts. A rhetorician, for example, might argue that the chaining out of the drama was a result of the skill with which the original drama was presented.

Bales distinguished three dimensions of the communication events coded into the "Dramatizes" category. The first dimension related to the content of the messages: What do the group members say? The second dimension of a shared fantasy was the drama as a mirror of the group's here-and-now experience and its relationship to the external environment. The drama played out somewhere else or in some other time often symbolized a role collision or ambiguity, a leadership conflict, or a problem related to the task dimension of the group. Just as an individual's repressed problems might surface in dream fantasies, so a group's hidden agenda might surface in a fantasy chain, and a critic might interpret the surface content with an eye to discovering the hidden agenda.

The third dimension of the dramatizing message, which manifested itself in some groups, was an expression in a given social field of the individual psychodynamics of the participants.

Bales argued that the past history of each individual affects the personal hang-ups that individual brings to a zero-history group. In this view, members bring concerns to the meeting only some of which they have in common. In a given group, for example, all members might have problems with their relationships with their fathers. Dramatizing messages that tap the participants' psychological problems with the male parent would then be shared, whereas if several members have had good relations with their mothers they would reject a dramatization that portrayed a mother in an unsavory light.

Individuals also bring to the group their personal fantasy lives and their past experiences in sharing fantasies in other groups. Suppose all the group members have previously, in other groups, shared dramas about the ineptness of the current President of the United States. When someone dramatizes a story about the President's ineptness, the members are likely to share it. When they do, they have publicly demonstrated how they stand on the persona of the President and that persona becomes a common symbol in the group's culture.

One of the more intriguing questions that has emerged from the study of group fantasies is the extent to which the chaining is inevitable or accidental or the result of a deliberate effort on the part of one or more members to generate a certain kind of symbolic world for the group.

Evidence from the Minnesota case studies suggests that the artistry with which the drama is presented is a factor in whether it chains through the group. One can never be sure whether a play will be a success; but if the playwright is talented and knows the craft, the play is more likely to be successful than if the writer is untalented and inexperienced. Something analogous to the playwright's success seems to be operating in the case of chaining fantasies in a small group.

Timing, too, appears to be a factor in whether a fantasy chains out once it is introduced. In much the same way that group decisions cannot be forced on a group before it is ready to make them, so the group members must be predisposed to respond by a common attitude or problem before they chain out a particular fantasy. Fantasies that are unsuccessfully introduced early in a group's life sometimes chain out when reintroduced later. Thus, proper timing, as well as the artistry of the manner of presentation, appears to be a factor in the success or failure of a fantasy to chain through a group.

In one case study, a woman had written up a fantasy for her diary on her group experience which took the form of a fable. She had depicted each member as an animal or bird. She was reading some of her diary to another member in a low voice while the others were going on about the group's business; the other person became intrigued and called the group's attention to the fable. He urged her to read it to the entire group. She was reluctant at first, but with some urging she started. She caught the group's attention, and they began to respond, at first tentatively, then with greater enthusiasm until, finally, all the others were actively participating, injecting comments, and roaring with laughter. She had not written her diary with an eye to the audience or with the conscious intent to persuade others to adopt a certain position or attitude. In other words, she did not have a rhetorical purpose. She had simply written the sketch for her own amusement. Her skill in writing it, however, contributed to the chaining of the fantasy. Moreover, the group had reached a state of tension because of interpersonal conflicts that it had not been able to handle in a direct way, and the fantasy personality analysis in her fable was presented to the group when all its members were at least intellectually aware that personality problems were crippling the group's effectiveness in the task area and were ready for her oblique analysis of their conflicts.

The fact that a person has more chance of having a drama chain through the group if it is presented skillfully makes a rhetorical approach to introducing fantasy themes into a new group possible. Indeed, some people do use group methods for persuasive ends, and they often use fantasies for their own purposes. Organizers of consciousness-raising sessions and other groups designed for conversion purposes frequently rely on dramas for their persuasive ends. The planners of groups used for rhetorical purposes usually arrange for a majority of the group to consist of people already committed to the position. Usually, the meeting will include only one or two potential converts. A person being rushed for a fraternity or sorority may find himself or herself closeted with four or five "actives." The woman attending a women's consciousness-raising session may find herself in a group in which the vocal and articulate members are committed to the movement.

Once a meeting gets under way, the insiders begin to introduce important dramas from their community's culture, and the committed then chain into them with the appropriate nuances and emotional responses. Under the pressure of the group, the potential convert often begins to participate in appropriate ways in the fantasies. Neophytes are particularly susceptible if their previous experiences have been similar to those of the already committed. One of the studies at Minnesota was of consciousness-raising groups associated with gay liberation. The pattern of fantasy themes in the sessions began with dramas that were widely disseminated nationally through underground presses and the gay liberation grapevine. Most of the committed knew the national rhetoric, although some of them were not personally acquainted with one another. When they had formed some common ground by participating in the nationally known dramas, they moved to the narration of personal experiences about the repressions they had suffered. All the dramas, however, were on themes related to the subculture of the gay liberation movement.

Although a conscious rhetorical effort to cause fantasies to chain through a group can succeed in igniting a chain reaction, the results are not always what was hoped for or intended. The fantasy often begins to take on a life of its own, and the member who first introduced the theme may well lose control of its development. When the fantasy gets out of hand in a rhetorical group, the organizers will judge that it was a bad session. As the others participate, they add new directions and new emphases to the drama. The originator may be astonished and frightened by the way the chain develops. The final fantasy event, viewed in retrospect, is the joint effort of all the members who contributed to it.

The fact that a person has more chance to have a drama chain through the group if it is presented skillfully makes possible a rhetorical approach to inducing fantasy sharing in a new group. Indeed, value-shift groups use fantasy sharing for persuasive purposes in just this way.

Of course, good storytellers, clever punsters, and imaginative users of figures of speech may do a lot of dramatizing in group meetings for the enjoyment they get from being the center of attention. After all, rhetorical skill marks a group member and draws both positive and negative attention. But when a person dramatizes only for the immediate effect of gaining attention, the group may accidentally create a culture that is more or less coping and enjoyable.

CULTURE AND COHESIVENESS

One of the more fruitful areas of study has been the analysis of chaining fantasies, both those accepted and those rejected, to gain insights into a group's culture. Investigators using a fantasy-theme analysis have worked with material hitherto often overlooked because it seemed trivial or irrelevant to the task-oriented group. When a shared fantasy impresses the members of a group to such an extent that they continue to recall it and respond to allusions to it with some of their original excitement, then the drama becomes part of the group's social reality and, therefore, important to their common and unique culture.

On occasion, one creative person may dramatize a powerful personal consciousness so skillfully that it is shared by others in the group until it becomes the basis for group culture. If this does happen, it happens rarely and in none of the case studies did an individual single-handedly create the culture. Culture building most often results from early small group meetings in which members share fantasies to which several more members contribute, in the process creating a new group consciousness and a new group culture.

Often the flow of communication in these consciousness-creating segments of meetings is not from speaker to listeners; rather, the chain triggered by the first dramatizing message is then picked up and elaborated by the others. People caught up in a chain of fantasies may experience moments similar to the creative experiences of individuals when they daydream about a creative project or an important problem and suddenly get excited about the direction of their thinking. Then the others feed back ideas and new dramatizations to add to the original comment. Messages begin flowing rapidly among the participants until, under the suggestive power of the group fantasy, the constraints which normally hold people back are released; they feel free to experiment with ideas, to play with concepts and wild suggestions and imaginative notions. Soon a number of people are deeply involved in the discussion, excitedly adding their emotional support and often modifying the ongoing fantasy chain.

The group's innovative dramas may be a radical departure from the fantasies that members have shared in other groups. They, then, leave the group meeting with new ideas. (That is, they have come to convergence about certain symbols and the meanings and emotional evocations which are novel for them.) The group may, alternatively, replay and share dramas that some know very well from previous groups.

When people join a zero-history group, they have no basis for knowing if there even is such a thing as "their group," for it has no history and no presence. One of the basic rhetorical problems for participants trying to build a new consciousness is to create in the members a sense of common identity. People create a common identity by becoming aware that they are involved in an identifiable group. Once they have discovered that there is something called "our group," the members have an opportunity to dramatize their group in ways that portray it as different from other groups. They also may share fantasies that portray members of their group as different from other people who are not symbolically tied together by being part of the group.

To come to awareness about the group and their relation to it, members need to identify their collective self. In early meetings of zero-history leaderless groups, members often shift from talking in personal terms about "I" and "you" and "he" and "she" and begin to use terms like "we" and "our group." At this point the members have mentioned a new social entity in the world: *our group.* Naming the group rhetorically creates the group. The new entity can now become the protagonist or antagonist in a dramatizing message. "Well, but you see our group, if it is really going to do well and get a good grade, is going to have to go to the library and interview people and in other ways get a lot of information about this question."

As noted earlier, personification is an important rhetorical device for dramatizing the group. Personification is the rhetorical figure in which an inanimate object or abstract notion is supplied with the attributes of a human being or a character in a drama. In the dramatizing message above, "our group" becomes the central character in a drama about the group going to the library and interviewing people for information. When the group appears as a persona in shared fantasies, the members come to symbolic convergence about what kind of group it is. If the members share a fantasy about a hardworking group that gathers good information and makes an A in the class, they have created part of their culture, including a celebration of achievement as defined in the class. Of course, the members might share a fantasy about "our group" which portrays it as taking it easy and having a good time and not worrying too much about getting an A so long as everybody passes.

Although the personification of "our group" is a common way to share fantasies about it and thus create a culture it is not the only way. Some groups select the name of an inanimate object and share a fantasy in which they apply that name to the group. Thus, they become the Stones or the Stars or the Cyclones. Athletic teams often use personification to make these inanimate objects into characters in their dramas: "The Stars really shone as they tamed the Cyclones 3 to 1 at the arena last night" or "The Stones again showed their toughness of character as they rallied from a 1-to-1 tie in the last period."

Groups may also select names for abstract concepts like *blues* or *reds* and give these concepts human characteristics so they can act in dramatic messages. "The Greens have managed to place several representatives in the newly elected assembly." Groups may also use animals, insects, birds, and other animate (but not human) creatures for their mascots or symbols. Thus, the members might refer to their groups as the Bears or Gophers or Eagles.

Professional and semiprofessional athletic teams often have cartoonists depict their names for use as a logo or identifying symbol. The University of Minnesota refers to its sports teams as the Gophers. The gopher caricature used as an identifying symbol for the teams looked much more like a human than a rodent. Some years ago, the Gopher football team got a new coach who, as one of his first official acts, commissioned an artist to prepare a new caricature of a gopher. The result was a symbol that looked as though the gopher had been pumping iron. The gopher was also wearing a new costume reminiscent of Superman's. Clearly, the coach felt that the way group members come to identify their group is important to their success.

Dealing with their identity often gets members to share fantasies about the boundaries of their group. Who are the outsiders? Typical persons who can symbolize the outsiders constitute a useful dramatizing device for identifying the insiders and drawing boundaries around the group. Sharing fantasies that clearly divide the sympathetic good people (we) from the unsympathetic people (they) aids the group's self-awareness and is crucial to the emergence of its culture. Indeed, an important question for a person evaluating a group relates to the way in which the members share fantasies that characterize insiders and their group.

We each have our own personal histories which are essential to our identity. Carl Becker, a noted historian, wrote an important essay entitled

"Everyman His Own Historian" in an effort to explain the uses of history. He noted that our personal histories are composed of authentic records such as birth certificates, but they also contain narratives from family members recounting what we did at a young age or our own recollections and reminiscences. Taken together, these records and narratives tell us where we have been and what we have done and provide a trajectory for our futures based on the arc of our past lives. When people suffer from amnesia, they lose their personal histories and sense of identity and future.

George Orwell, in his novel 1984, explains in fictional terms the subtle importance of the historical record. In his terrifying society, one of the important ways of manipulating the future is to rewrite the record of the past. The controllers of society continually rewrite history. The practice of totalitarian societies provides evidence in support of Orwell's insight that whoever controls the present controls the past and whoever controls the past controls the future. In short, efforts of native American groups to rewrite the history of the settlement of the West or of black groups to rewrite the history of the black experience in this country or of women's groups to rewrite the history of women in North America are not only of academic interest but of great importance to the future.

No small group can come to cohesiveness; no larger collective to a sense of community; no mass of people to a sense of nationhood without a common history. Sharing fantasies is the mechanism by which the members develop a group history and group tradition. When a series of fantasies has chained through a group dramatizing events that happened to the members because of their common activities and communications, the group begins to develop a collective memory. Once a group memory has been systematically developed, it is easy to perceive the group as unique and as something more than the people who compose it. The group history provides the old members with a sense of purpose and direction for the future. The history also allows new members to learn of the group's past and become socialized into the group's culture.

Organizations often have their histories carefully researched by a professional historian. Many fraternity manuals contain an official history, which each new member must read. Small task-oriented groups often recall their histories in a less systematic and authentic way. From time to time, members will reminisce about something that happened to them as they worked together. Such reminiscences fall into dramatic form, with the members or the group itself as characters in the drama. When the reminiscences chain out, they create the group's history.

On one occasion, a study group was meeting in a tower room of an old campus building. One member came late and found the building locked. He had to throw snowballs at the windows to catch the attention of the others. The meeting proved to be particularly productive and rewarding, and the members subsequently shared a fantasy about the event. It came to be part of their history, as a time of excitement and the point at which the group really came together. Whenever participants develop inside jokes or nicknames resulting from shared fantasies or from unusual happenings or adventures, they begin to feel part of an identifiable group.

One common fantasy type that appears again and again in group communication is the drama of the *founding*. The members recollect how they drew together and when they really became a group. Another set of fantasy types deals with the group's successes and another set with its failures. Many groups share a fantasy type dedicated not to the time a person joins the group but to some more significant moment when the individual "signs on" or "commits" to the group.

As groups evolve their cultures, they often develop repeated and scripted communication events growing out of their fantasy types. These take on the character of a *rite*, a formal ceremony or procedure prescribed or customary to celebrate important reminiscences. The more or less tightly scripted communication events may commemorate the founding and be called an anniversary or a founder's dinner or a founder's day. One rite may commemorate the successful completion of an important task. Another rite may be an initiation ceremony. Enacting the scripted communication makes the fantasy type live again in a solemn and impressive fashion or, perhaps, in a humorous and kidding fashion.

Cohesiveness and Common Ground

When five or six individuals meet together in a zero-history group or when newcomers join established groups, they have no way of knowing how their commonalities overlap or how their differences complement one another. Of course, neither do they know how their individual world views and psychologies will come into conflict.

The members may search for common ground directly by discussing their values and interests. A member may say, "I really believe that virginity and marriage are making a comeback, don't you?" Another might respond with agreement, and a third person may sit glumly, nonverbally suggesting disagreement, or may actively argue that attitudes toward marriage and virginity have not changed. Often, however, the primary tension of the early part of a group's history makes it difficult for members to launch into a direct consideration of such matters. The tension also encourages the members to tell jokes and personal anecdotes and experiences, or to dramatize other situations in an effort to relax the atmosphere and break the ice.

Many of the dramas do not chain out. The members find them dull or threatening or do not like the particular tone or interpretation of the drama. A member may say, "I'm sorry I'm late but my roommate decided to move in with this guy and I was helping her move her stuff." The member who thinks that the excitement and approval suggested by the way the first person presents the drama is laudable and that the roommate is doing the "right thing" will tend to chain in with something like, "Is she really? That's neat." The member who feels that the episode is deplorable is not likely to chain into the drama, but is much more likely to change the subject and might well suggest that the group get down to business.

When a number of fantasies have chained out, the members come to share a common symbolic world. Group members find it easier to grasp and to respond to many of the most vital political, military, economic, and social issues when they are presented dramatically in terms of concrete characters than when they are dealt with in terms of impersonal institutional analysis. The group finds it difficult to respond emotionally to a concept like the executive branch of the government, but the individual member can easily respond to a flesh-and-blood president in terms of love or hate or disdain or admiration if the character is presented in the suitable dramatic scenario. Often the radical campus groups in the 1960s dramatized their goals in terms of conflicts with some real individual such as the university president and tried to wrest their demands from a direct confrontation with the individual who symbolized the university. Usually the university president did not have the power or authority to deliver on the demands, but the group members found it easier to grasp the issue and mobilize support for their position if the question were presented in dramatic terms.

Against the panorama of large events and the seemingly unchangeable and often impersonal forces of society or of nature, the individual may feel lost and hopeless. One coping mechanism is to dream an individual fantasy, which provides a sense of meaning and significance for the individual and which helps protect the person from the pressures of natural calamity and social disaster. The group culture generated by chaining fantasies serves much the same coping function for those who participate in the group and often with much more force because of the power of group pressure and because of the supportive warmth of like-minded companions.

Members immersed in the fantasies that comprise the group's culture, surrounded by the traditions of the group, reminded of its history, often feel that the group is important and, when appropriate, they may feel that the group existed before they joined it and will continue to exist after they leave. When they commit time and effort to such groups the sacrifices seem worthwhile.

Bales points out that

> as the individual person creates and maintains a system of symbols with other persons in a group, he enters a realm of reality, which he knows does or can surpass him, survive him; which may inspire or organize him, and which may threaten to dominate him as well. . . . It is presumably this feeling that is referred to when people talk about "becoming a group," or "the time we became a group."

In the final analysis, group cohesion is not something that results primarily from member characteristics or from the composition of the group; rather, it is created by the communication of the group members. By their communication they create new meanings, new attitudes, and new emotions and motives as symbolized in the personalities and actions they dramatize. Cohesion and interaction do not have a reality outside of the communication of the group. Members do not usually communicate about their cohesiveness and their interaction; they create the meanings and motives associated with their group in the process of communicating with one another.

The case studies of group fantasizing at Minnesota reveal that groups vary greatly as to the amount of fantasizing they do. Some groups seldom dramatize their past or their future; members rarely tell jokes or stories or personal experiences; the group seldom chains into current events. Members stick doggedly to the here-and-now problems facing the group, and their communication is largely discursive. They discuss the facts related to their problem and the best way of proceeding. Some groups in the Minnesota studies have had only three or four fantasies that chained out in as many as 20 or 30 hours of meetings. Other groups set norms of fantasizing and may spend several hours in one meeting participating in loud boisterous fashion in a series of narratives.

Groups that do little fantasizing are seldom highly attractive and cohesive. Such groups tend to be boring and ordinary. The cohesive groups have usually done considerable fantasizing, but not all groups that fantasize a lot are rewarding and cohesive. The fantasies that chain may contribute to creating a social reality that is warm, friendly, and hardworking, that provides the group with a strong identity and self-image, and that gives the members a sense of purpose and meaning for their group's work. On the other hand, the fantasies may develop a group climate that is fascinating, frustrating, and punishing.

Some case studies at Minnesota discovered groups torn by dissension in which members were so frustrated by the group that they were aroused to hate other members and the group itself. Yet the group not only continued to meet, but the members would schedule extra meetings which would go on for hours. Fantasy-theme analysis provides a partial explanation for the apparent masochism of the members in frustrating groups. The members of the fascinating groups did a great deal of chaining into fantasy themes either in coalitions or in the entire group. The themes of the group's common fantasies, however, tended to be conflict-ridden and highly emotional. The humor associated with the dramas tended to be ridicule, sarcasm, or satire. The emotions aroused by the dramas tended to be scorn or hate. The dramatic action lines tended to be destructive or sado-masochistic. Participating in the groups came to have a fascination for their members something like that of attending a compelling horror film or observing an unpleasant accident.

The members often reported in their diaries that they were ambivalent about attending the meetings, yet they could not get the group off their minds, and in the end they could not stay away. One group, for example, was unable to stabilize roles or assign leadership because of a strong female contender in conflict with a strong but lazy male who felt that a woman's place was in the home. As the group continued and the woman remained active and adamant, the lazy man began to miss meetings; and, although the group failed to follow the woman, no man emerged to lead the group. Another man who was in early contention became ill and could not attend some of the crucial meetings. The group created a culture that was filled with dramas of conflict and cutting one another down. One of the continuing fantasies was the castration drama. The group was discussing population problems, and, in the course of discussing methods of control, one member jokingly said the group "could send a man around with a meat cleaver." The group laughed, and a male member chained in with "Ah, I have to go." Later in the discussion the group returned to the theme.

> MEMBER A: [male] We'll just have to start breeding smaller people, lighter people who don't weigh as much, don't eat as much.
> MEMBER B: [female leader contender] How can you do that . . . kind of regulated by genes?
> MEMBER A: All small people are getting bred out anyway.
> MEMBER C: [male leader contender] I'd volunteer to be a breeder, but I'm too big to breed little people.
> MEMBER B: Get the meat cleaver.

The castration drama became a major theme of their discussions, and all that was necessary for a strong emotional response was for a member to allude to it.

Sharing Fantasies and Value Formation

When a fantasy chains through a group, the members discover in an exciting and emotional way a common ground relating to values, actions, and attitudes. Group members create a common set of heroes, villains, saints, and sinners and the common scenarios in which these characters act out laudable and deplorable behaviors. The common set of dramatic characters and the actions, attitudes, and values that they symbolize become an important part of the group's culture. If a group of teenage men share fantasies in which the young heroes chew tobacco, try to score sexually with attractive women, and race cars at high speeds, the values inherent in their culture are apparent. If a group of college women share fantasies in which young male villains chew tobacco, treat women as sex objects, and take undue risks in racing their cars, the values inherent in their culture are equally apparent.

Sharing Fantasies and Emotional Response

The sharing of fantasies and the group culture that results provide the members with an emotional evocation for various symbolic events and for the things that happen to them. Hate, fear, love, laughter, jealousy, pride, and a host of other feelings and emotions are embedded in the fantasies. Physiological studies of emotions reveal that changes in heart rate, palm sweat, and so on, vary little from emotion to emotion. One way to account for the perception of many different emotions in the face of little evidence of physiological differences is to divide emotions into a physiological side and a psychological one and to argue that a person may interpret internally similar physiological states as different emotions.

An interesting study pointing up the difference between the physiological and psychological sides of emotions is one by Schacter and Singer. The investigators injected some subjects with placebos and some with a synthetic form of adrenalin which caused a state of physiological arousal. The experimenters told all subjects that the injection was a vitamin supplement. They told one part of the group injected with the adrenalin substitute to expect side effects such as heart palpitations. However, the remainder of those with the real drug were told nothing more than that the injection was a vitamin supplement. They divided the latter group into two experimental treatments. In one treatment they placed the deceived subjects with a collaborator who interpreted the feeling as one of euphoria and in another with a collaborator who interpreted the emotion as one of anger. Most subjects interpreted their artificially aroused physiological states in line with the fantasizing of the stooges.

The drama that accompanies an emotional state partly accounts for whether an individual interprets his feelings as hate or fear or anger or joy or love. The dramatic action in which the group participates provides occasion for humor and ridicule, for hatred and jealousy, for tragedy and catharsis. When prominent and colorful political figures suffer a setback, both their friends and their enemies will probably respond emotionally. Groups of friends will interpret their emotional response as sadness or despair, while groups of enemies will tend to interpret their response as joy and delight. Under group pressures built up during the excitement of a political race, members of both groups may cry at news of the politician's defeat, but enemies will interpret their tears as tears of joy.

Sharing Fantasies and Motives

The group culture contains the members' shared drives to action. People who generate, legitimatize, and participate in a fantasy chain may be moved to action by that process. Of course, some shared fantasies such as flight-taking dramas may result in inaction regarding a given line of endeavor. In short, participating in a group culture provides a person with impelling motives to action. Groups will often have a predominate number of fantasies that are affection or love dramas. The drama of the young man who falls in love with the princess and then has to do all sorts of difficult tasks to win her hand and finally does so to live happily ever after is an example. Groups may share many similar stories about who is well liked, what a popular person has been doing lately, how affectionate family members may be, how members had a great time and got on well at a good party, and so forth. Groups whose culture predominates in stories which have an affection or love motive will have members who spend much time and energy talking about and pursuing relationships.

Groups will often share a predominant number of dramas that imply a power motive. A group might, for instance, have members who share a drama about how they can take over the class. Fantasies about heroes who play politics until they climb to the top are other examples of dramas that imply a power motivation. Groups whose culture predominates in stories which have a power motive will have members who try to gain control over others and to rise to high-status positions.

Groups will often share a predominant number of dramas that imply an achievement motive. A group might, for instance, have members who share dramas about doing good work. The following hypothetical transcript illustrates how a group might share fantasies related to achievement.

"Last semester my roommate took this course, and he never worked so hard for a class in his life."

"Really?"

"Yeah. It was really great, though. He took field trips to hospital labs and everything."

"Yeah, I know this woman who took the course, and she said the same thing. She said you wouldn't believe how hard they worked. But she said she really got something out of it."

"You know, I don't mind working if I get something out of it."

"I'm really looking forward to it."

SUMMARY

For what reasons, then, might you want to study a group's communication to discover, describe, and evaluate its moments of fantasizing? This chapter has emphasized the theory of symbolic convergence and how group members create a group culture and its influence on cohesiveness. It has also laid the groundwork so that in future chapters about role emergence, leadership, and decision making only brief reminders need be made of the importance of the symbolic convergence theory and its implications for those features of group work.

Of course, as a group participant you are well advised to be aware of the rhetorical use of dramatizing to build a healthy and productive group culture. In that regard, it is good to keep in mind a popular T-shirt slogan: "I have given up my search for truth. Now I want to find a good fantasy."

An important general theory relating to small group communication is the way the sharing of group fantasies creates symbolic convergence.

Investigators studying small group communication discovered the process of sharing fantasies when they investigated dramatizing messages and their effect on group culture. A dramatizing message is one that contains a pun or other wordplay, a double entendre, a figure of speech, an analogy, an anecdote, a parable, an allegory, a fable, or a narrative.

Some dramatizing messages cause a symbolic explosion in the form of a chain reaction in which members join in until the entire group comes alive. Sharing group fantasies brings the participants into symbolic convergence and creates a common ground of meaning and culture that allows group members to achieve empathic communion as well as a meeting of the minds.

A fantasy theme is a concrete narrative that tells a story in terms of specific characters. A symbolic cue is an agreed-upon trigger which sets off the group members to respond as they did when they first shared the fantasy. A fantasy type is a stock scenario repeated again and again by the same or similar characters.

Individuals may share a fantasy because it taps previously shared dramas or personal hang-ups of members, because it reflects a common experience of the group members, or because the person who dramatizes has great rhetorical skill.

When members name their group, they rhetorically create it. Members often use the rhetorical device of personification as a way to dramatize and identify their group. Sharing fantasies is the mechanism by which members develop a group history. A group's culture often includes rites which makes the core fantasy types live again in impressive fashion. The deepest commitment and the strongest cohesiveness stem from the sharing of fantasies which generate attractive group cultures. Fantasy sharing also forms values, emotions, and motives which become important parts of the group's culture.

☞ Rules of Thumb

Practical Advice on How to Be a Good Group Member

Drawn from Chapter 5

- ☞ Like any good general theory, symbolic convergence has practical applications.
- ☞ You can use symbolic convergence theory to explain how members of a group come to share a common consciousness.
- ☞ You can use symbolic convergence theory to analyze common socioemotional problems in order to bring them to the attention of group members.
- ☞ You can use symbolic convergence theory to design and build productive and satisfying group cultures.

☞ Be sure to distinguish between the message and response, between the dramatizing and the sharing of a fantasy.

☞ The shared dramas (group fantasies) are what are important in analyzing group culture.

☞ What is happening in the group (the here and now) is not a shared fantasy.

☞ Fantasy themes are shared interpretations of human action taking place in a different setting and a different time.

☞ Learn to identify those moments when a dramatizing message causes a symbolic explosion in the form of a chain reaction.

☞ Remember, a shared fantasy often deals with real-life situations and people.

☞ Take steps to help build a common consciousness, which is essential to the development of cohesiveness.

☞ Fantasy chains do not need to be tacit or out of the awareness of the members.

☞ The rhetorical artistry used in developing a dramatizing message can contribute to triggering a fantasy chain.

☞ Proper timing can contribute to successful attempts to get groups to share fantasies.

☞ Do not use your knowledge of how to get groups to share fantasies for your own persuasion ends.

☞ Remember that a conscious rhetorical effort on your part can succeed in igniting a chain reaction but the fantasy may take an unexpected turn.

☞ When the group begins to share a drama that in your opinion would contribute to a healthy culture, you should pick up the drama and feed the chain.

☞ To build cohesiveness, use personification to identify your group.

☞ When your group begins to define its boundaries, be careful that the characterization of insiders and outsiders does not lead to hate and anger.

☞ Be sure to encourage the sharing of dramas depicting your group history early in your meetings.

☞ Select portions of your group's past with care when dramatizing your history because your past will influence your future.

☞ Defuse the incipient chains of potentially frustrating, flight-taking, and noncoping fantasies.

☞ Select your dramatizations for their implied value systems carefully because if shared they will influence group satisfaction and productivity.

☞ Select your dramatizations for their emotional evocation carefully because the emotional tone of your group will influence its communication climate.

☞ Select dramatizations that contain achievement motives for a productive task-oriented group culture.

QUESTIONS FOR STUDY

1. What are the differences between special theories of group communication like the public discussion theory and general theories like the symbolic convergence theory?
2. What is the nature of the communicative process of sharing group fantasies?
3. How might a fantasy theme and a dramatizing message be compared and contrasted?
4. How can fantasy types be used by group members to explain new experiences in old rhetorical forms?
5. Why do group members share fantasies?
6. What are some ways that participants can identify their collective self (their group)?
7. How can the shared fantasies that become the group's history contribute to cohesiveness?
8. How can group rites contribute to cohesiveness?
9. How might groups develop cultures that are frustrating and noncoping and fail to contribute to cohesiveness?
10. How can the sharing of group fantasies develop a culture that contains common values, emotional evocations, and motives?

EXERCISES

1. Select a group that you have been working with for some time and, if possible, tape-record some of its meetings. Describe several of the fantasies that have chained out in the group and analyze why the members shared the dramatization.
2. Do a case study of a class discussion group in terms of how the shared fantasies contributed to building a group culture.
3. Select a group of which you are a member and analyze the others to decide what sorts of dramatizations they might share. Develop five dramatizations that would appeal to the others in the group and contribute to a positive culture and group cohesiveness.

REFERENCES AND SUGGESTED READINGS

For studies demonstrating the presence and nature of fantasy chains in small group communication, see:

Dunphy, Dexter C. "Social Change in Self-Analytic Groups." In P. J. Stone et al., eds., *The General Inquirer: A Computer Approach to Content Analysis.* Cambridge, MA: MIT Press, 1966, pp. 287–340.

Bales, Robert F. *Personality and Interpersonal Behavior.* New York: Holt, Rinehart and Winston, 1970.

Gibbard, G. S., J. J. Hartman, and R. D. Mann. *Analysis of Groups,* San Francisco: Jossey-Bass, 1974.

Bormann, Ernest G., Linda L. Putnam, and Jerie M. Pratt. "Power, Authority, and Sex: Male Response to Female Dominance," *Communication Monographs,* **45:** (1978), 119–155.

For the original Bales categories and the revision of 1970, see:

Bales, Robert F. *Interaction Process Analysis.* Reading, MA: Addison-Wesley, 1950.

Bales, Robert F. *Personality and Interpersonal Behavior.* New York: Holt, Rinehart and Winston, 1970.

For another view of symbolic convergence, see:

Sharron, Avery. "The Mainstream of Consciousness: An Interactionist Analysis of a Phenomenological Concept," *Symbolic Interaction,* 8 (1985), 47–62.

For studies examining metaphors, narratives, and other symbolic imagery, see:

Ettin, Mark F. "Within the Group's View: Clarifying Dynamics Through Metaphoric and Symbolic Imagery," *Small Group Behavior,* 17 (1986), 407–426.

Fisher, B. Aubrey. "Leadership as Medium: Treating Complexity in Group Communication Research," *Small Group Behavior,* 16 (1985), 167–196.

Gustafson, James P., et al. "Cooperative and Clashing Interests in Small Groups: Part II. Group Narratives," *Human Relations,* 34 (1981), 367–378.

McLeod, John. "Group Process as Drama," *Small Group Behavior,* 15 (1984), 319–332.

Owen, William F. "Metaphor Analysis of Cohesiveness in Small Discussion Groups," *Small Group Behavior,* 16 (1985), 415–424.

Rossel, Robert D. "Word Play: Metaphor and Humor in the Small Group," *Small Group Behavior,* 12 (1981), 116–136.

Shambaugh, Philip W. "The Mythic Structuring of Bion's Groups," *Human Relations,* 38 (1985), 937–951.

For a collection of scholarly essays dealing with a dramatistic approach to communication, see:

Combs, James E., and M. W. Mansfield, eds. *Drama in Life: The Uses of Communication in Society.* New York: Hastings House, 1976.

For the description of fantasy chains by Bales and his quote on the relation between fact and fantasy, see:

Bales, Robert F. *Personality and Interpersonal Behavior.* New York: Holt, Rinehart and Winston, 1970, pp. 139 and 148.

For studies into attribution processes, see:

Berger, Charles R. "Attributional Communication, Situational Involvement, Self-Esteem, and Interpersonal Attraction," *Journal of Communication,* 23 (1973), 284–335.

Kiger, Gary, Ray P. Cuzzort, and C. Dale Johnson. "The Attribution of Positive and Negative Qualities to Social Actions," *Journal of Psychology,* 119 (1985), 322–333.

Smith, Mary J. *Persuasion and Human Action.* Belmont, CA: Wadsworth, 1982.

Taylor, Donald M., Janet Doria, and J. Kenneth Tyler. "Group Performance and Cohesiveness: An Attribution Analysis," *Journal of Social Psychology,* **119** (1983), 187–198.

For suggestions as to why group members share fantasies, see:

Bales, Robert F. *Personality and Interpersonal Behavior.* New York: Holt, Rinehart and Winston, 1970, pp. 140–142.

For the study of gay consciousness raising, see:

Chesebro, James W., John F. Cragan, and Patricia McCullough. "The Small Group Techniques of the Radical Revolutionary: A Synthetic Study of Consciousness Raising," *Speech Monographs,* **40** (1973), 136–146.

For the uses of history, see:

Becker, Carl. *Everyman His Own Historian.* Garden City, NY: Doubleday, 1976.

For a study of consciousness-creating small group communication and its relationship to cohesiveness, see:

Bormann, Ernest G. "The Symbolic Convergence Theory of Communication and the Creation, Raising, and Sustaining of Public Consciousness." In *The Jensen Lectures: Contemporary Communication Studies.* John Sisco, ed. Tampa, FL: University of South Florida, Department of Communication, 1982, pp. 71–90.

For the quote by Bales relating shared fantasies to cohesiveness, see:

Bales, Robert F. *Personality and Interpersonal Behavior.* New York: Holt, Rinehart and Winston, 1970, pp. 151–152.

For an analysis of the two sides of emotion, see:

Schacter, Stanley, and Jerome Singer. "Cognitive, Social, and Physiological Determinants of Emotional State," *Psychological Review,* **69** (1962), 379–399.

Chapter
6

The Social Climate
of Groups

The purpose of this chapter is to describe the social climate that
makes an attractive or unattractive group and to discuss the relationship
of that climate to productive disagreement and conflict in the group's
work. The social climate is an important part of the group's evolving
culture and relates directly to the level of group cohesiveness. As in
Chapter 5, this chapter will emphasize process analysis—that is, the
actual communication as it unfolds during the group meetings.

BALES'S CATEGORIES FOR INTERACTION
PROCESS ANALYSIS

Robert F. Bales and his associates at Harvard University have developed
one of the most widely used and helpful category systems for the study
of the communication process in small groups. Bales began his study of
groups with a large number of categories of interaction which were
gradually reduced to 12. According to the investigators, these 12
proved to be sufficient to account for all verbal and nonverbal
communication in small group meetings. The categories are evenly
divided between task-related responses and social responses. In
addition, each category has a converse category. Thus, category 1 is
the converse of category 12.

    The opening section of this chapter is organized around the six
categories of the Bales system that are useful in describing the social
climate of groups. The discussion that follows is organized around that
category system, but the material relating to the various concepts is

only partially an interpretation of Bales's work. The analysis has a different emphasis and includes additional material on social tensions and group solidarity taken from the Minnesota studies and from modifications as a result of using the concepts to teach small group communication.

As noted in Chapter 5, in 1970 Bales published a revision of his original category system that included changing the category of "Shows Tension Release" to "Dramatizes." He also changed the categories of "Shows Solidarity" to "Seems Friendly" and "Shows Antagonism" to "Seems Unfriendly." The latter changes were useful to researchers who found the older categories of little value when they were making observations of groups. For pedagogical purposes, however, they remain very useful in applying special theories of group work. Although shows of group solidarity and antagonism are relatively rare, they are very important when they appear. The tension analysis in this chapter remains useful and has not been changed from Bales's original findings with shows of group tension release. (The important new category of "Dramatizes" and the resulting group fantasy chains were dealt with in the last chapter.)

When people participate in a group, they perceive social cues not only from what is said but also from the way it is said: the pauses, pitch inflections, rate, and voice quality. A skillful actor can say a line so that the audience believes he means precisely the opposite. Such lines as "She's a great date" can be read in such a way that they communicate "I wouldn't go out with her on a bet." In addition, members get social cues from the language of gesture. If a person is expounding on her idea to a member who sits slumped in a chair looking away, she gets a much different social cue than if the other person sits erect, nods in agreement, and appears to listen to every word. Both verbal and nonverbal cues are important in developing the social climate of a group.

Shows of Group Solidarity and Antagonism

The first category of positive social response is "Solidarity." Each positive category is related to an opposite negative category—the opposite of *solidarity* is *antagonism.*

A show of group solidarity is any statement, comment, gesture, or cue indicating that the member feels the group is important and that she or he will help the group collectively and the other members individually. In larger groups, the pep talk plays much the same part as the less formal shows of group solidarity in smaller groups.

The shows of solidarity that are effective in small groups differ in quality from those that are useful for large organizations. In general, they are less formal and less inclined to be sentimental. They appeal to the more practical motives, rather than the idealistic or altruistic motives that are appropriate for shows of solidarity in larger groups. Appeals to patriotism and nationalism are essentially shows of solidarity.

The small groups in a discussion class use appeals of a different order to build group solidarity. Even a group set up in class to meet for only an hour will probably exhibit some signs of solidarity. The following example is from a small task-oriented discussion group composed of junior and senior students in the College of Liberal Arts at the University of Minnesota. The group was to meet for several months, but the following exchange took place toward the end of the first meeting.

MEMBER A: Why don't we just agree to look this thing over here, and any of us that are ambitious enough [*growing tentative*] to go to the library and read up some more do that . . .

MEMBER B: [*in agreement*] Uh-huh.

MEMBER A: . . . and then bring . . . bring your suggestions for organizing our report next Monday.

MEMBER B: I know one thing . . . there won't be anybody standing up . . . at least I know I won't be standing up and cussing anybody who does any research.

[*General agreement and considerable laughter from the other members of the group. The group is noticeably less tense after this laughter.*]

We gotta do research . . .

MEMBER A: Just the Alliance for Progress is so important that we have to do research on it . . .

[*Member A's first statement about research was phrased and said tentatively—". . . any of us that are ambitious enough to go to the library and read up some more do that . . ." This statement is now said with much more force and conviction. It receives general agreement and "Sure, sure" from the other members of the group.*]

MEMBER D: Everything is important . . .

[*General agreement: "Yeah," "Uh-huh"*]

MEMBER D: . . . the whole . . . the class is important . . . our group is important . . .

[*Another member of the group reinforces member D by saying "Yes." For the last several minutes the members of the group have been using collective pronouns and saying such things as "We gotta do research . . . ," but this is the first definite mention of "our group." At this point, the group has come to take on some identity of its own in the perceptions of its members.*]

MEMBER A: [*interrupting*] And the three credits of . . .

MEMBER E: [*overriding A*] Well, the thing that is probably most important to each of us individually is the interaction between all of us . . . because of the fact that . . .

MEMBER C: Right.

MEMBER E: All we're interested . . . I'm not saying all we're interested . . . our major interest . . . one of our major interests should be the grade that we get in this course . . .

MEMBER C: Right.

MEMBER E: And as we said earlier . . . what we . . . the grade we get depends on all of us acting as a unit . . .

MEMBER C: Uh-huh.

MEMBER A: It depends on how well we achieve our objective . . .

MEMBER C: And I . . . I personally would really like an atmosphere for myself where you would just bluntly come out and tell me something . . . I mean . . . maybe not in class or something but I won't be offended by anything and I mean I think we know each other well enough . . .

MEMBER E: Right . . .

MEMBER C: That we can do this . . .

MEMBER E: Right . . .

MEMBER C: I mean this . . .

MEMBER E: Right . . .

MEMBER C: [interrupting] I mean that . . .

MEMBER E: [interrupting] Why don't you carry matches?

[General laughter and cries of "Right, right." This bout of laughter dispels most of the remaining primary tension, and the social climate of the group exemplifies considerable warmth and rapport.]

MEMBER C: I mean something like that. It doesn't do any good for a group to go carrying . . .

[Several members of the group say "No no," with inflections that suggest they agree with C: that it doesn't do any good for a group to be that way.]

MEMBER C: . . . a chip on our shoulder.

MEMBER B: Let's face it if we can . . . if we can sit around like . . . like we are right now the first day . . .

[General agreement, including "Yeah."]

MEMBER B: We're going to get pretty informal . . .

MEMBER C: No, I think we should have that policy . . . you know . . . just tell each other what we think . . . I mean . . . in a nice way of course . . . you know . . . you can tell what other people mean . . .

MEMBER A: Oh, sure. I think we've already started off on a sort of free and easy . . .

MEMBER C: Right . . .

MEMBER A: Way of doing it . . .

MEMBER D: I think it's a fine group . . .

This transcript exemplifies several important principles of group processes. The first show of solidarity was tentative, but when it was reinforced by agreement, other members began to assert group solidarity. All the participants became more enthusiastic and made firmer shows of solidarity. The group atmosphere warmed up perceptibly within minutes, and the spiral effect of increased cohesiveness resulted in further shows of solidarity. The group went on to become an effective and cohesive group. If the group had rejected the first tentative show of group solidarity or responded in a halfhearted or ambiguous fashion, strong and positive shows of solidarity would not have followed. For these reasons, the group stood at one of the many crossroads relating to its social climate and took, on this occasion, a path that led to a more rewarding social environment.

Why did the group choose this path rather than the other? Research on this question at the University of Minnesota has not yet led to a definite answer. Apparently, this interaction took place by chance. But, when students of small group communication recognize the importance of such turning points in the life of a group, they can reinforce the tentative show of group solidarity or initiate signs of solidarity themselves. They will avoid cynical attempts to manipulate the group or insincere attempts to show group solidarity. They will remember that individuals who honestly want the group to be a good one can express sincerely their desire to work for the group and can help or reward others when feasible. Such concerns build a more socially rewarding and cohesive group.

Why must the group's time be occupied with shows of solidarity when it could be spent working on the task? Even though the members know that everyone is interested in the welfare of the group, it must be said from time to time. Expressions of interest reassure the members; the group is identified again as an entity. Even a tightly knit family suffers if its members do not tell each other that it is a good family and that they love one another. The cohesiveness of the family unit requires it. The same is true for less cohesive and more temporary groups such as discussion groups in speech classes.

The negative social interaction that corresponds to shows of solidarity is a show of antagonism. Antagonism may be directed to the group or to individual members. If a person punishes or lowers the status of another or indicates hostility, he or she creates social tension. Preschool children show antagonism by hitting other children on the head with a toy truck. Members of Ph.D. seminars and college discussion groups reveal antagonisms in more subtle ways, but the effect is the same.

Social Tensions

Bales's second category of positive social response was "Shows Tension Release," and the corresponding negative category was "Shows Tension." Smiles, chuckles, laughter, or other indications of pleasure serve to release tension. Members show tension in a variety of ways, which can be classifed into two main categories: primary and secondary tension.

Primary Tension Primary tension is the social unease and stiffness that accompanies getting acquainted. Students placed in a small task-oriented group with strangers will experience these tensions most strongly during the opening minutes of their first meetings. The earmarks of primary tensions are extreme politeness, apparent boredom or tiredness, and considerable sighing or yawning. When members show primary tension, they speak softly and tentatively. Frequently they can think of nothing to say, and many long pauses result. The following transcript is from the opening minutes of a group that experienced an unusual amount of primary tension. This group was plagued throughout its life by its inability to release tension.

> MEMBER A: *[softly]* Well, see now, here we got several topics that I can see that we aren't going to arrive at a definite conclusion on this nuclear testing . . . this, ah, policy in Berlin . . . *[dropping his voice]* what's that other one?
>
> MEMBER B: *[more strongly]* Well, I think policy in Berlin . . . we could . . . we could arrive at a pretty fair solution to the problem *[pause]*, don't you *[pause]*, really?

> *[There is a pause of five seconds, which seems longer because it is preceded by a question.]*

> MEMBER C: *[so softly as to be almost unintelligible]* Well, I think there are solutions to be arrived at . . . probably . . . probably we could *[dropping voice even more]* couldn't contemplate them now probably . . .
>
> MEMBER D: A lot of editorials . . . you know . . . in different papers . . . one way and another but *[pause]* common market is *[pause]* a nice one *[pause and dropping his voice]* interesting . . .
>
> MEMBER B: *[yawns]* I like these two . . . one of these . . . nuclear testing and the farm problem, but I don't want to throw any of them out either if anybody else likes them.

> *[Pause of four seconds.]*

> MEMBER D: I thought you had this one at first . . .
>
> MEMBER B: *[interrupting]* Oh, yeah, no that's *[strained laugh, but no one joins in]* that's, ah *[pause of five seconds]*, policy in Berlin *[noticeable sigh]*, but you see the trouble is our discussion and our outline . . . you know he said after we find a problem and discuss all our solutions . . .

People who experience a severe amount of primary tension (similar to stage fright) will often withdraw from the group and pretend to be disinterested in the meeting. They may pull their chairs back, look out the window, or look over their notes for another class.

The Minnesota studies included interviews with such members. They often reported that they were not sure why they did not take a more active part. They suggested that the reason was that they found the subject uninteresting. More extensive investigation revealed that a case of genuine disinterest in the work of a group as it gets under way is extremely rare. The member who seemed disinterested or who withdrew was really very tense and was exhibiting a high level of primary tension.

What is taking place that causes a high level of tension, interest, and worry? Five students meeting together for the first time have an item on their agenda that is so important to all concerned that it must be dealt with to some extent before any other business whatsoever. That item is the social relationships that will develop. These relationships raise questions that relate to each person's basic social and esteem needs. A student who sits in on a discussion group, even if it meets for only an hour, is offered an opportunity to enter in and develop social relations with the other people in the group. Students can take a chance, enter in, and win approval. Such approval is necessary and important to them. They feel primary tension until they begin to see evidence that their social and esteem needs will be gratified. When it becomes apparent that the group will accept them as individuals, they can relax and attend to business. There is the possibility of failure. They may be rejected, despised, or belittled. If this happens, they will respond with a feeling of unpleasantness and, perhaps, with frustration and anger. If they have participated in similar groups and similar situations before and have been accepted and liked as persons, they are more likely to participate. If the situation is novel, their feeling of primary tension is increased, and they are less likely to take part. In addition, in unusual situations they may lack necessary information. If the situation is like previous ones in which they have been rejected or hurt, they will have even more primary tension. If it seems likely that they will be rejected, they may not risk taking part. Of course, they also have a chance to win social approval. But if they think that punishment is more likely, they may escape by pretending to be uninterested.

Feelings of primary tension are common to all collections of individuals. Primary tension accounts for uncertain behavior of people when they begin working together. They speak softly, tentatively, and with great politeness. They all want to make a good impression and are therefore very polite. They do not insult other members, tell jokes, or express strong opinions. They are quick to laugh, although the laughter is always a bit strained. They will discuss almost any topic, such as the weather, in order to start getting acquainted. The group will listen to every word of the member who makes a statement about the weather and may devote several minutes of polite talk to the subject. Thirty minutes later, if the primary tension has been released, the group would not consider talking about the weather, because members have more important things to talk about.

Oddly enough, the group will experience a similar primary tension at the beginning of each meeting. Usually these periods of tension grow shorter as the group members settle into relatively stable relationships, but at the beginning of each meeting the participants feel the need to "warm up." They must find out if the others will treat them as they have in the past and if the group expects the same sort of behavior that it has in the past. Primary tension accounts for the universal phenomenon of small talk first and business later that characterizes interviews, conferences, and business meetings. The young man calling a young woman for a date seldom begins with "Would you like to go to a movie with me this Saturday?" He usually starts with some small talk or tension-breaking conversation. Obviously, this small talk at the beginning of a meeting meets a real and universal need. If it did not, it would be omitted in the hectic pace of modern living where so much time is spent in conference.

Figure 6 indicates a hypothetical construct that is useful in dealing with social tensions in a group. The horizontal line on the figure indicates the amount of tension that a given group can tolerate and still work on the task. When tensions rise above this level, the group cannot function on the task. Although many groups continue to go through the motions of discussing the problem at hand when the tensions rise above this level, the real item under discussion will be the problems causing the tensions. As the tension curve on Figure 6 indicates, the typical group finds the primary tension above the tolerance level at first, and they must release it before they can work.

The groups investigated by the Minnesota studies have handled the problems of primary tension quite well. A small percentage of them, however, have worked together for as long as two months without ever meeting the problems posed by social shyness and tension. They were plagued by apparent member disinterest and boredom, by considerable absenteeism, and a lack of cohesiveness. These groups usually talked of

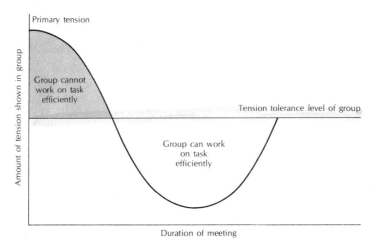

Figure 6 Primary tension curve.

nothing but the question they were discussing. They never got acquainted.

On occasion, when the tension level is high, a group should stop talking about the discussion question and consider the social problem. Some irrelevant talk at the beginning of the meeting may save time later. The good group, however, begins work as soon as the primary tension has been released. Some groups in the Minnesota studies continued the socializing well beyond this point and wasted time. They had a lot of fun, but they did not get much done.

As a rule, direct recognition of social tensions is a good way to release them. Primary tension is like the dog that distracts an audience by coming into the auditorium, walking up the aisle, and curling up beside the speaker on the platform. The audience will be distracted by the dog and unable to listen with undivided attention to the speaker. If the speaker ignores the dog and pretends it is not there, the audience grows more and more distracted. When the dog stretches, the audiences watches and smiles. When the dog yawns, the audience may snicker, and the speaker is soon faced with an embarrassing and unbearable situation. The speaker can meet the problem by recognizing the dog the moment it enters the auditorium and calling the audience's attention directly and explicitly to it. Discussing the dog discharges whatever attention the audience members may pay to the dog, and having considered the dog for a moment they can return to the speech without distraction. In the same fashion, if the primary tension is discharged by paying attention to it directly, the group can go to work. If the tension is ignored, however, it will build up and become a larger and larger burden for the group.

Secondary Tension Most groups manage to release primary tensions within a matter of minutes and can comfortably get down to work. As the group goes about its job, two kinds of group structuring take place simultaneously. First, the group works out a social structure and a network of social relationships. Second, the group establishes a pattern of work. Structuring generates tensions of another kind. Two persons may compete for the social approval of a third. They experience social tensions during their arguments and the others grow tense because of the emotion and antagonism of the two members. A similar sort of tension can result from working on the task. Two members may have different positions on a matter of policy and may try to secure adherents. In either instance, they have what is called a "personality conflict." Such conflicts lead to *secondary tension*. Secondary tension creates a different group climate than primary tension does. It is noisier and more dynamic. Voices are louder and more strained. Long pauses may appear, but often two or three people speak at a time. Everyone is highly interested in the proceedings. No one seems bored or tired. Members may fidget in their chairs, half rise, pound the table, get up and pace the room, run their hands through their hair, gesture excitedly, and exhibit a much higher level of excitement and involvement.

Figure 7 continues the curve of a group that has experienced primary tension above the tolerance level, has released the tension, and has gone to work. Often such a group will experience a rise in secondary tension that also goes above the tolerance level. When this happens, the group's task effectiveness is again in jeopardy.

Secondary tensions are much more difficult to deal with than primary tensions. The members most vitally involved are not as eager to have the tensions brought into the open and released. The group can seldom diagnose the problem clinically. Usually an analysis of the roots of these tensions results in the group blaming one or two people for creating them. Casting blame in this way hurts the status of the person, strains the bonds holding the group together, and creates frustration and anger.

Despite the difficulty of releasing secondary tensions, good groups develop mechanisms to handle such problems. Unfortunately, these mechanisms are not easily developed, nor are they universally applicable. Each group must work out its own salvation. To be successful, the technique adopted must have the support of the members. Trust and support come from trying several different approaches and settling on the one that works best for this particular group. Some groups will rely on one or two members to take the burden of releasing these tensions. They may joke about the problem or use irony or satire to cause laughter, deflate the tension, and *correct* the behavior that has caused the tension. They may engage in direct conciliation and negotiate a compromise. Some groups try, often without success, to have a member who is a friend of both antagonists see each person to discuss the problem privately. Finally, if all

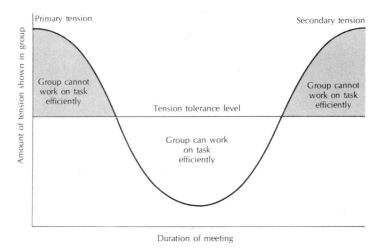

Figure 7 Secondary tension curve.

else fails, groups may consider the matter directly. The following transcription is such a case. It is also a good example of secondary tension.

[*The group had been meeting for several weeks. It was composed of
upper-division students in a discussion course at the University of Minnesota. The instructor had not assigned a leader or moderator or chair.
At the time of the incident, the group had no leader. Several members
had successfully led the group and then lost support. This exchange took
place when members A and B were contending for the leadership of the
group. B was very aggressive and fluent and defended his position by
talking over and through objections. Member A perceived the problem
to be member B's inflexibility and domineering manner; so he brought
the problem up for direct consideration by the other members. Member
A did not feel that he could bluntly confront B, so his tactic was to read
to the group from his textbook.*]

MEMBER A: I think there is absolutely *no* doubt about that. The procedures we've been using have not been those that
are . . . uh . . . for *good* discussion and I think each one
of us ought to analyze this fact and . . .

[*At this point member B begins a side conversation with member C.*]

MEMBER A: [*continuing but bothered by the fact that member B is not
paying attention to him*] . . . see if we can't . . . see if we
can't do something about it. I think that if I just read the
heads of these particular paragraphs here just . . . just so
you can think about the fact . . .

[*Member B is now listening carefully to member A, and gets up from
his chair and begins to pace the room.*]

MEMBER A: [*continuing*] . . . and uh . . . and uh just remember that
these things are uh . . . essential to uh group discussion.
[*reading*] "Good discussants, we believe, do not merely
tolerate the fact that other discussants who hold
that . . . who hold to opinions and attitudes different
from their own. They welcome this fact." We *welcome*
differences of opinion . . . we . . . we . . .

MEMBER B: You look at me when you say that . . .

[*Member A and member B begin to speak simultaneously.*]

MEMBER A: I'm not looking at you . . .
MEMBER B: . . . for my benefit? Or anyone else's?
MEMBER B: Just read it then.
MEMBER A: I *am* reading it. "We sense the uh presence of an attitude
uh of welcoming differences in groups . . . discussion
groups in which the leaders and members seem genuinely

eager to hear the opinions of all members of the group —
even minority opinions." *Eager* to hear minority opinions.

[*There is a pause. All the members of the group are tense, and they are
watching and listening intently.*]

MEMBER B: Uh [*pause*], you giving a speech or you reading?

MEMBER A: [*interrupting*] No.

MEMBER B: [*ignoring the interruption*] You emphasizing any particular
points?

MEMBER A: [*interrupting*] No, I just . . .

MEMBER B: [*ignoring the interruption*] . . . read . . . just read it
then . . .

MEMBER A: Well, I'm . . . I don't wish to read the whole book, I
just . . . you know . . . I thought that it might . . . if
we . . . if we seek to hear the minority . . .

MEMBER B: [*interrupting the words "the minority"*] You're not reading
now. You're commenting on it. Why don't you just read it
like you said you were going to without going back over it
two or three times?

[*There is a three-second pause. The secondary tension has reached an
uncomfortable level.*]

MEMBER B: [*in a tense voice*] If you're going to harass me, I'll harass you
a little bit.

MEMBER A: I'm not harassing anybody . . .

MEMBER B: Yes, you are.

MEMBER A: I'm not.

[*The tension level has now reached a point that is so high that neither
member A nor member B can tolerate it. The amount of tension that a
group can bear is related to the level of cohesiveness in the group.
Highly cohesive groups can stand more secondary tensions, and, therefore, the most bitter fights take place in highly cohesive groups such as
the family. Member A and member B both break out in strained laughter at this point to release the tension. The rest of the group does not
laugh.*]

MEMBER A: I'm sorry you're taking this attitude because . . .

[*Member B gives a half-laugh, half-snort of derision.*]

MEMBER A: I sincerely believe the discussion we held last time was
ah . . .

MEMBER B: [*interrupting*] I do, too.

MEMBER A: Didn't get us anywhere.

MEMBER B: I do, too.

MEMBER A: And I think that uh . . . unless we analyze these things and uh everyone . . . particular individual has . . . and I thought . . . you know . . .

MEMBER B: Well, right now we're not analyzing that discussion. We're talking about what's in the book there that someone [*member A tries to interrupt, but member B talks over the interruption and keeps the floor*] . . . everyone in the group is supposed to have read. You're reading it for . . . you're trying to relearn us here . . . what are . . . what are . . . [*member A tries to interrupt again — he says, "Yes, positive . . . positi . . . ," but member B keeps talking over him*] . . . you're wasting time on the discussion of the problem when you're reading the book, which we all already assume we've read . . .

MEMBER A: [*giving up*] Your point is well taken.

MEMBER B: All right then, let's forget the book. [*pause*] Thank you.

A good deal of the atmosphere of the meeting is lost in a transcription such as this one. The playscript is very different from a performance of a play. One reason these discourse analysis protocols are written in playscript form is to stimulate the reader's imagination to provide some of the important details of atmosphere.

In this case, direct confrontation did not succeed. The group was never able to mobilize even a majority of its members behind a move to solve its social and emotional problems. Member A received no active support from any other member of the group. The entire exchange took place between A and B. If one other person had supported A, the outcome would have been different. Member A's tactic of using the book backfired as well. It gave B an opportunity to bypass the issue by suggesting that A was "relearning" the group and "wasting time" by "reading the book, which we all already assume we've read."

Secondary tensions are inevitable in groups that have released their primary tensions sufficiently to engage seriously in the task. When they arise, the good groups included in the Minnesota studies worked out ways to handle them. Groups that ignore or withdraw from tensions develop a social climate that is uncomfortable and punishing. Groups try to ignore secondary tensions because dealing with them realistically is extremely painful. Groups are, if anything, more neurotic than individuals in their tendency to pretend that the social tensions do not exist. If they do admit that there is a problem, they often blame it on a member who is inherently "stupid" or "domineering." They dodge the problem. Often a group makes preliminary moves to deal with secondary tensions, but retreats when the climate becomes difficult by taking action that does not deal with the real problem. They leave the touchy area of human relations and return to the safe area of doing the job. The problem, however, never goes away and if ignored or dodged will continue to plague and impede their progress. Facing up to secondary tensions realistically is the best way to release them.

Agreement and Disagreement

The third set of climate-building interactions that Bales discovered he called "Agrees" and "Disagrees." The group cannot come to a consensus about policy, problem solving, or action without the liberal use of shows of agreement and disagreement. Ideas and suggestions are tested by disagreements. Even the highly task-oriented activity of processing information, of testing the truth or falsity of factual statements, requires shows of agreement and disagreement. Agreements and disagreements are double-edged. They serve a task function and simultaneously have strong social implications. Disagreements help criticize and process information, but they damage the social fabric of a group.

Brainstorming   Some years ago, a member of the large advertising firm of Batten, Barton, Durstine & Osborn became interested in the problem of encouraging creativity; his name was Alex T. Osborn. In his work with creating advertising themes and programs, he found a method of using a group of people to encourage one another to suggest good ideas.

Osborn labeled his method "brainstorming." He turned some of his promotional talents to publicizing his scheme for encouraging group creativity and imagination. The term *brainstorming* itself is something of a promotional triumph. In a short time, brainstorming became popular with some branches of the military services and with some industries.

The rules for brainstorming are relatively simple. People are assembled in a group and presented with a problem or a creative task. They are instructed to throw out as many ideas as possible in a short period of time. The core of the technique, however, is that *under no circumstances is anyone in any fashion to indicate disagreement* with a suggested idea. The wilder the idea, the better. The quantity rather than the quality of ideas is emphasized. Osborn had discovered the facilitating effect of agreement on the social climate of a group. One of the best ways to break primary tension is to have a high level of agreement. If a member feels uncertain and makes a tentative comment and receives agreement, he or she makes the next statement more easily and with greater conviction. If this too is met with general agreement, the member grows enthusiastic, soon loses self-consciousness and shyness, and no longer feels tense about how he or she will be accepted. By their agreement, the others have indicated their acceptance and liking for that member. In a few minutes, a brainstorming group can develop a highly permissive and pleasant social climate simply by arbitrarily ruling out disagreement.

Agreement as Reinforcement   Meanwhile, psychologists have been discovering experimental evidence in support of agreement as social reinforcement. The argument that underlies this research is behavioristic and suggests that the response of an organism can be shaped by the judicious utilization of rewards and punishments. Thus, when a dog is trained to "heel," the animal is conditioned to the command by the punishment involved in tightening the choke collar and the reward of praise when it obeys. Many laboratory experiments with rats, pigeons, cats, and monkeys indicate that a clever researcher can train these creatures to carry out complicated routines by the use of conditioning rewards and punishments. A number of psychological investigations of human verbal behavior have studied the changes resulting from the use of agreement as reinforcement. Sometimes the agreement was expressed verbally and sometimes in gestural terms such as nodding the head. Verbal behavior changed significantly when reinforced with agreement. Although most of these studies had a different purpose, they definitely establish the fact that perceived agreement is a social reward or reinforcement.

The Role of Agreement   Agreement serves as a powerful social reward for many reasons. It is the currency of social approval. When a person makes a statement and others all express agreement, she or he has received overt evidence of being a person of value and that of making a good contribution. If the members of the group agree and *act according* to one member's suggestions, that member is given the social reinforcement that comes from *influencing* other people. Most people are gratified when they know that their ideas and their suggestions have been accepted. Shows of agreement are the most definite signs of approval for a person's ideas.

Agreement is also the outward evidence of status or esteem. High-status people travel in an aura of agreement. If the people surrounding an individual listen to every statement and express their agreement, that person is undoubtedly a high-status individual. The same treatment will be accorded a highly esteemed individual within a small group.

Agreement also serves a valuable task function. By means of agreements, the group discovers its consensus. Group members accept factual information as true or false on the basis of shows of agreement. They accept or reject inferences from facts in the same way. Suggestions are made, plans laid, and action steps agreed upon by the same signs. There is a social edge to every task-oriented agreement. If the members agree that the factual information provided by member A is true and pertinent, they imply that A is knowledgeable and has done a good job. If they agree that member A's reasoning is valid and helpful, they imply that A is intelligent. If they follow A's plan of action, they imply that person is *their leader*. The esteem needs of many people are most gratified by acknowledged leadership.

The Need for Disagreement   Despite attempts such as brainstorming to eliminate disagreements, every group comes to some point when information must be tested for its truth or falsity. The discussion group that proceeds on the basis of false statements of fact will be misled.

The group must also test the inferences that are drawn from the information. If group members have accepted a fallacious line of reasoning, they may be rudely shocked. If their proposals have been tried and have failed, and if the undesirable effects of these proposals would outweigh the beneficial results, the group must reconsider those proposals. All such testing of evidence, reasoning, and policy requires shows of disagreement. Disagreement is vital to the task efficiency of the group.

Disagreement and Secondary Tension   The task requires disagreements, and yet disagreements cause the social climate to deteriorate. Disagreements strain the social bonds and are among the prime generators of secondary tensions. Where agreement reinforces behavior, disagreement extinguishes it. Disagreement, therefore, functions as social punishment.

Disagreement and Cohesiveness   Disagreements contribute to the stiffness of the social climate of the discussion. When group members disagree with an individual, they harm that person's status and self-esteem. The member finds the group socially punishing, and must have compensating rewards from the other dimension of group attraction to continue feeling part of the group.

Paradoxically, disagreements are a function of cohesiveness. The more highly cohesive a group, the greater the number of shows of disagreement that can be expected in its meetings.

The Handling of Disagreements   Good groups develop ways to allow for disagreements without unduly disrupting cohesiveness. A plausible and often repeated bit of advice is to preface the disagreement with a compliment or an agreement. Statements such as "I agree with you there, Bill. I think you are right about the need to take the military effect into account but . . ." are often recommended. Tact seldom hurts the social climate, but it wears off very quickly in a small group. Before the first hour of discussion is over, the members will begin to cringe when Jill starts to agree with them. They know that agreement is a cue from Jill for the inevitable "but we must also look at the other side."

A member cannot keep a disagreement from hurting. If the disagreement is to do its work, *it must be perceived as a disagreement.* If it is not, it does not do the job. If it is, it exacts its social toll. Members simply cannot have the best of both worlds in this regard. What happens when a person carefully words each disagreement as tactfully as possible or prefaces the disagreement with an agreement? At best that individual cushions the blow and, at worst, is gradually perceived as a person who is hard to pin down, slick, not to be trusted. Some groups, indeed, adopt a style that accepts the blunt, direct, and forceful disagreement as normal operating procedure and their members tolerate such disagreement as well as or better than the tactful kind. Other groups adopt as a norm the "I think you have a good point, Bill, but . . ." sort of disagreement, because the blunt disagreement would be more disruptive.

The proper attitude toward disagreements, according to the ideals of public discussion, is one of open-minded testing of the truth of factual statements and evaluating the advisability of action. Therefore, discussants should be objective, scientific, and uninvolved in the process of working out ideas.

Although participants in a public discussion can adopt such a discussion atitude, members of small task-oriented groups working on significant problems cannot do so. Even if the topic under discussion is not important, the group itself may be so important that members cannot remain scientific and objective. Even with the help of a status relationship, an age differential, and a context that establishes such activity as the expected sort of behavior, students often feel considerable resentment and frustration (secondary tension) when a teacher criticizes the ideas and information in a speech or theme. Although the students remind themselves that they have paid their fees for this service and that they need such criticism, they still feel some irritation when the instructor disagrees. Disagreements in speech-class discussion groups generate such social strains.

If disagreements inevitably cause social strains, is the situation beyond remedy? Not if the members are aware of the necessity for disagreements and of the social costs extracted by disagreements. The Minnesota studies discovered a number of moderately successful and unsuccessful groups that did not maintain an atmosphere that would sustain honest disagreement. Members agreed for the sake of agreement or remained quiet when they honestly felt they should disagree. Aware of the social toll, they would rather do a poor job than risk secondary tension. The task did not mean that much to them. They report that "We get along very well. But I don't know, I guess we just aren't very interested in the topic." The successful groups were those that had enough cohesiveness to disagree. Even in these highly cohesive groups, the disagreements caused trouble, but the groups worked out ways to mend their social fabric. One of the most common methods of repair was a great show of group cohesiveness and tension release after a period of disagreement. Quite often these disagreements were concentrated just prior to moments of decision. When these moments of decision are followed by activity in the three positive social categories discovered by Bales, the damage done by disagreements can be repaired.

An example of how groups work in this regard is furnished by one of the highly cohesive and successful groups studied at Minnesota. This excerpt from the diary of one of the members illustrates how the group handled disagreements. He reported in part,

> One nite [sic] . . . I had a long talk with the group attempting to narrow the scope of the problem . . . [the leader] finally decided we were too far along to change now and so we went along as previously planned. I agreed and received much concern and consolation. I'm not bitter. I wanted to do what I considered right and so stated my desire . . .

The key phrase in this report is "much concern and consolation." The group allowed the disagreement, and when the decision went against one member, the others hastened to assure him that he remained an important part of the group. They also closed ranks and showed solidarity by agreeing that since the decision had been made, everyone should support it.

Some groups solve the problem by settling the burden of disagreeing on one person. The critic is expected to disagree with anything and everything. When that person does so, the group finds it easier to release the secondary tension generated by the disagreement. They may say to a new member who is disturbed by disagreements, "Don't mind old Jack. That's the way he is. He disagrees with everything, but he's all right." If group members come to *expect* disagreements from Jack, then when he provides them, they do not find the criticism as irritating as if they had not expected it. Members discover that the habitual critic does not necessarily hurt their status.

CONFLICT MANAGEMENT IN THE SOCIAL AREA

Much of the discussion of disagreements and their effect on the social fabric of the group applies to those differences among members which cause extremely high secondary tensions. The way good groups manage disagreements productively is instructive in terms of how they deal with high-tension problems. Still, good groups can deal with the run-of-the-mill disagreements without too much difficulty by using their techniques for knitting the group back together and for rebuilding their social fabric. The extreme cases generally require special attention and treatment. *Conflicts* are those disagreements that cause such high secondary tension as to render the group inoperative.

Some communication contexts put people into competitive conflict. In group meetings with rules like a poker game, a certain amount of value goes into the game but is divided unequally as a result of the communication process that takes place during the session. Such rules bring the members into competition, and conflict often results. The task-oriented small group, however, should be a cooperative meeting in which the members work together to achieve high-fidelity communication by providing honest feedback to aid in overcoming confusion. The task-oriented small group is also designed to achieve a common goal. Such groups generally assume that by working together, they will create value which all members can then share. They are in the same boat and will sink or succeed together.

Some group contexts (and some games) are a mixture of cooperation and competition in that, by staying together and cooperating, the members achieve greater value than they could by working separately, but the group distributes the rewards unequally. Such mixed-motive situations result in conflict as well as cohesiveness.

Although much about the task-oriented small group is cooperative, it tends, in fact, to be a mixed-motive communication climate. The conflicts in a task-oriented small group are more likely to arise from the dynamics of the role structuring than from task discussion. The amount of value earned by productive work may grow and all may share in task success, but the internal social rewards are distributed unequally: Some members grow in status, influence, and attractiveness, while others sink into lower status, less influence, and less popularity.

Social conflicts arise from the three major areas of rewards. The emergence of leadership is a prime source of interpersonal conflict among members. Those individuals who remain as potential leaders after the group eliminates the obviously unsuitable will often come into conflict. The fact that some members acquire influence in the task dimension and assume exciting and interesting task assignments while others are encouraged to take on routine tasks often results in apathy on the part of the low-status members, in clique formation, and, on occasion, in actual efforts at sabotage of the group's work out of frustration because of unsatisfactory rewards from other members. That some members come to be better liked and more popular than other members is still another source of conflict. Less socially rewarded members may become jealous.

Groups often find conflicts in the social dimension difficult to deal with. When interpersonal conflict erupts, the level of secondary tension shoots up to destructive levels. Member discomfort is often so high that the group takes flight from the conflict.

The most common and destructive way that groups take flight is by ignoring the conflicts. Groups may also take flight into the task dimension, which is also destructive. Since the group is task-oriented, the members can, in good conscience, ignore their social conflicts by doggedly sticking to task discussion—*even though their secondary tensions have reached such levels that they cannot work effectively.* When classroom groups stop their meetings to discuss group process, they often report, "We were so task-oriented that we couldn't get anything accomplished." What they mean is that when social conflicts arose, instead of dealing with them, they took flight into the task area and discovered that unresolved conflicts in the social dimension crippled their ability to work. Groups taking flight from social conflict into dogged discussion of task topics generally conduct very tense meetings. They exhibit little tension-releasing communication. They seldom share fantasies. They do not disclose information about themselves. They do not joke around or laugh much.

When groups ignore social conflicts during formal meetings, the members often discuss their frustrations with one another in subgroups. Such discussions behind the group's back, as it were, seldom solve the difficulties. Generally, as long as the conflict is a hidden agenda item, it remains a destructive force.

Another common way that groups take flight from conflicts in the social dimension is by smoothing over the difficulty. When a group smooths over a conflict, the members mention the difficulty and begin to deal with it. Since the secondary tension is already high, however, opening a discussion of the sore spot causes great discomfort and the members may pull back. They may agree that they all feel much better with the problem "out in the open"; that having mentioned it, the problem is now solved; or that examining the problem revealed it to be much less severe than they had thought and probably really no problem at all.

A basic strategy that members use to smooth over a conflict is to fail to express their perceptions and feelings honestly when the subject is brought up in the meeting. Usually the member simply remains quiet and seems interested but noncommittal. Sometimes the member will physically move back a bit, away from the circle of the group, seeming to suggest nonverbally that he or she is becoming an observer rather than a participant. If someone asks a direct question, the member will deny his or her feelings and perceptions or play down their intensity. If several members of the group are involved in issues of leadership and power and the two contenders have come into conflict, the group may deny that a conflict exists by agreeing that the members are "all leaders," that they "do not need to have a leader," or that they can "all take turns being leader."

Difficult as it is for groups to discuss leadership, they often find it more difficult to discuss such matters as the influence of personal attraction, gender, and sex. They prefer to pretend to ignore the like – dislike relationships that are evolving, the influence of gender on the members' response to potential leaders and task influentials, and the influence of sexual attraction as revealed by nonverbal courtship routines.

As a rule, the leadership, influence, achievement, and gender conflicts need to be dealt with in order for the group to continue working productively. The sexual relationships and the like – dislike patterns may be ignored or smoothed over without a crippling effect. Members of task-oriented groups do not need to like one another in order to cooperate and work productively together, but they do need to evolve productive and stable role relationships.

The best technique for the management of conflict in the social dimension of the small task-oriented group is to confront the problem and work it out. The group should put the conflict on its agenda, devote sufficient time to its consideration to work it through, and pull itself back to the discussion of the conflict whenever the group begins to take flight. Of course, the group will have to pull back from time to time to release tension, and change the subject sometimes simply to allow members to relax, or they will not be able to continue. But such withdrawal must be allowed with the knowledge that the group will return, after the change of pace, to continue to focus on and work through the conflict. To fail to face social conflicts which are crippling a task-oriented group is to leave the group permanently disabled.

In a number of ways, confrontation of social conflict in the task-oriented group requires a different model of group work than that used to guide communication relating to the group's tasks. The group must achieve a level of cohesiveness such that the members can tolerate the tensions required to bring the conflict into the open. The group must also create a climate wherein members can honestly express their feelings and perceptions relating to the conflict. In one crucial respect, however, the session to confront and work though conflict in the social dimension of task groups differs from the sensitivity or encounter group meeting, and the distinction is an important one. In the sensitivity group meeting, the focus is on the individual's self-image, change, growth, increased awareness, and self-actualization, or on relationships among individuals. In the small task-oriented group, working through social conflict should focus *on the group.*

One of the more subtle ways in which groups take flight from working through their conflicts is by explaining away their difficulties as being caused by forces or persons beyond their control. They may argue, for example, that some external pressure, some accidental occurrence, or some unreasonable demands made by an individual outside the group caused their conflict. In a classroom group, students may argue that the illness and absence of a member, lack of time, or the unreasonable demands of the instructor caused their problems. One of the most destructive ways to take flight is to select one or two members and make them the scapegoats for the conflict. The group in conflict often finds it comforting to point to a bullheaded, unreasonable member who has single-handedly sabotaged the group. Usually the flight taking includes the explanation that "Stubborn Sue" acted destructively because of certain unchangeable personality traits which are beyond the power of the group to deal with. Under the circumstances, nothing can be done short of kicking Sue out of the group. By scapegoating, the other members can then get rid of their frustrations and guilt feelings by projecting them upon Sue.

Since scapegoating a member is a common neurotic tendency of groups in conflict, a productive confrontation session requires that the group *under no circumstance allow its session to degenerate into cattiness or comments about personalities.* The group must keep its focus *on the group* and the way in which role conflicts or status differences or achievement rewards are evolving or on norms that are destructive of a sound social dimension. The proper way to approach such conflict management is to remember that any person's behavior in a group is a joint enterprise worked out by the member and the group together. Whatever Sue's personality might be in social isolation, her role behavior as exhibited in the group is a function of that personality *and* the way that the group rewards and punishes her attempts to find a role in the group. Therefore, the question is not: What are the basic unchangeable miserable personality characteristics in Sue that result in her destruction of the group? Rather, the question should always be: What is the group doing to Sue to make her act that way? Groups that work through their conflicts in this manner often discover that Sue is a good deal easier to work with than they thought, and they may even come to like "good old Sue."

Some good questions to guide the group that finds itself needing conflict management in the social dimension are: Do the members of the group have stable roles? If not, is the group in the final stages of leadership emergence? Who are remaining contenders for leadership? Is the group ready to announce publicly that for most members a leader has now emerged? (Often a public avowal of leadership releases a great deal of tension and allows the person who has emerged to relax and perform the leadership role with security. Once the question of leadership is symbolically settled, the others in the group can concentrate on their own roles.) Are the apathetic or less interested members turned off because a few people are doing all the interesting and exciting things? Are the norms governing informal channels of communication such that some members seldom get the floor, and when they do speak, the others ignore their suggestions and ideas? Are the problems a function of gender? Are one or more of the leader contenders female and are the males (or other females) finding it difficult to take directions and orders from a female? Are the females becoming a power center because of industrious gathering of information? Does the female power center cause apathy on the part of the males? Are females disturbed because they feel that, despite talent and ability, they are not given roles that match their contributions?

Confrontation of conflict and working through to more productive and less tense social climates are encouraged in the task-oriented group because cooperation is rewarding. The group that works like a team and has high esprit de corps tends to be successful and fun to be a part of. If the members can keep their common goals before the group continually and remember the rewards of cooperative effort, the forces for cohesiveness can help in conflict resolution.

One final word of warning. When a zero-history test-tube group first tries to confront a conflict in the social dimension, the success or failure of the effort becomes a very important precedent for the future success or failure of the group. If the group should probe the conflict, raise tensions, take flight, and fail to work the problem through, then that failure is taped into its history. When the next conflict arises, the members will find it more difficult to deal with it directly. If they fail a second time, then they may not deal with other conflicts at all. On the other hand, if the first confrontation is successful, the members will find it easier to deal with future conflicts, and conflicts are inevitable. A second success begins to establish a healthy norm for dealing with conflicts in the social dimension, and gradually the group sees itself as a social system that knows how to handle conflict. The members are able to work through social conflicts at the appropriate times and thus free much more of the group's energy for undertaking productive tasks.

CONFLICT MANAGEMENT IN THE TASK AREA

While conflicts are more likely in the social dimension of group interaction, they are not uncommon in the task dimension. One of the difficulties in resolving conflicts in general is that the content of the communication does not always reveal whether the conflict is a task disagreement or actually a problem in the social area. Members in a role conflict or in a power struggle often will wage battle over what appears to be some task issue. People may view the fate of their suggestions and ideas as evidence of their own status in the group. "Reject my idea and you have rejected me" is their attitude. A member may gleefully report that the group has accepted his or her plan of action. Sometimes a member says that it was "my idea and the group liked it." On the other hand, a member may be very upset and report that an idea was rejected only to have the group accept the same idea, or a very similar one, introduced by someone else later on. Very probably there is always a mixture of social status, control, and achievement involved in every task conflict. Still, small task-oriented groups do deal with important substantive matters, and many conflicts are primarily related to the group's work.

Groups often get feedback from the external environment to indicate how well they are doing. An athletic team wins or loses games. A task force has its report accepted and praised or rejected and ignored. A business unit thrives and makes a profit or begins to lose money. A class discussion group puts on a program and the audience likes it or is bored by it. Feedback causes the group to evaluate its work norms and decisions, and the importance of doing a good job often results in conflicts which are largely substantive. Group members should, however, analyze the nature of the conflict before attempting to resolve it. If the argument over the task issues is really a power struggle, then the group which assumes that the conflict is over substantive differences may find itself taking flight into the task dimension and fail to deal with the real problem.

Interestingly enough, groups may take flight from task conflict into the social dimension. Groups which take flight into socializing generally have very pleasant social relations. The members like one another and have built good relationships. The minute they begin to work on a common task, however, they come into conflict. Instead of fighting through the disagreements to some task consensus, they make a decision quickly, and members who do not like the decision do not disagree; they "go along." Members of such groups report "pseudo-agreement because we did not want to cause trouble." Members assert that they do not want to "make waves" or that "we have such a good group that we didn't want to hurt our cohesiveness by getting into an argument about the task." Of course, members who talk of cohesiveness in terms of dodging disagreements because they might strain their sociability do not truly understand the concept of cohesiveness as explained in Chapter 4. Members of cohesive groups are tightly drawn to the group and *can tolerate more disagreement and conflict* than can members of groups that have low cohesiveness. Groups that must take flight from task conflict into socializing are not very cohesive at all. Cohesive groups handle the task and social dimensions of their group life with equal success.

Some task conflicts relate to work norms and procedures. The group should deal with task conflict related to matters of standard operating procedures much as it would with a conflict in the social dimension.

Although it is difficult to do, if groups can create a flexible work climate, they can often become exceptionally productive. Such groups gain an added bonus from the creativity and novelty of the people who score low on the high procedural order scale during the opening phases of group problem solving while retaining much of the structured members' administrative efficiency in the application phases when the group divides up work and mobilizes its resources.

An important part of the task conflicts of any work group will relate to the substance of the discussion. Groups may ignore such problems by simply ruling out certain topics from consideration. "We never talk about the honors program because Mary is in it and very excited about it and Joe tried it for a term and hated it." Members may smooth problems over and not raise the disagreements they feel because of the anticipated unpleasant conflicts. As a result, the group may well make poor decisions, and some members may be less than committed to what the group is doing.

When a group brings a task conflict into the open, it may decide rightly or wrongly that the conflict cannot be resolved. (Sometimes, indeed, conflicts are irreconcilable even in cooperative groups.) The group may then bring in a majority report and a minority report. Not all groups have the luxury of making two reports, however, and the external environment (for instance, the parent organization) may require one recommendation or decision. The majority may then submit its conclusions and the minority may have to accept them or withdraw. (Of course, sometimes high-status members submit the conclusions and they are, in effect, a minority acting as a majority.) Such a situation leaves the conflict unresolved and such procedures are unsatisfactory. Still, many conflict situations are handled in this manner, and some at least are probably of such a nature that they cannot be worked through.

A group may bring a task conflict out into the open and discover great differences, which it then resolves by negotiating a compromise. Usually the discussion quickly reveals two polar positions of considerable intensity within the group. One or more members, however, will be undecided (on the fence) or more committed to the group's coming to some decision than to either of the two polar positions. The middle-of-the-roaders will then try to work out some position which requires each of the conflicting camps to give a little in order to keep some of their important ideas in the final conclusion. If both sides are willing to give and the negotiators in the middle are skillful, a compromise that the members can support and work to achieve may be worked out. Managing conflict by compromise is less than satisfactory for the members of the rival factions, and it may set a work norm which carries over to other tasks, thus reducing group efficiency. Sometimes, however, compromises are wiser ways of managing conflict than are majority or minority reports, splitting the group apart, or resorting to violence.

A group may bring a task conflict out into the open and confront differences, come to some common-ground positions, and work through to a consensus that all members can support wholeheartedly. During the conflict, members may be stimulated to express all their objections and disagreements forcibly and without reservation. The end result of confrontation and working through to consensus is often a thoroughly tested and wise decision or solution to which the members are committed. Such conflicts are productive in that they contribute to better problem solving and wiser decisions.

Task conflicts about message content tend to relate to one or more of the following kinds of issues: (1) questions of fact, (2) questions of policy, and (3) questions of value. Groups generally find it easiest to work out conflicts relating to questions of fact. Questions of policy are difficult, but consensus is often possible. Members who come into value conflict frequently cannot achieve satisfactory consensus.

Members of groups in task conflict should, therefore, sort out what kinds of issues divide them. If the issue is related to facts, they may be able to resolve the conflict by gathering additional information and by testing the available sources more carefully. If the group is studying whether there should be a change in the way instructors grade student work, members may come into conflict over the number of A's, B's, C's, and D's given in courses in psychology, sociology, and speech communication as compared with the number given in chemistry, geology, physics, and mathematics. Conflicts over such matters are factual, and the members can often resolve them by making further investigations and getting the distribution of grades by classes for the last several terms from the records office. Task groups which make decisions and try to solve problems on the basis of wrong information often fail to do a good job. All members thus have reason to try to agree, using the best information available.

Closely related to the conflicts over factual matters are those differences that grow out of group problem-solving efforts. A group may face an important common problem, perhaps even a crisis situation, and seriously disagree about its nature and causes. Here again, careful investigation of the conditions surrounding the difficulty and thorough testing of possible reasons for the problem should aid the group in coming to consensus. Without productive resolution of the conflict, group members are likely to try solutions which leave them no better off than they were before. The feedback from other individuals, groups, and organizations to group messages resulting from collective problem solving is often direct and clear and, when the attempts are unsuccessful, painful.

If the members come in conflict over questions of policy, consensus is less likely than when the question can be convincingly resolved by observation of the facts. Questions of policy relate to the group's general philosophy and overall objectives as well as to the important courses of action that it should follow. A policy question might be: What should the College of Liberal Arts do to improve grading procedures? Because policy questions often relate to matters of philosophy, they may arouse conflict relating to basic world views, ethical systems, and values of the members. Members often will come into conflict over the amount of resources, energy, or effort that the group should invest in various courses of action. The value questions, as we shall see, are the most difficult to resolve. However, if the group can find some common goal or common philosophical ground, one which is broad enough to include the various courses of action under consideration, it can often work through the policy conflict to consensus.

Here is where symbolic convergence becomes important. Resolution of task conflicts, therefore, often requires a careful consideration of where the members agree and where they disagree. If the group's attention can be focused first on areas of agreement and these commonalities can be kept in mind, then the conflict may be resolved by continually checking various positions against the common goals. Again, the task-oriented group provides a context in which such conflict resolution is facilitated because of the group's common task and purpose and the fact that success may generate additional value which all can share.

If the members come into conflict over questions of value, they will face many difficulties in trying to reach consensus. A value question might be: Ought one human being be given institutional authority to evaluate another publicly? One faction of a group may assert that it is ethically and morally deplorable for one person to have the right to evaluate another human being's intellectual effort and worth and to put down the evaluation in a public record that is available to the student's family, friends, enemies, and potential employers. Another faction may assert that evaluation is not only inevitable but necessary, and therefore honest evaluation reflecting the actual worth of the student's work is not only desirable but the only ethically justifiable course for the faculty to follow. Polar positions on the basic question of the morality and value of grading itself reflect a conflict over values and are most difficult to resolve.

Many times groups will have to give up on the resolution of conflict over values and simply recognize that if they are to act as a unit they will have to work around or within the restrictions that the differing value systems place upon their efforts. Successful resolution of value conflicts usually requires *changing the value systems of some or all of the members.* People change their value systems reluctantly, and usually only when the group has high saliency for them. That is, you are a member of a number of task-oriented small groups and of other important groups, such as your family. Any given group you belong to can be compared with other groups as to how important it is in your life. You are not likely to change your value system in a classroom task-oriented small group that meets for five or six hours when your values are supported by another strong, salient group that has a long history.

SUMMARY

This chapter has provided an overview of the social climates of groups that create attractive or unattractive contexts for decision making and problem solving. The socially facilitating interactions discovered by Bales and his associates include shows of solidarity, tension release, and agreements. The socially punishing interactions include shows of antagonism, tension, and disagreements.

Shows of solidarity are verbal and nonverbal communications that raise the status of members, offer to help a member of the group, or show commitment to the group. Tensions are generally released by laughter, smiling, chuckling, or other genuine expressions of shared mirth or amusement.

Shows of tension often change quality during the course of a group meeting. The early shows, primary tension, are generally more quiet and less obtrusive than the later, secondary tensions generated by role conflict and task differences. In general, primary tensions are easier to release because group members welcome the relaxed social atmosphere that results. Secondary tensions are more difficult to handle. Nonetheless, good groups develop ways that work for them in releasing secondary tensions.

Disagreements are important to the successful functioning of a task-oriented group. By means of disagreement, the group tests information and reasoning. Disagreement, however, exacts a social toll and tends to stiffen the social climate. Successful groups develop ways of handling the inevitable secondary tensions that result from disagreements.

Conflicts are those disagreements that result in such high secondary tension as to render the group inoperative. Conflicts in both the social and task areas need to be dealt with directly to ensure maximum group morale and productivity.

Although much about the small group is cooperative and the special theories require cooperative communication, the workings of the general theories tend to ensure that the climate is, in fact, one of mixed-motive communication.

Conflicts arise from three major areas of social reward: contention for leadership, task influence, and popularity. The best way to deal with conflicts in the social dimension is to avoid taking flight from them or smoothing them and, instead, confront and work them through.

Conflicts arise from task deliberations involving factual matters, decisions about wise policy, and value questions. Again, confronting and working through to group consensus is a good way to deal with task conflicts. Factual conflicts tend to be the easiest to resolve. Policy matters are more difficult, and value questions are the most difficult of all.

Rules of Thumb

Practical Advice on How to Be a Good Group Member

Drawn from Chapter 6

- If you honestly want the group to do well, sincerely express your desires for group solidarity when feasible.
- Keep an eye open for turning points in a group discussion when you can initiate shows of group solidarity to build cohesiveness.
- Keep an eye open for when others offer tentative shows of group solidarity and reinforce them.
- Avoid cynical attempts to manipulate the group with insincere signs or shows of solidarity.
- Learn to recognize the signs of primary tension in a small task-oriented group.
- Learn to estimate when primary tension rises above the tension tolerance level and then take steps to release it.
- Release primary tensions by getting acquainted, joking, kidding, making small talk, and doing and saying things to break the ice.
- If primary tensions are severe, have the group discuss them directly and seek the sources of the tension and ways to deal with it.
- Learn to recognize the earmarks of secondary tension in a small task-oriented group.
- Learn to estimate when secondary tension rises above the tension tolerance level and then take steps to release it.
- When dealing with secondary tensions, be careful not to scapegoat one or two people for creating them.
- It is not a good idea to have the two or three people centrally involved in a disagreement deal with it outside of group meetings.
- Help your group develop its own productive ways to handle primary and secondary tensions.
- Facing up to tensions realistically is the best way to release them.
- Authentic agreement serves as a powerful social reward and can raise a member's status and esteem.
- Authentic agreement serves to aid the group in evaluating information and making decisions.
- Agreement for agreement's sake can serve socioemotional needs but go counter to task requirements for culling out bad ideas and decisions.
- Disagreements are necessary for sound decisions; you should disagree when you feel it in the best interests of the group to do so.
- Although disagreements are necessary for sound decisions, even

productive disagreements result in hurt feelings and social tensions.

☞ Do not preface a disagreement with an agreement or a compliment in the hopes of defusing the negative impact.

☞ In order for a disagreement to work as a rejection of ideas, it must be perceived by other members as such a rejection; and when it is, a complimentary preface will not prevent the secondary tensions.

☞ Work for a group that has enough cohesiveness to disagree.

☞ Learn to tell when a disagreement has become so crippling (when secondary tensions are so high) that it must be dealt with as a conflict.

☞ Learn techniques to help your group develop a cooperative communication climate (win-win) to ensure that fewer disagreements become conflicts.

☞ When conflict arises, decide whether its root is a socioemotional or task problem.

☞ When your group has a socioemotional conflict, decide whether it is caused by contention among members over leadership, power, gender, or status.

☞ Do not let your group take flight from dealing with the conflict.

☞ Do not let your group ignore the conflict by pretending everything is all right.

☞ Do not let your group smooth over the conflict by mentioning it in a meeting but dropping the topic before the conflict is resolved.

☞ As a group member, you must decide whether the conflict can be worked through or whether it is best to work out a compromise.

☞ In working through social conflict, keep the focus on the entire group and its responsibility and its possible courses of action.

☞ Remember that the group's successes and failures in working through conflict become part of the group's history and make future conflicts easier or more difficult to resolve.

☞ When conflicts arise over factual matters, the best approach, when possible, is to engage in further research to find out the cause.

☞ In dealing with conflicts over policy, search for a common ground and common goals and stress what holds the group together.

☞ In dealing with conflicts over values, work around basic differences as best you can.

☞ Consciousness-raising groups can be powerful tools for changing values, but the task-oriented group is not well adapted to changing deeply ingrained values quickly.

QUESTIONS FOR STUDY

1. What is meant by shows of solidarity? How do they work to create a positive communication climate?

2. What is the difference between primary and secondary tension?
3. How might the concept of "tension tolerance level" be used to increase group productivity?
4. Why is agreement often rewarding to a group member?
5. In what ways do disagreements both facilitate and inhibit group success?
6. How may groups ensure sufficient disagreement?
7. How might disagreements and conflicts be distinguished?
8. What are some typical ways of dealing with conflicts?
9. What are some recommended ways to deal with conflicts?
10. How do social conflicts differ from task conflicts?

EXERCISES

1. Select a classroom group that you are working with and write a short paper analyzing the way members disagree. Evaluate the group's effectiveness in handling the social tensions produced by disagreements.
2. Select an acquaintance who is expert at releasing social tensions. Write a brief analysis of that person's techniques and evaluate their success.
3. Set up a role-playing exercise in which each member prefaces every disagreement with a compliment or sign of agreement. In class, perform a panel discussion program of 20 minutes with these roles. Discuss the effect of such disagreements on the program.
4. Set up a role-playing exercise in which several members have a discussion and come into conflict over leadership. Have the group confront and work through the conflict. Discuss the way in which the group managed the conflict.
5. Set up a role-playing exercise in which several members have a discussion and come into conflict over task. Have the group confront and work through the conflict. Discuss the way in which the group managed the conflict.

REFERENCES AND SUGGESTED READINGS

Bales's category system is explained in detail in:

Bales, Robert F. *Interaction Process Analysis: A Method for the Study of Small Groups.* Cambridge, MA: Addison-Wesley, 1950.

Bales, Robert F. *Personality and Interpersonal Behavior.* New York: Holt, Rinehart and Winston, 1970.

The tendency of groups to turn from attention to task matters to attempts to mend the social fabric is discussed in:

Bales, Robert F. "The Equilibrium Problem in Small Groups." In T. Parsons, R. F. Bales, and E. Shils, eds., *Working Papers in the Theory of Action.* New York: Free Press, 1953, pp. 111–161.

The case studies of secondary tension were part of a doctoral dissertation by:

Geier, John. "A Descriptive Analysis of an Interaction Pattern Resulting in Leadership Emergence in Leaderless Group Discussion." Ph.D. dissertation, University of Minnesota, 1963.

The literature on the reinforcement of verbal behavior is extensive. For a survey of some early studies, see:

Aiken, Edwin G. "Interaction Process Analysis Changes Accmpanying Operant Conditioning of Verbal Frequency in Small Groups," *Perceptual and Motor Skills*, 21 (1965), 52–54.

Krasner, Leonard A. "Studies of the Conditioning of Verbal Behavior," *Psychological Bulletin*, 55 (1958), 148–170.

For studies of conflict and conflict management, see:

Baxter, Leslie A. "Conflict Management: An Episodic Approach," *Small Group Behavior*, 13 (1982), 23–42.

Bell, Mae Arnold. "A Research Note: The Relationship of Conflict and Linguistic Diversity in Small Groups," *Central States Speech Journal*, 34 (1983), 128–133.

Fogg, Richard W. "Dealing with Conflict: A Repertoire of Creative, Peaceful Approaches," *Journal of Conflict Resolution*, 22 (1985), 330–358.

Hare, A. Paul, and David Naveh. "Group Development at Camp David Summit, 1978," *Small Group Behavior*, 15 (1984), 299–318.

Tjosvold, Dean, and Richard H. Field. "Effect of Concurrence, Controversy, and Consensus on Group Decision," *Journal of Social Psychology*, 125 (1985), 355–363.

Wall, Victor D., Jr., and Gloria J. Galanes. "The SYMLOG Dimensions and Small Group Conflict," *Central States Speech Journal*, 37 (1986), 61–78.

Wall, Victor D., Jr., and Linda L. Nolan. "Small Group Conflict: A Look at Equity, Satisfaction, and Styles of Management," *Small Group Behavior*, 18 (1987), 188–211.

Chapter
7

Roles

A popular psychological concept is that of individual personality. Usually, personality is thought of as the sum of an individual's physical, mental, emotional, and social characteristics. Personality in this sense might be accounted for in several ways. Personality might be regarded as the stable behavior patterns exhibited by a person in a wide variety of situations. A more detailed explanation of individual characteristics is furnished by dividing up the distinguishing features and labeling each part as a *trait*, such as intelligence, extroversion, dominance, verbal fluency, or flexibility. The trait approach furnishes a theoretical basis for describing a person as having a bright, vivacious, and charming personality.

This way of describing personality is useful because it allows psychologists to name an individual's dominant traits or dominant behavior. An individual can be described as usually acting intelligently even though on occasion he or she has been observed to do stupid things. A woman could be characterized as being frequently dominant and verbal even if on occasion she is quiet and submissive. Given the theory of personality traits, attempts can be made to measure the amount of various personality traits within a given person by standardized testing procedures. A clinical psychologist can, therefore, describe an individual in terms of his intelligence test scores, his critical-thinking test scores, and his scores on the Minnesota Multiphasic Personality Inventory or some other personality index. Such descriptions are particularly helpful if they enable the tester to predict how that individual will perform in a given situation. When a psychologist can discover traits that help to predict that a particular student can graduate from college or that she should be a successful business manager, the definition of personality as stable behavior patterns is useful.

The concept of individual personality may also be defined in social-psychological terms — that is, personality is the individual's predisposition toward certain stable behavior patterns *as actualized within a given social field.* The variables that affect an individual's behavior within the group comprise the *social field.* Some personality traits remain stable — that is, they do not change appreciably as a person moves from group to group (changes social fields). These traits are termed *field invariant.* But the social field *determines* a number of behaviors — whether or not a person is talkative, charming, dominant, aggressive, submissive, funny, serious, solemn, stupid, and so forth. The young woman, for example, who is charming and pleasant on a double date may be shrill, unpleasant, and bossy at home with her brothers and sisters. What kind of person is she really? The second way of defining personality implies that what sort of person she is depends on both her stable personality traits (field-invariant behavior) *and* her role within a given group (field-variant behavior). The first approach to defining personality can only note and disregard the exceptions to otherwise stable behavior patterns. The second approach is more useful for the student of group methods because it provides a more complete explanation for the behavior of individuals within groups and organizations.

Bales and his associates worked out an elaborate framework to account for individual personality in social-psychological terms. Bales developed the system using data from his interaction process analysis technique (described in Chapter 5), but he also used data from the Minnesota Multiphasic Personality Inventory and other personality tests and from a procedure for studying value statements in small group communication. The system is based on the technique of factor analysis, which is a statistical procedure designed to take a complex set of relationships and boil them down to a few basic "factors" on the assumption that if a number of relationships seem to vary together, they may reflect a more powerful underlying feature in the data.

Bales developed an account of group roles that explained behavior in terms of three basic dimensions. He interprets role positions by presenting them geometrically. He defines group space in terms of upward–downward, forward–backward, and positive–negative dimensions. One can, theoretically, observe a person in a group and plot that individual's place in group space. The account contains 26 types of group roles and their value directions. The group role types include such positions as the upward dimension of group space (U), the upward positive dimension (UP), and the upward, positive, forward dimension (UPF), until 26 different positions are described.

A final important outcome of the framework of analysis is a paper-and-pencil "Interpersonal Rating Form." Participants in a group can use the form to rate fellow members after they have worked together for a period of time. The rating form also resulted from a factor-analysis procedure and consists of 26 items that are loaded with one, two, or three of the factors. Each question is typical of one of the positions in group space, so that a yes answer to one question is loaded on the upward dimension (U), one on the upward positive (UP), one on the upward, positive, forward position (UPF), and so forth. One person can evaluate another's role by answering yes or no to such a question as "Is his or her *rate of participation* generally high?" A yes answer is loaded on the upward dimension of group space, and a no answer is loaded on the downward dimension.

Group members or nonparticipant observers may use the Interpersonal Rating Form to get an index of perceived roles in a group with little expenditure of time and effort. Assume that member A rates member B after several hours of group meetings, and the summed index of answers to the 26 questions yields a UPF position in group space. Participant or nonparticipant observers can use the rating to diagnose role ambiguity, conflict, stability, and structure. Bales further presents a relatively detailed analysis of each of the roles which includes such things as how people in a type such as UPF see themselves, how others see them, how they tend to participate in the communication process and networks, and what values they express. The role analysis also includes an account of the way a person in a certain position tends to participate in coalitions or comes into conflict with other role types.

Bales takes the position that the way members perceive an individual's interpersonal behavior is a function of both personality and group role. Bales sees a *group role* as consisting of all the group members' perceptions, evaluations, and expectations of an individual. He views *personality* as the relatively enduring characteristics of the member. Bales argues that a member's personality is not the same as her or his role in a group, since a person's behavior in any given group reflects only one side of the personality elicited by that particular group. Interestingly enough, Bales suggests that the line of inference ought not to go from the analysis of individual personality to conclusions about role behavior, but rather that one can, on the basis of observed and perceived behavior, place an individual into group space and then make inferences about the kind of personality traits usually associated with that position. Thus, group behavior is studied both to discover an individual's personality and to assess the influence of the group on the individual's role.

Bales's framework of analysis of role and individual personality plus the empirical verification for it essentially agrees with the results of the Minnesota studies as described in this chapter. Whenever independent investigators arrive at essentially similar findings, they provide corroboration for one another. By contrast with other research efforts such as Schutz's FIRO (discussed in Chapter 4) and the attempts to estimate group behavior on the basis of personality profiles, Bales's account provides a much more detailed and complete explanation that includes data from personality tests, value scales, and the process analysis of group communication.

THE CONCEPT OF ROLE

The process by which roles emerge in a leaderless group discussion furnishes a detailed explanation of the way an individual who already has a set of field-invariant personality traits learns the additional (field-variant) behavior unique to a particular group.

In the theater, *role* means assuming or being assigned a part in a play. In small group communication a member is assigned a role, or he or she assumes one. In this regard the discussant is much like the actor. However, participants differ from actors in an important way: Their parts are not written for them.

Role, in the small group, is defined as that set of perceptions and expectations shared by the members about the behavior of an individual in both the task and social dimensions of group interaction. Quite often, role is defined as a set of behaviors appropriate to a specific position within some formal organization, but here the term is used to indicate the *informal* group norms that place an individual within the group. The part an individual plays within a task-oriented small group may continue for weeks, months, or even years. When the other members know what part a person will play and that person knows what part they expect of her or him, that person has assumed a role. Individuals who work with a wide variety of groups may find that they play a diversity of roles. Students in small group communication classes often participate in many other groups. Some are active in church groups. Some are members of athletic teams. Some are active in campus politics. One of the case studies at Minnesota included a student who played the role of a quiet, interested worker. This same student was quarterback on the football team and played the role of a field leader — a take-charge player. Was he really a field leader and take-charge guy? Or was he really a quiet, interested follower? The answer is that his personality was dependent, to some extent, on the group.

Another case study contained a handsome, fast-talking young man and an equally fast-talking, attractive woman. Before the end of the first meeting, they had a severe and disagreeable personality clash. Within a week the woman left the group. When interviewed about her experiences, she reported that after one acrimonious session the fellow had invited her to a campus coffee shop. They had spent several hours over coffee, and she was puzzled by how much nicer he really was outside the group. But the minute they returned to the group the fighting began again. The point is that a number of socially important behaviors are field-variant. Individuals change their personalities in important ways depending on the roles they play in a particular group. Think of yourself in various groups and see if you are not serious in some groups, joking and laughing and clowning in others; taking charge and leading the way in some groups, and quietly going along in others.

The role a member takes in a group is, to the objective observer (that is, someone watching but not part of the group), what the member says and does as the group interacts; for the group members, it also includes what they *expect* the participant to say and do. If they expect the person to disagree, they will turn to that individual for such disagreement when it seems appropriate. If they expect a member to crack a joke when the group feels primary tension, they will turn to that person when they feel primary tension. The role a member takes includes what he or she thinks the group expects in terms of interaction and work.

There are two sides to the concept of role as it applies to small groups. One side is the objective and overt behavior. Several independent observers can verify directly and can agree about the truth or falsity of statements describing this behavior; for example, observers might agree that a person got up from his chair and wrote "Time remaining — 15 minutes" on the blackboard. The other side is the subjective perception of the individual members of the group. One may perceive writing "time" on the blackboard as getting the group to work and increase its efficiency. Another may consider the same action as an attempt to wrest the leadership of the group from the assigned leader. And another may perceive the action as an attempt to show off. The Minnesota studies indicate that each member perceives a slightly different group than does every other member. At the same time, the subjective perceptions of the participants will exhibit some commonality. They often reach a consensus on what has happened and what is *expected* from the various members in the future. When these expectations stabilize, the roles within the group are stable. For the group member, the subjective side of role perception is more important than the objective side. Once common expectations about what the person will do and say have been reached, the participant has a role in the group. The member knows what he or she is to say and do while working with the group. And like some actors, members are happier if, in effect, they know their lines and the way the action should go.

THE MECHANISM OF ROLE EMERGENCE IN NEWLY FORMED GROUPS

The Basic Model

The Minnesota studies used the zero-history *leaderless group discussion* (or LGD) as the basis of test-tube groups for the study of the mechanism of role emergence and specialization. The basic model of group functioning is that of a generalized process typical of the LGD. Quite often, descriptive models that identify basic processes can be used to predict and explain phenomena. For example, investigators began the study of the acceleration of a freely falling body by positing a simplified condition in which the object fell in a vacuum. They first determined this basic rate and then applied the model to more realistic conditions by adding such complicating factors as the effect of the resistance of the atmosphere and the force and direction of wind currents. With these additions, they were able to apply their theory to such practical problems as aiming cannons. Much the same procedure can be followed with the general theory in this chapter, although the knowledge about the LGD is not as exact as the knowledge a ballistics expert has about the firing of the cannon. The model is, thus, scientific rather than a touchstone, as are the models of special theories discussed in Chapter 1. There are no groups in which the process of role specialization described by the model does not take place. The model has been successfully adapted and accommodated to the functioning of such groups within formal organizations. Roger Mosvick, a professor at Macalester College, St. Paul, Minnesota, has applied the model to the specific case of project-organized groups in his capacity as communications consultant for Minneapolis Honeywell. The author has made the same use of the theoretical model as consultant to such firms as the Rochester, Minnesota, branch of IBM, the Control Data Corporation, and the Minneapolis Honeywell Ordnance Division.

The test-tube groups used in the Minnesota studies were composed of strangers and had no formal structure. Every member was a peer. Many of the groups were set up in small group or organizational communication classes and had a clear objective and a specified time limit, but a number of the groups were part of ongoing organizations. The groups that were newly formed had no history. Those from continuing organizations had a history.

The first important discovery in these studies was that after several hours of discussion, the members began to specialize, and some people gained status and esteem. The case studies of many discussions indicated that specialization of function and its resultant status arrangement occurred in the majority of groups.

The second important discovery was that the discussants did not take roles, but rather each worked out a role jointly with the others. The process by which a given individual came to specialize within the LGD was a dynamic set of transactions in which the person tried out various role functions and was encouraged or discouraged to continue by the responses of the group. The dynamics of the give-and-take by which members of a group work out their roles are intricate and complicated, but the basic model emerges from the study of these test-tube groups. That model assumes the conditions of the leaderless group discussion. The theoretical explanation of the mechanism by which roles emerge in newly formed groups consists of two parts. The first is a list of components of the LGD including the requisite social and task functions matched against the talents, skills, and abilities of the people assembled to participate in the discussion. The second part of the model diagrams the basic transactions used by the group to test and develop specialization.

Turning to the first part of the model, Figure 8 presents some of the behaviors required for group discussion and supplies a hypothetical breakdown of how the various skills might be distributed. Thus, member A is good at initiating action, dividing a group's work, assigning tasks, and gathering information. Member B is best at initiating action, testing the soundness of information, dividing the group's work, assigning jobs, gathering information, and drawing inferences. Member C is talented in being funny and releasing tensions, testing soundness of information, suggesting possible ways to do a job, and evaluating inferences and plans. Member A could do all these things, but as an individual he is best at the activities listed.

The personnel of the LGD, of course, must do many other things than the items listed in Figure 8. These 10 role functions are among the most important, however, and the same basic model of reward and punishment is used by the group to teach additional role functions to the members.

The second part of the model of the basic process of role specialization is an application of psychological learning theory to the group context, as indicated by Figure 9. At a given point in time, T_1, the group requires that certain social or task functions be performed. The social field exerts pressure on the discussants to do what is needed. A given individual, member A, is stimulated to display the required behavior, role function RF_1. The group responds to A's behavior with ambiguous feedback, or with approval, or with disapproval. At the next point in time, T_2, that the group requires someone to perform RF_1, the social system already has some history which affects the response of all members to the pressure of the social field. If the original response to A's display of RF_1 was ambiguous and if member A has a strong drive to assume that role function, she or he will tend to repeat the RF_1 activity at T_2. However, another member

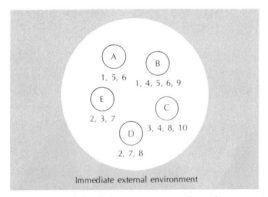

Figure 8 Model of the LGD. Members have native or acquired abilities to do the following tasks better than any other tasks: (1) initiating action; (2) doing routine chores; (3) being funny and releasing tension; (4) testing soundness of information; (5) dividing up group work and assigning jobs; (6) gathering information; (7) following orders carefully and doing the job assigned; (8) giving suggestions as to possible ways of doing a job; (9) drawing inferences; and (10) evaluating inferences and plans of action.

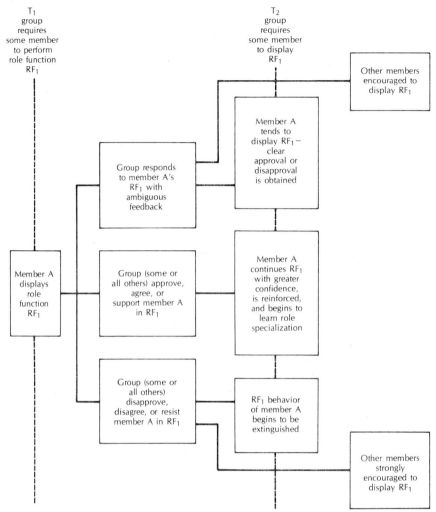

Figure 9 The dynamics of role specialization.

with similar drives will also be encouraged to display RF_1 at T_2. If some or all of the others approved, agreed, or accepted A's behavior, she or he was reinforced at T_1 and will tend to display RF_1 with greater confidence at T_2. If the group again reinforces the behavior at T_2, member A will continue to perform RF_1 as the need arises. In this fashion, RF_1 becomes part of member A's repertoire of behavior within the group. The member is, in a sense, taught a specialization by the reinforcement the group provides. To be sure, members tend to try out first for those parts that they have played successfully in other groups and for those role functions that they most enjoy and find most rewarding; but the dynamics of the process move individuals into roles that they work out with the approval of the others. When member A has been reinforced at T_1, others who may wish to perform that role function will tend not to do so at T_2.

Disapproval, disagreement, and resistance at T_1 are punishing to the individual, and the member will be more reluctant to exhibit the RF_1 behavior again at T_2. If the participant tries and continues to receive disapproval from the others, the RF_1 behavior is extinguished, and the individual will begin to try other role functions in order to find a place in the group. Sometimes, a person has an extremely strong drive to assume a set of role functions and continues RF_1 behavior in the face of strong and continued resistance. When the individual fails to learn a role from the usual group feedback of reinforcement and resistance, the member may be characterized as being inflexible and insensitive. The group often finds such a person frustrating to work with, and members wonder how to deal with her or him.

The operation of the basic model is well illustrated by the typical first meeting of an LGD. The first task facing the LGD is to release primary tension. Both member C and member E have a capacity to be funny (skill 3). Having had some experience, they are sensitive to primary tensions and make attempts at releasing them. Member C has a characteristic style of being funny. He makes small talk and watches for the response. When he thinks another member will respond favorably, he makes a mildly insulting personal comment about the member and laughs to indicate that it is all in fun. He then waits for the reaction of the others. If his attempt at humor fails, he is less likely to try again. Early in the meeting, however, the typical responses are ambiguous; that is, some people smile or laugh a little, but C cannot decide whether they like his little jibe or not. Probably the members themselves are not yet sure. The primary tension remains, and E takes the opportunity to try to break the tension. She, too, has a unique way of being funny. She is clever at impersonations, a good panto-mimist, and she relies to some extent on visual gags for her humor. Member E comments that she is feeling ill at ease. She shrugs her shoulders into her coat and pantomimes to show the coldness of the group atmosphere. Her grimaces and shakes are tentative, but indicate what she could do if she really let herself go. She, too, waits for the group's response. There are many other styles of being funny demonstrated by contenders for the "best liked" role. They may be gracious, smiling, and agreeable. They may have a stock of funny stories memorized and handy for most occasions. They may kid themselves. You can supply from your own experiences the kinds of behavior that act to release group tensions and contribute to an individual assuming the most popular role.

Typically, member E will also receive ambiguous responses to her attempts at humor, unless she is clearly much better in the eyes of the group than member C. The stage is now set for a competition between C and E as to who will do this particular job.

The competition between E and C will continue for a time until the group decides that E will be their tension releaser, or that C is more to their liking and that he will be their joker, or that E and C will share in doing this job. This sharing may involve a relatively equal balance, or one may do most of the tension releasing with the other supporting and adding to the clowning.

The group reaches the decision about member E and member C in the following way. They watch the two demonstrating their wares for a time and then vote for either E or C or the two together. The voting is done by cues that are interpreted as reinforcement or resistance. As long as E and C perceive the response to their kidding and cutting up as unclear or ambiguous, the issue is in doubt, and they will continue the contest. When A begins to relax and laugh with what E perceives as genuine delight at E, and when A groans or frowns or remains disapproving of C's attempts at humor, then A has cast a vote for E. Should B now begin to support C's attempts at humor the group would still be evenly divided, and the issue could only be resolved by D clearly indicating which contender he will support. When a clear consensus has been reached, the question is decided. The votes cannot be forced and, with the exceptions of such duties as secretary, chair, or moderator, are seldom dealt with directly.

With the release of primary tension, the group often feels pressure to begin work. Members A and B have in their repertoire of skills the initiation of action. Member A suggests to the group that they get down to business. She is met by silence. Member B suggests that before they begin work they should consider the best procedure for working. Member D is now confused. Member E does a little pantomime about how really confused she is and the group laughs, this time not with primary tension but releasing some secondary tension because A and B are marked members. They have both made *leadership* moves, and each member of the group is directly concerned with the question of whether A or B will initiate the group's action. A contest now ensues between A and B as to who will get this job. Again, the decision may be that either A or B will be responsible primarily for this function or that they will share it. And again, the consensus comes from social interactions that are perceived by the contenders and the others as supporting one of the two members.

In the same fashion, all other tasks that the group must perform are delegated after a period of interaction during which the members try their hands at the various chores. Some functions may become almost the exclusive specialization of a particularly adept person. For example, the function of disagreeing may become the special duty of one member. Many functions, however, will be shared by several members and sometimes by everyone. All might gather information and bring it to the group for processing. Nonetheless, one or two members would spend more of their time in the activity, and the group would expect them to furnish the bulk of the information. After working together for some time, the LGD makes assignments in this indirect way by reinforcing or resisting the interactions of the participants. When a consensus is reached on the assignment of jobs, the *roles* have clearly emerged, and members know what the group expects them to do. At this point, the roles in the group have stabilized. The stabilization of roles releases both primary and secondary tensions. People know where they fit in. The question of what the group will think of them is now answered. When the participants know what to expect and what others expect of them, there are fewer indeterminate situations, fewer rude shocks, fewer punishing and surprising social interactions. They can relax and concentrate on the job without having to wonder how people will react socially. With a few exceptions, the group's cohesiveness increases rather dramatically when roles are stabilized.

The Idiosyncratic Nature of Individual Roles

To clarify the diversity of functions that go into role development, one might label the typical role patterns as clarifier, initiator, information giver, tension releaser, and information tester. More dramatically, students of LGD might label such roles as Mr. Pessimist, Mr. Egoist, Ms. Vivacious, Mr. Best Liked, and Ms. Joker. Such labels are oversimplifications of the roles that actually develop in groups and should be considered as illustrative rather than descriptive. Actually, an objective description of the behavior and interactions of the members of a particular LGD would reveal that all members at one time or another function in all 10 of Bales's categories. If an investigator made an analysis using the Bales category system or any other system, he or she would find that all participants had some interactions coded in every category. However, some individuals would have a larger percentage of their total interactions clustered in one or several categories.

Obviously, the concept of role cannot be limited exclusively to several categories of behavior. The 10 items of the illustrative (and also somewhat oversimplified) list may divide as follows: Member A largely does 1, 6; member B does 1, 4, 5, 9; member C does 4, 8; member D does 2, 6, 7; member E does 3, 7. All the members participate in doing 6, although A and D are looked to by the group to gather most of the information.

This particular clustering of chores associated with each role and the amount of sharing of functions (A, 1, 6; B, 1, 4, 5, 9; C, 4, 8; D, 2, 6, 7; E, 3, 7) is unique to the hypothetical group. For example, if 25 students are placed by random selection in five LGDs and work until the basic process is completed and a role structure is stabilized, observers can describe their roles. If five new LGDs are set up using the same 25 students, and the process is repeated, observers will agree that an individual does not perform the same functions for the second group that he did for the first. Member B, who did functions 1, 4, 5, 9 in the first group, would not have an identical cluster in the second group, although the role may be very similar (say, 1, 5, 10) and the participant might be perceived as the leader by both groups. (But she or he would not be quite the same kind of leader in the second group as she or he was in the first.) On the other hand, the role might be composed of quite a different set of functions, such as being funny and releasing tension. In the latter case, the participant would be perceived as leader in the first group, but not in the second.

Students often bring to a group meeting a simple trait framework for stereotyping the others in the group. The unstructured social field of a zero-history group is tension producing, and a trait stereotype provides an immediate short-term reward because it allows one to structure the group quickly. Unfortunately, the trait framework does not anticipate the way the group develops, and people who persist in using a stereotyped-trait approach to get their bearings in the group find themselves continually frustrated, disturbed, and confused by the way people act in what they consider uncharacteristic ways. A person with a trait viewpoint may join a zero-history group and soon come to the conclusion that member A is quiet and unassuming, that member B is a loud extrovert, that member C is frivolous, and so forth. Once he labels any member as being a certain kind of person with one or two distinguishing personality traits, he may assume that these members will not change their personalities. When member A grows more and more active and assertive in the meetings, the individual who has stereotyped A as quiet and unassuming will often write in a diary response to a group meeting that A is changing in surprising and unexplainable ways and that it was wrong to judge A as being quiet and unassuming. Actually, the individual will add, A is a much more talkative and pushy person than was first thought; the participant has been misled, and now A's "true" personality traits are emerging.

Students often find it difficult to transcend the simple stereotyping of traits and adopt the more complex and adequate framework for interpreting roles such as is presented in this chapter. Once they move from a simple trait viewpoint, they often adopt an oversimplified set of role stereotypes. They evaluate the roles of group members in static terms according to one salient role function such as: member A was an information seeker, member B was a leader contender, and member C was the socioemotional leader. This is still too narrow a view for a realistic evaluation and for the ongoing adjustments needed for effective group endeavor.

To better understand the dynamism and complexity of group roles, one must move past the tendency to make static stereotypes that assume that every group will contain a limited number of roles and that these will consist of one or two kinds of salient communication and behavior. People act in extremely complex ways, and no static labeling of one or two salient role functions for each member can do justice to human behavior in a small group. What is required is a concept that sees each role in a group as a dynamic set of expectations and behaviors that are part of a complex communication system and are thus sensitive to changes in others' roles and to external pressures on the group. Despite the dynamic complexity of the small group as a social system, particularly as the group is beginning work and structuring itself, clusters of expectations and behaviors do emerge in time to form discernible patterns, and these profiles, as they stabilize, make up the roles of the group members.

Field Variance of Roles

The mechanism of role emergence accounts for the *field-variant* portion of an individual's personality. It works like the "operant conditioning" model of the behavioral psychologists. By offering social rewards and punishments, the LGD sets up operant conditioning schedules that teach each person his or her role. When a person behaves properly, the group members reward him or her; and when the participant behaves in a different fashion, they exact punishment. In successful groups, each member's behavior is, to some extent, shaped by social reinforcements, such as shows of agreement and of tension release, that he or she receives. People tend to have a history of success and failure at doing the chores demanded of them, but they never know if a particular group will decide that they should continue to do what they have done successfully before.

Why does a group reinforce one sort of behavior rather than another for a given member? This explanation is somewhat speculative and is based largely on clinical insights drawn from case studies. Quite often the decisions seem to come fortuitously. A chance remark, an interaction that is perceived as a slight or an insult, a mistake that causes laughter, or a sudden group crisis may play a determining part in role emergence. However, groups often exhibit several tendencies that play a part in the role specializations. Although individuals may selectively resist or reinforce behaviors of other members for personal reasons, the vector of the group's reinforcement tends to support the behavior of each that is best for the entire group. When an individual does things that the others perceive as attempts to manipulate the group for that person's own personal satisfactions, they resist vigorously. After a time, group members seem to make some decisions as to the skill with which each functions in a given task, and they tend to reinforce fellow members in their areas of greatest competence.

To return to the list of functions, assume B is perceived by the other members to be the most competent in functions 1, 4, 5, 6, and 9. The star is B, who does almost everything well and better than anyone else in the group. However, she does not do everything. The LGD conditions her behavior into certain special channels. The members perceive these as being the most vital for the group; they then turn to the second- and third-best choices for the other important chores. In this situation, something analogous to the law of comparative costs in economics seems to be operating. For example, California soil can produce oranges for 15¢ apiece and corn for $1.00 a bushel, and South Dakota soil can produce oranges for $1 apiece and corn for $2.00 a bushel. According to this principle, it is to the advantage of each state to produce its best product and trade with the other even though California can produce both crops more efficiently than South Dakota. California should use its soil to raise oranges and trade oranges for the corn they need, rather than raise oranges and corn. Thus, although B is best at gathering information, the group allows her to specialize in other things and turns to the next best members, C and D, for the gathering of information. Member A, who has been the leader of a number of similar groups, finds himself at a disadvantage because of B's greater skills and does not emerge as leader of this group. Should the group contain very little talent for releasing tension, members might call on someone to do these things who has seldom played this role. A student may discover that although he is normally task-oriented, industrious, and serious, in one group he is the "life of the party."

Despite tendencies to structure the roles within a group to make maximum use of resources, there is considerable waste in the way most groups arrive at role structures, and sometimes they make mistakes. A person with ability to perform a certain function may be rejected because of his "style," and group members may assign the task to someone with a more pleasing style but with less competence. Group members have considerable difficulty describing what "style" involves. They report that there was "something" about the individual that they "did not like." Sometimes they focus on slight cues such as tics or mannerisms or facial expression or vocal inflection. Sometimes such things as verbalism, language usage, and sentence structure cause the group to reject a member's bid for certain functions.

Many role functions are assigned gratuitously during the course of group interactions. Sometimes a person is inadvertently qualified as an authority by another participant. A member may ask, "Who is the political science major?" Joe responds that he is, and another member says, "Well, I guess we know now who is the authority." The group begins to treat him as an authority, and he begins to act like one. Although Joe is a political science major, he may not be the member best equipped to do the job for the group; however, because he mentioned his political science major and because a member who was trying to break the tension asked who the political science major was, Joe assumed a certain task function. Other such chance occurrences in the early meetings can influence the way role clusters develop. Usually, if the groups develop sufficient cohesiveness and continue for a long enough time, they recognize their mistakes and reshuffle the roles.

FANTASY THEME ANALYSIS OF ROLES

One important reason for a fantasy theme to chain through a group is that it can reflect a common problem for the members. If the problem is one that is likely to arouse social tensions if the members attempt to discuss it openly, they may repress it, and it then tends to surface in symbolic form as a fantasy chain. Often, when a group is in the process of discovering its role structure and status arrangements, people come into conflict with one another or feel resentment and frustration because the group seems to be pushing them into roles they find unrewarding and unattractive. On occasion, the group members feel that they cannot teach a particularly inflexible member a suitable role because, despite all of their verbal and nonverbal resistance to the unwanted behavior, the individual continues to act in the same way. Many times group members find the problems of power, leadership, and authority particularly tension producing. They may feel one of the participants is too domineering, too bossy, and too pigheaded, and yet have difficulty confronting that person directly about the frustrating behavior.

Freud argued that individuals often repressed needs or problems that the conscious mind found embarrassing or painful and that these difficulties then tended to surface in distorted symbolic terms in the person's dreams. A trained person could thus use dream analysis to discover the repressed difficulty. Freud used the analogy of a country under heavy censorship so open discussion of problems was repressed. The people would, under such circumstances, express their criticism of the repressive regime and their political problems in the form of jokes, parables, and fables which could not be censored because their manifest content was not closely and clearly related to the realities of the situation; but, for someone who understood the context, the application to the immediate situation would be clear. In much the same way, a group may bring its difficulties concerning the emergence of suitable roles for its members to the surface in the form of a fantasy chain on a theme that has a double meaning. The overt meaning would relate to other people in other contexts, but the covert meaning would relate to the interpretation of the story by finding applications to the group's role problems.

One of the case studies at Minnesota was of a task force investigating curriculum changes in secondary education. All the members of the group were in their thirties and forties, and most were secondary school teachers or administrators. Very early in the group's life, a basic conflict over the role of leadership developed between two inflexible and aggressive males. The meetings often became debates between the two members over procedural matters. As a result of the bickering, the group's progress on the task was very slow, and the meetings dragged on for several hours each session. After several meetings, a new member joined the group and soon became aware of the basic conflict. Very tactfully the new member began to try to compromise differences and to give the group structure and direction. The remaining members began to support the new member's efforts at leadership, but the two antagonists continued to bicker and to monopolize the discussion, and the group remained at an impasse despite the fact that all the members were dedicated, hardworking, and conscientious.

One of the female members had been working particularly hard at collecting information and preparing materials for curriculum revision. In the course of discussing the problem, she began to dramatize the difficulty of getting innovation into a school system. She noted that it was "particularly true of new teachers going into a system where everything is cut and dried already, and no one wants to rock the boat."

The group began to chain into the drama of the difficulty of innovation. One member asked, "Does the system tend to just perpetuate itself?" and a bit later asked again, "Where does change come from then?" To which the woman who began the chain replied, "As people die off, leave, or move and new ones come in. Then as new administrators come in it's much easier. For example at Olson Junior High—they have administrators who are very flexible." The group grew more excited about the drama of the hopelessness of trying to get anything accepted by the typical secondary school administration, and the plight of a "new young teacher" who was "on the ball," but had a hard time. She was characterized as spending "more energy in fighting for what she knows is right than in teaching." The woman who began the chain then noted, "I've even had trouble introducing ideas I know have worked into a traditional speech program. . . . When I make a recommendation to the team teacher he feels defensive, as if I'm criticizing what he's done in the past." The chain continued for a few minutes longer and the woman finally said, "A teacher can't reach the administrator 'til she's allowed to know him honestly as a person . . . and not as someone who's supervising the system. Out of three administrators, there's only one I would feel confident to go confide in because he's personable, he's human . . . he's a person. The others are on cloud nine, and we see them only at faculty meetings." The fantasy was now cutting very close to the here-and-now problems of the group, and another member broke it off by saying, "Getting back to the paper now. . . ."

Clearly, the drama of the inflexible and unheeding school administrators versus the flexible and willing-to-listen principal was a drama with a double meaning, and the analogy of the school administrators to the administration of the group was a useful starting place to analyze the group's problems.

An observer, facilitator, or instructor can thus use fantasy theme analysis as a diagnostic tool to help the group bring to the surface the hidden agenda items relating to role emergence which may impede their progress. Group members may listen to the tapes of their meetings and discover the fantasy themes that relate to their problems as well. Not all fantasy themes that chain through a group will relate to role problems, of course, and one must always be careful not to overinterpret a group's fantasies.

STATUS AND ROLES

Status Assignment of Roles

Once roles have clearly emerged and stabilized, members arrange the roles in order of importance—the most important, the next most important, and so forth. An observer can arrange the roles in order of importance on the basis of certain behaviors exhibited by the group members. For example, group members tend to direct more talk to the people they consider important (playing an important role). The members in the more important roles tend to talk more to the whole group. The person in the most important role receives the most consideration from the others. Members of the group perceive this ordering of roles; and in groups with stable role structures, there is considerable consensus about the status of various roles. This is particularly true of the more important roles. *Status* is the importance of a role in the group. A status ladder organizes the roles that have emerged in order of their importance. Each group with stable roles has a "pecking" order.

The functions that the group will consider important depend to some extent on the kind of group. If the group clearly succeeds or fails, such as a basketball team that wins or loses, and if the individual's contribution to victory can be clearly measured, then the task specialist (highest scorer) may have high status. In organizations in which success or failure is not so easily measured, the best-liked person may be of higher status. In college discussion classes, the leader often holds the high-status role.

No common pattern of status describes groups of similar composition and functions. Some individuals may be so skillful that they are perceived as having higher status than another less skillful person whose role may often be more important. Sometimes, for example, a leader emerges because she is the best of the contenders, although the others are not too happy with her. If the best-liked person is extremely talented, he may have a higher place on the status ladder than his role implies.

Status and Need Gratification

The social esteem and material rewards that members receive are closely associated with their status. High-status positions are pleasant. The group makes a high-status person feel important and influential. They show her deference, listen to her, ask her advice, and often reward her with a greater share of the group's goods. She gets a bigger office, more secretaries, better furniture, more salary, a bigger car, and so forth. Even in communication class discussion groups, the high-status members receive considerable gratification of their social and esteem needs. One of the most powerful forces drawing people into groups is the attraction of high status.

Since the high-status positions in the group offer such substantial rewards there is always a considerable struggle for them. Indeed, primary tensions in newly formed groups result from the uncertainty about who will become the "important" people in the group. The resulting struggles generate a considerable portion of the secondary tensions that a group experiences.

GROUP STRUCTURE AND COHESIVENESS

As stated previously, when a role structure emerges in a leaderless group discussion, the cohesiveness of the group generally rises rather dramatically. There are, however, some exceptions to this general tendency. When people do not like the roles they receive, they find the group less attractive. They might not like their roles because they are of little importance and the others treat them like recruits in the rear rank. Of the roles in the hypothetical group, for example, member D, whose tasks include gathering information, doing routine chores, following orders carefully, and doing the job assigned, is the one most likely to feel this way.

When members of the group do not like the way someone performs the functions assigned — whether they were fooled by early behavior or had accidentally given that person an important role that he or she could not handle — they will depose the person from the position. Such reshuffling extracts a high toll on the group's cohesiveness. It creates secondary tension and upsets the role structure to the point where the group must examine not only the two changing roles but the other roles as well.

SUMMARY

For the purpose of examining the roles assumed by individual members in small groups, personality is defined as the field-invariant potential for behavior plus the field-variant conditions that actuate that potential. The actuated behavior results from the conditioning of the individual by the group.

A nonparticipating observer may describe the role a member has in a group in terms of what the person says and does as she or he interacts with the group. For the participants, however, the roles are often defined in terms of their expectations. When these expectations stabilize for all or most members of a group, the role structure has stabilized.

Each group has certain tasks that must be done if the group is to succeed. Each individual brings to the group native or acquired potentials to perform some of these functions. During the course of their early interactions, members try one and then another of these functions, and the group then reinforces or punishes the attempts. Gradually the reinforced behavior is learned by the members and they expect to perform these functions and be rewarded for doing so.

Some of the assignment of role functions seems to be gratuitous, yet there are two general tendencies within the dynamics of most groups: (1) the behavior perceived by the members as most beneficial to the entire group is reinforced, and (2) the behavior of each member is channeled into the functions that he or she performs most efficiently. Fantasy chains often provide a useful diagnostic tool to discover problems relating to role emergence.

With the assignment of roles, the group also awards status. The group rewards valuable roles with shows of deference and other social reinforcements. Most groups experience considerable struggle among at least some of the participants for the high-status positions.

General role stability usually results in a higher level of cohesiveness. However, if a number of members are disgruntled by their roles, they become inactive and actually reduce the cohesiveness of the group.

☞ Rules of Thumb

Practical Advice on How to Be a Good Group Member

Drawn from Chapter 7

- ☞ Remember that you cannot assign roles successfully ahead of the actual meeting.
- ☞ Remember that a person cannot single-handedly take on a role in a group.
- ☞ You work out your role jointly with the others in the group.
- ☞ You should clearly support or reject the efforts of others in order to encourage role emergence in your group.
- ☞ Be alert to the responses of others to your communication and take up those role functions on which you all agree.
- ☞ If you receive ambiguous responses when you try out various role functions, you should continue until you get a clear indication of rejection or support.
- ☞ Do not use a simple trait framework as a basis for stereotyping the others in the group.
- ☞ Do not oversimplify group roles by thinking of them in static terms according to several salient dimensions.
- ☞ Role stabilization is like a pattern in a children's top that changes until at peak speed the pattern stabilizes only to disintegrate again as the speed slows.
- ☞ If you have some standard opening moves that have worked in the past, go ahead and try them in new groups; but if the others reject them, move on to other role functions.
- ☞ Respond positively and clearly to the communication that you find in the best interests of the group.
- ☞ Your understanding of the general theory of role emergence will help you avoid some of the frustrating, wasteful effort often associated with the process.
- ☞ When conflict arises as roles emerge, keep a lookout for shared fantasies that can help group members analyze their problem.
- ☞ If you understand that there is no simple way to bypass the period of secondary tension and conflict while roles emerge, you should be able to better tolerate and deal with it.

QUESTIONS FOR STUDY

1. How does the personality-trait theory account for individual behavior?
2. How does the social-field theory of group roles account for individual behavior?
3. What is the difference between the field-variant and the field-invariant dimensions of personality?
4. What is meant by *role* in the small group?
5. What is the mechanism by which the group encourages role specialization among its members?
6. What is meant by *role emergence* in a leaderless group discussion?
7. What is the relationship between role stability and group cohesiveness? Why are they related?
8. How does the theoretical model of role emergence account for the field-variant portion of individual personality?
9. What is the basis on which the group assigns status to individual roles?
10. Why do members often come into conflict over roles?

EXERCISES

1. Form a leaderless group discussion with a specific task and objective. Tape-record the meetings. Keep a diary of your experiences in the group. Record your impressions of the role specialization, struggle, and stabilization. Listen to the tape recordings, and check your perceptions. Hold a group postmortem session in which you discuss one another's perceptions of the role structure. Isolate the group's fantasies, and see if they relate to the role emergence in the group.
2. Form a small task-oriented group with a specific task and objectives. Assign each member certain set role functions. One member may be asked to help release tension, another to initiate action, a third to control the channels of communication, a fourth to disagree and test ideas, and so forth. Tape-record the meetings. Hold a postmortem session in which you discuss the effect of assigning role functions on the development of the group structure.
3. Select a group that you have worked with for several months which has been characterized by considerable tension, conflict, and lack of productivity. How much of the group's difficulties can be accounted for by role struggles and lack of role stability? Map out a course of group therapy designed to deal with the role problems in the group.
4. Form a zero-history leaderless group discussion with a specific task and a clear goal. After each session, have all the members rate one another on one of the forms of the interpersonal ratings test found in Robert F. Bales, *Personality and Interpersonal Behavior* (New York: Holt, Rinehart and Winston, 1970, pp. 6, 12, 13). All members should also fill out one form as they estimate how the others will rate them. After a number of sessions, tabulate the results and

discover if members' perceptions of one another's positions in group space grow more compatible as the group continues.

5. Read the descriptions of the role types and value directions in Bales above, and see how they agree with the members' anecdotal reports of their perceptions of the roles in the group.

REFERENCES AND SUGGESTED READINGS

The basic model describing group process as it relates to the emergence of roles is drawn largely from the results of the Minnesota studies. These results are in substantial agreement with the discoveries of other investigators of small groups. The Minnesota studies provide evidence for a general theory of role emergence, since they investigated many groups composed of students enrolled in small group communication classes as well as those in groups functioning in nonclass contexts. Bales's framework of analysis of position in group space and interpersonal rating systems are found in:

Bales, Robert F. *Personality and Interpersonal Behavior.* New York: Holt, Rinehart and Winston, 1970.

Bales, Robert F., and Stephen P. Cohen. *SYMLOG: A System for the Multiple Level Observation of Groups.* New York: Free Press, 1979.

For studies of personality and the relationship of the field-variant and field-invariant behaviors of individuals in small groups, see:

Alderton, Steven M. "Locus of Control-Based Argumentation as a Predictor of Group Polarization," *Communication Quarterly,* **30** (1982), 381–387.

Andrews, Patricia Hayes. "Ego Involvement, Self-Monitoring, and Conformity in Small Groups: A Communicative Analysis," *Central States Speech Journal,* **36** (1985), 51–61.

Borg, Walter. "Prediction of Small Group Role Behavior from Personality Variables," *Journal of Abnormal and Social Psychology,* **60** (1960), 112–116.

Gruenfeld, Leopold W., and Thung-Rung Lin. "Social Behavior of Field Independents and Dependents in an Organic Group," *Human Relations,* **37** (1984), 721–741.

Mann, Richard D. "A Review of the Relationships Between Personality and Performance in Small Groups," *Psychological Bulletin,* **56** (1959), 241–270.

For studies relating to the process of role emergence, see:

Baker, Paul Morgan. "The Division of Labor: Interdependence, Isolation, and Cohesion in Small Groups," *Small Group Behavior,* **12** (1981), 93–106.

Goetsch, Gerald G., and David D. McFarland. "Models of the Distribution of Acts in Small Discussion Groups," *Social Psychology Quarterly,* **43** (1980), 173–183.

Rees, C. Roger, and Mady W. Segal. "Role Differentiation in Groups: The Relationship Between Instrumental and Expressive Leadership," *Small Group Behavior,* **15** (1984), 109–123.

Tuckman, Bruce W. "Developmental Sequence in Small Groups," *Psychological Bulletin,* **63** (1965), 384–399.

See also:

Cloyd, Jerry. "Patterns of Role Behavior in Informal Interaction, *Sociometry,* **27** (1964), 160–173.

Gouran, Dennis S., Randy Y. Hirokawa, and Amy E. Martz. "A Critical Analysis of Factors Related to Decisional Processes Involved in the *Challenger* Disaster," *Central States Speech Journal,* **37** (1986), 119–135.

Guetzkow, Harold. "Differential of Roles in Task-Oriented Groups." In Dorwin Cartwright and Alvin Zander, eds., *Group Dynamics: Research and Theory.* New York: Harper & Row, 1960, pp. 683–704.

Haiman, Franklyn S. "The Specialization of Roles and Functions in a Group," *Quarterly Journal of Speech,* **43** (1957), 165–174.

Chapter
8

Norms

*I*f the members of a leaderless group discussion (LGD) work together for several weeks, they begin to share expectations about social interaction, values, styles of manner and expression, and a group tradition with its associated rituals and myths. These characteristics will be similar to those of other LGDs in similar environments, but the details of behavior and language will usually be unique to that group. These unique details comprise a group's subculture, which, in addition to shared fantasies, will include group norms.

THE DEVELOPMENT OF GROUP NORMS

A *norm* is a shared expectation of right action that binds members of a group and results in guiding and regulating their behavior. A stable role structure is a complex pattern of differentiating norms that are binding on each member and regulate that person's behavior according to her or his assigned role; that is, each person is expected to specialize and thus exhibit a somewhat unique set of behaviors during the course of group interactions. Shared behaviors comprise another important set of norms. For example, in some groups all members may express themselves in blunt, crude, direct language, regardless of their roles.

In Chapter 7 the basic model for role emergence furnished an explanation for the differentiating norms and how they developed. The concern here is to describe and explain the way shared norms develop as a group discovers, agrees on, and teaches members its subculture.

The Shakedown Cruise

Before a ship or an aircraft is put into regular service, the officers and crew test it under operating conditions in order to become acquainted with the craft and with one another. Whenever a task-oriented small group begins its work, it must undergo a similar testing under operating conditions. The members must become familiar with the group's purposes, resources, and personnel. Also, when the role structure is disrupted in established organizations, members must reorient themselves in order to stabilize roles and norms. During this preliminary period of testing, the group develops norms related to its task of dealing with the external environment. By interacting with its environment, the group will learn if its control measures (norms) are successful; the group may need to modify its norms in order to deal more successfully with the environment. Norms such as these are clearly related to statements of fact. Observations serve to correct faulty norms; thus, if the group is systematically misled, it will learn about its mistake directly—the environment will punish the group.

Another set of norms relates primarily to the social interactions among the members. This behavior is often idiosyncratic and tied to the external environment by tenuous connections, if at all. The participants may adopt a low-key or high-pressure style of work. They may function in a continual atmosphere of crisis and disorder, or they may work quietly and compulsively. They may adopt a common mode of dress or strive for as much individuality as possible. While conforming to norms developed during their social interaction, members may exhibit unusual and bizarre behavior, because these norms are largely divorced from external feedback. The same freedom to develop a similar diversity of norms relating to the task does not exist. Norms grounded largely in task requirements are limited to those that prove successful as the group interacts with the environment.

Several features of the first few meetings are important in forming the context in which normative behavior develops. First, the primary tensions in the shakedown period often are a factor. Behavior typical of people experiencing primary tension may become the norm if these tensions are not released early. In the Minnesota studies, several groups adopted a style of politeness, apathy, boredom, and sighing. The case study used to exemplify primary tension in Chapter 6, for example, continued to exhibit the same style for the rest of its meetings. Participants slouched in their chairs; they spoke softly, seemed apathetic; when they spoke they were polite, but not involved with the group or the topic.

Second, the primary tensions typical of first meetings emphasize the sensitivity of people to social interactions. During this period, participants are alert to the social implications of all interactions, even those that are ostensibly task-related. Comments that are perceived as personal slights are more impressive in this period. Members may report subsequently that another person made a cutting comment in the first meeting; they may indicate that they have forgotten what it was, but that they still resent it. At this point in a group's development, antagonisms may develop that establish the tone for a long period.

When a person enters the delicate social field of the first meetings with blunt statements and flat assertions, the behavior often creates norms that remain part of the group's culture. One group in the Minnesota studies developed a style that was extremely noisy and unruly. Often two or three people would talk at the same time, each trying to override the others. It was not unusual for everybody to be talking at once. There were few pauses in the meetings, and people stood up, pounded on the tables, and paced the floor. During the first meeting, one member ignored the primary tension by leaping into a consideration of the problem at hand. He talked at length, loudly and aggressively. Soon others were imitating his manner. Early in the second meeting, members were discussing the goals of American foreign policy when a key exchange took place that set the norm for subsequent discussion.

MEMBER A: Just how might the United States bolster . . . ?
MEMBER B: In what ways . . .
MEMBER A: In what ways . . .
MEMBER B: Because we're going to come up with several ways when I'm finished ramming them through the committee . . .

[*The primary tension is still quite high, and the group does not react to member B's amazing declaration immediately. Rather, participants continue on as though nothing unusual has been said.*]

MEMBER C: We're going to have many ways after . . .
MEMBER D: So this is the goal we set upon as our group: In what ways can we strengthen U.S. prestige around the world?
MEMBER A: Uh-huh.
MEMBER B: And by prestige . . .
MEMBER D: And by prestige we mean the influence and respect . . .
MEMBER B: Uh-huh . . .

[*The tension is building up as the group absorbs the implications of member B's declaration of intent to "ram the program through the committee."*]

MEMBER D: [*self-consciously and jokingly*] That is defining of a term.
MEMBER A: OK.

[*The group now does a collective double take and begins to react vigorously to member B.*]

MEMBER E: Well, I just put down a couple of goals myself here . . .
MEMBER B: Uh-huh.
MEMBER D: I think we all did as a matter of fact . . .

MEMBER E: And ah . . .
MEMBER B: We all . . . we all . . .

[*Member B is interrupted by both members D and E, who try to override him. He does not yield the floor, and all three speak at once.*]

In the subsequent battle to prevent the aggressive member from ramming his plan through the committee, the norm of active, unruly participation was firmly established.

Another person immediately emerged as a central participant in one case by glibly attacking the other members' value systems. He felt college was a waste of time. He was primarily interested in gambling and in having a good time. He had already dropped out of school several times for periods of several years. In the early meetings, whenever others suggested that more information was needed to make a wise decision, this member systematically ridiculed the idea. The group had selected a problem relating to gambling, and he indicated by word and manner that he knew all there was to know about the subject. Soon the group members adopted his attitude toward work. They established a cynical "inside dopester" style of belittling all published information and confined themselves to exchanging ignorances, as though they had privileged information unavailable in print. Associated with this no-work norm was another relating to a characteristic mode of expression. Since the group had little factual information and little authoritative opinion or advice, the discourse was largely filled with fantasy themes composed of figurative analogies and hypothetical examples. One person adopted the role of a hypothetical evangelist called the Reverend Ham and then delivered long satirical diatribes against the sinfulness of gambling. As long as these norms remained characteristic of the group, it continued to be unproductive.

The third way in which normative behavior develops is through traumatic experiences. In one case study, a member emerged as leader during the early meetings by exhibiting a congenial discussion-moderator technique and by doing extensive preparation for the project. He prepared voluminous notes and was the most informed member. After his leadership was established, one of the participants was absent for several meetings. During his absence, the other participants began to perceive their leader as a soft-sell manipulator. When the absentee returned, he began to challenge the leader's directives. The leader was caught off guard and off balance. He responded with the behavior that had resulted in his originally emerging as leader. He began to refer to his research notes. The challenger then got up and walked around the table to the leader's side. He picked up the sheaf of papers and asked the other members to look at all that research. "Isn't it ridiculous?" he asked. The others agreed and laughed and reinforced the challenge. For the next 15 or 20 minutes, the challenger continued to ridicule the leader. The leader tried to reply with factual information, but the challenger simply ridiculed "research" as belittling the intelligence of the others and as unnecessary. After some minutes, the leader was deposed, and he sat quietly for the rest of the meeting. From then on, no one indicated in any way that he or she had done any "research." This interchange was sufficient to set the norm that no member would use the claim of gathering information as a means of establishing status.

The Basic Model

Roles can be viewed as a special kind of norm. The group develops its norms and roles by the same process. The basic model described in Chapter 6 needs only slight modification to account for the way an LGD develops norms. One important norm concerns the way the group deals with the primary tensions of its early meetings. If members do not release the primary tensions, the climate common to such tensions may be incorporated as normative behavior. However, if several people begin to break the primary tensions and a majority begins to reinforce this behavior, a norm will gradually be established. Often the person who successfully breaks the tension will set another norm. People are emotionally involved in the problem posed by primary tensions. When a certain type of tension release is used successfully, the group tends to adopt that style as a norm. For example, if primary tensions are released by shows of sarcasm and personal insult, the participants develop a norm of treating one another in a friendly, but sarcastic way. Nicknames may be insulting — *Meathead, Stupid, Fatty, Lamebrain* — and even shows of solidarity, indicating affection or raising another's status, may be accomplished with sarcasm. If people release their original tension by gossip, they may adopt a norm of gossipy small talk and interlace their work meetings with such digressions.

Norms of this sort are established simply by behavior that indicates support for one way of proceeding. Since most people exhibit primary tensions at the beginning of their first meeting, the earmarks of primary tension will become a tentative norm. It is not a comfortable norm, however; people do not like such a social climate. They search to release the tension. Someone steps forward to do so. At first, she is unsuccessful. She may try again. If she is again unsuccessful and does not try a third time, the norm of apathy may be established. If she tries again and gains one supporter, she will be encouraged to continue. If one after another joins in, the rest will soon follow. In this case, the dynamics of the small group are illuminated by the pressure for conformity exhibited by large crowds. If a few people in an audience rise at a certain point in the meeting and no one else does, they soon sit down again. However, if they are joined by a few more people, and then more, until a third or more of the audience is rising or already standing, a larger number of people will stand. When the majority are on their feet, a flurry of people will rise. The few remaining seated will feel pressure to stand, simply because everyone else is standing. The pressure for conformity is not as powerful in the intimate setting of the small group, but the same process accounts for the development of some norms.

Some social norms originate with the mannerisms of influential people. This is illustrated by the way in which the kind of joking and humor in a group is influenced by the individual playing the role of tension releaser. Often norms relating to formality or informality of dress, behavior, or language develop because of the styles of behavior exhibited by central people. For example, every group makes some decisions about the right and wrong ways to express emotions, strong attitudes, and opinions. At some point in the early proceedings, a participant may curse. He may say, "Personally, I say to hell with it." If the discussion proceeds with no one else cursing, this member may insert a "goddamn" in his next comment. If another and then a third person curse, their example and influence could set the norm.

A number of groups discussed questions relating to the population explosion and birth control. Each set norms to deal with sensitive areas related to these topics. One group discovered early in its first meeting that its members included Protestants, Catholics, and Jews. This group quickly established a norm of not talking about the moral issues relating to birth control. Each group had to decide how to talk about birth control techniques and the reproductive system. Some groups adopted norms that included very abstract and euphemistic linguistic conventions. Some adopted norms that substituted vague references for explicit language. They used phrases like, "you know," "things like that," and "problems of that sort." One group developed the norm of using explicit clinical language to discuss the reproductive process and contraceptive devices. No one in the group, male or female, found this norm embarrassing. However, when the group presented a symposium discussion to the class, the first speaker continued to use this language norm, which *was not the norm* of the class. As a result, everyone was embarrassed.

Groups may develop norms relating to modes of dress or hairstyle. They may develop norms relating to ethical conduct—that is, right and wrong behavior *within the group.* Of course, highly cohesive organizations may determine the values of its members when they interact in other, less cohesive groups.

Goals

Every task-oriented group has some ostensible goal or goals, which are often clearly indicated. These may be imposed by the external environment. In organizational structure, upper management may set production goals for a unit of workers. The group may discuss and set its own goals. These ostensible goals can become norms to guide behavior. Such norms often increase cohesiveness; those working gain a sense of purpose from a clear and realizable goal. If they know what is required for success, they can work for it and recognize when they have succeeded. Reaching goals contributes to the satisfaction of the individuals; it is tangible evidence of the excellence of the organization. The members can say that the group exceeded the production goal or collected more money for charity than required. The cohesive force of a clear goal is often employed to unify volunteer organizations in charitable fund-raising campaigns. Professional fund raisers commonly use the technique of assigning an overall goal clearly expressed in terms of money and time. They may divide an overall goal into small segments and assign part of the total to a series of subgroups. Clear goals relating to production are frequently established in industry. Each unit has a production goal, and each subunit may have an optimum daily or weekly output as a goal.

The group may have a set of ostensible goals that are not norms for behavior. In that case, the group has hidden goals that govern the members' behavior. Such disparity is more likely to exist when the goals are imposed from outside the group. Industrial psychologists studying production schedules occasionally discover units in which management's attempts to increase production always fail. In these groups, the norms for production are set, not by the ostensible goals furnished by upper management, but by the work group itself. Cohesive units can enforce their own norms so effectively that the organization's incentive system cannot shake the worker's tendency to conform to them. Similar findings emerge from the study of the classroom, in which highly cohesive cliques establish norms of classroom behavior that are more effective than those set by the teacher.

PRESSURES FOR CONFORMITY

The Pressure of Group Action

One of the most definite conclusions of small group research is that groups exert great pressures on their members to conform to the group norms. Even perceptions of such phenomena as an illusion of moving light or the comparative lengths of lines may be distorted by social pressure. The discovery that everybody else is doing something puts powerful social pressure to follow suit on the one who is not doing it. The fact that everyone is doing something with a certain style often causes the recruit to do the same thing with the same style. When a pedestrian finds a group in which all are shading their eyes and peering into the sky, he or she will be under strong pressure to do likewise. The tendency of crowds to cause members to stand, cheer, or sing *when everybody is doing it* is a common occurrence.

Once a norm emerges and stabilizes during the course of the shakedown experience, people will tend to conform to it simply because most do so. If the norm is established that participants will not swear, even the person who usually swears will not do so in the group. New members adopt the norms almost subconsciously simply because of the pressure of being in a group in which everyone else is acting and talking in a certain way, *even though the veterans make no conscious effort to change the recruit's behavior.*

The Pressure of Cohesiveness

A group with a high level of cohesiveness exerts greater pressure on its personnel to conform than one with only a low level of attractiveness. People who find the group attractive are willing to work harder and change their behavior to become and remain members. They also find that participating in the group's normative behavior publicly identifies their membership and their commitment to the group. Some norms result in ritualistic behavior which observers may find silly or foolish, although participants may take the behavior very seriously because it serves to structure the cohesiveness of the organization. Idiosyncratic norms that developed accidentally because of the participants' unique experiences during the shakedown cruise often continue because they serve such ritualistic functions.

Members of a highly cohesive group are sensitive to failure to act in accordance with norms. They see deviant behavior as a threat to the cohesiveness of the organization and act to make everyone conform. Members of groups with little cohesiveness find deviant behavior much less disturbing because they do not care very much about its threat to the group's welfare.

Overt Pressure for Conformity

People who perceive deviant behavior as a threat to the collective good often take steps to reduce the danger. They may delay action, hoping that the model of all the others doing the right thing will inspire the nonconformist to change. Or they may use nonverbal cues to indicate that the behavior is not appropriate. If these tactics do not work, they may talk among themselves about the disturbing activities. They will begin to direct more communication to the nonconformist. The preliminary communication is often light and humorous. They make genial fun of the member because of his or her nonconformity. The man who grows a beard when the norm is for the shaven look will be kidded about forgetting to shave. Humor in all forms can serve as a corrective mechanism. It tells the deviating member that the behavior does not have group approval in a way that allows a laugh to release the tension.

If the nonconformist does not change, the others will increase their communication. The genial kidding will become a more cutting use of satire or ridicule. The mood changes from laughing *with* the offender about his or her foibles to laughing *at* the offender as being ridiculous, not one of them, different. If the nonconformist remains adamant, the communication pressure increases and changes to serious persuasive efforts. The atmosphere changes from kidding and ridicule to complete seriousness. Is the nonconformist going to be one of them or not? The deviant behavior is damaging to the entire group. All sorts of arguments, reasonable and unreasonable, may be directed to the "outsider," depending on the level of cohesiveness and the importance of the norm in the group's hierarchy of values.

An example of how others begin to pressure a person to conform is provided by an excerpt from the diary of one subject included in the Minnesota studies:

> At the start of our meeting we decided each member should report his findings. Unfortunately, the first person "didn't find time to look up the subject." The group laughed at him and told him he had better be prepared next time. However, you could tell they were a bit concerned and I thought the group lost some of its cohesiveness then.

If the nonconformists do not finally conform to group expectations, the others will reject them and isolate them from the group. Even if they continue to attend the work sessions, they will be ignored and frozen out. This drastic step tends to occur only when the others perceive that the behavior cannot be changed. As long as they think that the deviant member will change, they will try to bring the nonconformist into line.

Although the general tendency is for the group members to communicate their concern about nonconformity in the manner indicated above, there is some research evidence that there is a difference in the way members communicate with a deviant member that depends upon the individual's status in the group. High-status members tend to be allowed more freedom to deviate than low-status members. It is as though the high-status members have some freedom-to-deviate credit stored up and can break group norms for a while without receiving the corrective communication. Perhaps the group's need for some flexibility in order to adapt to changing situations accounts for this tendency toward lenience for high-status nonconformity. Still, if a high-status member continues to break norms, that individual will lose status and the corrective communication will come into play.

Competing Norms

When people are members of several groups and discover contradictory norms, they will have conflicting loyalties. If they conform to the norms of group A and group B discovers what they have done, they will be subjected to overt pressures. If the high school clique adheres to a certain style of haircut and a boy's family follows a different norm, he will have difficulty with his family or with his friends at school. Many norms, of course, can be adopted and shed more easily than clothing and certainly are less obvious than a haircut. A high school student could easily change her language, depending on whether she was at home or with her high school crowd. She might do the same with her eating, smoking, and drinking habits. However, the conflicting demands of highly cohesive groups cause conflict within such individuals. They often try to resolve the conflict by adopting one norm consistently. When this happens, they will adopt the norms of the more attractive of the two groups.

CONFORMITY, CREATIVITY, AND INDIVIDUALISM

A common misconception is that conformity to norms must necessarily stifle individual identity or creativity. To be sure, an organization may require every person to think alike. The participants may have common scapegoats, prejudices, and attitudes and may enforce such conformity. Some movements require this unity of purpose in order to be effective. If a crusade requires a totally mobilized fighting power, immediate, unquestioning compliance with orders is required.

Many organizations, however, require the opposite set of norms for efficient functioning. They may expect participants to be creative and individualistic. A graduate student in art at the University of Minnesota developed a modification of a standard test to measure meaning to give to a group composed entirely of abstract painters. The subjects resisted the notion of the test because it implied standardization, and after they finally agreed to it, each attempted to respond in a way that was as unique as possible. This group demanded that everyone respond in a new and unique way to every stimulus. Triteness was perceived as deviant behavior.

Groups develop their customs by repeating them. In many respects, the norms of a group function like the habits of an individual. They provide a guide and a sanction for behavior. Thus, the members' attention and energy can be focused on other matters. Norms provide a stable social environment and reduce the shock of interacting with other people. Just as an individual's habits may be good or bad for that person, so a group's culture can be facilitating or crippling in terms of its goals and the satisfactions of its members. When the participants perceive norms as damaging, they attempt to change them.

ESTABLISHED GROUPS IN THE PROCESS OF CHANGE

If the external environment suddenly creates unusual pressures for the group, the established culture may prove inadequate. The role structure may crumble, and the basic model of the LGD will be in evidence as roles are reshuffled. In this process, some members may begin to act in ways contrary to the established norms. If they gain support from others who also adopt the *new* ways, the old norm may be replaced with the new one.

New members of an organization may resist certain norms and substitute other behaviors. If a sufficient number of old members are dissatisfied with the original norm, they may adopt the new way of doing things. Even without a change in membership, people may decide that certain norms are undesirable and adopt new ones. If others begin to follow their behavior, the group may change its norm. If high-status and highly esteemed people change behavior, the group often adopts a new norm.

Some norms emerge so accidentally that they are unrelated to the task and unsatisfactory in dealing with the environment. The discussants who adopted a norm of rejecting evidence were attacked when they presented a panel discussion to the class. Their pleas that there was no sound evidence available on the subject did not convince their audience, and their program was a failure. Norms have considerable inertia. The group tends to continue a pattern of behavior after the conditions that established the norms have disappeared. A role struggle or crisis may have been resolved for weeks, but the group may still follow a norm established during that crisis. Such norms hinder effectiveness and cohesiveness. Spontaneous corrective action may not develop. Dissatisfied participants may try conscious and direct orientation, evaluation, and control of the group's style. Norms, like habits, can be identified, evaluated, and changed consciously. On occasion, a task-oriented group is so preoccupied with its work that it ignores its role structure and style. It continues to use nonfunctional norms simply because it does not pause to ask whether or not they are useful.

The core of much work in T-groups, sensitivity training, and group dynamics is the discussion of roles and norms. Frequently, a discussion will expose matters that have hindered performance. The intent and interpretation of communication are often different. Discussion will reveal that first impressions were erroneous. Comments made during the early stages that were perceived as attempts to lower status can be put into proper perspective. Often, inadvertent norms develop that can be changed simply by having everyone talk about them.

Some cases included in the Minnesota studies conducted a series of discussions on their own group after it had completed several tasks in a period of six weeks. In one group of three men and two women, the men were surprised to discover that they had ignored the suggestions and comments of the women. When they replayed the tapes from the first meetings, they found evidence of such response. One woman responded to being ignored by withdrawal, the other by joking and ridicule. When the men discovered this norm, they immediately and consciously changed their behavior. They listened carefully to what the women said, and if they fell into the old norm, they were reminded. This one modification did much to increase the participation of the two women and to improve the group's cohesiveness.

A student of group methods should recognize the importance of talking about group roles and norms in improving the operations of a group. One must remember, however, that indiscriminate use of such self-evaluative sessions can create more tensions and problems for the group than it dissipates. Some people may enjoy postmortems on social relations and try to work out their own neuroses through them. The difference between a healthy discussion of ways to improve a task-oriented group and the use of the task-oriented group for a therapy session is not always clear. When evaluation sessions become an excuse for gossiping or cattiness about other individuals, they disrupt cohesiveness.

If certain procedural norms have become troublesome or the role structure seems too unstable, the participants should plan to discuss these matters. The group must establish the norm that what is said about roles and norms is honest and dedicated to the good of all. These sessions should emphasize the perspective that the *group* is somewhat responsible for the role behavior of its members. The discussion should center around what the *group* can do. Blame, in most cases, should be placed on the group. If the organization adopts a norm of scapegoating individuals for its problems, the evaluation sessions are less likely to prove helpful. Several people may point to a participant and say, "You are the one who is causing all the trouble. You have been domineering, inflexible, and impossible. If you would just be quiet, we might accomplish something." If blamed in this way, the scapegoat is very likely to fight back in kind, and a new, more destructive norm may be established.

SUMMARY

A norm is a shared expectation of appropriate behavior. Norms are binding on the members of the group. A stable role structure is the result of a complex set of norms that differentiate among the behaviors of the participants. The group also develops other norms — for example, shared behavior norms, procedural norms, and the social norms evolving from the interaction among group members.

The very existence of a group of people exerts some pressure for conformity. If a majority begins to behave in a certain way, this common behavior exerts pressure on the rest to follow. In addition, participants exert some overt pressure on deviants. This pressure consists of additional communication addressed to the nonconformist, until the group decides that he or she cannot be changed. At this point, members typically close ranks and isolate the nonconformist from the group.

The subculture of a small task-oriented group results from a long and complicated process of acculturation. It includes the role structure, the traditions and rituals, and the common norms developed during the group's history. However, *the group employs the same basic process to create its norms that it used to allow roles to emerge.*

Norms may cripple the group's task efficiency and social dimension. The group may take corrective action spontaneously or may place the problem of its normative behavior on an agenda for direct consideration.

 Rules of Thumb

Practical Advice on How to be a Good Group Member

Drawn from Chapter 8

> ☞ Be alert during the opening sessions of your group for emerging norms, and support those that promise to be productive.

☞ During the opening sessions of your group, try to block the emergence of norms that would be unproductive.

☞ Break primary tension early, before it becomes set in the form of group norms.

☞ Be alert to the social implications of ostensibly task-related comments in the first meetings of a group.

☞ Be careful not to make flat assertions and blunt, inflexible statements during early periods of high primary tension.

☞ Do not assume that the communication norms of your group will transfer to other groups and audiences.

☞ Aid your group in developing clear goals that all members can share.

☞ Encourage the group to have an overall goal that is clearly expressed.

☞ Encourage the group to divide the overall goal into subgoals and help make these smaller goals clear to all.

☞ When the group reaches a goal, remind the members of their success and comment on the importance of the event.

☞ Help your group develop ways to change norms when they are no longer useful.

☞ If you feel a norm needs changing, urge the others to put the topic on the agenda and to discuss the change directly.

☞ Make sure that your discussions of group norms do not become excuses for gossiping in general or scapegoating others in particular.

☞ Help your group develop a norm that what is said in evaluation of the group's socioemotional dimension is honest and dedicated to the good of all.

QUESTIONS FOR STUDY

1. What elements in the early meetings of a new group affect the development of normative behavior?
2. What is the relationship between pressures for conformity within a group and the development of group norms?
3. What is the relationship between group norms and group goals?
4. What is the relationship between group goals and group cohesiveness?
5. What mechanisms do groups use to make members conform to group norms?
6. How might conformity to group norms encourage individual creativity?
7. Under what conditions might group norms continue even though their usefulness is at an end?
8. How might a group change its norms?

EXERCISES

1. Do a case study of one of your class discussion groups. Describe the norms that developed and account for their emergence.

2. Select a group that you have been working with for several months and analyze its task behavior. Are the work norms productive and realistic in the group's present circumstances? Are there better norms that could be adopted? How might you initiate change in the group's work norms?

3. Select a group that you have been working with for several months and analyze its social norms. Are these norms conducive to a socially rewarding group environment? Are there better norms that could be developed? How might you initiate change in the group's social norms?

REFERENCES AND SUGGESTED READINGS

For studies relating to norm emergence, see:

Bettenhausen, Kenneth, and J. Keith Murnighan. "The Emergence of Norms in Competitive Decision-Making Groups," *Administrative Science Quarterly*, **30** (1985), 350–372.

Chalofsky, Neal, and Ralph Bates. "Using Group Process Techniques to Increase Task Force Effectiveness: A Case Study," *Journal for Specialists in Group Work*, **9** (1984), 93–98.

Spich, Robert S., and Kenneth Keleman. "Explicit Norm Structuring Process: A Strategy for Increasing Task Group Effectiveness," *Group and Organization Studies*, **10** (1985), 37–59.

For studies of conformity and the operation of norms, see:

Festinger, Leon, Stanley Schachter, and Kurt Back. "Operation of Group Standards." In Dorwin Cartwright and Alvin Zander, eds., *Group Dynamics: Research and Theory*. 3rd ed. New York: Harper & Row, 1968, pp. 152–164.

Insko, Chester A., et al. "Conformity and Group Size: The Concern with Being Right and the Concern with Being Liked," *Personality and Social Psychology Bulletin*, **11** (1985), 41–50.

Tesser, Abraham, Jennifer Campbell, and Susan Mickler. "The Role of Social Pressure, Attention to the Stimulus, and Self-Doubt in Conformity," *European Journal of Social Psychology*, **13** (1983), 217–233.

For studies of deviance from norms, see:

Katz, Gray M. "Previous Conformity, Status, and the Rejection of the Deviant," *Small Group Behavior*, **13** (1982), 403–414.

Miller, Charles E., and Patricia Doede Anderson. "Group Decision Rules and the Rejection of Deviates," *Social Psychology Quarterly*, **42** (1979), 354–363.

Chapter
9

Leadership

Of all the roles that emerge in a task-oriented group, none has fascinated the philosophers, novelists, and social scientists more than the top position. The most influential role has been the subject of much fiction, drama, poetry, and conjecture; and, lately, it has been the concern of many systematic empirical investigations.

People discussing this role usually refer to it as that of the *leader*. Citizens of the United States have a preoccupation with and a cultural ambivalence toward leadership. If a member of a class discussion group suggests that another would be a good leader, the typical response of the one suggested is "Oh, no! Not me. Someone else could do a better job." Despite such protestation, most members of many groups want to be the leader. In the Minnesota studies, Geier* interviewed 80 students who participated in 16 discussion groups. All but two students reported that they would like to be the leader. One student acted as though she were disinterested in leading, but the other was actually very much in contention for leadership. This study was done in an academic setting in which subjects might be more likely to be interested in leadership. However, our case studies of other groups indicate the desire for leadership is quite widespread.

On the one hand, our democratic traditions suggest that all people are created equal, and that nobody is better than anybody else. The whole mystique of a classless society rejects the phenomenon of status.

---

*See the Appendix for the titles of theses and articles by John Geier, Calvin Mortensen, Jerie McArthur Pratt, Debora Baker, Charles Larson, and other contributors to the Minnesota studies.

In the popular culture of this country, there is a strong cult of the "common person," and some rancor against the elite. Candidates for public office often make a fetish of identifying themselves with common activities, goals, and aspirations. Experts in propaganda analysis give this device special consideration under "just plain folks" and "common ground" appeals. In this tradition, the candidate does not seek the office for fear of appearing immodest. Only an egotist would publicly assert that she or he is better than other people. Instead, candidates allow the job of leadership to seek them, and if they are called, they will humbly do their best to live up to the high responsibility and great challenge.

On the other hand, our culture inherited from the rugged individualism of the past a strong tradition of driving for the top. The status positions at the top are the symbols of success. Young people today are expected to be a success. They are educated for leadership and encouraged to become chief executive officers. Activities ranging from joining the Scouts to delivering newspapers are supposed to prepare young people for leadership. In turn, our society gives rewards to leaders. In view of this ambivalence, the American preoccupation with the top role in a group is to be expected.

A FRAME OF REFERENCE

The Trait Approach

Among the early explanations of leadership was one that attributed it to divine inspiration. God, or the gods, selected a man and guided him to leadership. He led a charmed life and was unlike ordinary mortals. It was futile to challenge his lead, since he was the chosen one of God. He had supernatural sanctions and was thus predestined for greatness. The tradition of supernatural inspiration culminated in Western Europe in the divine right of kings. The king, according to this idea, held his throne directly from God. This idea of leadership fell into disrepute, but the *form of the argument* remained; only the content changed.

A leader like Napoleon was different from others. He led a charmed life because he was possessed of some inner quality. Goethe called this the *daemonic* and thought of it as a mystical, inexplicable power. To this day, some political scientists use the concept of *charisma* to explain the power of some political leaders. Charisma is a certain magic power to capture the popular enthusiasm.

One branch of early experimental psychology in this country modified the idea that leadership was inherent. These psychologists were preoccupied with measuring personality traits by means of psychological testing procedures. They assumed that an adequate battery of psychological tests could identify the cluster of personality traits associated with leadership and thus explain it.

Investigators studied the relationship between physical factors such as height and weight and leadership. They correlated intelligence and personality test scores with formal leadership. These investigations were synthesized in the 1940s, but the results were inconclusive. Many critics evaluated the progress of this line of research at that time and concluded that the results were disappointing. Since then, the notion that some individuals have a certain amount of leadership that will cause them to emerge as the top person in any group has been rejected in most literature on the subject.

The trait approach simply reflects the viewpoint of those who hoped to study individual personality by examining personality traits as separate from the social field surrounding a person. Leadership proved too complicated a phenomenon to be explained in this fashion. Yet the fact remains that certain people do become "stars" in almost all the groups they join. Although it is not the complete explanation, the trait approach does account for some everyday experience.

The Styles-of-Leadership Approach

When the trait analysis of leadership proved unsatisfactory, several other perspectives generated considerable research. One of the most important was that kinds of leadership could be distinguished and correlated with evaluations of excellence. The basic assumption was that there was an ideal type or style of leadership. In this view, excellence resided not in the individual, but rather in an ideal procedure that could be learned. An important study by Lippitt and White distinguished among three kinds of leadership. They named the three leadership styles *authoritarian, democratic,* and *laissez faire.* In the 1950s, various investigators and theorists used different labels in the same enterprise. They compared autocratic with democratic leadership, group-centered with leader-centered leadership, production-oriented management with employee-oriented management. Some theorists distinguished between leaderless and leadershipless groups. A school of industrial psychologists and management experts developed an approach to *participative management* which was essentially the same as democratic management. The first results indicated a clear superiority of the democratic style of leadership. Occasionally, studies revealed that other styles of leadership created productive, cohesive groups. Such cases were explained away by saying that even better results would be obtained in the same situation with democratic leadership.

Nonetheless, in some kinds of group activity the democratic style was inappropriate. The quarterback on the football field was not democratic, nor was the sergeant in a fire fight. Clearly, the external environment and the purposes of the group played a part in evaluating leadership styles.

Questioning what style of leadership is best is a more sophisticated approach than asking what qualities in individuals make them leaders. Research into the styles of leadership was conducted by observing groups in action. Investigators went into factories, organizations, and laboratories and learned a good deal about groups and leadership. They developed the idea that if excellence in leadership resided not in a person but in a way of leading, then the style could be taught. Leaders are not born, but trained. Students could learn a *style* of leadership by participating in groups rather than by developing individual traits. The democratic style was learned by taking part in groups and by practicing it in a realistic situation.

The Contingency Approach

Fiedler and his associates have developed an account that considers individual traits, leadership styles, and several situational factors. The account assumes that leadership effectiveness is contingent on a clearly specified and limited number of factors and is called a *contingency model* or *approach*. Fiedler developed a scale to test for individual traits of leaders, such as concern with good interpersonal relations versus interest in task success and desire for self-esteem as opposed to preoccupation with task performance. In addition, his approach uses a sociometric test to scale a group's atmosphere and to estimate the relationship between the leader and the others. Finally, Fiedler developed a way to evaluate group situations in terms of *favorability* for the leader. Fiedler argued that a situation might include more or less authority for the leader in that an organization might provide a leader with a formal position that had sanctions to reward or punish subordinates. The more such sanctions a position had, the more favorable the situation. A person might also have earned influence with other members because of the excellence of past performance in the group. The more such earned power a person had, the more favorable the situation. Fiedler also developed a technique for the evaluation of the difficulty of the group's task. The more difficult the task, the less favorable the situation for the leader.

Fiedler used four criteria to evaluate task difficulty: (1) the higher the degree to which the correctness of a decision could be verified by feedback or by checking logical procedures, the lower the difficulty of the task; (2) the higher the degree of clarity of the goal, the lower the difficulty; (3) the fewer the number of different paths or procedures to reach the goal, the lower the difficulty; and (4) the fewer the number of different solutions that might be judged as correct, the lower the difficulty. Fiedler argued that the least difficult tasks were those in which decisions were clearly correct or incorrect, in which the goal was clear, in which one or very few paths could lead to a correct solution, and in which only one solution was correct.

Fiedler weighted the criteria for evaluating the favorability of leadership situations by giving the greatest weight to the leader's personal relationships with the others, next greatest to the difficulty of the task, and the least to position authority.

Fiedler's approach assumes that his testing procedure resulted in identifying individuals who were directive or authoritarian as opposed to those who were democratic and less directive. Fiedler argued that leaders preoccupied with task success would tend to be more directive than those preoccupied with social relationships.

Fiedler and his associates conducted a number of studies to test the hypothesis that the right combination of leadership style and situation would result in task efficiency. Although the studies do not provide unequivocal support, they do give some empirical verification for the contingency approach. The studies suggest that if investigators evaluate a situation as highly favorable or highly unfavorable on the basis of the four criteria described above, then a directive task-oriented leadership style will result in more task effectiveness than the less directive style. When investigators evaluate the situation as moderately favorable, a more democratic and member-oriented style of leadership is more effective than the authoritarian.

The argument is that when a situation is extremely favorable, a leader can be authoritarian because the goal is clear, the path is evident, and the group can easily judge its success or failure. In addition, the leader has many sanctions from an external organization to reward or punish the members and has earned the respect and esteem of the others. Thus, in the highly favorable situation, being bossy does not hinder the willing cooperation of the followers. The more democratic style of people-oriented leadership, on the one hand, is likely to waste effort on needless fence building in the social dimension. When the situation is extremely unfavorable, the group is likely to be facing a crisis, and authoritarian leadership is required. When things are moderately favorable, the leader cannot rely on institutional authority or sanctions nor the rewards of task success as much as in the favorable situation and must keep mending interpersonal relationships to keep earning esteem in order to get the willing cooperation of the others.

Although too simple for an adequate account of leadership, the contingency approach is an improvement over either the trait or styles-of-leadership account. One virtue of Fiedler's work is that it focuses attention on factors in the task requirements as important to leadership. The criteria for evaluating the difficulty of a group task are insightful and useful for the person participating in work groups. The notion that different tasks require different styles of leadership is an important concept, and anyone who is a group leader for a period of time during which the group changes tasks could profit from the insights furnished by the contingency approach.

The contingency approach seeks to discover testing procedures that scale potential leaders and discriminate among them so the right kind of leadership can be assigned to the proper kind of leadership situation. The approach would have important practical applications if, indeed, some simple paper-and-pencil testing procedures would allow administrators of organizations to appoint people to leadership situations so that no square pegs would be fitted into round holes. For instance, personnel managers could test several candidates for a leadership position as to task orientation versus people orientation and appoint the one who best fit the leadership situation, confident that the result would be the most effective leadership for that particular unit of the organization. The difficulty with testing, scaling, and evaluation procedures is that to be useful they must be both reliable and valid. To be reliable, the test must yield essentially the same results when applied to the same individual by several different testers or when given to the same individual on different occasions. To be valid, the test or scale must correlate with actual behaviors in the group or, in the case of the evaluation of task difficulty, with the actual difficulty of the work. The Minnesota case studies contain groups in which the members discussed their leadership difficulties and succeeded in changing the leadership style of an individual so that their leader was structuring the group in a more acceptable way, and the result was an increase in group effectiveness. In other words, task orientation versus member orientation is a field-variant feature of the leadership role and a paper-and-pencil test that assumes that it is field-invariant will be misleading. One would not rely on a test for knowledge of an individual's ability in a foreign language if the person were taking a class in the language so that his knowledge was in the process of change. In the same way a paper-and-pencil test for task orientation is not valid for those situations in which the person who is testing for the leadership role changes orientation because of what the group teaches him or her about the kind of leadership style it prefers.

Nonetheless, the contingency approach and its empirical support provide evidence that an adequate account of leadership must be much more complex and detailed than either the trait or the styles-of-leadership approach. The most satisfactory framework to date has been the contextual study of leadership.

The Contextual Approach

The contextual study adds to the contingency approach the notion of the dynamic interplay of the communication in a group. The contextual account includes all the factors of the contingency explanation and adds to it the emergence of group norms and roles, the chaining fantasies that contribute to a group culture with their implications for leadership, the evolving communication networks with the amount and direction of the flow of messages, and the verbal and nonverbal contents of the communication.

The contextual viewpoint provides a more sophisticated and complete explanation of leadership than any of the other accounts. It incorporates the idea that leaders are, to some extent, born, but it also suggests that potential leaders can achieve skills and improve talents with training. Since some of the leadership behavior will be unique to a particular group because of the communication and interaction which contributed to its development, *a case history of the group is the only way to provide a complete explanation of its leadership.* Thus, the case study method is one of the most fruitful ways of examining the complexities of leadership. Investigators can take a number of carefully developed and detailed case studies and by comparison and contrast discover similarities and patterns that generalize across many groups. The procedure is analogous to the techniques used by medical doctors and psychiatrists in the study of disease and psychological problems.

Certainly the contextual view will frustrate people who wish a quick and easy formula that will make them leaders in every group. They will also be frustrated, however, by advice and procedures stemming from another perspective that provide them with an easy formula; the easy formula that works in one situation will not work in another. Still, the possibility of generalizing about leadership from the contextual point of view depends to some extent on the level of analysis. If the student of group methods wishes to generalize about the one set of personality variables that will result in an individual's always assuming leadership, or about the likelihood of a given group accepting a leader whose style is autocratic or democratic, the possibility of generalization is limited. At a different level, however, generalizations are possible. This chapter, for example, is written from a contextual perspective and reports general patterns of leadership emergence based on situational and interactional grounds.

In addition, the contextual view explains a good many facts that the other positions must rationalize or note as exceptions. The trait approach does not adequately explain why an individual emerges as leader of one group, but does not in a second similar group. It does not account for the change in leadership that often accompanies a marked change in the purpose of the same group. The one-best-style approach cannot fully explain the groups that are equally successful in terms of cohesiveness and productivity; similar in size, composition, and purpose; and yet exhibit different styles of control.

Different explanatory systems may emerge within the same school of thought. Within the contextual view of leadership, two major explanatory systems account for most differences of opinion among theorists. The first rejects the idea that one leadership role emerges from group interaction and that this role is played by one individual. Instead, leadership functions become part of the roles of all members; it is therefore misleading to refer to one person as the leader of the group. A better explanation would be that leadership functions are distributed through the behavior repertoires of all group members. The members thus share in the leadership of the group. A slightly different variation on this theme suggests that the leadership role is assumed first by one member and then another.

The second explanation asserts that one leadership role emerges from group interaction and that until this role is played by one member, the role structure of the group is not stable. Further, this explanation asserts that the dynamics of group process tend toward such stability. The perspective of this book is, of course, the second version of the contextual approach. The empirical support for the perspective comes from detailed case studies compiled at Minnesota.

LEADERSHIP EXPLAINED

In everyday conversation, people talk about a group's lacking sound leadership, or about the need for more leadership in politics, the community, or the fraternity, and they know generally what they have in mind. However, when social scientists study the phenomenon of leadership systematically, they must clarify the commonsense concepts to eliminate as much ambiguity as possible. If they wish to study leadership in experimental groups, they must define terms very carefully so that other investigators can repeat the studies. Early investigators gave widely varying definitions to the concept of leadership. It would require an entire chapter to explain all the conventional definitions that have been established as ground rules for empirical studies of leadership.

In a highly disciplined, authoritarian organization such as a symphony orchestra or a football team, leadership is easy to observe. When the coach maps a play and the quarterback calls the signals, the team follows the orders without question. In general, leadership includes setting goals, making decisions, giving orders, and evaluating performance. Of course, it is implied that the decisions are implemented, and the orders are followed. In everyday conversation, the term *leadership* often implies that the decisions are good in terms of the organization's goals, and that the personnel willingly follow the orders. Fans praise the football coach and his quarterback for leadership when they make wise decisions about the sequence of plays and the players follow through effectively.

Leadership in an authoritarian organization is easily defined, but many groups do not have an authoritarian structure. What of the committee chair who asks the group what it would like to do? What if the group makes suggestions and then votes on them? What if some person other than the chair makes the suggestion that is eventually used? What if someone other than the chair persuades a majority to accept this position? Who is the leader of such a group? Does the group have a leader?

Leadership might be defined as the behavior of the top person in an authoritarian group. But this definition is too limited because of the tradition of democracy and the assumption that authoritarianism is bad. People in our culture do not like bosses, dictators, and domineering people. Many American groups are "democratic" in the sense that *the group* rather than *the leader* is supposed to make decisions. This is true of educational classes, voluntary organizations, political clubs, and some families.

Investigators in the field of leadership have not restricted their studies to authoritarian groups. They needed a definition of leadership broad enough to include groups in which members reach a consensus about decisions. One approach was to define different types or styles of leadership. As stated earlier, Lippitt and White distinguished three types of leadership as authoritarian, democratic, and laissez faire.

Such distinctions solve only part of the problem, since they do not specify the nature of democratic leadership. Some investigators have suggested that the democratic group may not have a leader, but rather that an analogous role is played by a neutral arbiter who keeps the group within procedural bounds. Labels other than leader have been used — for example, *chair, moderator, facilitator,* and *spokesperson* — to refer to this person in the democratic organization. The shift of labels does not avoid the problem, for members continue to follow the group tendency to develop a role structure and a status ladder. Participants differ as to talent, commitment, and the roles they assume. Some are more "influential" than others in structuring the group and making decisions. Some theorists have reacted to those facts by defining leadership in terms of the action or behavior that moves a group toward its goal. This broad a definition might sometimes include everyone in the group; and when everyone is participating in leadership, the proper study of leadership then becomes the study of leadership functions as well as the study of leaders per se.

Investigators have a right to restrict their studies by means of the operational definitions they use. They can study leadership functions rather than leaders if they wish; but in so doing, they miss some important nuances that are part of the ordinary meanings associated with leadership, whether democratic or authoritarian. In one sense, democratic groups and societies have *leaders* who perform similar functions and are perceived in much the same way as the leader of an authoritarian group.

Other investigators have defined leadership in terms of influence. If the group changed its behavior because it was influenced to do so by one of its members, leadership was exercised. This definition is closer to the usual meaning of the term, but it can be questioned. What about the attempt to influence that is resisted? Is this not negative influence? Does not the person who follows really influence the member who leads? Does not every member, by her or his presence, influence every other member in some way?

The point of this brief review of definitions of leadership is that these definitions have often fallen prey to the philosophical disease of starting with a stipulated definition and then discovering new meanings in the definition until a factual argument emerges which is based purely on assumptions hidden in the definition. The Minnesota studies also required an operational definition of leadership: A leader was that individual perceived by all participants as the group leader. When all participants including member A reported that they perceived member A to be their leader, then that member had emerged as the leader. The Minnesota studies discovered such consensus in the great majority of groups that developed stable role structures. Subjects had little difficulty responding to questions in interviews and questionnaires using the term *leader* in this context. Their observed behavior gave further evidence that they perceived a given individual as their leader. The group members showed deference to this person, looked to him or her for directions on procedural matters, and often expected the leader to make unpleasant decisions.

This operational definition raises the question of what objective behaviors relate to the perception of leadership. Mortensen made a content analysis of the communication associated with the perception of leadership and discovered that, although others communicate some of the same things that the perceived leader communicates, the leader's communication differs in a statistically significant way from that of the other members. Mortensen discovered that the perceived leaders specialized in communication that could be reliably coded into such categories as introducing and formulating goals, tasks, and procedures; eliciting communication; delegating and directing action; and integrating and summarizing group activity.

If all members of a group do and say some of the same things as the perceived leader, why do they pick a leader rather than regard each member as sharing leadership functions? People participating in groups perceive the interactions of others in general terms. They do not tabulate the percentage of member A's directing actions as compared with the total number of orders and directions given. If A performs a high percentage of directing actions, as tabulated by an observer analyzing group interactions, that person is eventually perceived as a leader. One suggestion for action made by member A at a time of crisis may impress the group members as forcibly as many directions given at moments of less involvement. The psychological principles of learning provide a partial explanation for the impact of isolated interactions on the perceptions and recollections of participants. The primacy of an interaction is often an important factor. Early in a group's life when primary tensions are high, a suggestion for action supported by the group can aid the perception that member A is a leader. Some interactions have greater impact because they are more recent. If member A has been active in structuring the group at the last meeting, she or he may be perceived as leading even though earlier A had not been as active. In the context of a group, intensity of perception, as well as the importance of the leading at a given time, may give the impression that A is the leader.

Members often carry some stereotyped role structures with them to each new group. They strive to make sense and order out of a socially insecure situation. Stereotypes serve to structure the flow of the meeting. One of the major stereotypes is that of the *leader*. Many people would like to be the leader and "run things," and "get their own ideas across." Even when members perceive that they will not assume the role of leader, their interest in who will become leader is considerable no matter what stereotype they have of the role. Group members want someone they can "follow," a leader they can admire and trust. They do not want to be "dominated to the point of being subjugated," or to be "led around by the nose." These last comments, drawn from diary accounts collected by the Minnesota studies, indicate the nature of some typical leader stereotypes.

The interactions that are closely correlated to the perception of leadership in the task-oriented groups are those that relate to procedural matters. If a person suggests that the group should get down to business or that the topic should be divided into military, economic, and political aspects, that member is perceived as making a leadership move. Early in the LGD an individual who exhibits a great deal of knowledge and authority in the task area is often perceived as a potential leader, but as the group continues, the procedural directions relate more and more directly to leadership. Very early in an LGD, the participants may perceive the person who talks the most as a potential leader. Indeed, some investigators were so impressed with this phenomenon that they investigated it and discovered that leadership did correlate positively with talkativeness.

For some groups, the ability of a person to structure the work is closely related to the ability to do the job. A guide for a mountain-climbing expedition must be a good climber. A college president, on the other hand, may administer the college without being an expert in atomic physics, classical rhetoric, or small group communication.

The role of leader is closely related to the status rankings within the group. Usually the final decision as to status must wait until this role emerges. When a leader emerges, the group can agree about where that role fits in the status hierarchy and where other roles will be placed in relation to it.

The basic theoretical model of the LGD discussed in Chapter 6 explains why no two perceived leaders play precisely the same role in two different groups. It also explains why the same individual does not play precisely the same role in two different groups *even though she or he is perceived as leader of both groups.*

An important principle of role development is that *the role a person takes is worked out by the individual and the group together.* Thus, the observed behavior of a given group leader is to some extent *idiosyncratic.* An investigator can best explain the behavior of a particular leader by understanding the case history of the group and determining how the role was worked out. The idiosyncracies of expectations associated with the role of leader make it difficult for investigators to discover broad patterns that account for leadership behavior. To some extent, these idiosyncracies explain the puzzling results of much research literature on leadership; for example, why studies that attempted to correlate leadership style with group cohesiveness and productivity were inconclusive. One group and one individual may work out a leadership role that includes an autocratic style, yet the group may still be cohesive and productive. Another group

PATTERNS OF INTERACTION RESULTING IN THE EMERGENCE OF A LEADER   205

may, under similar conditions, work out a more democratic style of giving directions. Nevertheless, there are some typical patterns to the process by which leaders emerge in the LGD.

PATTERNS OF INTERACTION RESULTING IN THE EMERGENCE OF A LEADER

Struggle for Role and Status

Since the internal esteem rewards are closely related to status within the group, they are always awarded unequally. Some individuals receive greater esteem gratification because the others perceive them as more important to the welfare of the group. As a result, people with high esteem needs contend for the top positions and, in this struggle, come into conflict and disagreements. The conflict generates secondary tensions, and much of the group's energy is directed to the question of who will win. When these struggles are protracted and intense, the group becomes split and gets little done.

The General Pattern

The groups included in the Minnesota studies were divided into two categories: groups in which leaders clearly emerged, and groups in which the roles never stabilized. The majority of cases are in the first category. The groups that developed stable role structures experienced consider-able release of secondary tension and a dramatic increase in cohesiveness at the point when a leader clearly emerged. The continual shifting of roles in groups that failed to find a leader created an unstable social field, high levels of secondary tension, reduced member satisfaction, lower levels of cohesiveness, and less effective work.

The basic principle governing the emergence of leadership in the LGD is that *the group selects its leader by the method of residues.* The group does not pick a leader, but instead eliminates members from consideration until only one person is left. The one outstanding impression that people report having in early meetings of the LGD is that there is difficulty in estimating who will emerge as leader, but little disagreement about who will *not* be the leader. People seem to come to the first sessions looking for cues that will eliminate other participants from the struggle for high-status roles. One possible explanation of this tendency is that eliminating some persons is relatively easy and it helps the individual begin to structure the social field. The members can then concentrate on those people who are still in contention. If they are personally ambitious, they may find themselves eliminating others from leadership in order to remain in contention. When they select a leader, they eliminate themselves from the high-status place.

The First Phase The general pattern of role emergence consists of two movements. The first phase is relatively short and often terminates after a matter of minutes. It seldom lasts more than a session. During this phase, the group eliminates people who are perceived as definitely unsuitable for leadership. Case studies indicate that roughly half of the members were eliminated as potential leaders in this early phase. They were eliminated on the basis of very crude and limited evidence. Participants found certain patterns of interaction so impressive that people who exhibited them were uniformly eliminated from contention. Among those first eliminated were the quiet ones, those who "did not take part." The participant who said nothing or very little during the first meeting was always eliminated. Although silent participants usually reported that they would like to be leaders, they testified that they would not emerge as leaders because they were not taking an active part.

Some active persons were perceived as being uninformed, unintelligent, or unskilled. They did not seem to know much about the task, or what they said "did not seem to make much sense." They irritated the group because they introduced unnecessary distractions. These people were eliminated from contention early.

Another group of people eliminated in the first phase were those who often took a most active and vociferous part in the discussion. They took strong, unequivocal stands, expressed their position in flat, unqualified assertions, and indicated that no circumstances would change their ideas. They were perceived as "too extreme" or "too inflexible."

Sometimes the others perceived an individual to be extreme and inflexible, but they did not reject that person immediately. The members did not recognize the individual's inflexibility because the participant phrased positions tactfully. On other occasions, the members found the participant so articulate, well informed, and intelligent that they did not reject his bid for leadership until later.

The Second Phase The second phase of role emergence typically found about half of the group still actively contending for leadership and was characterized by intensified competition. Members felt irritated and frustrated by the meetings. The group was "wasting time," and "nothing was accomplished." Animosities developed among some participants, and the group began to avoid questions relating to its social structure. Some ignored the role struggle by pretending it did not exist or by withdrawing from the group. Others began to find scapegoats to account for their failures. Quite often, the participants testified that little could be done to improve the group. They said they were victims of circumstances or at the mercy of some unfortunate, inherent, unchangeable personality traits of one or more members.

The groups that finally eliminated all but one contender used some additional negative evidence as a basis for rejecting a leader contender. If they failed to reject an inflexible person in the first phase, they rejected him or her in the second. In addition, the group rejected the contender whose "style" of leadership they found disturbing. The rejected styles were perceived as inappropriate to the situation, task, and group. In groups formed in discussion classes, the authoritarian style was often rejected. Contenders who were too "bossy" or too "dictatorial" were eliminated in the second phase. In Geier's study of 16 groups, only one contender with an authoritarian style emerged as the leader.

Although an authoritarian style was perceived as inappropriate to task-oriented groups in discussion class, other groups in other situations might find the authoritarian style necessary. Certain situations demand instant and unquestioning obedience, and the authoritarian style may be appropriate for their purposes.

Baker's study of style and leadership found that a complex pattern of word usage was related to early elimination of participants from leadership in leaderless zero-history groups. An important part of that complex pattern included the finding that people also rejected leader contenders whose personal style they found irritating and disturbing.

If the members were predominantly interested in the task area, they sometimes rejected the contender who was considered unduly interested in the social dimension — that is, too worried about hurt feelings or too busy socializing. On the other hand, members who were preoccupied with social and esteem needs sometimes rejected the contender who seemed too task-oriented. In the final analysis, groups accepted the contender who provided the optimum blend of task efficiency and personal consideration. The leader who emerged was the one that others thought would be of most value to the entire group and whose orders and directions they trusted and could follow. In some instances, members were not too pleased even with the best contender.

About one-third of the groups included in Geier's study did not complete the second phase and after three months were still contending for high-status roles.

Within the second phase of struggle for position, certain archetypal patterns tended to be repeated. The following discussion will describe four of the most important and illustrate each with a case history.

Pattern I

Groups that have a relatively easy, short, and painless period of role struggle often follow archetypal pattern I. A hypothetical group of five might exhibit this pattern as follows. Member A has emerged as the tension releaser and is thus removed from contention. Members C and D are eliminated because they seem uninvolved or uninformed. Members B and E are left to contend for the top position. During the second phase, A perceives B to be arbitrary and tactless, but finds E understanding and better organized. A begins to support E. Members C and D also soon perceive B as less desirable and eliminate that person. At this point, E clearly emerges as the leader. *E may not maintain the role.* He or she will be on probation for a while. But by continuing to lead in a satisfactory manner, E solidifies the role and grows in power and esteem. If the others begin to dislike E's style, a new contender will arise to challenge the position. A number of leaders in the Minnesota studies were deposed after several weeks.

Of course, not all role problems are solved by the emergence of a leader. The group may still have serious difficulties. The person who loses in the final, clear-cut struggle is a potential source of trouble. She or he may be upset enough to sabotage the group. Such "runners-up" are always among the more capable people in the group. When they lose their bid for leadership, their esteem needs are unsatisfied, and they will be frustrated and upset. They often perceive the group as unreasonable and disorganized. They report that in their opinion many of the members' decisions about how to organize and do their work have been wrong. They usually find the leader less than capable and personally obnoxious. The others now perceive individuals to be troublemakers. Everyone else gets along fine, and the group could accomplish something without them. Members are often tempted to reject or ostracize them.

The group can fit unsuccessful contenders back into its role structure and find a useful and productive place for them, but this is not an easy task. The newly emerged leader often has just as much animosity toward the individual he or she defeated as the loser has for the winner. The greatest mistake the leader can make at this point is to exploit the power of the new role and make life miserable for an antagonist. If the leader punishes the loser, trouble will continue as long as the unsuccessful contender remains with the group. The wise leader, with support from the others, is always especially careful at this crucial point to support the antagonist in moves to assume a high-status role commensurate with his or her abilities. The loser seldom becomes completely reconciled to a secondary role, but usually assumes this place and works for rather than against the group's goals.

Pattern I exhibits the emergence of a role function that is crucial to the structuring of the group. It can be thought of as the *lieutenant* role function. When member A begins actively to support E, A becomes E's lieutenant. Member A's role then includes, among other things, being the tension releaser, best-liked member, and E's lieutenant. The emergence of a lieutenant is often a key development in determining a leader.

One of the cases included in the Minnesota studies exemplified pattern I and also illustrated the successful integration of the loser. This group was composed of five discussants, three of whom were men. One woman was poised, vivacious, and smiling. She soon emerged as the tension releaser. Both women were eliminated from leadership contention in the first phase. The second phase settled down to a contention among the men. Two members were most strongly in contention. One of them was soft-spoken but fluent and assertive. He was tactful and serious.

The other was intense, fast-talking, and task-oriented. After a short period of work in the second phase, the third man began to withdraw from the discussion. He eventually entered the deliberations by strongly supporting the more soft-spoken and tactful of the two remaining contenders. The women members quickly began to support this same member. Four members — the leader himself, the lieutenant, and the two women — now perceived the tactful member to be their leader.

The task-oriented member reported only that the group was wasting too much time and that a number of members did not seem well informed. In the next meeting, he began to challenge the leader vigorously on a point of procedure. At this crucial point the *lieutenant stepped forward to meet the challenge and defend the leader's suggestions.* The women members supported the lieutenant, and the leader remained above the battle. When the eliminated contender capitulated to the pressure, the leader stepped in as a noncombatant with many shows of group solidarity. He suggested that they all work together to make their group a good one. He raised the status of the contender by praising his challenge of the procedure and assured him that the group expected and appreciated vigorous questioning. In this way, the group found a high-status and productive role for the considerable talents of the eliminated leader contender.

Pattern II

Archetypal pattern II is a longer, more frustrating, and tension-producing path to the emergence of a leader and to stable roles in a task-oriented group. Some groups that fell into pattern II never reached completion and remained without a clearly perceived leader. In a group of five, the first phase of this pattern sees the elimination of three members from contention for leadership. During the second phase, each of the remaining contenders gains a lieutenant. Such support encourages each to strive more vigorously and to hold out for a longer time. In a four-person group, such a division may prove disastrous. A number of groups included in the Minnesota studies did follow pattern II to the conclusion of stable roles and a clearly perceived leader. The following case history describes such a group, composed of five men.

During the first meeting, the group spent its time getting acquainted and dissipating primary tension. The only role to emerge clearly during this hour was that of member E, who kidded around and entertained the group.

During the second meeting, member B made a strong and determined effort to "run" the group and get his ideas across. No other member was equipped with the information or speaking skills to challenge his suggestions and ideas at this meeting.

In the interval between the second and third meetings, B met E in the library and discussed "his" solution with E. Member E reported:

I ran into B today while doing research. He spent fully one hour convincing me of a solution for our assigned task. His arguments were logical enough, and I finally agreed after I became convinced of the feasibility of his plan. In fact, I was so convinced that I was determined that he be given a hearing by the rest of the group and, further, I was determined to help him shove this solution through as the group's document.

Member B came to the third meeting prepared to "shove" his solution through the group with the help of member E. He began the meeting by "instructing" the group about economic principles with the aid of several economics textbooks. In B's own words: "My major is business administration, so I'm more qualified than others to speak on economics and economics policy. . . . I explained many technical terms. . . ." At this point in the group's life, A and C were eliminated as leader contenders because they were uninformed. Member E was eliminated because he was the best-liked and was B's lieutenant. This left B in the major position, except for opposition from D. Member D reported his impressions as follows: "The first phenomenon observable was the attempt of member B toward leadership. He is a business major and with unmitigated gall let us know he had the whole discussion topic under control. . . . I clocked him at 15 minutes for one talk." A bit later, member D reported:

I could see signs that the other members were falling in behind him and I began to fear that the group would accept his proposals without any deliberation or critical analysis on their part. Consequently I began to question his position, not because I disagreed with him so much as I disliked the thought of having any one idea go through unopposed and not analyzed.

When D began suggesting alternate modes of procedure, he was immediately supported by A. The meeting continued with B and his lieutenant, E, and D and his lieutenant, A, conflicting on almost every substantive issue. Member B reported in his diary that D's first challenge "was to go on record as favoring rewording the topic. . . . Two were for his motion, and two were against. The two against argued and argued that this procedure was not cricket."

As the discussion grew more acrimonious, E became more and more disillusioned with B. He reported that "D openly challenged the plan [member B's] and I, feeling incompetent about the matter, let B face the challenge alone. . . . I occasionally nodded my head and added a few statements." However, E was publicly on record as supporting B's plan, and he found it difficult to withdraw that support.

The group had a "lively" discussion for most of the third hour even though it often consisted of quibbles about relatively unimportant substantive matters. Secondary tensions arose, and the talk grew louder and louder. Meanwhile, member C remained neutral. He took little part in the proceedings, and his responses remained noncommittal. Finally, toward the end of the hour, B directly challenged C by asking, "Where do you stand?" Member C responded, "Directly in the middle."

Under these circumstances, groups that fall into pattern II continue the role struggle. Sometimes they fail to find a satisfactory conclusion. In the case of this particular group, C finally suggested a compromise between the positions of B and D. This gave E an opportunity to sever his support of B without losing face, and he gratefully leaped to the support of the compromise. The group released great amounts of secondary tension and made a number of shows of group solidarity. Members A, C, D, and E were now definitely in agreement and supportive of member D as their "leader." The highly competent and aggressive member B remained a source of potential disruption. Member D, with the full support of the other three members, skillfully reinforced member B into the high-status role of task expert.

Pattern III

Archetypal pattern III is also more difficult and complicated than pattern I. However, it typically results in the emergence of a leader. In successful groups that fall into this pattern, the leader who emerges proves satisfactory, and the group follows willingly. Occasionally, the leader who emerges from pattern III is unsatisfactory, and such groups are often unsuccessful.

Groups that fall into pattern III are faced with an external or internal crisis of such magnitude that the group is seriously threatened. Under the stress of this unexpected threat, the group often turns to a member who provides a solution for them. She or he becomes their leader. Pratt's study comparing a set of groups in which women emerged as leaders with another set in which men emerged replicated the earlier investigations by Geier and Larson of leadership emergence in leaderless group discussions, but Pratt discovered that pattern III was more widespread in her sample of groups than in Geier's (Pratt's study is described more fully later in this chapter).

External factors that pose a crisis for the group are usually unexpected and capricious, such as acts of nature that destroy material resources, health problems that withdraw key members when they are needed, and other unusual and unforeseen demands.

Equally important are the crisis situations within the social structure of the group. When the group's drive for a stable social field is disrupted so violently that the members are seriously disturbed, they face a crisis that opens the way for a leader to emerge. If one of the contenders in the second phase solves the internal problem satisfactorily, she or he will usually survive the eliminations. Groups whose patterns include internal social crises contain members whose early attempts at finding a role in the group are so impressive that the others focus attention on them. The group may become so fascinated by the behavior of a particular member that its attention is distracted from the normal considerations of role structuring. Such members are *central persons*. Redl developed the concept of *central persons* to aid in his psychoanalytic interpretation of group process. His analysis resulted in the discovery of specific forms of central persons. The concept is used here in a more general and less psychoanalytic way. Central persons may be *stars* in the sense that they are perceived as so good and potentially helpful to the group that they stand out from it. They may be stars in the social area in that they are exceptionally pleasant, charming, and amusing. Such positive central persons seldom raise the kind of internal crisis that precipitates pattern III. Central persons may also be perceived as extremely hostile to the organization and its purposes, a great threat to the success of the group. And when the central person is unusually apathetic or uninvolved, he or she is very likely to precipitate an internal crisis.

Member B in the case history for pattern II soon became a central person, and member D emerged as leader partly because of his ability to challenge him. Since D was strong enough to stop B's efforts, he gained support from A and, eventually, from C. Other negative central persons included in the case histories reflect the range of behavior that, if extreme enough, can cause the member to become a central person. One member was so apathetic and uncommitted to the group's purposes that he was called "Mr. Negative," and the group turned to a leader who could handle him, even though the leader had a strongly authoritarian style, and the group remained ineffective. Another central person was a voluble and articulate individual, who systematically demolished all values important to the group's success. He belittled the goals of the group, strongly asserted that he would do no more work than necessary, and laughingly admitted that he was irresponsible and lazy.

The groups that follow pattern III to conclusive and stable roles select leaders who demonstrate that they can effectively handle the problems posed by the central person. Often leadership decision results from a dramatic crisis attributed to the central person. Group members testify that they supported the leader because she or he was "strong" enough to handle an inflexible member or was able to successfully defend the group's rights and jurisdiction. Pratt's groups were part of simulated organizations. She found that external crises relating to the defense of a group's boundaries were important in the third pattern of leadership emergence.

Pattern IV

Groups following the path of archetypal pattern IV do not achieve role specialization and stability. They are fraught with social tensions and frustrations; people find them punishing. Groups that follow pattern IV try to eliminate contenders in the second phase, but falter just before a decision or depose any leader who does emerge.

During the second phase, a particularly disturbing contest often develops between two contenders for leadership. The group is involved in endless bickering over unimportant points. Group decisions are reversed shortly after they are made or are reconsidered in the next meeting. The group seems to be getting nowhere and to be wasting time. Finally, in desperation, participants bring the problem out into the open, saying that the group needs direction and leadership. At this point, in some groups, a member changes the subject and the group gratefully drops the topic. Sometimes a participant argues against the need for leadership. The participant asserts that the group is doing fine with everybody leading and with nobody leading; members are all equals and working democratically. Sometimes the group decides that it needs leadership and agrees to an election. At this point, the group avoids the issue by electing a leader (moderator, spokesperson, chair) from among those eliminated in the first phase. Members might elect a quiet woman, or a man who has been uninvolved and seems uninformed. Subsequently they justify their selection on the ground that they wanted someone who was "neutral," who would not "take sides" between the two warring contenders. Interestingly, the elected leader begins *to behave like a leader* after election. In all the cases in the Minnesota studies, when groups selected a leader in this fashion, the elected leader *was not followed* and, within a matter of minutes, *stopped trying to lead.* Selecting someone not in contention does not solve the problem of selecting a leader.

In a variation of pattern IV, a person emerging as leader for a brief period is then challenged and deposed. Another leader emerges and in turn is rejected after a short time. A typical group following this variation had the following case history. The panel was composed of two men and two women. At the end of the first movement, a woman, member B, was eliminated from contention because she was perceived as being quiet and shy. The others were all verbal and aggressive. Member A, a man, was particularly task-oriented and driving in his attempt to structure the group. The woman who remained in contention, member D, fought against A's attempts to run the group. The third member, C, was more relaxed in his manner and might have been the leader except that neither A nor D would support him. In short, no one assumed the role of lieutenant. The group members were continually assuming new roles, and the situation was in a constant state of flux. Whenever one of the contenders seemed to be emerging as leader, the other two would combine against her or him. In the course of successfully rejecting that individual, one of the two others would seem to be left in the leadership role, but at that point, the third member would switch and combine against the one emerging as leader. The three contenders thus ensured that no member would become leader.

A group often follows pattern IV when the contenders for leadership in the second phase all have substantial handicaps and there is little basis to choose among them. A typical case history that illustrates this point found three of the five members eliminated in the first phase. Of the two remaining, member A had a strong, aggressive style of structuring the group. He moved to the blackboard and began dividing the work very early in the first meeting. Several of the others perceived him as a manipulator and resisted his efforts to organize the work. Member D began to challenge A. The others began to alternate their support from A to D. D was congenial and showed consideration for the others when structuring the group. The others much preferred his leadership style to that of member A. However, they discovered that D had not prepared very well for the task and was not as well informed as A. He was quite tentative and fuzzy in his thinking and rather indecisive. Member A was more capable of developing a clear, coherent course of action and was clearly most able to lead the group to its task goals. The members perceived the contenders as roughly equal, but both had serious handicaps as leaders. The members did not follow either, and the role structure never stabilized.

SPECIAL PROBLEMS

Because leadership is crucial to the establishment of role structure for the group, it is the focus for many secondary tensions that inhibit group efficiency and satisfaction.

The Manipulator

Groups frequently have difficulty resolving the leadership struggle because of the presence of individuals who are in many respects stars. They are fluent, intelligent, and hardworking. However, they plan to exploit the group for their own purposes. They try to be *manipulators*. The most acrimonious role conflicts arise when people come into the group to "run" it or to get ideas across. Manipulative efforts are first perceived by the others as attempts to assume the role of leader. Eventually the group perceives that the manipulative person is trying to exploit the group for her or his own advantage. At this point, no matter how brilliant or clever, the manipulator is rejected as the leader.

Member B typifies one sort of manipulator. Member B was a hard-sell manipulator. He reported in his diary, "I have been in many, many discussion groups and I believe I can manipulate most people to predetermined ends." He subsequently reflected this preoccupation with "winning" the discussion when he evaluated his record within the group. "I convinced the group of several things. First of all, I was against limiting the question . . . and I won."

Members who come into the group to manipulate it are usually frustrated because they are rejected. They quite often react strongly. They feel that they have been unable to run the group because they have not been tough enough. They must bluster more, make more definite plans, argue more — the actions that created the initial trouble become more offensive. They soon become the focal point of group attention. The other members see them as bull-headed and domineering; they think that if the manipulators would just be silent or leave, the group might be able to accomplish something.

Manipulators of a second type are more subtle in their approach. They are congenial, good listeners, persuasive, tactful, and complimentary. They employ all the techniques commonly found in lists of what to do and what not to do in order to improve social relations. They paraphrase disagreements carefully and ask leading questions with skill. They seize the appropriate moment to assert group consensus in line with their own desires. For a time these tactics succeed, but gradually the group becomes aware that it is being led. An emergent leader undergoing his or her probationary period in the role may be challenged at this point by another member and may be deposed. If the group discovers a member making use of skillful leading techniques for the purpose of exploiting the others during the second phase of leader contention, the group will eliminate the participant as a possible leader.

One case history included in the Minnesota studies was of a group judged unsuccessful by both participants and observers. It contained both a hard-sell and a soft-sell manipulator. Member B was smooth, a bit older than the others, and congenial. Member D was fast-talking, aggressive, and driving. B emerged as the leader of the group during the first meeting. Member D was absent for the next two meetings. When he returned, he sensed the group's dissatisfaction with B and began a systematic attack on all B's suggestions. He got considerable support and within 30 minutes, B was deposed as group leader. B reported of himself that during "the third meeting I deliberately ran the group my own way, rather subtly I thought. I gave suggestions and called on those who I knew would give me support." During the course of this meeting, the other members became aware that B's friendly, democratic style of asking for opinions and directions masked an intent to control and manipulate. Another member reported, "B tries to tell us what to do too often. . . . You can only take so much of that." Another recorded in his diary, "B gets a little worse every meeting. It's as though he were the captain of the ship."

D, having deposed B, was not accepted as leader. The top spot was then open, and a number of the others were in contention. D was soon perceived as a hard-sell manipulator. One member said, "I've never worked with anyone who tries like he does to manipulate the entire group. He just won't listen to reason." D expressed his position as follows:

> When I was in the army, the guy who won out was the one who spoke the loudest and the fastest. You had to keep up with the other guys. I've been using the same thing ever since I got out.

Member D was as unsuccessful as B in emerging as leader. Indeed, the group resisted his efforts even more vigorously than it had B's leadership. D, however, was less sensitive to the group's resistance, although he did recognize it. He reported, "I can't understand it. I gave suggestions, I called on participants, I volunteered to write the paper. But in the end the group just wouldn't listen."

The Inflexible Member

Another special problem that delays successful structuring of the LGD is the perception by participants that another member is inflexible. Members who take an unequivocal stand and express it with flat certainty, indicating by verbal and gestural messages that they will under no circumstances change their position, cause the group trouble. Such members become central persons and the other members are soon preoccupied with deciding what to do with them.

One group in the Minnesota studies contained two inflexible members and was judged to be unsuccessful. The group was studying medical care for the aged. Member B flatly and unequivocally stated he was against government insurance programs. Member C was equally strong in her commitment to such programs. She reported:

> Participant A appears to be the diplomat—he seeks to establish compromises between the extremists—mainly B and me. Participant B admits he's one-sided since he sells health insurance. . . . I admit B makes me see red the way he throws out statements without proof for the most part. . . . I don't see how we'll ever get together.

A member may be inflexible in the social dimension as well as in the task area. Some participants are insensitive to the cues that small groups use to extinguish behavior. Despite such verbal and nonverbal indications as disagreement, noncompliance, and having their suggestions or evaluations ignored, these rigid participants continue to do and say the things the group dislikes. The participant who does this confuses and frustrates the other members. They do not know how to teach her or him a suitable role in the group. College and high school debaters have often been desensitized in this regard because, in their experience, the proper response to disagreement is a tenacious reaffirmation of the debater's position.

Engineers and other specialists whose training and work experience have stressed productivity and the manipulation of machines and materials often exhibit some of this social rigidity. They sometimes feel that other group members should act sensibly and predictably, as materials and machines do. The virtue of sensitivity training for managers in business and industry is that it makes engineers and other production specialists who find themselves in management positions aware of ways in which groups teach members their roles.

The Female Contender

The first edition of this book, published in 1969, contained a section on the woman who contended for leadership, a section written before the movement for equality for women was well under way. The section reported the results of case studies at Minnesota in which a woman was an active and able contender for leadership. Essentially, women rarely emerged as leaders in coeducational discussion groups containing two or more men. The Minnesota studies also contained case histories of all-female groups, all-male groups, and groups containing only one man or one woman. One reason for studying such groups was to compare the process of role emergence to see if all-female groups were different from all-male groups. In the all-female groups included, the two-phase elimination of leader possibilities and the emergence of a leader by the method of residues was similar to that followed by all-male and by coeducational groups.

In groups composed of women and two or more men, the woman who contended for leadership apparently posed some problems simply because she was a woman. Men usually refused to follow directions given by a woman in the presence of other men. Some expressed the opinion in their interviews, questionnaires, and diaries that women should obey and men should lead. In some groups in which a woman was in strong contention, the men even expressed doubts as to the advisability of women receiving higher education.

The groups that included a female contender who was considered extremely able had the most difficulty resolving their leadership problems. If the woman who remained in contention demonstrated exceptional brilliance and good sense and seemed best qualified to lead the group, the fact that she was also female caused considerable ambivalence on the part of the men.

The results of these early case studies caused much discussion, argument, resentment, and antagonism in classes in discussion and group methods. Interestingly enough, it was the women in the classes who were, for the most part, upset by the results. Very seldom did any of the male students raise the issue in their groups, or in the class meetings. Women were upset with the material, not because they felt it was inaccurate, but because they found it all too accurate, and they felt it was unjust. With the rise of feminism and the concern with equality for women, research began to focus on the question of women as leaders in task-oriented small groups. Several seminars at Minnesota also dealt with the topic.

Case studies from 1969 to 1979 indicated that the emergence of women as leaders in small groups at Minnesota was not as rare as it was in the 1950s and 1960s. More men reported in their diaries and interviews that they would be willing to accept direction from an able woman leader, and a considerable number behaved as though they meant what they said. In group discussions of role emergence and in class discussions of the question, the male response tended to be one of surprise that there was much of a problem, often followed by a quizzical or humorous reaction. The female response tended to be much more emotional, and more women testified to the frustrations they had experienced when working in a coeducational group and being unable to lead, even though they felt certain they were the best qualified to do so, because of the unwillingness of the others to follow. In some case studies after 1969, women raised the question of influence and leadership directly and confronted the males with their concern about making a greater contribution to the group than simply doing routine chores. In many of the cases, the issue focused on who would perform the role function of recordkeeping, the traditional secretarial role. Many women absolutely refused on principle to be a group recorder or secretary.

In short, the earlier case studies no longer accurately reflect the problems faced by a female in contention for leadership. The question of female leadership is clearly a culture-bound feature of small group communication. It may well also be a geographically bound feature to some extent, even within the United States. Much of the earlier laboratory research on the influence of sex on small group dynamics is thus probably more indicative of historical attitudes and roles than of current or future conditions.

Even through the 1970s, women continued to have difficulty emerging as leaders in groups containing two or more males, and the situation certainly had not come full circle in the case studies at Minnesota. Women continued to emerge in influential roles in small groups largely through avenues other than as recognized and sanctioned leaders.

One avenue of influence often used by women was the path of hard and dedicated effort for the welfare of the group. Often one or two women would provide the group with most of its information and would provide a dedicated, responsible, and dependable core for the group. Sometimes a woman would form a coalition with a male and, by playing a lieutenant role, would rise to influence. Women who assumed such a role often did much more than simply support the leader's efforts at structuring the group's work. They often suggested courses of action, administered details of programs and plans, and ensured that the group mobilized its resources.

An important area of recent research in small group communication relates to the influence of gender on leadership emergence. A number of scholars have studied women's role as group leaders.

The results that have accumulated from these studies are sometimes difficult to compare because investigators used different research approaches and different tests and measures. On balance, the results are often a function of cultural norms about women's roles in society rather than generalizations suitable for an overall theory of group process. In a survey of research on sex differences, Shaw concluded that women are less self-assertive and less competitive in groups than men, use eye contact as a form of communication more frequently than men, and conform more to majority opinions than men. But he also noted that differences between men and women in the studies were probably due to different socialization patterns for the sexes and would probably disappear as differences in socialization narrow.

In her study of groups in which males emerged as leaders as compared with groups in which females emerged, Pratt found that women were emerging on a basis approaching equality. As mentioned earlier, Pratt's study replicated Geier's earlier analysis of leadership emergence, except that she also compared and contrasted the patterns of leadership emergence of women with those of men in mixed sex groups. Pratt found the same two-phase overall pattern, with the three basic patterns of emergence common to both male and female leaders. She found about the same proportion of groups in pattern I as did previous studies. However, she found more groups in the crisis pattern (third path) and fewer in the two-lieutenant pattern (second path) than Geier did. She also found a possible fourth pattern, which was predominately a female path to emerging as group leader.

Pratt documented an avenue to leadership that involved two women who provided much of the information and became a dependable, responsible, and dedicated power core for the group. The women not only provided information but also suggested courses of action, administered details of the plans and programs, and ensured that the group mobilized its resources to achieve its goals. They dominated in both the task and social dimensions of group work. The group members, when questioned, selected one of the powerful two as the group leader.

The other members of the group accepted the new leader and recognized the efforts of the two central members, but they still expressed some resentment because the core group was doing so much that little interesting work remained for the others. Also, they were sometimes resentful because of a perceived dominance over group work by the two women. For these reasons, the pattern that Pratt found is quite different from the other three patterns noted above.

As a by-product of the investigation, Pratt also noticed that the woman leaders did not delegate as much as did the male leaders, that men did not confront women in contests for leadership as they did other men, and that men did not form coalitions as easily and effectively as women. Pratt's findings have been supported by the case studies at Minnesota and indicate that in certain cultural circles in the United States, women are emerging more often than they used to in leaderless zero-history small task-oriented groups.

From the beginning of the case studies in 1959, investigators at Minnesota have assumed the hypothesis of no difference in the investigation of male and female communication in the small task-oriented group (until proved otherwise, men and women are assumed to be similar). Even in the early 1960s, the case studies included many assertive and even aggressive women. Early research findings that women were essentially passive, submissive, nurturing, and person-oriented, whereas men were aggressive, domineering, assertive, and task-oriented, were simply not borne out in the case studies. Investigators did find that men resisted supporting the woman contender who emerged as clearly the best person to be the group leader. This resistance has been slow to fade. Bormann, Pratt, and Putnam's study of the groups in a simulated organization in which women emerged as holders of the most powerful positions also indicated that the majority of males resisted female leadership efforts by becoming nonparticipant or apathetic.

Some studies suggested that women communicated in a different style from men. The notion was that women characteristically used language in such forms as tag questions (asking for confirmation of what was said) and qualifying words (implying a tentativeness about what was said). Men, on the other hand, used far fewer tag questions and qualifiers and had their own characteristic way of speaking. Baker's study of the language usage of male and female speakers in relationship to their emerging as leaders in zero-history leaderless groups used complete transcripts of the group meetings and submitted them to word and phrase analysis with the aid of a computer program. She found little statistically significant difference between the styles of women who emerged as leaders and the styles of those who did not. She also found little significant difference between the styles of men and women who emerged as leaders.

There may be some important communication differences between men and women that are inherent, genetically based traits, but the research evidence to this point is unclear. Again, probably most of the findings on the role of gender in leadership, including those from the most recent Minnesota studies, are culture-bound. How group members respond, either male or female, to the female contender for leadership is probably heavily influenced by the cultures of the various small groups and communities in which people were socialized. This does not mean that women, or men for that matter, are on an equal basis in their efforts to work for the good of the group and rise to a role of prominence and importance in a given situation. The group context and the socialization of its members will often result in women encountering resistance, prejudice, and frustration in their efforts to achieve leadership. However, many of these problems are not inherent, sex-linked traits but matters of socialization which can be changed.

Good Politician, Poor Administrator

In some groups, a member who has been very skillful at emerging as the leader fails to hold the position. This member is preoccupied with the power struggle and explores various avenues to the top position. Such members are less interested in the group's work than in the social structuring of the group. They are very sensitive to group opinion and watch carefully for indications of approval or disagreement. They get to "know" the members and show interest in them as people. They weigh the members in terms of their possible alignment in the jockeying for top position. Often, they perceive the group in terms of who will support them or other contenders. An excellent example of this is furnished by the emergence of roles in a group composed of five men and two women.

Between the second and third meetings, member A made an appoint-ment to discuss the group with the instructor. He felt that the group needed direction, that it had floundered and was not progressing. He revealed that he would like to be the leader of the group. Finally, he asked the instructor's advice as to how he might become the leader. The instructor was nondirective. He suggested that member A knew the group intimately and that there really were no simple formulas. Member A finally decided to do a little "politicking." He would call some of the others and discuss the group's problem with them. He might even suggest that they ought to elect a leader.

Between the second and third meetings, member B also made an appointment with the instructor. He explained why he had been absent from the group and promised to attend future meetings. He said that he had talked to some members and that the group was apparently getting nowhere. He had decided that the group needed leadership and that he could provide it.

The third meeting brought the role struggle to a head. B arrived early and took the chair at the head of the table. He introduced himself to the group and explained that he had discussed its progress with the instructor. He misquoted the instructor as saying that the group was "spinning its wheels" and that it was in "trouble." Immediately he aroused a lively response from the other members, who came to the defense of the group. Dynamic member B overrode their objections and asserted that in his opinion the group needed a leader. He then outlined the requisites of a good leader and included, among other things, experience in working in groups and an understanding of group dynamics. He told them that he had 20 hours of group theory in sociology.

The new member upset the tentative role structure the group had established. He posed a crisis of the type characteristic of pattern III. Finally, he suggested that the group elect a leader. The suggestion was quickly supported by A, and the two women agreed. B opened the nomi-nations, and one of the women nominated A. In a few moments, a rather surprised B discovered that A had been elected leader by a vote of 6 to 1.

In his diary, member A recorded: "Meanwhile, back at the ranch, I won the election . . . cohesiveness was restored, and we were ready for the task." He was wrong. After his election, he became a very fastidious, authoritarian leader. He made no moves to reconcile B to the group. Neither did he perceive the problem posed by two other former con-tenders. Within two weeks, mutiny was brewing among the three. As B put it in his diary:

> He performed his role well, although some members have talked among themselves as to how good a leader he was. The conclusion is, had he been leader for a longer period of time, other members may have replaced him.

Another of the unsuccessful contenders commented:

I think at times A was a little too authoritarian in his leadership and that although we recognized him as a leader, we didn't want to assume a position of being subjugated to a complete position of dominated. I think that some of us felt that he was perhaps a little too zealous in his method of attaining leadership.

The Unsuitable Assignment of Leadership

A final problem that often occurs in the small task-oriented group is that posed by the formal assignment of a leader who then proves unsuitable. Or the group may make a mistake and elect an unsuitable leader. Member A, in the last case, was such a leader. He was formally elected because he had prepared the way and was able to exploit the crisis presented by the new member. The group accepted him, until he showed that he was not a good administrator.

In many other situations, leaders are assigned by the organization. This is quite often the case with ad hoc and standing committees. The organization usually appoints managers, supervisors, chiefs, or sergeants for the small task-oriented groups within it. In small group communication classes, the instructor may assign a chair, moderator, or leader. Such assigned leaders typically begin by leading the group. They take charge, give direction, control communication, and intiate action. The group does not accept these people as leaders without a period of testing. Challenges to the assigned leader's control arise. If the assigned leader proves unsuitable, the group faces the same situation as if it had formally elected the individual and then discovered that the leader was unsuitable.

The advice on leadership that stems from the contextual perspective relates only to natural or emergent leadership. A distinction must be made between the formal position of leadership and the leadership role that emerges in the LGD. The insights from the contextual theory of leadership relate only to the LGD. A person may come to formal leadership, headship, or a position of status and authority within an organization by a number of routes. Leadership can be attained through birth, seniority, or luck, or it can be earned. It is this latter process of emerging as the leader — through interacting with the members and earning their esteem and allegiance in order to gain the power to structure and mobilize the group's resources — that is the focus for the following advice.

Even when a person attains a position of leadership because of election, inheritance, seniority, or luck, actually earning a leadership role within the organization is of great importance. The person in a position of leadership must emerge as the natural leader, or *someone else will*. The dynamics of group process tend inexorably to the emergence of a leader. If there is a vacuum because of lack of leadership, the LGD follows the pattern of the basic model of role emergence.

EMERGING AS THE LEADER OF A SMALL TASK-ORIENTED GROUP

Developing an Understanding of Group Method

Some people have learned sets of opening moves that apply to different kinds of groups and enable them to emerge rather consistently as the leader, if they wish to do so. Such skill represents a kind of unconscious competence or instinct. A good many people, however, are not competent by instinct. A grasp of group process and method will help both kinds of people understand why they are successful, or why they are not. An understanding of group process helps competent practitioners to increase their competence and incompetent ones to achieve some measure of success. Students who understand the material in Chapters 4 through 10 — particularly the operations of the basic model that governs role emergence and the patterns that groups follow in eliminating leader contenders — are in a much better position to become natural leaders.

The first principle of emergent leadership is that participants who wish to become leaders *must respect the laws that govern group process.* If they work against such laws, the group not only will resist them and their attempts at influence, but will raise the level of secondary tensions.

Members who wish to lead must recognize that they are not free to lead the group arbitrarily in the direction they wish or they feel to be the best. The group limits their area of choice to *those leadership moves that others will follow.* It does little good for the leader to march off at the head of a column in what seems to him or her to be the wisest direction if the members take another path. Studies have indicated that the individual who emerges as leader may be quite influential in setting the group norms during the early period of role struggle; but, once these norms are established, the group will not follow a leader who departs too widely from these expectations (even if he or she had been influential in establishing them). Leaders who persist, will be deposed. In one study, people who emerged as leaders were removed from a set of experimental groups and then placed back in the groups after the group norms had been changed. When the subjects rejoined the group, they did not again emerge as leaders unless their behavior conformed to the new group norms.

Members who wish to lead must recognize the drive for specialization and role stabilization within the group. Instead of concentrating on resisting and rejecting behavior which they interpret as striving for high-status roles within the group, they should spend some time thinking about the best roles for individuals within the group — *not in terms of their own, but in terms of the group's welfare.* They should examine the talents and achievements of each member, including themselves. They will wonder: What task functions can member A best perform for the good of the group? Will A accept the status associated with this task role? What social maintenance functions can this person best perform for the good of all? How can A be reinforced to learn this role? How can A be assured shows of solidarity and esteem sufficient to gratify her or his social and esteem needs? How can this role assure member A an opportunity for self-actualization?

People who wish to lead must expect the period of role struggle to be frustrating and difficult. Even a thorough understanding of the laws of group process will not make things easy during this period. They must give the process sufficient time to work to a conclusion. If leaders attempt to force things before the members are ready to accept them, they will simply build up the secondary tensions. With practice, they will develop a sensitivity to the importance of timing. A clearly formulated plan (agenda) may be completely rejected on Monday; however, by Wednesday, the group may be demanding some sense of direction and be ready to accept with enthusiasm essentially the same plan of action. A group may point-edly ignore the call to elect a leader on Tuesday and welcome an election on Friday. In short, a person with a good understanding of group method, who has participated in groups and learned their rhythm, will know when to push for structure and when to wait. He or she will know when to step forward with a plan or an interaction to facilitate the stabilization of roles and when to be silent. Several strong shows of group solidarity at the right moment can do much to build the cohesiveness of the group. The transcript on shows of solidarity in Chapter 6 highlights such a moment. Strong agreements interjected at the crucial moment will help to guide an individual into a good role for both the person and the group. A suggestion that the group has reached a decision, when inserted at the appropriate point, can structure the group's work, mobilize resources, and save meeting time.

The best plan for emerging as the natural leader of a group is devised for each particular situation by a person who knows group methods and the history of the group. Such a plan is an artistic enterprise somewhat similar to designing a house. The architect understands the laws governing mechanics. She must design the house so it will not fall down. She also knows some principles of esthetics and has some theory of art. But to design a particular building, she must study the environment, the uses to which the building will be put, and the personalities and wishes of the people using her services. Similarly, the problem of emerging as the leader of a task-oriented group poses particular problems that are unique to that group, to its purposes, to the interactions members share in their common history, and to the pressures of the environment. There are no easy tactical plans that encompass a wide number of groups.

The Strategy of Leader Emergence

Strategy in this sense refers to the overall plan, the big picture, the general attitudes and objectives of the person who emerges as leader. The following is a composite strategy built up from aspects of individuals who emerged as leaders in the Minnesota studies.

The Desire to Be Leader   The first element in this strategy is that participants who emerged as leaders wanted to be leaders of the group enough to do what was required to achieve the role. Others felt that they really deserved to lead or could do a very good job of leadership, but they did not want to do the required work or make the requisite personal sacrifices; their stereotype of the role included the notion that the *leader did all the work*. One reason that individuals refuse positions of formal leadership in community organizations such as the PTA and the League of Women Voters is that they think the rewards of such positions are not commensurate with the time and trouble involved. The person who wants to be leader without effort seldom emerges as leader. Members who adopt the strategy that they will work hard enough and make whatever sacrifices of time and resources are necessary to achieve leadership are much more likely to be successful.

The Manipulative Versus the Nonmanipulative Attitude   Second, successful leaders adopted a nonmanipulative attitude and set of personal goals. Their basic strategy was to *work for the good of the group*. From the beginning, they were interested in self-transcendence. They wanted the group to succeed; they wanted the members to be happy and to enjoy their roles. The good of the group became the basic criterion against which they judged and selected tactics.

Not every person who used this kind of strategy emerged as a leader, because some accepted a lesser role for the good of the group. However, most people who became leaders in the Minnesota studies did follow this strategy. The impressive thing about those who adopted the opposite strategy, what has been called the manipulative approach, is that they rarely emerged as leaders. Yet those with a manipulative strategy were the most willing to work, and most preoccupied with achieving leadership, in order to get their way and have their ideas accepted.

The Tactics of Leader Emergence

Tactics refer to those things members say and do to implement their overall strategy. For the person sincerely dedicated to the good of the entire group, a careful examination of the group's development, its role structure, and its members and their resources precedes the development of a specific strategy. Even if the group has never met before, certain opening moves can be planned if the participant does some investigating before the meeting. He or she should first ask: What style of leadership is suitable for this group? Would members expect a democratic, moderator style? Does tradition require authoritarian control? What style of leadership is best suited to my background and temperament? Am I particularly skilled in democratic moderating? In authoritarian leadership? Do I have the patience and ability to restrain my own compulsion for organization and efficiency? Am I indecisive in crises? Can I make snap judgments quickly and then implement them with great decisiveness? Am I good at sensing the feelings of a group? Can I judge when members have come to a decision, whether they have verbalized it or not? Can I be an effective administrator?

No matter what style of leadership seems most appropriate, the opening moves of a would-be leader should emphasize group commitment, concern for other members, and willingness to make sacrifices. Contenders should resist the impulse to bring order to what may seem a time-wasting, chaotic meeting. They should not be surprised or disturbed if suggestions that seem eminently logical and wise are resisted or misunderstood at first. They should realize that some of what seems groping and useless in the early meetings is really hard and careful work on the social structuring of the group. This stage might be thought of as the collective preparation stage, and it is absolutely necessary if important work is to be done later.

When the group is deeply involved in the second phase of eliminating potential leaders, the member must watch secondary tensions. When tensions break the tolerance level, he or she should deal with them, or reinforce and encourage the members who do. The best tactic for dealing with these tensions is to talk about them directly. Two general approaches may be used. Would-be leaders can talk to individuals outside the group meetings. They can indicate their concern for the welfare of the group, ask for opinions about the personality conflicts, and give suggestions for solutions. If a number of members in these conferences suggest that an inquiring contender would make the best leader, she should accept the role, making it very clear that her only interest is the success of the group. If these conferences suggest that another member would be a better leader, she should consider assuming the role of lieutenant and supporting the other person. If the other members clearly understand that she is sincerely and unselfishly dedicated to the good of the group, they will accept her leadership much more willingly. They will perceive her directions not as evidence that she feels superior or is exploiting or manipulating the group to satisfy her own power and esteem needs, but rather as a necessary structuring of the group's work, which she is doing for the good of all. Groups which require a highly authoritarian style of leadership to meet crises with a quick, efficient mobilization of group resources will accept crudely barked orders without a great deal of resentment.

The second general approach is to devote part of a regular meeting to a direct examination of the secondary tensions and their causes. This approach may bring the whole problem into the open. New courses of action and new roles may emerge, solve the problem, and result in increased cohesiveness. A group that demonstrates that it can survive this approach impresses on its members its importance and durability.

SUMMARY

The major perspectives that have guided research into various aspects of leadership include the trait approach, the styles-of-leadership approach, the contingency approach, and the contextual study of leadership. The trait approach assumes that leadership can be studied in individuals by isolating clusters of traits that are required for it. The styles-of-leadership approach searches for an ideal way to lead. The contingency explanation seeks a limited number of factors in the leader's personality, the difficulty of the task, the leadership style, and the relationships among group members on which group success is contingent. The contextual position explains leadership in terms of all the factors considered by other approaches, but adds to them a consideration of the dynamic interplay of communication within the group's processes.

This chapter reports the results of the Minnesota studies of leadership emergence in leaderless group discussion. The results support the variation of the contextual approach that explains leadership in terms of group process driving toward a stable role structure, with one role being perceived by the group members as that of leader. The leader is defined as the member who is perceived by the participants as their leader and who is judged by observers to be the member whose directions are followed. The interactions that are closely related to the perception of leadership in the task-oriented discussion group are those related to procedural matters. The role a person takes is worked out by the person and the group together. The principle is true of leadership as well as the other roles. The behaviors associated with the leadership role in any given group are to some extent idiosyncratic and can often be best explained by a case history of how the role was worked out in a given group.

Despite the idiosyncratic nature of role behaviors, there is a general pattern to leadership emergence. The group rejects people as unsuitable for leadership until it is left with one person who emerges in that role. There are two general phases in this pattern. The first, early phase ends when the members have perceived all participants who can be quickly and easily eliminated from contention. These include members who seem uninformed, nonparticipative, or inflexible. The second phase is characterized by intensified competition among the remaining contenders.

Within this general pattern of leadership emergence, at a more detailed level of analysis, four archetypal patterns apply to the majority of case histories. Pattern I is a relatively short and easy route to the emergence of stable roles. In the second phase of the role struggle, one of the two remaining contenders gains a strong lieutenant and the other does not. After a period of time, the contender and her or his lieutenant swing the uncommitted members to their support, and this contender emerges as leader. Pattern II is a more difficult route to the emergence of a leader, since both contenders gain a lieutenant. In archetypal pattern III, the group faces some crisis posed by the external environment or by the behavior of a central person within the group. The contender who provides evidence of being best able to handle the crisis emerges as the leader. Archetypal pattern IV is typical of groups that never stabilize their role structures. Support is thrown from one contender to another in such a fashion that no leader emerges, or the struggle is bypassed by the formal election of a noncontender to the leadership position. Quite often, pattern IV results from the members' inability to discern a difference among the remaining contenders.

Special problems reflected in these four archetypal patterns include those posed by the hard- and soft-sell manipulators, the rigid member, the politician who is a poor administrator, and the formally appointed or selected leader who proves unsuitable.

Individuals who wish to emerge as natural leaders should adopt appropriate strategies and tactics. The most successful overall strategy is that of being willing to work hard enough for the group to achieve leadership and of adopting a sincere desire to work for the good of the group even at the expense of a high-status position. Appropriate tactics are dependent on the given situation. They essentially involve communicating this strategy to the other members of the group by word and deed.

 ## Rules of Thumb

Practical Advice on How to Be a Good Group Member

Drawn from Chapter 9

- ☞ If you want a complete explanation of leadership emergence in your group, make a case history of the process.
- ☞ Do not expect quick and easy recipes and formulas to ensure leadership in small task-oriented groups.
- ☞ Helping leadership to emerge in your group will result in increased cohesiveness and task efficiency.
- ☞ In the second stage of leadership emergence, take an active part in giving the unsuccessful contender a productive high-status role.
- ☞ If you are emerging as the group's leader, take care not to exploit the power of your new role to punish the unsuccessful contender.
- ☞ If it becomes apparent that you will not emerge as leader, consider playing the lieutenant to your candidate for the position.
- ☞ If two contenders are vying for leadership in the second phase, do not elect a noncontender to the position as a way of taking flight from a decision.
- ☞ If you wish to emerge as leader, you must respect the general theory that governs group process.
- ☞ If you wish to emerge as leader, you must be sure to lead only where others will follow.
- ☞ Spend some of your time thinking about the best roles for members in terms of the group's general welfare.

☞ Do not try to force the process of leadership emergence.

☞ If you wish to emerge as leader, you must anticipate the period of role struggle to be frustrating and difficult.

☞ If you wish to emerge as leader, devise a plan based on the general and special theories governing the group communication.

☞ If you wish to emerge as leader, you must be willing to do the necessary work.

☞ If you wish to emerge as leader, do not be a manipulator.

☞ If you wish to emerge as leader, adopt the strategy of working for the good of the group.

☞ If you wish to emerge as leader, take an active part in the meetings and reveal a commitment to the group, an understanding of the task, and consideration for other members.

☞ If you wish to emerge as leader, do your homework and understand the group and its tasks.

☞ If you wish to emerge as leader, make personal sacrifices for the good of the group.

☞ If you wish to emerge as leader, raise the status of other members.

☞ If you wish to emerge as leader, build group cohesiveness by dramatizing a group vision, history, and identity.

QUESTIONS FOR STUDY

1. What are some of the cultural ambivalences toward leadership in the United States?
2. What is the trait approach to leadership?
3. What are the advantages and disadvantages of the contextual explanation of leadership?
4. How would you define *leadership*?
5. What are some of the communications closely related to the perception of leadership in the small group?
6. What are the implications of the discovery that "the group selects its leader by the method of residues"?
7. What are the characteristics of the two major phases of leadership emergence in the leaderless group discussion?
8. What is the first pattern of leadership emergence? The second? The third? The fourth?
9. What is the lieutenant role function in a small group?
10. What is meant by a *central person*?
11. In what ways may a group take flight from the leadership problem?
12. What is the difference between a soft-sell and a hard-sell manipulator?
13. How may leadership emergence in women's groups, men's groups, and co-educational groups be compared and contrasted?

14. What effect does the assignment of leadership have on leadership emergence?
15. What behaviors do members who emerge as leaders in initially leaderless discussion groups commonly exhibit?

EXERCISES

1. Form a leaderless group discussion with a specific task and objective. Tape-record the meetings. After the first meeting, guess who will emerge as leader. List the names of those who will not be the leader. Describe the role that you will most likely assume in the group. After the second and subsequent meetings, make a similar evaluation of the leadership. After four meetings, write a short paper in which you describe the way your group handled the question of leadership. Fit your group into the overall pattern and the appropriate specific subpatterns of leadership emergence. Did your group have a lieutenant? A central person? Hold a postmortem, and discuss the leadership emergence in your group with the other members.

2. Select a group you have been working with for several months. Write a short paper discussing the assigned chair or leader. Is the assigned leader the natural leader? If not, who is? What is the relationship between the assigned leader and the natural leader? Why did the group accept or reject the assigned leader?

3. Form a group from your class, and work out a role-playing exercise to demonstrate the principles of leadership emergence. Conduct a class meeting as a group in which you use the role-playing exercise to demonstrate and illustrate leadership principles.

4. Work out a case study suitable for a leadership-training session. Divide the class into groups, and have them discuss the case; then reassemble the class for a general discussion.

REFERENCES AND SUGGESTED READINGS

Most of the discussion in this chapter is drawn from the results of the Minnesota studies. The literature on leadership is voluminous. For a survey of major studies of leadership, see:

Bass, Bernard M., and Ralph M. Stogdill. *Handbook of Leadership: A Survey of Theory and Research.* 2nd ed. New York: Free Press, 1981.

For studies reporting and evaluating the trait approach to leadership, see:

Fiedler, Fred E. "Leadership and Leadership Effectiveness Traits: A Reconceptualization of the Leadership Trait Problem." In Luigi Petrullo and Bernard Bass, eds., *Leadership and Interpersonal Behavior.* New York: Holt, Rinehart and Winston, 1961, pp. 179–186.

Stogdill, Ralph M. "Personal Factors Associated with Leadership: A Survey of the Literature," *Journal of Psychology,* **25** (1948), 35–71.

For a summary of research relating to styles of leadership, see:

Hare, A. Paul. *Handbook of Small Group Research.* 2nd ed. New York: Free Press, 1976.

Studies based on the styles-of-leadership perspective are too voluminous to catalog. For illustrative works, see:

Jurma, William E. "Effects of Leader Structuring Style and Task-Orientation Characteristics of Group Members," *Communication Monographs*, **46** (1979), 282–295.

Lippett, Ronald, and Ralph K. White. "Leader Behavior and Member Reaction in Three Social Climates." In Dorwin Cartwright and Alvin Zander, eds., *Group Dynamics: Research and Theory*. 3rd ed. New York: Harper & Row, 1968, pp. 318–335.

For the contingency approach to leadership effectiveness, see:

Fiedler, Fred E. *A theory of Leadership Effectiveness.* New York: McGraw-Hill, 1967.

Wofford, J. C. "Experimental Examination of the Contingency Model and the Leader-Environment-Follower Interaction Theory of Leadership," *Psychological Reports*, **56** (1985), 823–832.

The studies relating to the contextual approach to leadership are:

Baker, Deborah. "A Rhetorical Analysis of Communication Style in Initial Meetings of Small Groups." Unpublished Ph.D. dissertation, University of Minnesota, 1983.

Geier, John. "A Descriptive Analysis of an Interaction Pattern Resulting in Leadership Emergence in Leaderless Group Discussion." Ph.D. dissertation, University of Minnesota, 1963.

Larson, Charles U. "Leadership Emergence and Attention Span: A Content Analysis of the Time Devoted to Themes in the Task-Oriented Small Group." Ph.D. dissertation, University of Minnesota, 1968.

Mortensen, Calvin David. "A Content Analysis of Leadership Communication in Small, Task-Oriented Discussion Groups." Master's thesis, University of Minnesota, 1964.

Olson, Clark. "A Case Study Analysis of Credentialing in Small Groups." Ph.D. dissertation, University of Minnesota, 1987.

Pratt, Jerie McArthur. "A Case Study Analysis of Male-Female Leadership Emergence in Small Groups." Unpublished Ph.D. dissertation, University of Minnesota, 1979.

For women and leadership, see Baker and Pratt's dissertations above. See also:

Alderton, Steven M., and William E. Jurma. "Genderless/Gender-Related Task Leader Communication and Group Satisfaction: A Test of Two Hypotheses," *Southern Speech Communication Journal*, **46** (1980), 48–60.

Andrews, Patricia Hayes. "Performance-Self-Esteem and Perceptions of Leadership Emergence: A Comparative Study of Men and Women," *Western Journal of Speech Communication*, **48** (1984), 1–13.

Bormann, Ernest G., Jerie McArthur Pratt, and Linda L. Putnam. "Power, Authority, and Sex: Male Response to Female Dominance," *Communication Monographs*, **45** (1978), 119–155.

Mamola, Claire. "Women in Mixed Groups: Some Research Findings," *Small Group Behavior*," **10** (1979), 431–440.

Reed, Beth G. "Women Leaders in Small Groups: Social Psychological Perspectives and Strategies," *Social Work with Groups*, **6** (1983), 35–42.

Spillman, Bonnie, Richard Spillman, and Kim Reinking. "Leadership Emergence—Dynamic Analysis of the Effects of Sex and Androgyny," *Small Group Behavior*, **12** (1981), 139–157.

Wentworth, Diane K., and Lynn R. Anderson. "Emergence Leadership as a Function of Sex and Task Type," *Sex Roles*, **11** (1984), 513–524.

Wood, Julia T. "Sex Differences in Group Communication: Directions for Research in Speech Communications and Sociometry," *Journal of Group Psychotherapy, Psychodrama, and Sociometry*, **34** (1981), 24–31.

For a study of central persons, see:

Redl, Fritz. "Group Emotion and Leadership," *Psychiatry*, **5** (1942), 573–596.

Chapter
10

Group Decision Making and Problem Solving

*S*tudents of group problem solving and decision making have developed a range of perspectives in their efforts to study and teach about the task dimension of group work. These perspectives fall on a continuum with the rational, step-by-step approaches which stress planning and systematic, structured, organized, conscious group thinking on one end and holistic, intuitive, creative, natural, spontaneous, and expressive approaches on the other.

Many have made the argument that groups should develop a "group mind" and then should think the way individuals do when individuals think reflectively, creatively, or productively. Thus, organized approaches and synthesized research results relating to individual decision making have served as the basis for prescriptions on how groups might best make decisions and solve problems.

GROUP RATIONALITY

The rational, systematic end of the continuum has been the most popular and has been supported by the development of computer systems which essentially work by using the assumptions of logic and by systematic step-by-step information-processing procedures. The rational approach is illustrated by Kepner and Tragoe's recommendations on rational management, by the Program Evaluation and Review Technique (PERT), and by Janis and Mann's vigilant information-process approach to decision making. The rational end of the continuum, however, has been dominated by Dewey's original formulation of how people think reflectively. Kepner and Tragoe's approach to problem solving is essentially taking the Dewey pattern of reflective thinking and breaking the steps into substeps, thus making a finer-grained analysis. Kepner and Tregoe developed a decision-making procedure that is popular in business and industrial training programs. They define a problem as a deviation from a standard and identify the nature and extent of the problem by an elaborate set of step-by step comparisons. They first compare the "should" with the "actual" — that is, the ideal situation with actual conditions. Next, they compare the "is" with the "is not" to find out what factors are clearly part of the problem. The boundaries of the problem are located by repeated applications of the "is" and "is not" to features of the environment. The smaller steps are indicated by four questions: What is the deviation? Where is the deviation? When is the deviation? What is the extent of the deviation?

Even more closely modeled on computer experience is the Program Evaluation and Review Technique. People using PERT have arrived at a major policy decision that sets a goal. They use PERT to aid in solving the technical and practical problems involved in mobilizing resources to reach that goal. The PERT model provides a step-by-step checklist of procedures to establish priorities, estimate time, and allocate resources. Step 1 is to specify the final event or goal. Steps 2 and 3 are to determine the events that must precede the final outcome, and order them. What events must take place to ensure the final outcome, and what is their most sensible order? Step 4 is to determine the activity time for each event. Step 5 is to break up important links between the major sequence of events into sub-PERT events. Thus, the model proceeds in computer-programming fashion to analyze the administration of a project into ever smaller activities and time segments. Additional steps plan the needs and priorities relating to personnel, finances, and facilities.

Shaw's discussion of factors that aid group problem solving is essentially a restatement of the steps in the discussional process drawn from Dewey's analysis of reflective thinking.

Dewey has, thus, made one of the most important analyses of how individuals think in terms of a scientific, rational, step-by-step process; his ideas have been used for many years by students of group discussion. They were used for making the recommendations on problem solving in the one-time meeting in Chapter 2.

As we have seen, a number of people have modified Dewey's pattern of reflective thinking by making additions or breaking up each part of the pattern into smaller steps to make the search for solutions more systematic and ordered. The core of these variations retains the basic notion that good group problem solving should start with a focus on the problem and then move on systematically to consideration of possible solutions and that solutions should be examined in detail before the group makes a final decision as to which solution to put into practice.

GROUP CREATIVITY

At the opposite end of the continuum from the rational, systematic approach is the holistic, intuitive, and creative emphasis. Scholars of small group communication have also investigated the extent to which the group mind might solve problems in a creative way.

What Dewey's work is to the conscious, rational end of the continuum, Graham Wallas's analysis of creative thinking is to the other. Wallas described creative thinking in terms of a moment of conception during which a creative idea gets started and results in a period of preparatory work. Usually the project gets bogged down, and the individual puts the work aside for a time. The period of putting aside is an incubation phase when the subconscious is at work. The individual might fantasize about the project in an aimless way while driving a car, walking, jogging, or doing routine chores. The incubation phase peaks in a moment of illumination when the "light goes on" and the individual sees the solution to the problem. Such moments of illumination are an emotional and exciting part of creative work. The solution that pops into the mind "feels right." The final stage of the process is one wherein the individual carefully tests the solution to see whether that which seemed so good at the moment of inspiration really turns out to be good in practice.

Howell, whose work in intercultural communication has brought him in contact with Far Eastern communication and group work, stresses the difference between *analytic* and *holistic* approaches to decision making. He sees the Western style as predominately analytic—that is, the problem solver breaks the matter into small parts and analyzes each part and then puts them back together again (synthesizes) in ordered fashion. The results of such careful analysis and synthesis should be understanding and wise decisions. He sees the Eastern style as predominately holistic— that is, the problem solver or decision maker processes the necessary information largely out of awareness. When people process information holistically, they do not break the matter into parts or even think about it consciously. Instead, they absorb the whole pattern and react to it as a whole. The correct answers then surface as behavior or moments of illumination.

Some students of small group communication have tried to apply the principles of individual creativity to the group mind. Chapter 2 discusses the use of brainstorming and the nominal group technique. An important part of creativity is fluency, the ability to generate many ideas quickly. The brainstorming and nominal group techniques stress the fluency feature of group work and are aimed at generating many ideas quickly.

Another feature of creativity is flexibility, the ability to break out of the routine way of looking at a problem, to adopt a new set or way to approach the question. Practitioners such as Prince and Gordon who advise people about how to run productive business meetings have developed an approach to group creativity that they call *synectics*, which includes both fluency and flexibility.

The synectics approach suggests that in many business meetings there is a norm of antagonism to new ideas. Antagonism can be illustrated by the following hypothetical transcript:

MEMBER A: I think it would be a good idea to design the exteriors of our new computers so they seem more human and lovable.

MEMBER B: Marketing gimmicks have never gotten us anywhere. What counts is high technical quality and results. Looks don't matter.

MEMBER C: We're short of time. I think we ought to get down to serious business.

The immediate criticism of new ideas dampens creativity. Often member A (above) is too sophisticated and mature to admit that the criticism dramatized above irritated him. However, it is often the case that when member A gets the opportunity he will give as good as he got and the rewards of submitting new ideas only to have them shot down become smaller and smaller.

The creative group climate, according to this perspective, is open and nonjudgmental and involves members examining possibilities, hitchhiking on original suggestions to improve them, and accepting far-out ideas for further amplification. In terms of flexibility, the synectics approach stresses a variety of dramatizing techniques to break the participants out of their typical ruts. Synectic suggestions as to how to encourage flexibility include making the strange familiar and the familiar strange, using metaphors and analogies, personification, illusion, and daydreams.

Other ways to encourage flexibility include such things as taking a position and standing it on its head ("We have been assuming that men hold the powerful positions and women are powerless. What would happen to the communication if women were to hold the powerful positions and men were powerless?"); magnifying the question ("What if the mosquito infestation in the area were to become worldwide?"); minimizing the question ("What if we were after not world peace but peace in a small group like this one?"); and identifying with the nonhuman elements in the problem ("Suppose that we become the cancer cell and look at this question as a cancer cell would?" "How would we feel if we were a metal spring?").

In an organizational context, the prescriptive model of creative group work developed by those working with synectics stresses the importance of the leader having a creative rather than a critical set. The creative set views the suggestion in terms of its positive features and how it might be improved to work more effectively. The critical set views the suggestion in terms of all possible shortcomings, and raises such typical argumentation questions as "Is it unnecessary?" "Is it unworkable?" "Would it make matters worse?"

With a creative set, the person leading a creative group meeting should keep the following guidelines in mind:

1. Don't compete with group members. That is, don't state your own position until others have had a chance to thoroughly air theirs. If you insert ideas all through the creative meeting, you will often inhibit the free flow required for creativity.
2. Listen to group members. By modeling careful listening, the group leader can increase the productivity of the entire meeting.
3. Step in when someone is in danger of being put on the defensive.
4. Keep the meeting interesting. Be interested and involved; add humor if you can; use surprise, a new angle, a striking set of facts, an interesting illustration or example; throw out challenges. Use nonverbal communication to communicate your own interest; use gestures, facial expressions, and vocal intonation to communicate your personal involvement.
5. Creativity should be fun. A creative session should generate interest and excitement.

FANTASY SHARING AND PROBLEM SOLVING

Some case studies of the sharing of group fantasies suggest that symbolic convergence can explain how groups may deal with problems in a creative manner. Thus, a group might discover it has a problem (in Graham Wallas's term, the moment of *conception*) and begin by discussing information related to the problem in an attempt to solve it (*preparation*). After the problem is mulled over unsuccessfully for a time, the resulting secondary tensions might stimulate a member to dramatize about something that is apparently off the subject. If the drama is shared, the group may indulge in a period of fantasy sharing which contains a double meaning applicable to the problem, much as an individual might daydream without conscious purpose while working on a creative project (*incubation*). Suddenly the group may experience a moment of insight because something in the shared fantasies reminds them of the problem, and quickly all members realize that they have found a good solution to it. With mounting enthusiasm and excitement, the group realizes that a solution has emerged (*illumination*). Finally, the group carefully and systematically evaluates the solution to make sure that it is as good as it at first seemed (*verification*).

A group member reported on a moment of illumination in the group as follows:

> We had picked our topic at the first meeting. By the third meeting, it was going nowhere in a hurry and not a soul was interested in pursuing it any further. However, we had 10 days before our presentation, and we all thought that the others wanted to continue with our first choice. This near-transcript is of our fourth meeting at Riverbend.

"Hi, how was your weekend?"

[*General comments: "Fine," "Okay."*]

"Well, it was pretty eventful for me." [*A stack of information literally three inches thick is placed before our eyes.*] "That lady I talked to at the courthouse sent me all this information. There is some good stuff in here."

. . .

[*Some brave souls pick up some sheets and scan through them.*]

"It says here that there were three murders allegedly committed by juvenile offenders in the state of Minnesota last year and only one went to jail."

. . .

"So we are dealing with an issue that isn't a problem."

"It's still a good issue."

"Come on, you can't call one thousandths of a percent a problem."

"Yeah, but look at all the information she brought. We must be able to use it."

"Look, there just aren't that many kids committing murder in the state of Minnesota."

"What about [*name*]? She was murdered by kids."

"That was gang-related."

[*Short yet powerful pause.*]

"GANGS!!!"

"Yeah! We can do it on gangs!"

"We can call Tony Bouza and talk to him!"

"We can dress up like gang members during our presentation and walk in to *West Side Story* music!"

"We can go to North High and speak to the principal there!"

"This is great! It's gonna work! We're going to be great!"

[*General euphoria and cohesion set in. The group was indeed great.*]

Ferguson conducted a case study of the fantasy themes among a group of teenagers working on a "tot lot" which was to become a playground for small children. The teenagers were to help plan details for the playground and would work as volunteer supervisors when it was set up. She found that some of the fantasies of the group were very analogous to the period of incubation in individual problem solving. For example, at one point group members were considering the problem of rules for the children, and they broke off their direct analysis of the problem to fantasize about how teenagers did not obey their parents.

In such a way, some fantasy chains probably contribute to solutions in a productive way because they stem from problems relating to the group's task dimension. Of course, other fantasies may contribute to solutions that are not very good because they stem from internal conflicts in the social dimension.

Some practitioners of synectics have also discovered the importance to creative group work of such dramatizing messages as wordplay, figures of speech, analogies, and narrations which result in group fantasizing. Prince, for example, suggested that when a group bogs down, the members can take a "fantasy vacation" from the hard, rigorous, step-by-step analysis of the problem and agree to talk about something completely different.

Scheidel has discussed the uses of divergent (creative) and convergent (rigorous, step-by-step) analyses in group decision making and has pointed to the strengths and weaknesses of both. Certainly at some point the ideas generated in a brainstorming or synectic context need to be evaluated and winnowed for quality and applicability.

At any rate, the Minnesota studies of good problem-solving groups lead to the conclusion that there is a time for a freewheeling, creative period of discussion and a time for more ordered procedures and for organized, step-by-step planning. The studies fall somewhere near the center of the continuum and suggest that groups develop flexibility in their work norms so they can be both creative and reasoned.

PHASES IN GROUP DECISION MAKING

A number of scholars have studied the changes in small group communication over time from the point at which members first begin to work on a problem to the point at which they come to a decision or a solution.

The earlier studies, such as those of Bales and Strodbeck, found a unitary sequence composed of an orientation phase, an evaluation phase, and a control phase. Fisher also found a unitary sequence composed of an orientation phase, a conflict phase, a decision-emergence phase, and a reinforcement phase. Recently Poole and his associates have argued persuasively for a multiple sequence account of how groups make decisions. The argument is that group decision making is too complex to be explained by one pattern of action and that, indeed, groups exhibit a number of different patterns. In order for group decision making to be understood in all its complexity, the process must be viewed in a context which involves at least three threads of communication: (1) task work relating to problem and solution analysis; (2) relationship messages which reveal how members get along in terms of focused work and conflict; and (3) the topic (substantive communication relating to a specific decision). In addition, Poole added the concept of *breakpoints*, which could cause the typical pattern of decision making to shift. Breakpoints include topic shifts, dropping a point to cycle back to an earlier point and rework it, and major disruptions which halt the group's progress or cause it to reconsider the entire decision anew.

Although much work has gone into the search for a unitary pattern of problem solving, the new emphasis on groups following many or several paths to decisions and problem solutions is a good one. It points out again the complexity of group work and the need to be aware of the difficulties that arise in group decision making. The new theoretical formulations are promising and should aid the student in participating in group decision making and problem solving.

The studies of group problem solving have found that communication generally changes in systematic ways as the problem-solving process continues. Of course, the cycling back feature reported by Schiedel and Crowell and supported by the Minnesota case studies would be a breakpoint in these changes, as Poole suggests.

THE DECISION-MAKING PROCESS IN SMALL TASK-ORIENTED GROUPS

Another approach to the decision-making process assumes that problem solving does not follow a rational model, but rather reflects and affects the social and emotional tone and climate of the meeting. Zaleznik and Moment, for example, emphasize the relationship between emotional effect and work. Starting from essentially Freudian psychoanalytic assumptions, they discuss the work meeting as analogous to a psychotherapy session and describe the participants' tendency to vacillate between hostility and affection, aggression and passivity, fight and flight. These swings of mood and reaction relate to such problems as handling external and internal authority. The group may swing from extreme independence to overdependence on an external authority, or from fighting authority to fleeing from it. Zaleznik and Moment regard work as just one of a number of group modalities, the majority of which are emotional. They suggest that each group must develop its own work norms and discover for itself how it can best solve problems.

Bales also establishes an explanatory framework that accounts for both the socioemotional responses and the task dimension of group process. He suggests an equilibrium model in which the group strives to establish an equilibrium of tensions. When social tensions rise to uncomfortable levels, the group attends to them until it reaches a comfortable state of equilibrium, when it turns again to the task. In this way, the group swings from work to establishing social equilibrium and back to work. In a study of 16 experimental groups, Bales discovered that over one-third of the responses were socioemotional in nature. The proponents of a purely rational model of decision making might consider such a high proportion of social activity a waste of time. Those who assume that cohesiveness and social interactions are just as important as productivity might view these social interactions as evidence of group health.

Zaleznik and Moment use a somewhat different explanatory framework to present essentially the same description. They discuss *levels of work*. The first level is characterized by personal needs of the individuals. Each participant talks about his or her personal experience as it relates to the problem at hand. Members react to one another personally, and when they do offer new information, it is largely unevaluated. Except for providing individuals with information about the personal needs of the members, little constructive work on the problem results.

The second level begins when participants question information. They begin to ask for reasons to support suggestions. At this level, they are satisfied with conventional answers. They rely on common knowledge and common sense. The testing and analysis are still ego-involved and do not help them to relate to the external environment. The contributions serve mainly to justify the views of each individual.

The third level finds participants raising basic questions. They consider a point for a longer period of time. Participants learn about each other's real position on the important questions and the possible alternatives open to the group.

The fourth level finds participants becoming members of a group. Feedback is increased; people relax and do not hide things from one another. Members say what they think, and misunderstandings are clarified. They stimulate one another to generate new ideas, and these ideas are tested openly and bluntly. The first three stages are preparation for this final level of work. In the first level, individuals get to know one another and confine themselves to safe, conventional behavior. In the second level, ideas are suggested, with the covert understanding that no one will get hurt. In the third stage, members start to disagree. They are getting ready to begin the real work.

For a number of years, Tavistock Psychiatric Institute in London has been conducting human-relations-training workshops based on the work of Bion as expanded and applied by Rice. The analysis of the dynamics of a work group that emerged from the Tavistock group is analogous to those described by Zaleznik and Moment. According to Bion, groups face socioemotional and work problems. The tendency for newly formed groups is to go through stages of immaturity and neurotic behavior before achieving the level of work. Bion outlined three basic neurotic conditions for groups: (1) dependency, (2) pairing, and (3) fight or flight. Bion refers to the neurotic conditions as basic-assumption groups. When the group is making the basic assumption of dependency, it is neurotically preoccupied with power and comes to depend on a strong leader or a strong force external to it. The group expects its strong leader to serve a savior function. When the basic assumption is pairing, the members tend to form coalitions based on compatible needs. The third assumption group is one of flight or fight in which the group tries to preserve itself by avoiding or attacking things it finds threatening. The emphasis is, however, on group survival. Finally, groups that mature move from the basic assumptions to work groups able to focus their energies on a common task.

Zaleznik and Moment as well as Bion and Rice are describing in somewhat more psychoanalytic terms the same dynamics that emerged in the Minnesota studies. The period of tension in which people are quiet and polite is what Zaleznik and Moment call the first level of work. The period in which participants test one another and find a role structure is equivalent to the second level. The stabilizing of a role structure and the development of a common group culture is the third level. The final level describes the work of successful, highly cohesive groups with stable role structures such as has been evident in the cases included in the Minnesota studies.

The basic assumptions outlined by Bion and Rice also appeared at Minnesota. The second pattern of leadership emergence in which two leader contenders both gain a lieutenant and thus continue the struggle is much the same as the pairing-assumption group described by Bion. Occasionally a strong, assertive person seemed to be running the groups in the Minnesota studies because no one raised a challenge immediately, although the members were very dissatisfied with the person's leadership. The group always challenged and then rejected the strong, assertive person's leadership sooner or later, but during the portion of the group's history when that individual seemed to be in charge, the group would behave as though it were making the dependency assumption. Of course, many observers in addition to Bion have reported the tendency of small groups to take flight or to vent aggression. The fight-or-flight behavior has also been a prominent feature in the Minnesota studies, as has the analysis of role emergence and stability which parallels the basic-assumption groups described by Bion. When several research groups, working quite independently, arrive at descriptive conclusions that parallel and support one another, the assumptions gain credence, and when the results appear in two somewhat separate cultures as well, the empirical support for the analysis is strengthened.

The following description of the dynamics of the group's task dimension is drawn from the case studies conducted at Minnesota, but it is supported by the analysis of Zaleznik and Moment and by the experience of the Tavistock workshops.

THE PROBLEM-SOLVING AGENDA
AND THE TASK DIMENSION

Empirical evidence indicates that groups do not follow a linear path through the recommended steps of a problem-solving model. For example, Scheidel and Crowell developed a set of categories to study the development of ideas in discussion groups. They discovered that discussions do not follow a linear path through the testing of ideas, but rather that ideas are introduced spontaneously. Someone may extend an idea by changing the emphasis or suggesting a modification. Someone else may simply affirm or reject the idea. Scheidel and Crowell characterize the process as an "idea-in-the-making" in which the original idea is changed through oral modification until it represents the discussants' cumulative, developing, mutual point of view. They discovered that discussions drawn from a course on the principles of group discussion devoted only 22 percent of their thought units to the initiation, extension, modification, and synthesis of ideas. About one-fourth of the group effort was used to clarify and substantiate ideas already displayed before the group. These workers decided that group thought moves forward in a reach-test cycle rather than in a straight line; that is, one discussant reaches forward with a new idea which is then tested by elaboration and acceptance or rejection. When this thought is "anchored" in group acceptance, a procedure that occupied almost half the time of the discussions, a participant will reach forward with another idea, and the cycle will be repeated. Scheidel and Crowell suggest that the typical linear development of group problem solving should be replaced with a spiraling model.

Taylor and Faust justify their use of the game of Twenty Questions in a study of the relationship between problem-solving efficiency and group size on the basis that the game is a realistic approximation of everyday problem solving. In this game, players are told that they must find an object by asking a series of yes–no questions. Taylor and Faust maintain that solutions to everyday problems are seldom reached by a linear pattern of rigorous, well-defined steps, but that individuals often begin with a vague problem about which they ask a series of vague questions. When these questions are answered, they have a clearer impression of the problem and can ask a series of sharper questions. The same authors discovered that groups of people were more efficient than individuals at playing the game of Twenty Questions. They suggested that this occurs because a group has more relevant information and is more flexible than an individual in its approach to a solution. Individuals who played the game were sometimes unable to stop an unproductive line of questioning.

Group Attention Span

One striking feature of groups is their relatively short attention span. Berg studied over 100 discussions by student, faculty, religious, political, and professional groups. He made a content analysis of the themes introduced and measured with a stopwatch the length of time a particular theme was discussed without interruption. In all, he coded 5079 themes and discovered that the mean time per theme (group attention span) was 58 seconds. The range, on a group basis, was from 28 to 118 seconds; the small amount of variance is indicated by a standard deviation of 18 seconds. Berg further coded the themes into categories and discovered that substantive themes were attended to on the average for 76 seconds and that procedural topics were attended to for 47 seconds. The groups' attention span for topics irrelevant to the task was 29 seconds. The most interesting feature of these data was their uniformity. When groups composed of three to five members were compared with groups of five to eight, and when class discussions used as training exercises were compared with groups dealing with "real" problems, the attention span remained very stable.

Larson refined Berg's category system and gathered further normative data that essentially supported Berg's findings. Faffler used Berg's categories in a cross-cultural study of American and Middle Eastern students in Beirut and found similar results, as did Ryberg in a study of bilingual North and South Americans discussing in both Spanish and English.

Group Risk Taking

A number of investigators of small group communication have been preoccupied with the discovery by Stoner that groups tend to make riskier decisions than individuals. Stoner's notion, which came to be called the *risky shift*, was intriguing because one widely held stereotype of groups prior to that time was that they were essentially average or even conservative in their decisions. A number of subsequent studies investigated the risky shift usually by giving subjects descriptions of hypothetical situations and asking them how sure they would have to be of success before they would risk a course of action. The subjects first responded to the questionnaire individually and then took part in a group discussion until there was consensus on the same list of hypothetical situations. Investigators using the technique of hypothetical situations replicated the results of the original research so that the phenomenon was, for a time, generally accepted as having been demonstrated, at least for the hypothetical situations.

Subsequent research was directed to discovering the process that accounts for the increased risk taking by groups. Among the hypotheses put forward was the notion that risk taking is a cultural value and that most North Americans see themselves as above-average risk takers. Further, when they discover in a discussion that they are average or below average, they shift to a riskier decision. Another hypothesis was that risky individuals are more influential in groups than cautious ones. A final hypothesis was that a group decision diffuses responsibility and thus makes it easier to take a risky position with the support of like-minded group members.

Several studies have reported historical examples of groups making risky decisions. Janis's work dealt with important foreign policy decisions in the United States in the 1950s and 1960s, such as the Bay of Pigs invasion and the escalation of the Vietnam war. Raack applied behavioral theory to historical materials relating to the anti-French conspiracy in Prussia in 1808 and discovered that forces within the small radical groups heightened the influence of the risk takers and stifled that of the moderates. In addition, he judged that the plot developed a momentum of its own which seemed to force the leaders to act more precipitously than they wished and to take action counter to their original plans.

Clearly, groups often make riskier decisions than the individuals composing the groups might make singly; however, recent research into the risky-shift phenomenon demonstrates that groups vary as to conservatism or risk taking depending on their norms and culture. Studies by Dion, Miller and Magnan, and Kroger and Briedis, for example, demonstrated cautious decisions by groups in which cautious norms were experimentally induced. Although groups may develop either a cautious or risk-taking culture, the research into the risky-shift phenomenon demonstrates that the stereotype of groups as more mediocre, average, or cautious than individuals in decision making is not adequate. Rather, the group culture, the motivations generated by the group's chaining fantasies, and the group's norms provide a better account for risky or cautious decisions than the hypothesis that groups invariably make either cautious or risky decisions. The most recent research has used the term *polarization* to describe the tendency in groups to make risky or conservative decisions. Studies by Alderton, Alderton and Frey, Cline and Cline, DeStephen and Major provide further support for the polarization conclusion.

Approach – Withdrawal Behavior

Another feature of group discussion is the participants' tendency to explore a topic until they discover that it is related to a role struggle or has other status implications. They deal with the topic until the secondary tension becomes uncomfortable and then typically withdraw. They approach the problem by getting a quick and superficial survey of the ground. They find the areas of easy agreement and the points of difficulty. When they feel that the rise of tension is a threat to cohesiveness, they withdraw and introduce a different theme. They must, of course, return to the difficult questions in order to succeed. After a time, they try another probe of the difficult area. If it seems less difficult than they first suspected, they may make a decision. The really crucial and divisive themes are withdrawn from and approached several more times until the external pressures and deadlines force participants to a decision.

A Basic Model of Group Decision Making

Work by Fisher in the small group seminar at Minnesota suggests a hypothesis that explains much of the data relating to group decision making. When the Dewey model or some variant of it is used, it is assumed that a group uses one process in establishing roles and norms (the model developed in Chapter 6) and another (Dewey's reflective-thinking model) in solving problems related to the task. The research results outlined above can better be explained by a simpler hypothesis: *Decisions emerge from group interactions in the same way that roles emerge and normative behavior develops.*

Decision Emergence   Bales's equilibrium model reflects the tendency for decisions to emerge the way norms do. His discovery of a swing from task to social responses supports the basic model. Zaleznik and Moment's suggestion that groups probe deeper and deeper into the entire problem as they proceed through levels of work also is accounted for by the hypothesis that decisions emerge as do roles and norms.

The basic model of decision emergence in the small task-oriented group is as follows. Participants attack a problem in a cyclical fashion rather than in a linear way. They approach the entire problem several times. Someone submits an idea. Others contribute statements of fact, advice, and opinion. A number of ideas are displayed. Some information is rejected quickly and easily, just as some leader contenders are eliminated in the first phase of role emergence. The members accept some ideas just as quickly because of their source or because all find them clearly meritorious. As people discuss the idea, they sharpen their questions and discover areas of disagreement. Some significant ideas are not acceptable to all. Discussants do not follow a rational step-by-step model at this point because they cannot do so. They must find the areas of consensus and of difference, the touchy points and the safe ones. The participants approach the problem in its entirety at a rather superficial level, then return to the problem again and dig into a deeper analysis, swing away, and return again to probe deeper.

Early in their deliberations, participants may display a number of solutions and discover that several are clearly unsuitable, but that one has strong support from several members. Participants may drop consideration of the solution at that point to discuss the problem. The proponent of the solution may introduce the plan again and relate it to the discussion. Others may now disagree with the solution, and tensions will grow. At this point, an irrelevant tension-releasing theme is introduced. After a time spent releasing tension, someone may ask what the group is trying to do. The members respond by considering goals, which enables the proponent of the solution to suggest its usefulness again. If the solution is again rejected, another participant may be encouraged to propose a solution. The group swings from problem to solution to goals to problem to goals to solution to solution, with tension release and group solidarity comments inserted at points throughout the deliberations.

At some point during this process, the participants will discover that a decision has emerged, a decision to which they are committed and which they are willing to implement. Often the decision is reached without a vote or a formal show of consensus. On occasion, the discussion does not result in the clear emergence of a decision; the participants may then vote and settle the question on the basis of majority rule. Such a situation is analogous to the problem faced by a group that is unable to structure its roles and perceive that a leader has clearly emerged. Problem solving is similar to peeling an onion, layer by layer. The group removes the superficial layers of the problem until the participants become uncomfortable. They withdraw for a time and then return to it. This process occurs many times until participants are forced to return to the task by the pressure of the problem, and they must reach the core and make a decision.

Task Decisions That Emerge by Accident   Just as some norms develop as a result of chance happenings during the course of a discussion, so some decisions emerge accidentally. Early in one group's first meeting, for example, a participant asked if members should elect a chair. As might be expected, posing a status issue so early flustered the others. Finally another discussant broke the tense silence by asking if they should vote by a secret ballot or by a show of hands. Still flustered, several others suggested that a show of hands would be better than a secret ballot. Member A then turned to member B and said that in his estimation, B was the best person to be chair. Member B protested modestly that someone else would be better. When the others urged B to be chair, however, he capitulated and said that he would do his best. The decision to elect a chair was made by accident. The group withdrew from the issue through a question on procedure that *assumed it would elect a chair.* No one questioned this assumption.

Task Decisions That Emerge Through Role Struggles   In the second phase of leadership contention, a substantive decision may be a by-product of role struggles. For example, in one discussion, a leader emerged, but his style of leadership proved unsatisfactory. The showdown came during the course of a work meeting devoted to writing a committee report. The leader arrived for the meeting with the preamble to the resolution already drafted. He had an agenda to guide the group's deliberations on the substantive sections of the report, but he felt he would facilitate matters by writing the introduction. After explaining this to the others, he began to read the preamble. He started with considerable enthusiasm. Perhaps he expected the group to reward him for his extra time and effort in preparing for the meeting. He received no compliments; instead, he was interrupted by a participant who asked that a certain phrase be read again. The leader was puzzled, but he read the phrase again. The participant then challenged the wording of that section. The leader tried to brush off the challenge by reminding the committee that the introductory material was relatively unimportant and that it should begin work on the substance of the report. The challenger repeated the demand that the phrase be reworded and suggested new language to be substituted. The leader was now aroused to defend his language. For some minutes the leader and the challenger quibbled about the wording of the innocuous phrase. Finally the challenger received support from a lieutenant; and, after a few more minutes, the remaining members supported the changed wording. The leader held out a little longer and then capitulated. The phrase was changed; and, from that point, the challenger assumed the role of leader. The group had deposed an unsatisfactory leader and selected a new one without formal election. An observer with a rational bias would criticize the session because most of it was devoted to an argument over an essentially trivial point. Yet the group made an important decision in regard to its social structure. As a by-product of that social structuring, it also made a task decision about the wording of the report.

Another committee drafted a proposal heavily influenced by fantasy chains relating to the socioemotional problems the discussants faced. In the first meeting, one individual complained about being placed in an all-female group. She felt such a committee could not make an intelligent study and report. Immediately, she became a negative central person. The others found themselves working to integrate her into the group. Subsequently, she missed several meetings. When she returned, the group was in the middle of a study of the problem posed by police brutality. She expressed her opinion in strong terms and argued that local police forces were hampered by unrealistic restrictions on their ability to question suspects and obtain confessions. After some discussion, the others perceived that she would not change her position. The members withdrew from a decision until the deadline for their report forced them to act. They approached the topic again, and when secondary tension rose, they went into a period of prolonged group fantasizing. Using the Supreme Court—whose decisions, they said, made the job of the police untenable—as a scapegoat, they argued that nothing could be done about the Court. Obviously, their analysis had taken them to a dead end. They responded with loud satirical attacks on the Court. The leader dramatized, "Let's all march on Washington!" Another participant suggested a mayors' conference to which the committee would "present a huge, long document." Members were now laughing and speaking loudly. "Citizens to overthrow the Supreme Court!" the leader fantasized. After a moment, they began to consider somewhat seriously the possibility of public opinion's changing the Court's decisions. "What can one mayor do about it? That's the problem!" "So what can four college kids do about it?" Clearly, they were in an untenable position. The leader started to laugh again and said, "We'll have everyone meet. And we'll deputize everybody!"

After a prolonged period of near-hysterical fantasy chains which had the theme of attacks on the Court, the members proceeded to write a report. It was a one-sided analysis which suggested that police brutality was nonexistent and that police officers were unable to function effectively because of the Supreme Court decision that allows suspects to have legal counsel and does not allow confessions obtained without counsel to be admitted as evidence. The report concluded that the main problem was the philosophy of the Court, which admittedly could not be changed. It then suggested that better training for police officers, more money, and more personnel would enable the police to do a better job despite the restrictions imposed by the Court. The committee's final decision was made partly in response to the information about the group's external environment and partly as a response to the needs of the group's internal social structure. The shape of the decision was heavily influenced by fantasies which stemmed from the problems posed by the negative central person.

Task Decisions Based on Authority   The highest level of efficient work takes place in organizations with stable role structures. One feature of such work is the tendency for task decisions to be made on the basis of role expectations. Participants make many procedural decisions largely on the basis of the source of the recommendation. Thus, minor decisions concerning the structuring of the work are quickly made because the leader suggests them. A group may follow any one of five or six different agendas, for example, and achieve task goals with equal efficiency. During the process of achieving a role structure, people discuss these procedural plans at great length, because they furnish the battleground for the leadership struggle. After a leader emerges, he or she will make frequent procedural suggestions, and many will be accepted because the leader makes them.

Other kinds of decisions are made on the basis of authority. If an influential person suggests or agrees with information about the external reality or a suitable solution, the others often accept the information or solution.

Task Decisions Based on Factual Analysis   A good group, in which members work efficiently as a team, will make significant decisions on the basis of a thorough and accurate examination of the facts and will make plans with a clear perception of the problems posed by the external environment. At those moments when a good group reaches the highest level of work, it is an exciting thing to watch. It is just as exciting to participate. Ken Kesey, in his novel *Sometimes a Great Notion*, describes three men cutting timber, a scene that captures the spirit common to all task-oriented small groups when they are functioning at peak efficiency.

> Until the three of them meshed, dovetailed . . . into one of the rare and beautiful units of effort sometimes seen when a jazz group is making it completely, swinging together completely, or when a home town basketball squad, already playing over its head, begins to rally to overtake a superior opponent in a game's last minute . . . and the home boys can't miss; because everything—the passing, the dribbling, the plays—every tiny *piece* is clicking perfectly. When this happens everyone watching *knows* . . . that, be it five guys playing basketball, or four blowing jazz, or three cutting timber, that *this bunch*—right now, right *this moment*—is the best of its kind in the world! But to become this kind of perfect group a team must use all its components, and use them in the slots best suited, and use them all with the

pitiless dedication to victory that drives them up to their absolute peak, and past it.*

Of course, even highly cohesive groups working efficiently achieve such moments only rarely, but they do achieve them, and they are among the most gratifying experiences of people who work with and participate in groups. Some groups in the Minnesota studies made detailed analyses of their own dynamics. One of the more successful case studies contained the following description of the group's work norms:

> Cooperatively we arrived at an illustration or hypothesis of how the group frequently works when we all meet. It is obviously a great oversimplification, but we still feel that it has some validity and also somewhat clarifies the role structure; Stig throws out an idea for consideration. Pam — "the first filter" — picks up the idea, feels out the consensus of the group, and attempts to establish the attitude. If it is positive, Jim as "the second filter" in his turn picks it [the idea] up, twists it about, jokes about it, and ends up by reinforcing or rejecting it. Barb then questions the idea, adds some comments of her own, and occasionally seriously criticizes it — if so, it will normally be dropped right away. Finally Mark, who has remained silent up to this point, usually summarizes, crystallizes, and explains the revamped idea by adding another dimension to it; he then throws it back to Stig for final approval.

Clearly, a group that processes ideas in a relatively orderly and specialized fashion requires a stable role structure. The members of this group perceived the role structure in this way: Stig was the leader; Jim was the tension releaser; Pam gathered information, questioned ideas, and initiated certain kinds of action; Mark was a summarizer, a clarifier of ideas, a philosopher; Barb was a questioner of ideas and "a (not too frequent, and consequently all the more powerful!) critic."

Of course, the group did not process all ideas in the same way. When participants dealt with an important decision on which there was disagreement, they did not run it through an assembly line as the above description might suggest. They, too, followed the general model of a cyclical or spiral path through the superficial layers to the basic issues of the problem. Yet various people did specialize in task functions, and a particular individual did influence the group in certain ways. They were using their components in the "slots best suited." They had achieved a level of cohesiveness such that each member felt free to respond to an idea with an honest opinion. Stig was the leader, but his ideas were criticized as thoroughly as everyone else's. When the group rejected Stig's ideas, he did not lose status or esteem. The same stability protected people playing the other roles. Stig was realistic and generally made a sound analysis of the requirements of the task. Pam was more sensitive to the internal stresses a course of action might evoke. She was alert to the meshing of the work modality with the social effects within the group. In

---

*Ken Kesey. *Sometimes a Great Notion.* New York: Bantam, 1965, p. 476.

Barb, the group had an intercollegiate debater thoroughly trained in argumentation who was able to do a superior job of testing evidence and reasoning. Mark was a capable philosopher who saw the ramifications of a course of action as they related to both immediate and long-range goals.

With stable roles and healthy work norms, the group dealt with the demands placed on it by the external environment in superior fashion. They did not go through the steps of the Dewey pattern, but they did work out their own normative pattern. The group's task norms were tailored to the skills of its personnel, and they enabled the group to make sound decisions.

IMPROVING THE TASK DIMENSION OF GROUP INTERACTION

Ensuring That Work Norms Are Efficient

The student who wishes to improve the productivity of a small group should first observe and describe the way it goes about its work. What are the task roles? What are the work norms? Group norms are analogous to individual habits. Just as habits may be good or bad for an individual's physical health, so norms may be good or bad for the organization's productivity.

Bad habits are not easy to change; neither are unproductive norms. Both habits and norms, however, can be evaluated and modified by conscious effort. One group discovered that it had developed a norm of withdrawing into socializing and tension release whenever it had a business meeting. Members were, in many respects, congenial and cohesive as long as their interactions remained on a social level. However, they did not achieve a high level of work. The group was divided, two against three, on a basic question about the kind of information required to do a good job. Three members felt that secondary sources from popular magazines would furnish adequate information if supplemented by interesting personal experience. Two participants felt that, for a public discussion, more information from primary sources was required and that group members should do much more intense library research. To some extent, the alignment represented cliques that developed during the second phase of leadership contention. Member A and his lieutenant were clearly task-oriented. Member B and his supporters were more interested in social cohesion. The clique led by B was composed of people who felt inadequate because of lack of time or training to gather information from the library. When the group failed to get a good grade on its class discussion, members talked over the reasons for the poor performance. They discovered the norm of fleeing into socializing and discussed the best way to find information. They determined to change the norm for future assignments and largely succeeded.

Another common norm that develops out of the social structuring of a group, which often inhibits the quality of work, is the use of a sensible division of labor for gathering information as an excuse to withdraw from the tensions of group work. People often approach a new committee with the stereotype that the others will be lazy. The myth of minimal effort is widespread in our society. Douglas McGregor, in his book *The Human Side of Enterprise*, suggests that the traditional perspective for business management assumes that average human beings have an inherent dislike for work and will avoid it if they can, and that they must be coerced, controlled, and threatened to put forth effort for the organization. McGregor argues that work is as natural as play or rest and that the average person will not only accept responsibility, but will seek it out under proper conditions. People who have the stereotype that human beings are lazy typically approach any suggestion that would require work from any or all committee members with great reluctance. They would prefer to have someone volunteer to work rather than face the decision of directing or appointing someone to do a job. Quite often an appointed or elected chair will, in the early meetings of a task-oriented group, ask for volunteers. If no one steps forward, he or she will do the work rather than ask or order another person to do it. Task-oriented groups often establish experts to deal with the division of labor in a fair and just fashion. If it is an intellectual task such as studying a question of public policy, the group may "divide the topic" so that each member is responsible for one area. The following transcript is typical.

MEMBER A: Should we break it up into magazines? We should each be responsible for like — *Time, Newsweek, America, Nation* — rather than all going over the same . . .

MEMBER C: But you know you are still going to have a lot of overlapping if . . . and to prevent that, so that we won't take up quite so much time getting out extraneous material . . . maybe if we decided to take various separate things, either divide up according to country, or divide up according to areas, political, economic . . .

MEMBER A: Yes . . .

MEMBER C: We cut down on this overlapping . . .

MEMBER A: Yeah. That's all right with him, isn't it? If we do it that way?

MEMBER D: He mentioned in class that if we do that, more than one person is bringing in one kind of information and then no one else really knows.

[*This comment refers to the instructor's warning, while explaining the assignment, that dividing the work into content areas was likely to result in a lack of thorough testing of information.*]

MEMBER A: Yeah. But if we break it up into areas I think . . . in order for the paper to be complete, we are going to have to . . . otherwise we are going to have this mish-mash of junk sitting there and we are going to have to painstakingly take each thing out and that would be awfully hard . . .

MEMBER C: Yes, I don't see how we really . . .

MEMBER A: Let's see, economic would be important . . . political, social . . . what does social include? Sort of conditions?

At this point, the group has decided to divide the topic according to sets of categories, including political, social, and economic. Notice how this decision emerges. Member A makes the suggestion and is supported by C's immediate consideration of how the division might best be accomplished. Member D suggests that the instructor might not approve, but her disagreement is quickly drowned out by A and C. By the time A begins trying to find a suitable set of categories along the lines suggested by C, the group has decided to divide the work. The next thing members do is volunteer to take certain sections.

Committees that divide the work in this way develop specialists in content areas. In this instance, one participant became a specialist in economic conditions, and another a specialist in political affairs. When the group began its work, a norm was established in which economic problems were referred to the economic specialist, and her word was never challenged by the other members. In return, when the political specialist offered ideas involving political affairs, her information was not challenged or tested by the others. They referred all questions to the appropriate authority and accepted the expert's information without question.

If each person in a small task-oriented group becomes a specialist in some content areas, information can be processed with a minimum of social tension. The others simply turn to the appropriate authority and accept his or her testimony. Disagreements about the truth of statements of fact are largely ruled out by this procedure. Participants can also avoid the questioning of advice in this fashion. The committee's productivity is thus dependent on the skill of its experts. The work may suffer because some of the experts are not competent. In addition, content specialists reduce group interaction, cohesiveness, and commitment.

In groups with such division of labor, a typical information-processing session proceeds as follows. The committee meets and the economic authority delivers a 15-minute lecture while the others take notes. Next, the expert on political affairs reports, and so forth, until all have given their speeches. On the other hand, a group that has each person specializing in a task function, such as testing the truth or falsity of statements of fact, is not handicapped in the same way. If, in addition, the task roles emerged during the shakedown cruise and are performed by the most capable people, the job is done effectively.

Channels of Communication

A considerable body of research literature reports the relationships among artificial channels of communication — restricting feedback and who can talk to whom — and task effectiveness and the social dimension. The research is usually referred to as studies of *communication networks.* The investigators used research designs that differed as to details, but usually the channels of communication were experimentally manipulated, and the effect of various channels was estimated by scaling or testing variables such as task efficiency and member satisfaction. Researchers controlled the flow and direction of messages by such devices as having subjects separated by partitions and then allowing them to communicate only by written messages, telephone connections, and so forth. For instance, an investigator might use three-person groups in which member A is allowed to talk to B, and B to C, and C to A, but the subjects are not allowed to talk freely to one another. In another experimental treatment, the researcher might allow all three subjects to speak to one another as much as they wished. In still another, the design might include five-person groups arranged so that one member is the center of the network in that the other four can talk to that person and he or she can talk to all the others, but they cannot talk with one another. Investigators have used considerable ingenuity in working out variations of networks. In a survey of the research, Shaw noted that the literature contained as many as five variations for three-person groups, six for four-person groups, seven for five-person groups, and five for six-person groups.

The main finding of the research that is useful for the student of the small task-oriented group in the natural setting is that feedback in the message communication manner increases task efficiency in the experimental groups. In addition, the unrestricted flow of communication tends to improve member satisfaction. Some research evidence suggests, however, that unrestricted communication *takes more time* under conditions of free, unlimited feedback than it does without feedback. In other words, to facilitate maximum understanding on the part of all, the meetings must take considerable time. Too frequently, the planners of a conference try to do too much in the time allotted. They often cut off feedback by nonverbal communications such as looking at the clock, talking rapidly, growing restless when questions are raised, and in other ways indicating that everyone is in a hurry and, if people will be quiet, the meeting will end on time.

The main lesson to be learned from the study of communication networks in the laboratory is that norms that restrict the flow of information tend to reduce the productivity of the group.

Often the communication flow that actually takes place in a discussion is restricted by the role structure and the norms. Observers who chart the flow of communication within a meeting discover that there is a wide variance in the amount of participation. Bales and his associates have compiled a large amount of normative data that demonstrate this variability. One study by Stephan and Mishler presented data that in 17 groups of six persons each, the leaders contributed, on the average, 43 percent of the communication; the next most active participant, about 24 percent;

and the next 15 percent; with the least active people contributing only 2 percent. Empirical investigations demonstrate that participation in discussion groups is seldom balanced. People are often unhappy with the lack of equal participation. They hold the stereotype that in a good discussion everyone should participate equally and are disturbed if one person monopolizes the discussion or some people do not participate. Balanced participation is a virtue in a discussion *program* because of the common audience expectation that all experts should have equal time. It can be approximated by careful planning and rehearsal, following the suggestions in Chapter 3; but in task-oriented groups, unequal distribution is the inevitable concomitant of specialization and structure. Bales, for example, discovered that the leaders generally participated more than the best-liked people.

The communication within a group is not only distributed unevenly among the participants, it is also often restricted in other ways by the norms that develop to form the communication network. One person may seldom receive any direct verbal communication from any other member. Two people may talk to each other more than they talk to anyone else or to the entire group. Norms of this sort usually develop during the early stages of role emergence or during the periodic status struggles. Often they reflect the pattern of those struggles. Leaders and their lieutenants may talk things over frequently. The leader and the loser in the status struggle may seldom speak directly to one another.

The status ladder influences the flow of messages. People tend to direct more talk upward on the status ladder. They talk more with peers than they do with those on a lower status level. The participants with the highest status tend to direct more communication to the whole group than to the individual members. As the size of the group increases, the communication tends to focus on one individual.

Investigators have accounted for who-talks-to-whom patterns by member choices on a sociometric index. The sociometric index is a simple questionnaire in which the subject is asked to select other people on the basis of social attraction or rejection. Participants may be asked such questions as: Whom would you most like to have serve on another committee with you? Whom would you least like to have serve on another committee with you? Stemming from the pioneering work of Moreno, the sociometric technique has been used often to investigate and explain communication flowcharts and other phenomena.

Informal channels of communication are inevitable and may serve to increase task efficiency. Certain people will assume roles that require them to talk more than others. The job may demand that certain workers communicate more with one another than with other personnel. However, an organization may have norms governing the flow of communication that grew up during the status struggle. The resultant network may be inefficient for the present demands placed on the organization, and it may persist only because it is habitual. The participants can discuss, evaluate, and change norms in order to increase the group's productivity. In general, the communication network should be such that each person has access to the information she or he requires to do the job successfully. Each person should also have channels to social and esteem rewards so that she or he will be committed to the successful completion of the work. The network needs to be diverse enough to ensure a free flow of messages back and forth among the members. The level of cohesiveness must be high enough so that the listener furnishes the speaker with sufficient feedback to ensure high-fidelity communication.

Cohesiveness

The highly cohesive group provides a social climate that encourages feedback and thus ensures efficient communication. Bales and his associates developed normative data comparing the ratio of questions to answers in a wide variety of discussions. Their content analysis of the communication revealed a *much higher proportion of answers than of questions.* Discussions are characterized by a large number of answers looking for questions. The Minnesota studies corroborate these findings, particularly in the period of group structuring and role struggle. People do not ask many questions in the period of searching for a role and for status, because they do not wish to appear ignorant or stupid. They may, therefore, act as though they understand much more than they do and have considerably more knowledge than they have. People are very polite at this point, and they often do not ask questions for fear of insulting the person who is making the comment. Asking a question might imply that the speaker is not capable of clear expression or even that the speaker's reasoning is not cogent or logical. Finally, participants often cannot ask a question because they have not listened to the previous comment. During the period of role testing, people are eager to demonstrate their talents. They wait for a cue from the discussion that makes them "think of something to say." They then plan how they will say it, and they watch impatiently for an opportunity to gain the floor. When they do get the floor, they say as much as they can as effectively as possible, and when they must relinquish the floor, they try to think of another good comment. When one occurs to them, they look for another opportunity to get the floor. Often the person who has not done well in demonstrating skill by active participation will be disturbed enough to review the proceedings and "replay" the meeting, this time mentally providing the good comments he or she might have made. The "quiet listeners" may be so busy mentally that they are not listening well at all. People generally feel that they should participate. If they do not, they fear that they have not made a good impression and are disturbed.

Since people do not listen well during the early discussion, they often say something unrelated to the topic raised by the previous speaker. They say what they have on their minds when they get the chance to speak, even if the comment is no longer pertinent. They often say as much as they can even if they introduce several ideas within one speech. Berg's discovery that the group has a very short attention span is somewhat accounted for by these facts.

When a group achieves a stable role structure and a high level of cohesiveness, the need to "show off" is largely eliminated. Participants are secure in their positions and do not worry about appearing ignorant when they ask a question. They are confident that another person will not take offense if they ask for clarification or test another's information. Participants begin to listen and, when confused, will ask for clarification.

People who are strongly attracted to a group and wish the group well will want to maximize the communication efficiency. They know that the group will do a better job if they are thoroughly briefed and if they clearly understand what they are to do. Therefore, if they do not know, they ask. Knowledgeable people will search for feedback and welcome it in the highly cohesive group. They may even ask for it. They are alert to non-verbal cues that others are confused or unsure about.

Displaying knowledge and demonstrating expertise are different from communicating knowledge or explaining technical matters. People who are primarily interested in making a good impression may talk rapidly and introduce complicated concepts in technical jargon. By using language to confuse and obscure, participants can impress people with their under-standing and knowledge without becoming subject to embarrassing ques-tions. Most professions have developed a tradition of protecting the ex-pertise of their members from the questions of the lay public by means of a complicated technical vocabulary. Medical doctors, for example, de-scribe common ailments in technical terms. A runny nose might be de-scribed as *allergic rhinitis; contact dermatitis* may simply mean that the doctor does not know what is causing a skin rash. Lawyers use Latin words and phrases for the same purpose. Small group specialists may use terms like *syntality* and *vectorial measurement of group synergy.* The layperson is thus often reduced to relying on the expert's judgment. If the others are untrained in statistics, they may request the statistician to interpret the statistics. Technical terms can serve a useful function in naming clearly defined concepts. Experts may change their purpose from defending their status to explaining technical matters to their listeners. When they do so, they may still use the technical vocabulary; however, the change in atti-tude should result in a change in presentation. Generally, when trying to inform, the expert will introduce the technical concepts more slowly, define them carefully, and encourage questions and feedback.

The personnel in an organization will vary as to their skills in the art of communicating. Some may have difficulty listening carefully, others may have trouble expressing their ideas clearly, and others may be unable to hold a chain of inferences in mind to see if they relate in a consistent or inconsistent fashion. Achieving communication appropriate to the group's task under such circumstances often takes considerable time and tension-producing effort. Communication is hard work. The group should develop norms that encourage such effort at feedback and communication. It should establish the norm that sufficient time will be spent (not wasted) to ensure the proper level of understanding.

TECHNIQUES FOR THE TASK DIMENSION

Relating to the External Environment

Too often the group is provided with undigested and unevaluated information. If the internal data-processing structure is inefficient, the group may waste time with irrelevancies and falsehoods. It may also find itself unable to deal with the external environment and achieve its task goals. Participants should work to develop the presentational skills necessary to convey their knowledge to the group with efficiency. Presentations require preparation, analysis, and structure. The resource people should examine the data and discover the central issues. They should estimate the importance of the information and decide how much time the group should devote to processing the data. They should then prepare suitable messages to disseminate the information. With reproduction facilities at the disposal of most important task-oriented groups, resource people should consider using both written and spoken messages. Too often, a student will come to a meeting with notes jotted in a notebook, which he or she reads or refers to while making a series of disjointed comments about his or her discoveries. The bulk of such information can be provided in a duplicated memorandum, brief, or outline distributed before the meeting. The participant can use the allotted time in the session to clarify ambiguous points, and the others can devote their efforts to testing the soundness of the information.

Processing Information

A sound and healthy social dimension is necessary, but it does not guarantee that a group will process information in such a way that it will do a good job. The first skill that participants must have is the ability to describe the facts in clear report language. They must have the basic expository skills required to draft specific topic sentences and to support these topic sentences with sufficient illustrations and materials to make them clear to the others. Presentational skills require that resource people provide interpretations of statements of fact. They should also provide background information and draw out the implications of the facts for their group.

The presentation of information requires dialectical skills as well as expository techniques. The knowledgeable member must cultivate the art of fitting the information into the flow of the group's deliberations. Good groups usually have at least one philosopher or big-picture person, who can relate the information to the project at hand. All participants should use transitions that relate their comments to a major theme under discussion. Periodic summaries and stock-taking comments help the participants to remember the theme. Summaries often become part of the role functions of one or two people, but if each participant works to develop a sense of the overall pattern used by the group to process information, he or she can help eliminate those moments of aimless confusion when members stop and wonder where they are and what has happened.

The group must develop work norms that include careful testing of information. The art of asking questions is crucial to this process. If one member, as part of his role function, asks, How do you know? with monotonous regularity, the ability of the group to work effectively would be increased. The art of asking questions involves skill in thinking of and posing questions, as well as a certain attitude toward communication. A participant cannot ask good questions without listening carefully to the speaker.

Earlier chapters have presented some of the reasons for a participant's initial tendency to interpret the flow of verbal and nonverbal messages in these terms: What does this message imply for me as a person? Does it raise or lower my status? Does it show agreement or antagonism to me? Participants also tend at first to interpret messages in terms of the person who sends them: Is she leadership material? Is he ignorant? Intelligent? Quick tempered? Humorous? Once the role structure is stable, the discussant can focus on ideas rather than status.

The presentation and testing of information assault the emotional health of the group. Knowledgeable people, even if they are primarily concerned with the job at hand and have little desire for status, will cause secondary tensions. They are immediately perceived as potentially high-status members. The ambitious member who is not so well informed finds it difficult to compete with them. In their desire to participate, ambitious individuals may make some false statements. The knowledgeable member may prove with specific information that the statements are false and thereby anger the ambitious person. The ambitious member may try to save face by belittling statistics or questioning the relevance of library research or scholarship to "real life," or by ignoring or misunderstanding the information. Thus, informed members who have no motive other than to help the group may nonetheless find the others misunderstanding, rejecting, or resenting their contributions, simply because they give their presentation with great eagerness and are not aware of the resentment they arouse.

Testing information by asking speakers how they know that something is true or false also causes secondary tensions. The speaker may view the question as a threat to her or his authority or integrity. If people have developed norms during the period of role struggle that cause them to resist the questioning of their information, the group should, after it reaches the level of real work, discuss these norms.

One of the most interesting factors controlling the communication within an organization is the status structure. As noted, status arrangements are closely related to the channels of communication and to the flow of messages through those networks. Status differences determine the quality of the messages as well as their quantity and direction. Frequently, status differences inhibit the free flow of information and restrict feedback. High-status people often do not know of the discontent and grievances of low-status people. They think the morale of the organization is higher than it is. Although they think their talk is clear and straightforward, the low-status listener searches for hidden meanings and interprets much that was not intended. Often, unpleasant information is not revealed to high-status levels until such a crisis occurs that it can no longer be withheld. Subordinates frequently tell their supervisor only the good news. They do not tell the boss upsetting things or information that makes them look bad.

Efficiency in group discussion may be increased if the members discover that they can say "I do not know" without losing status. Units within an organization often work better if participants discover that their status is not jeopardized by having others test their information. The engineer who discovers that having her blueprints criticized by a machinist does not hurt her standing within the project or within the company will tolerate such testing, and the efficiency of the unit will increase.

Testing Solutions

Solutions need to be thoroughly questioned. Testing course of action creates more tension than testing factual information. Examining a solution requires estimates of probable outcomes if the plan is adopted, and opinions as to right and wrong come under discussion. The group not only must predict outcomes, but must agree on goals. Often each course of action entails costs as well as rewards; the gaining of time may cost wasted effort and materials, or a short-term gain in efficiency may exact a toll in cohesiveness. The organization often must balance production goals against the morale of employees. A hierarchy of value statements will aid in the selection of solutions, but hierarchy is difficult to shape; there are often disagreements. Courses of action always raise questions of ethics. Discussants must ask not only if the plan will work, but also if the plan is right. Questions of ethics often generate secondary tensions.

Mobilizing Resources

When the unit mobilizes its resources, it assigns tasks to various people and sets a schedule of completion dates. It assigns resources such as equipment, money, and materials to the various workers responsible for particular parts of the plan. The division and integration of work require the giving of directions to others. Few features of a task place a greater strain on the group's social ties than the giving and taking of orders. People who control and divide the material resources and give directions and orders inevitably grow in importance. The workers who need the resources find themselves dependent on the one who controls them. The administrator who sets salaries and distributes new machines grows in importance. Participants are often sensitive to perceived injustices in the distribution of workloads and material resources. They resent someone who is not ordered to do her or his share. They are dissatisfied if they feel they do not have the equipment they deserve and need. Group resources must sometimes be distributed unequally in order to meet external pressures. Usually the leader is forced to make the unpopular decisions. Former President Harry Truman was often quoted as saying of the presidency, "The buck stops here." If members are forced as a unit to make a decision, they may withdraw from the problem by dividing the resources equally. If, for example, the decision of how to divide salary increases is forced on the members as a group, they may raise all wages an equal percentage, even though there are important reasons to give individual merit raises.

Directions are hard to take. They often imply that the person giving them is better than the persons receiving them. The worker may perceive nonverbal communications in a supervisor's orders that imply that the boss thinks she or he knows more and is better than the worker. Yet, if the group is to do its job, members must take and follow orders or directions. Good groups develop norms that encourage the facing of emotional effects directly. Ignoring, repressing, or avoiding the open expression of emotions is often damaging. Participants should respond directly and not dodge shows of either antagonism or liking. Often an honest, antagonistic response will clear the air just as a sincere acceptance of a show of affection will preclude embarrassment.

Making Decisions

When students of group methods understand the way decisions emerge, they can be alert to the ways in which the process goes astray. Frequently, a committee will act as though it has made a decision only to have the participants begin to question the action. They may find the solution untenable and ask to reconsider the decision. Hasty decisions usually occur because the group has pushed too hard. Often people need time to mull over the various solutions. Participants should develop a sense of timing and watch for the cues that indicate the group is ready to act. Also, they should guard against the acquiescence that occurs without everyone knowing what the decision is or why it has been made.

Quite often, a consensus should be explicitly stated. Getting direct expression of support, neutrality, or nonacceptance will often avoid drifting decisions. Consensus may come quite naturally through nonverbal agreements, such as vigorous nods of approval and verbal assertions of

"Right" or "I agree." Some members may ask for a vote. If the timing for the request is right, the direct show of support may aid the group in making a decision.

Bales discovered that many groups experienced the highest levels of disagreement just before moments of decision. When courses of action are decided on, secondary tensions often reach their high points. Decisions about solving group problems relating to the control of the external environment are often those that groups approach, withdraw from, and approach again and again before finalizing. They are the most damaging to the group's social dimension. If group members are not careful, they may select a solution that eases the internal social strain, but does not solve the real problems. In other words, the reality of the external environment will punish the group. Decisions should be made with a clear understanding of their implications: Are the internal tensions more important than the external environment? Is the present social reward sufficient to justify a loss in task efficiency? Obviously, these are difficult questions, and it is to be expected that decisions about dealing with the external conditions lead to the highest levels of disagreement and secondary tension.

SUMMARY   PERT   Program Evaluation + Review Technique

Computer programs / logical steps

Recommendations for group work fall on a continuum, with rational, step-by-step procedures on one end and intuitive, creative approaches on the other. One common assumption is that groups can be taught to think as individuals do when they deliberate reflectively, creatively, and productively. One important recommendation on the rational end of the continuum is that groups should learn to think reflectively as Dewey suggested individuals should.

Brainstorm / Flexible / open & nonjudgemental

Another important recommendation on the creative end of the continuum is that groups should learn to think creatively along the lines that Wallas suggested individuals should. Symbolic convergence theory can explain group creativity along the lines suggested by synectics, brainstorming, and Wallas.

Scholars who have conducted research in the group problem-solving process have found that it changes in systematic ways through time. Earlier formulations that sought to explain group work in terms of one unitary pattern have been replaced with multiple sequence accounts.

The beginning of group problem solving should include an opening-up stage for generating many ideas, fantasizing, and joking. Once a decision has begun to emerge, the group should enter a zeroing-in phase of organized planning procedures.

Groups which have decision-making power need a series of long, hard, careful deliberations to solve problems. Groups, like individuals, have short attention spans. Real work groups do not have briskly conducted work meetings in which members march through an agenda. In addition, participants approach the problem several times in order to find areas of consensus and difference. Decisions emerge from group interaction in the same way that roles emerge and normative behavior develops.

Some decisions emerge by accident. Others are a by-product of status struggles. In groups with stable role structures, some decisions are made on the basis of esteem for the individual making the suggestion. Important decisions, however, ought to be made on the evidence of a thorough and accurate examination of the facts.

The group's work norms should be periodically evaluated to see if they still meet the demands of the external environment in realistic fashion. Norms can often be changed if the group discusses and evaluates them. Communication patterns that encourage feedback and ensure the distribution of information are important to success.

Even under ideal conditions, discussants must have speaking skills that enable them to prepare and report on factual conditions and listening skills that enable them to understand others and ask sensible questions.

The processing of information causes social strain because the person who presents knowledge may be resented and the respondent's probing question frequently seems to be a personal attack. The status hierarchy often presents a barrier to effective communication. If the group establishes the norm that a member can admit ignorance without loss of status and that ideas and plans can be questioned without threatening a member's position, the effectiveness of communication is enhanced.

The control phase of group operations—when plans are implemented, resources allocated, and work orders distributed—frequently generates secondary tensions. Good groups develop norms that devote some time after a difficult decision to repairing cohesiveness.

☞ Rules of Thumb

Advice on How to Be a Good Group Member

Drawn from Chapter 10

- ☞ When adopting the rational perspective of group decision making, use high procedural order and a problem-solving agenda to organize the meetings.
- ☞ When adopting the creative perspective of group problem solving, develop an open and nonjudgmental communication climate.
- ☞ When adopting the creative perspective of group problem solving, encourage flexibility by dramatizing and fantasy sharing.
- ☞ When you are leading a group, encourage flexibility by such techniques as making the strange familiar and the familiar strange, and by magnifying or minimizing the problem.
- ☞ When leading a creative group, do not compete with the group members.
- ☞ When leading a creative group, listen carefully to group members.

☞ When leading a creative group, step in and change the communication when a member is in danger of being put on the defensive.

☞ When leading a creative group, keep the meeting interesting.

☞ When leading a creative group, build an atmosphere of fun, interest, and excitement.

☞ When a creative group bogs down, it is sometimes helpful to take a "fantasy vacation."

☞ Because of the approach–withdrawal behavior of groups, help the group return to important questions until members finally make a decision.

☞ Because groups have short attention spans, your ideal model of a good group should not include a rigorous sticking to the topic for long periods of time.

☞ Do not expect a group to do as much work as an individual could do in the same amount of time working alone.

☞ Do not develop an agenda that contains many topics with the most important items left until last.

☞ Be alert for when a decision has emerged and then state the decision and test your assumption with the other members.

☞ A clear statement of group decisions, with shows of consensus or formal votes, aids follow-up and action.

☞ Be on the lookout for and short-circuit any decisions that seem to be emerging by accident.

☞ Be on the lookout for and short-circuit any task decisions that are by-products of role struggles.

☞ Push for task decisions that are based on factual analysis.

☞ For good group work, ensure that task norms are efficient.

☞ For good group work, ensure that the specialists in the group have their ideas challenged and evaluated by the nonspecialists.

☞ Be careful to watch for and defuse incipient norms that restrict the flow of communication.

☞ In task-oriented groups, the unequal distribution of tasks is highly probably.

☞ Maximize the communication efficiency in your group in order to ensure productivity.

☞ When speaking in the group, search for feedback to maximize high-fidelity transmission of information.

☞ Introduce technical concepts and terms slowly, define them carefully, and encourage questions.

☞ Do not assume that silence means either understanding or consent.

☞ Take sufficient time to ensure that your communication has been successful.

☞ Develop the presentational speaking skills necessary to convey information and opinions to your group.

☞ Learn to describe facts in clear reporting language.

☞ Cultivate the art of fitting the comments you make into the flow of the group's deliberations.

☛ Cultivate the art of asking perceptive questions in order to understand and test ideas.

☛ Be aware that your well-intentioned efforts to help the group may lead to misunderstandings and resentment of your contributions.

☛ Work to encourage high-fidelity communication despite status differences in your group.

☛ Strive for a group climate in which members can say "I don't know" without loss of status.

☛ Help your group develop norms that allow members to take directions without creating crippling secondary tensions.

QUESTIONS FOR STUDY

1. What are the advantages and the disadvantages of evaluating the small task-oriented group on exclusively rational criteria?

2. What is the difference between the context of rationality and the context of creativity?

3. What is the relationship between the social dimension and the task dimension in terms of group decision making?

4. What is the difference between a linear problem-solving model and a spiral problem-solving model?

5. What is the difference between the decision-emergence model developed in this chapter and the steps in the discussional pattern as adapted from John Dewey's reflective-thinking analysis?

6. In what ways might task decisions emerge from group interaction on non-rational grounds?

7. What are the advantages and disadvantages of a group that bases its task decisions on external reality?

8. In what ways can specialization and the development of task experts hinder a group's task effectiveness?

9. What is the relationship between feedback and cohesiveness?

10. What informal restrictions may inhibit the free flow of communication within the small group?

EXERCISES

1. Form a problem-solving group in your class, and work out a careful agenda based on the Dewey reflective-thinking process. Hold a meeting in which the group attempts to follow the agenda carefully. Allow for no digressions. Tape-record the meeting. Analyze the tape to discover how closely the group stayed with the agenda. Did the group do a good job? Was the agenda an aid or an impediment to the work of the group?

2. Form a problem-solving group in your class, and begin with a period of "kicking the topic around," without any agenda to restrict the deliberations. Let the members free-associate if they wish. After a time, if the group feels the need for

a plan of procedure, work one out. Let the group decide what topics to take up and in what order. Use the outline as a guide, but allow digressions. Tape-record the meeting. Analyze the tape to see how the group went about its task. Did the group do a good job? Hold an evaluative session in which the entire group discusses its work norms and possible ways of improving task efficiency. Hold another work session. Tape-record and evaluate the second meeting.

3. Select a group that you have been working with for several months that in your judgment is cohesive and productive. Write a short paper analyzing the group's fantasy chains as they relate to group problem solving.

REFERENCES AND SUGGESTED READINGS

For an expansion of the Dewey pattern, see:

Kepner, Charles H. and Benjamin B. Tregoe. *The Rational Manager: A Systematic Approach to Problem Solving and Decision Making.* New York: McGraw-Hill, 1965.

A discussion of PERT can be found in:

Phillips, Gerald M. *Communication and the Small Group.* Indianapolis: Bobbs-Merrill, 1966.

For Wallas's model of creativity, see:

Wallas, Graham. *The Art of Thought.* New York: Harcourt Brace, 1926.

See also:

Gordon, W. J. J. *Synectics: The Development of Creative Capacity.* New York: Harper & Row, 1961.

Howell, William S. *The Empathic Communicator.* Prospect Heights, IL: Waveland Press, 1986.

Prince, G. M. *The Practice of Creativity.* New York: Harper & Row, 1970.

The reference to a fantasy vacation is from:

Prince, G. M. "How to Be a Better Meeting Chairman," *Harvard Business Review,* **47** (1969), 98–109.

The reference to Scheidel's divergent–convergent approach is from:

Scheidel, Thomas M. "Divergent and Convergent Thinking in Group Decision Making." In Randy Y. Hirokawa and Marshall Scott Poole, eds., *Communication and Group Decision Making.* Beverly Hills, CA: Sage, 1986, pp. 113–132.

For phases of group decision making see:

Bales, Robert F. "The Equilibrium Problems in Small Groups." In T. Parsons, R. F. Bales, and E. A. Shils, eds., *Working Papers in the Theory of Action.* New York: Free Press, 1953, pp. 111–161.

Fisher, B. Aubrey. "Decision Emergence: Phases in Group Decision Making," *Communication Monographs,* **37** (1970), 53–66.

Fisher, B. Aubrey, and R. K. Stutman. "An Assessment of Group Trajectories: Analyzing Developmental Breakpoints," *Communication Quarterly,* **35** (1987), 105–124.

Poole, Marshall Scott. "Decision Development in Small Groups," *Communication Monographs*, **50** (1983), 321–341.

Poole, Marshall Scott, and Joel A. Doelger. "Development Processes in Group Decision Making." In Randy Y. Hirokawa and Marshall Scott Poole, eds., *Communication and Group Decision Making*. Beverly Hills, CA: Sage, 1986, pp. 35–61.

On the relationship between affect and work and the levels of work, see:

Zaleznik, Abraham, and David Moment. *The Dynamics of Interpersonal Behavior*. New York: Wiley, 1964.

The discussion of Bales's equilibrium model and the data on percentages of social interactions are to be found in:

Bales, Robert F. "The Equilibrium Problem in Small Groups." In T. Parsons, R. F. Bales, and E. A. Shils, eds., *Working Papers in the Theory of Action*. New York: Free Press, 1953, pp. 111–161.

The Tavistock approach is described in:

Rice, A. E. *Learning for Leadership: Interpersonal and Intergroup Relations*. London: Tavistock, 1965.

Rioch, Margaret J. "Group Relations: Rationale and Technique," *International Journal of Group Psychotherapy*, **10** (1970), 340–355.

The spiraling model is from:

Scheidel, Thomas M., and Laura Crowell. "Idea Development in Small Discussion Groups," *Quarterly Journal of Speech*, **50** (1964), 140–145.

The game of Twenty Questions was used in:

Taylor, Donald W., and William L. Faust. "Twenty Questions: Efficiency in Problem Solving as a Function of Size of Group," *Journal of Experimental Psychology*, **44** (1952), 360–368.

The studies of group attention span are by:

Berg, David M. "A Descriptive Analysis of the Distribution and Duration of Themes Discussed by the Task-Oriented Small Group." Ph.D. dissertation, University of Minnesota, 1963.

Faffler, Irene. "A Cross-Cultural Study of the Task-Oriented Small Group in the Middle East." Ph.D. dissertation, University of Minnesota, 1971.

Larson, Charles U. "Leadership Emergence and Attention Span: A Content Analysis of the Time Devoted to Themes Discussed in the Task-Oriented Small Group." Ph.D. dissertation, University of Minnesota, 1968.

For research relating to the risky-shift and polarization phenomena, see:

Alderton, Steven M. "Locus of Control-Based Argumentation as a Predictor of Group Polarization," *Communication Quarterly*, **30** (1982), 381–387.

Alderton, Steven M., and Lawrence R. Frey. "Effects of Reactions to Arguments on Group Outcome: The Case of Group Polarization," *Central States Speech Journal*, **34** (1983), 88–95.

Beniot, John H. "The Application of Expectation States Theory to the 'Risky Shift,'" *Canadian Journal of Sociology*, **7** (1982), 167–179.

Cline, Rebecca J., and Timothy R. Cline. "A Structural Analysis of a Risky-Shift and Cautious-Shift Discussions: The Diffusion-of-Responsibility Theory," *Communication Quarterly,* **28** (1980), 26–36.

Cline, Timothy R., and Rebecca J. Cline. "Risky and Cautious Decision Shifts in Small Groups," *Southern Speech Communication Journal,* **44** (1979), 252–263.

DeStephen, Rolayne S. "Group Interaction Differences Between High- and Low-Consensus Groups," *Western Journal of Speech Communication,* **47** (1983), 340–363.

Dion, Kenneth L., Norman Miller, and Mary Ann Magnan. "Cohesiveness and Social Responsibility as Determinants of Group Risk Taking," *Proceedings of the Annual Convention of the American Psychological Association,* **5** (1970), 335–336.

Kroger, Rolf O., and Irene Briedis. "Effects of Risk and Caution Norms on Group Decision Making," *Human Relations,* **23** (1970), 181–190.

Mayer, Michael E. "Explaining Choice Shift: An Effects Coded Model," *Communication Monographs,* **52** (1985), 92–101.

The studies of high-level decision-making groups which indicate the complexity of such a process as compared with the simplicity of the groupthink analysis are:

Ball, Moya Ann. "A Descriptive and Interpretive Analysis of the Small Group Decision-Making Culture of the Kennedy and Johnson Administrations Regarding Decisions Concerning the Expansion of the Vietnam War." Ph.D. dissertation, University of Minnesota, 1988.

Callaway, Michael R., and James K. Esser. "Groupthink: Effects of Cohesiveness and Problem-Solving Procedures on Group Decision Making," *Social Behavior and Personality,* **12** (1984), 157–164.

Gouran, Dennis S., Randy Y. Hirokawa, and Amy E. Martz. "A Critical Analysis of Factors Related to Decisional Processes Involved in the *Challenger* Disaster," *Central States Speech Journal.* **37** (1986), 119–135.

Hare, A. Paul, and David Naveh. "Group Development at Camp David Summit, 1978," *Small Group Behavior,* **15** (1984), 299–318.

Janis, Irving L. *Victims of Groupthink.* 2nd ed. Boston: Houghton Mifflin, 1982.

Moorhead, Gregory, and John R. Montanari. "An Empirical Investigation of the Groupthink Phenomenon," *Human Relations,* **39** (1986), 399–410.

The study of decision emergence is by:

Fisher, B. Aubrey. "Decision Emergence: Phases in Group Decision-Making," *Communication Monographs,* **37** (1970), 53–66.

The discussion of the inherent laziness or lack of it in human beings is from:

McGregor, Douglas. *The Human Side of Enterprise.* New York: McGraw-Hill, 1960.

For a survey of research on communication networks, see:

Shaw, Marvin E. *Group Dynamics: The Psychology of Small Group Behavior.* New York: McGraw-Hill, 1971, pp. 137–148.

For some typical studies of communication networks see:

Bavelas, Alex. "Communication Patterns in Task-Oriented Groups." In Dorwin

Cartwright and Alvin Zander, eds., *Group Dynamics: Research and Theory.* 3rd ed. New York: Harper & Row, 1968, pp. 503–511.

Lawson, Edwin D. "Changes in Communication Nets, Performance, and Morale," *Human Relations,* **28** (1965), 139–147.

Miraglia, Joseph P. "Communication Network Research and Group Discussion," *Today's Speech,* **12** (1964), 11–13.

The percentages of communication are from:

Stephan, F. F., and E. Mishler. "The Distribution of Participation in Small Groups: An Exponential Approximation," *American Sociological Review* **17** (1952), 598–606.

See also:

Burleson, Brant R., Barbara J. Levine, and Wendy Samter. "Decision-Making Procedure and Decision Quality," *Human Communication Research,* **10** (1984), 557–574.

Donohue, William A., Leonard C. Hawes, and Timothy Mabee. "Testing a Structural-Functional Model of Group Decision Making Using Markov Analysis," *Human Communication Research,* **7** (1981), 133–146.

Geist, Patricia, and Teresa Chandler. "Account Analysis of Influence in Group Decision Making," *Communication Monographs,* **51** (1984), 67–78.

Hirokawa, Randy Y. "Group Communication and Problem-Solving Effectiveness I: A Critical Review of Inconsistent Findings." *Communication Quarterly,* **30** (1982), 134–141.

Moreno, Jacob L. *Who Shall Survive?* Washington, DC: Nervous and Mental Disease Publishing, 1934.

Raack, R. C. "When Plans Fail: Small Group Behavior and Decision Making in the Conspiracy of 1808 in Germany," *Journal of Conflict Resolution,* **14** (1970), 3–19.

Chapter
11

Ethics

Many statements in this book are what a student of ethics would call *value statements*. They support and shape what has been said about the ends and uses of discussion in our society; the relationships between discussion, democracy, and science; the gathering and processing of information; the development of group cohesiveness, roles, norms; and the nature of decision making. The purpose of this chapter is to outline and explain a value system for the student of discussion and group methods.

THE NATURE OF ETHICS

What distinguishes the ethical from other concerns is the act of choice. The inevitable is not ethical. People should not be held responsible for events that are beyond their control. However, individuals may be held responsible when they deliberately choose to lie, to steal, or to blacken another's reputation with malicious half-truths, innuendoes, and suggestions. Choice is the prerequisite for praise and blame, and the most important ethical considerations reach the ultimate question of "What is praiseworthy?" Choice implies both the freedom and the ability to make the praiseworthy decision. A person who is unable or incompetent to choose should be neither praised nor blamed.

Participants in small task-oriented groups make ethical decisions largely about ends and means; that is, members must sometimes choose between their personal goals and the goals of the group because the two are in conflict. They must sometimes choose between the goals of their group and those of other groups or the larger society because such goals also come into conflict. In addition to ends, purposes, and goals, an ethical scheme should give equal weight to the means used to reach the ends. Participants must choose the personal code they will follow in dealing with their fellow group members as well as weigh the common code the group follows to achieve its goals. They may find the end praiseworthy but reject the tactics of their group as too dirty, violent, or extreme for their personal value system.

The student of small group communication is thus faced with a two-step ethical problem. The group has an internal ethic that causes its members to praise ends and means that aid the preservation and success of the total group. The first major point of tension is therefore between individual and group. In addition, the participant must make choices about means and ends in terms of their impact on other groups, institutions, and society. The second major point of tension is between the goals and tactics of the particular group and those of other groups and the general welfare. Answers for the ethical problems posed by participating in a group come largely from two contexts, which roughly parallel the two points of greatest tension. First, one set of answers is contained in the specific ethical code that emerges from the study and practice of small group communication. The specific code pertains to the proper, correct, and accepted information, techniques, and practices and is similar to the professional codes of medical doctors and lawyers. A second ethical system stems from the more generally accepted and widely held system of time-honored values common to the general culture.

This chapter begins with an examination of the tension points and the major ethical dilemmas they pose, summarizes the value system reflected in this book, outlines an appropriate professional code, and, finally, presents some of the ethical insights pertinent to small group communication, which are part of the cultural heritage upon which our society rests.

ETHICAL PROBLEMS

The Individual Versus the Group

Conformity and Nonconformity Journalists and essayists writing on contemporary American culture often berate the general public for its "conformity." They deplore mass culture, mass humanity, and standardization. If there is a value to which the contemporary American conforms, it seems to be nonconformity. Too frequently, critics use *conformity* as a convenient oversimplification with which to belittle actions or values that they dislike. Because conforming behavior relates so closely to the ethics of working with small groups, the student of group methods should examine this widespread tendency to deplore it.

Shepherds who live for months without seeing another human cannot comply or fail to comply with a norm. They conduct their business as they see fit. If abstract artists do not adapt to the norms of the Teamsters' Union local or Farm Bureau chapter, it is an idle exercise to compare their behavior to the norms of these groups. Artists usually do not care what the teamsters or the farmers think of them or their work. The critic of conformity should watch the painter at work with fellow abstract artists. The critic will find that the artist turns out to be a conformist. The hero of those who deplore conformity in the abstract, the mythical person who hears a different drummer, is not, as we are led to suppose, the only one to hear it. Such a person hears the beat of a different group.

The point is that everyone who takes part in any group is a conformist to some degree. Conformity is a necessary phenomenon associated with all groups. When members fail to comply with the role expectations or with the norms, they distract the group from its job. Other members become uncomfortable. Having failed their expectations once, they reason, the nonconformist might act in other unexpected ways. Will he fail to do his share of the work? Can he be counted on in the future or must the whole group reorganize itself to be sure that the jobs will be completed? Nonconformity results in role struggles, secondary tensions, and backbiting. Systematic and continuous nonconformity will result in an organization that is torn with dissension and socially punishing to its personnel. Rather than introducing new and challenging ideas, the nonconformist makes himself and others unhappy, in the most destructive and unproductive sense. He may choose to undermine a group in this way because he wishes to destroy it for some ulterior purpose.

A simple stereotype suggests that the nonconformist is the creative person. She is supposed to be the individual who introduces new ideas, great discoveries, and works of art, and she must therefore be encouraged. Again, the stereotype should be examined in terms of a relevant group. Every organization that requires creativity, or needs open and extended debate and discussion, develops norms that encourage such behavior. One goal of the university faculty, for example, is the discovery of new knowledge. The faculty members do not punch time clocks when doing research. The work norms for research teams encourage the creative process by allowing individuals to work in their own way at their own pace without close supervision. The faculty also has academic freedom in its work. Scholars are allowed a wide latitude of investigation. They may study the nature of snails or the way bees find their way back to the hive; they may study ancient Egyptian drama or the history of the Communist party in the United States. But if a professor became a nonconformist by suggesting that the norm of academic freedom be restricted, considerable alarm would be aroused in the university.

Industrial research and development groups, government research facilities, play casts, and advertising agencies all develop their own norms to encourage creativity and innovation on the part of their personnel. Some of the often satirized linguistic innovations of the advertising agency are a function of the norms that encourage new and different gimmicks. Nonconformists in such groups would discourage rather than encourage creativity.

The United States Senate has developed a norm called *unlimited debate*. The code of the Senate encourages full discussion of legislation. Any senators who suggested a serious restriction of the right of debate as a permanent change of procedure would be nonconformists.

Clearly, a person might still praise nonconformity, but she would logically do so because it is harmful to a group she dislikes. The critic of conformity might applaud an FBI agent who infiltrated a Communist cell or the Ku Klux Klan and failed to conform to the group norms, because she dislikes the goals and activities of these organizations. Of course, the conservative who wishes to restrict the academic freedom of a socialist professor, or the liberal who criticizes the style of life of the upper middle class is not a *non*conformist. Such attacks on the outgroup do not violate the norms of the ingroup. Attacking the outgroup simply increases the pressure for conformity within the group.

Some organizations have norms that are restrictive and discourage creativity. They encourage conformity to the party line. Militant action groups, which must move quickly and with firm discipline in order to win, establish such norms. Revolutionary organizations are tightly organized and disciplined, and they follow the party line. Religious organizations, during periods of change, often punish the heretic. Conforming to the norms of such groups discourages innovation and creativity.

Many groups may have ways of doing things and may advocate goals that a person dislikes. Individuals have every right to deplore an organization for its goals, but they should understand that it is not conformity but the norms themselves that are at fault. They may not like the goals of a gang of juvenile delinquents and thus may pronounce moral judgments about its behavior. They may not like the norms of the Ku Klux Klan or a street gang and may be disturbed by the way these organizations operate.

They will have the most fun when they are criticizing another group's conformity in the company of colleagues, who reinforce their feelings by supporting their criticism. When they belong to a highly cohesive group that has a norm of belittling the conformity of people in other groups, they enjoy poking fun at the mindless way other people follow the dictates of the herd.

When an individual joins a group and works for it, he or she must give up a certain amount of liberty. The group exacts a toll in return for the social, esteem, and security rewards it furnishes. The group may require individuals to do work that they do not enjoy, or it may demand discipline that they do not demand of themselves. Membership may require a distasteful compromise of principle, or restrict individual freedom of expression. A given group may exact all these costs, and a person may find the price too high. However, if an individual weighs all the costs and still joins the group to work with and for it, that person must then understand that conforming to norms and goals that are good for the group is a basic requirement for the group's success.

Group Efficiency Versus Member Satisfaction   In the days when rugged individualism was dying out and even the farmers were joining alliances and granges and forming political parties and cooperatives, the priests of the new urban culture were at work inculcating the new ethic. *Cooperation* and *organization* were the good words, and *competition* was bad. Since the heyday of progressive education, children have been taught to adjust to the group and to work with others. Many students of contemporary American culture, however, have discovered that cooperation — although absolutely necessary for the effective functioning of groups in an urban, corporate society — is not without its problems. Some yearn for an older, simpler individualism. Yet today's citizen lives in a society that requires cooperation or, in contemporary terms, conformity.

Groups inevitably make demands on their members that reflect the pressure of the external environment. The good of all is often at variance with each member's personal good as he or she sees it. The tension between the good of the unit and the rights of the individual creates an ethical dilemma for all participants. Organizations often ask members to make a personal sacrifice for the good of all.

History furnishes many examples of organizations whose norms forced their members to sacrifice personal goals for the good of the group. One was expected to die, if need be, for the efficiency of the unit. On the other hand, some groups have developed a set of norms that place member satisfaction above group efficiency. The issue is raised in many contemporary situations. If a classroom group is under pressure of time, facilities, and teaching resources, what are the rights of individuals when compared with the overall goal of providing maximum opportunity for all? What are the rights of students with little ability? What are the rights of those with extraordinary potential? Often task efficiency exacts a toll in the social dimension. Some years ago, a new kind of specialist emerged who studied the "time and motion" of workers. Called *efficiency engineers,* they conducted careful studies of the ways workers do their tasks, and then developed more efficient ways of performing the jobs. However, workers often resented being taught to redo their jobs according to step-by-step directions, because they feared becoming extensions of the machinery. The result was a loss of employee morale.

One of the troublesome ethical issues facing contemporary management is balancing the profit-making goal against the employee's social and esteem needs and the belief that a person's work should contribute to the quality of her or his life. The question of balancing an organization's effectiveness against individual rights and needs is not unique to industry. For example, the discussion group may find that for the good of all, certain students will have to give up a prominent part in the final program. Member A may have to talk less than she or he wants to or feels that she or he should.

Authoritarianism Versus Democracy   To a large extent, the question of the individual versus the organization is focused on the tensions between authoritarianism and democracy. Often democracy is defended on the ground that, although it is slow, cumbersome, and inefficient, it recognizes the rights of the individual and protects them. Totalitarianism, on the other hand, is efficient, but makes its members cogs in the overall structure, subservient to the demands of the unit. The group, left to its own devices, will tend to act for the good of all and thus crush the minority that opposes it. If the goal is clear and within the grasp of the group, an authoritarian set of norms and leadership roles will increase the speed with which the group attains its objectives. Authoritarianism is characteristic of athletic teams and military units. When speed is a crucial commodity for its self-preservation, the unit often turns to an authoritarian mode of operation.

Authoritarian groups may be healthy in terms of both task efficiency and member satisfactions. Athletic teams can be highly cohesive, and playing on such a team, even though the coach is a dictator, can be very satisfying. If the group is an elite organization, making the team can furnish a player with great prestige. It may also provide people with an opportunity to play positions that they enjoy. Team players sublimate their own desires to the goal of winning; the joy of participating in a team victory largely replaces the enjoyment they would normally get from individual achievement.

Democratic organizations may also fulfill the criteria for a good group. Leaderless group discussions, which have achieved a stable role structure and in which leaders emerge who adopt a democratic style, may yet reach a level of work that results in a high-quality product. The democratic style is appropriate to policy-making and decision-making organizations. The ethical problem is not answered by the simple decision that authoritarianism is bad because it emphasizes the group and neglects the individual. The rejection of the democratic style because group decisions are complex and experts should make them is not an adequate answer either. What right does the family group have to tell its children what they should do and think? What right does the federal government have to tell its young people that they must serve in the armed forces? What right, on the other hand, do individuals have to reject the decision of others if their actions will jeopardize the entire group? What right does a student have to fail to appear at the planning session of a discussion group?

Freedom of Dissent   Small groups often develop norms that restrict communication. Although freedom of speech is the law of the land, expressed in the Bill of Rights and buttressed by the legal system, the organization will often restrict the flow of communication. Lincoln said in his first inaugural address that "perpetuity" was implied in all governments, and that no government contained within its structure the mechanism for its peaceful dissolution. To some extent, small groups fight for their lives against people who seek to destroy them. The participant who challenges the basic purpose of the group, who fights its norms and foments malingering, sabotage, and absenteeism often finds personal freedom of thought and expression within the group restricted. The question that must be faced is to what extent participants who are perceived as destructive to the group itself should be given the opportunity for free expression within the organization? Even the most authoritarian organizations require some questioning of norms and goals in order to ensure adequate flexibility to deal with changing circumstances. Yet unlimited freedom for those who challenge the group may destroy it. For example, what right does the family have to restrict the freedom of expression of the children within the home? But what right does a daughter have to attack the basic norms and values of the family? Both sides of the issue pose an equally difficult ethical consideration. Participants do not challenge the group's culture as often as they absorb it. What right has a college fraternity to change the pledge's norms and value systems? Students who bring a set of religious beliefs to the university may experience a crisis during their first few years. The faculty may say that it had no responsibility in the matter because it merely provided a context in which students were exposed to knowledge, and they made up their own minds about religious matters. But the students inevitably felt the pressure of the group to conform to the norms of the college.

The cultural heritage of the United States emphasizes democratic values and institutions. The implication is that the member must be considered in any group. He or she is to have equal opportunity with others in the group to climb in status, power, and esteem. The member is to be able to choose which of the group's goals and norms to follow. Individual members are to be respected as people and the group is to serve them so that they will have a maximum opportunity to develop their full potential as people of worth and dignity. Democratic values imply freedom of speech. Each person has the right to make choices on the basis of as much information as possible. Individuals should have the right to challenge a group's goals and norms even if they push the group to destruction. The group, in turn, has no right to impose its opinions and advice on the individual. Members may listen to the others' arguments, but they should be free to reject or accept the group's value system on their own. Carried to the extreme, democratic values suggest that neither the family, the church, nor the university has a right to impose its norms on the individual.

Democratic values are often violated by the actual practices of institutions and organizations in the United States: The group has a dynamic that forces it to defend itself, and it destroys individuals who stand in its way. One of the large ethical problems to be faced in the last decade of the twentieth century is the extent of an individual's allegiance to the group and the extent to which he or she will strive to protect the older democratic values.

Groups and the General Welfare

Just as a weed might be an especially healthy specimen, so might an outgroup be extremely efficient and cohesive. A gardener, however, might consider the healthy weed bad for the garden, just as a larger view of the public good might yield a judgment that a cohesive band of delinquents is bad because of its effectiveness in theft and vandalism. An adequate ethic for the judgment of groups requires external as well as internal criteria.

Group Versus Group   Many groups have a dynamism that forces them to expand. A business firm often drives to expand its share of the market and increase its size and influence; at the same time, within its corporate structure, as within the corporate structure of most bureaucracies, empire building is rampant. One way to gain prestige is to be part of a successful unit. Within a bureaucracy, success is measured by group power and a broad base of control. As the organization grows, there are new domains for conquest. The small groups that have a chance to stake out claims move into the new territory and compete. Inevitably their goals conflict, for if one achieves dominance, the other loses its chance. The groups fight each other for new territory, and fight encroachments on the areas they already control. In this regard, the study of small groups tends to support the territorial-drive theory of naturalists, which states that the drive to own and defend territory is basic to animals, including humans. In our corporate society, this territory, or field of influence, becomes the area of contention. The more successful units build empires within the bureaucracy to the glory of their leaders and members.

Some groups are prohibited from growing in size, but are placed in direct competition with other groups. A common example is furnished by athletic teams. Many other groups compete with one another in less clear-cut ways.

Ethical tensions between the individual and the group are strong, but even stronger are problems posed by conflict among groups. A person often finds it more difficult to treat members of her or his group in unethical ways than to do so to strangers or enemies from competing groups. A football player may find it more difficult to trip a teammate during practice than to topple an opponent in a close game. The support of the group may even encourage the player to commit acts of violence and to harbor feelings of hatred toward the members of a competing group. Often people with the lowest status within the group will show the greatest rancor toward the enemy. Conflicts among groups thus may result in actions that are blatant violations of the ethical codes governing the internal pattern of social relationships. The issue is illuminated by the example of athletic contests; for here the pressures are strong to adopt a win-at-any-cost ethical code, and values such as good sportsmanship conflict with success. "It does not matter if you win or lose; it is how you play the game" is answered by "Nice guys finish last!" Playing dirty to win is condoned, and blame is cast only on the member who is caught. Breaking the rules of competition, whether these are codified in a book or entrenched in the mores of the culture, gives the rule breakers a competitive advantage if the opponents are caught by surprise. Such tactics, however, increase the losers' frustration, and they often adopt similar measures in the future. Thus, competition among groups encourages participants to ignore ethical questions relating to means and to justify any action on the basis of good ends—that is, group success.

Group Versus Society   Often small groups develop goals and tactics that are counter to the general welfare. Extreme examples are furnished by gangs of delinquents or groups of criminals. Equally relevant ethical issues are raised by the business corporation that increases prices, indulges in deceptive advertising, or conspires to fix prices, and by the labor union that demands unproductive featherbedding or restricts its membership. Even praiseworthy goals may raise ethical issues relating to means. Civil rights movements may provoke questions concerning the use of violent versus nonviolent means. The fraternity whose goal is to improve the chapter's grade average may face the ethical issues relating to stealing examinations, cheating, and providing less able members with term papers.

In more subtle ways, group ends and means may be destructive to the general social welfare. Public discussion and freedom of speech inevitably come under attack from the new corporate values. The attack on the freedom of political expression is most dramatic and well publicized, because powerful groups have always tried to restrict the rights of expression of their opposition. From the Alien and Sedition Acts through the Know Nothing party to the Anarchists, Bolsheviks, Communists, and Fascists, history is replete with attempts to restrict political advocates. Elaborate safeguards now exist to protect the rights of political speakers. That such rights need continual defense goes without saying, but there are more subtle erosions of free expression that are of recent development.

In an agrarian society, citizens had three major groups with which they identified: their family, their church, and their homeland. In an urban society, they identify with a multitude of groups. On the farm in 1800, the child absorbed the norms of the family with few outside distractions. In today's suburbs, the child becomes part of groups outside the family before starting school. Soon the norms of the family conflict with the elementary school peer group, and children reproach their parents with, "But Jane doesn't have to. . . ." The more relevant attack on freedom of speech comes in the restriction of the flow of communication as a group defends itself from other groups. Information is kept confidential or secret, in order to achieve a better competitive position. The widespread practice of marking communications "secret" or "top secret," because of the danger to the group if outsiders discover the information, is a pervasive and subtle restriction of freedom of speech. In the aftermath of the incident in the Democratic party headquarters at the Watergate during the 1972 presidential campaign, a series of investigations, including one by a senate select committee, revealed the extent to which the executive branch of the government had become addicted to "top secret" documents, clandestine meetings, and information drops reminiscent of intelligence agents in a foreign country. Much the same story was told about secrecy during the televised hearings related to the Iranian arms sale in 1987. The restriction of the flow of information by the executive branch and its attempts to manage news are a prime, but by no means isolated, example. Finally, the development of the mystique of experts — the specialization inherent in group structure — erodes freedom of expression. Experts develop their own jargon and thus defend their status. They hoard information and typically rely on presenting judgments as conclusions, which they say are based on secret knowledge too important or too technical to reveal. Even within the group, the expert may protect status by hoarding information. The bureaucratic structure is so complicated, and the flow of communication so restricted by the boundaries of organizational structures, ad hoc committees, and distributed responsibility, that much information is lost in transit.

Small group meetings provide a mechanism by which the free flow of communication within a corporate and urban society can be encouraged. Values have inertia and often are gradually transformed rather than radically altered. Skill in small group communication continues to be an important way in which freedom of speech can serve the ends of society. Technological advances in the mass media give public discussion an added power. If the restrictions inherent in bureaucracy could be loosened and information released through public discussion on television, the democratic values of free speech and inquiry might be preserved in a viable form for an urban society.

SOME BASIC ASSUMPTIONS

Throughout this book are hints and implications relevant to the ethical issues raised by the relationship of the individual to the group, groups to groups, and groups to the general welfare. One of the major assumptions is that there is a close connection between discussion and a democratic society. Both share a common set of values. These include the belief that citizens can rule wisely if they are given the opportunity; that each individual has an innate worth and dignity; that groups, institutions, and political structures must take into account, preserve, and uphold that dignity.

A second major assumption is that discussants have a right and obligation to make up their own minds. Their participation implies individual rights, with their concomitant obligations. Discussants should be allowed to decide for themselves without being coerced, duped, or manipulated. This assumption further implies that every person should acquire and process information in such a way that he or she can make sound decisions. The channels of communication leading to the group and those within the group should be such that maximum freedom of expression is coupled with maximum feedback. Becoming a group member means choosing to conform to the group's norms. The ethical standard is simply that members ought to make the choice for themselves, with a full understanding of its implications for them as individuals as well as for the group.

A third major assumption is that each individual ought to have the opportunity to grow and develop his or her potential within the group. A praiseworthy group does not neglect the desirable (those things that meet the needs on the deficit ladder: material goods, security, social approval, prestige, and esteem), but it goes beyond the desirable to the ends and means that transcend the self. The praiseworthy group, therefore, is one in which the member's potential for achievement and self-transcendence is realized. Role struggles, hostilities, and destructive norms that are barriers to such growth should be overcome as soon as possible.

A fourth major assumption throughout this text is a faith in reason and communication. Human beings differ significantly from other animals in their ability to use symbols in connected discourse to reason not only about the things present in their immediate perceptual field, but also about the past (they are capable of history and tradition) and about the future (they are capable of purpose, ends, and goals). Human beings are able to plan and evaluate. They are the only ethical animal; only human beings can conceive of future ends and means and judge when they are desirable or praiseworthy. When they bring language and reason together, they exhibit some of their unique and best human characteristics. When people see the facts clearly and reason about them consistently, they are knowledgeable; but when they praise intelligently, they are wise — and wisdom should be prized above knowledge.

A final major assumption is that in the conflict Karl Menninger characterizes as *man against himself* and *love against hate*, the instinct for life and the capacity for love are more praiseworthy than the death wish and the ability to hate. Conflicts and aggressions among group members and among groups that result in destructive attacks on either the persons or personalities of others are bad. This book assumes that lowering the status of others, showing antagonisms, and creating social tensions are destructive to the group and to the individuals.

A CODE FOR THE PRACTITIONER
The Ethics of Participation

No ethical principle emerges more clearly from the study and practice of small group discussion than this: The person who deliberately chooses to use the group or any of its members as means to achieve personal ends is to be censured. Such people ought to be labeled *manipulators*. They are unethical, for even if they fail to achieve their own ends, they nonetheless create a destructive group environment. On the other hand, the person who forgets his or her own welfare in seeking to work for all is to be praised. Like the individuals who forget personal happiness in working for the good of others and often find a meaning and purpose in life that make them happy, so people who forget their own status in order to work for the good of the group often win esteem. Thus, building cohesiveness by showing solidarity for the group, raising the status of others, volunteering to help, releasing social tensions, and showing affection and regard for colleagues are all praiseworthy means.

Karl R. Wallace has suggested that there is a close connection between persuading and giving advice. Participants, too, find themselves advising their colleagues. When they view the facts, examine a course of action, and contemplate means to achieve ends, they take the role function of group adviser. Advisers have certain duties and responsibilities. They must present information honestly, fairly, and accurately. They should be open about their sources and cooperate with the others in testing the truth of their statements of fact. Lying is intolerable in a group. It breaks the trust members have in their information-processing norms. Lying disturbs both the task and social dimensions of group process. An adviser should be prepared to defend her or his advice in terms of the common good, rather than for selfish interests.

When participants receive advice, they in turn have a responsibility. They must do more than say, "Tell us what to believe or do and we will believe or do it." They must test and determine for themselves. This does not mean "Buyer beware," but both the giver and receiver should assume their proper responsibilities in the evaluation of the advice.

The ethical code suitable for the practitioner in small groups ought to be pertinent to the wholeness and mental health of participants. The connection between group experience and mental health is weak in brief and transitory groups and grows impelling in those basic groups to which one devotes much of life. The discussion group that meets for only one night in a religious center may mark a person superficially, whereas the family group will bend that person for life. The basic person-to-person ethics that govern interpersonal relations develop an individual's self-image and may result in inferiority complexes, loneliness, neuroses, depression, and even psychoses. Our inhumanity to others has always been a source of evil. Nowhere is it more damaging than in the confines of a small group. An ethical code that views each person as significant, having dignity, and being worthy of respect is of vital importance. Whatever the status arrangement, the human relationships ought to reflect the values of trust, respect, and honesty.

The Ethics of Teaching

As students gain knowledge about small group communication, they face new ethical choices as a result of that knowledge. The expert on small groups must follow a more professional ethical code. In many respects the expert's problem is similar to that of the student of persuasion whose knowledge may be put to the service of praiseworthy or evil ends.

An adequate ethical code for the small group practitioner requires that the expert as well as the participant not manipulate groups for personal ends or for the ends of an employer that hires them to achieve its own ends. It is quite possible for group techniques to be used as persuasive devices, but when they are so used without a clear label of the intent, the practice is unethical.

An expert in small group communication should not tease or use groups for personal amusement. A hypnotist is able to use his or her powerful skill for self-amusement and the amusement of others. An expert in group methods could also arrange demonstrations and projects that make the participants look amusing or ridiculous. The indiscriminate use of either hypnotism or knowledge about groups may result in permanent damage to the subjects.

Experts should use their knowledge to develop better, healthier groups. The student of discussion ought to be dedicated to improving small group communication, increasing cohesiveness, and developing efficient productive groups.

Experts should not pretend to have greater knowledge and understanding than they possess or that the state of the art will support. Since the interpersonal dimension of group process is so clearly allied to mental health and has so many psychiatric implications, students of small group communication are often tempted to play, if not God, at least psychiatrist. Practitioners have an ethical obligation to make clear to the layperson the extent of their knowledge in the difficult area of mental and emotional health. They must be careful not to damage the personality of an individual in the course of role-playing exercises or group evaluation sessions. If an expert in group methods criticizes a person in front of a group, he or she has an obligation to be objective and fair and to indicate the good as well as bad qualities of that person. The expert ought not to justify such behavior on the basis that the purpose of the criticism is to make the person aware of shortcomings. When dealing with another's self-image, the expert should treat it with reverence and care.

Finally, the expert should not simplify the problem of learning to work productively with or to lead groups. The demand for training in leadership and small group communication is so strong that unscrupulous people are often tempted to offer patent-medicine-type panaceas. An expert who cloaks knowledge in mystery, talks some impressive and unintelligible jargon, and promises quick and easy success may develop a lucrative practice in bilking the general public. Many people have so vital a stake in working with and leading groups that they will pay considerable amounts of money to achieve success. They may be more reluctant to invest the time and effort required for genuine understanding, so the promise of painless, quick competence is tempting.

Ethical Guidelines for Public Welfare

Participants in a group must make choices relating to their allegiance to the group when they find their norms and ends in conflict with the larger purposes and norms of society. They must decide what goals they will suggest and fight for within the group. If their programs and tactics are not adopted, they must decide whether to support the group or not. When they can no longer subscribe to purposes or means, what should they choose to do? When does their responsibility to the group cease and their duty to the larger public welfare begin?

Irving Janis has made a perceptive study of the way group pressures can pose ethical issues in his book *Victims of Groupthink,* in which he discusses the effects of group norms and pressures for conformity on such high-level decisions as the Kennedy administration's move to invade Cuba at the Bay of Pigs and the Johnson administration's move to escalate the Vietnam war. Certainly, the same issue was posed for members of the Reagan administration who perjured themselves to keep secret the extent and nature of their dealings with Iran in regard to hostages and arms and their diversion of money from those transactions to *contra* rebels in Nicaragua. In less world-shaking ways, the same issue develops whenever one works for a period of time in a small group.

Does our culture contain some general universal values suitable to aid the participant with such choices? One should not take the more general value statements as rigid and unbending principles, but they do furnish starting places to reason about a given problem. In addition to the values already summarized as the basic assumptions of this book, several other widely held and time-honored insights deserve consideration.

Small group communication has much in common with public speaking. Some of the best minds of ancient and modern times have puzzled over the question of the ethical responsibility of the speaker. Most have come to a consensus about certain basic values. The next few paragraphs must of necessity have an old and familiar ring. The fact that sages in succeeding generations have sought in vain for a better ethic testifies to the power and validity of these basic values.

Two important insights from the classical rhetoricians may be adapted to guide workers in groups. The first is Aristotle's imperative that rhetoric should be used to defend the truth. In an age when speech often was used for attack and defense of individuals, his notion that rhetoric ought to be dedicated to truth was an ethical revolution. Thus, instead of personal aggrandizement or attack of one's enemies, Aristotle suggested that knowledge and skill be used to discover and defend truth. The second important guide from classical times is Quintilian's dictum that a praiseworthy speaker is a good person, as well as a skillful and effective technician. The orator, according to Quintilian, ought to be a good person speaking well.

The group participant should defend the truth and be a good person participating effectively and skillfully. The group itself should defend true statements of fact, praiseworthy value statements, and sound advice. It ought to be a good group when judged within the context of the larger society.

In terms of human relations, the biblical commands "Love thy neighbor" and "Do unto others as you would have them do unto you" remain basic general values of our culture against which to judge choices in a group context. The same insight was given a slightly different twist in Kant's ethical imperative that a choice is praiseworthy insofar as it ought to be generalized to all similar situations. One might ask of a given decision: Would it be a good thing if all others who faced a similar choice made the same decision?

Finally, and of utmost importance in any consideration of the ethics of communication, is the necessity of judging means in terms of a general framework of ethics, rather than in terms of the end to be reached. History furnishes many instances in which people have justified lying, cheating, aggression, hate, physical violence, and psychological destructiveness on the basis that the end was praiseworthy. One of the most frightening aspects of the propaganda and persuasion of the international communist movement under the leadership of Stalinist Russia and of the Nazi movement in Germany under the leadership of Hitler and Goebbels was the wholehearted and cynical adoption of the ethic that the triumph of that system justified the use of any means whatsoever. A similar argument is often an element in the tactic of the demagogue. Huey Long proclaimed that he was the official "thief" of Louisiana State University and on one occasion told a group of educators that the politician would always be with them and that politicians would always steal, but what the school officials ought to do was to get the politicians to steal for the schools. When Joseph McCarthy of Wisconsin was a senator in the 1950s, he often charged individuals with being Communist party members or sympathizers on tenuous evidence, and his tactics were justified on the basis that the elimination of the communist menace required such means. Gandhi's ethical insight, "Evil means, even for a good end, produce evil results," continues to serve as a sound touchstone for the student of small group communication.

① indiv + then group.
② group goals + tactics

SUMMARY

What distinguishes the ethical from other concerns is the act of choice. Participants of small task-oriented groups make ethical decisions largely about ends and means. Students face a two-step ethical problem in their work with small group communication. The group has an internal ethic, and the first point of tension is between the individual ethical system and the group code of ethics. The second major point of tension is between the goals and tactics of a particular group and those of other groups and the general welfare.

Everyone who takes part in a group is a conformist to some degree. Nonconformity within the group context is often disruptive and damaging to the group's social and task dimensions. Creativity is not necessarily related to conformity to group norms, since norms may be encouraging or discouraging to creativity.

Groups make demands on their members that reflect the pressure of the external environment. The tension between the good of the unit and the rights of the individual creates an ethical dilemma for all participants. Organizations often ask members to make a personal sacrifice for the good of all. Often the question of the individual versus the group is focused on the tension between authoritarianism and democracy. Still, authoritarian groups may be appropriate in certain contexts, and they may be healthy in terms of task efficiency and member satisfaction. Democratic groups may also be healthy and rewarding but they, too, can be unethical in terms of their goals and norms.

Small groups often develop norms that restrict communication. The ethical question is: To what extent should participants who are perceived as destructive to the group itself be given the opportunity for free expression? Every group requires some questioning of norms and procedures in order to deal with changing circumstances. Yet unlimited freedom for those who challenge the group may destroy it.

For ethical purposes, groups need to be viewed from the perspective of the larger society. Many groups have a dynamic that encourages them to expand, and such expansion is often at the cost of other units. Other groups are placed in direct competition with similar units or teams. Strong ethical problems are posed by conflict among groups. Group loyalty may even result in unethical actions against members of competing groups.

Often small groups develop goals and tactics that are counter to the general welfare. The general tendency of groups to restrict the free flow of information can easily be abused to protect wrongdoing. In addition, the mystique of experts erodes the freedom of expression. Experts often develop their own jargon and procedures to protect their work and use similar tactics to assure that their efforts go unchallenged.

An ethical code for practitioners in the United States should recognize the close connection between discussion and a democratic society. Included in such a code would be the belief that citizens can rule wisely if they are given the opportunity; that each individual has innate worth and dignity; and that groups, institutions, and political structures must take into account and uphold that dignity. The code is based on the assumption that each individual ought to have the opportunity to grow and develop his or her potential within the group. The code emphasizes that human beings are ethical; that they use symbols in connected discourse; and that they are capable of reason. Finally, the code suggests that the instinct for life and the capacity for love are more praiseworthy than violence, death, and the ability to hate.

Practitioners should not be manipulators; they should be responsible givers of advice and should care for the wholeness and mental health of other participants.

Teachers and consultants have a special responsibility in regard to ethics. Using groups for persuasive purposes or manipulating them for personal gain is unethical. Teachers and consultants should not pretend to have greater understanding than they possess or than the state of the theory and practice can support. They should not oversimplify the complexity of group communication in order to gain students or clients.

Two important insights from classical rhetoric have relevance for the practitioner of small group communication. Aristotle's imperative that rhetoric should be used to defend the truth and Quintilian's dictum that a praiseworthy speaker is a good person as well as an effective technician are still worth applying today.

The biblical commands "Love thy neighbor" and "Do unto others as you would have them do unto you" are still important. Kant's ethical imperative that a choice is praiseworthy insofar as it ought to be generalized to all similar situations also applies.

Finally, the dictum that the end does not justify the means is a useful guide for the student of small group communication.

the saying
authoritative pronouncement

Rules of Thumb

Practical Advice on How to Be a Good Group Member

Drawn from Chapter 11

- ☛ When you choose to communicate a value system, you are acting in an ethical or unethical manner.
- ☛ Do not praise or blame a person who is unable or incompetent to choose.
- ☛ In the task-oriented group, you often make ethical decisions about ends and means.
- ☛ When your personal goals and the goals of the group come in conflict, your choice has ethical implications.
- ☛ When the goals of your group are in conflict with those of larger segments of society, your choice has ethical implications.

☛ You must develop your personal code of working in, teaching about, or evaluating small group communication.

☛ You may find the group's goals (ends) praiseworthy but reject the tactics (means) the members use to reach the goals.

☛ Remember that a certain amount of conformity to norms is necessary for a cooperative group.

☛ Despite the importance of conformity, groups also need to have some successful deviance from norms in order to adapt to changing circumstances.

☛ An important ethical choice for you as a group member relates to conforming or not conforming, to supporting or not supporting the deviant.

☛ When you join a group, you should make the group's goals your own, and that means choosing the group's goals on occasion.

☛ In most task-oriented groups, each person has the right to make choices on the basis of as much information as possible.

☛ Small groups may restrict the free flow of communication, and you often have a responsibility to push for changes in such restrictive norms.

☛ Be careful not to share fantasies unthinkingly and absorb the unethical features of the group's culture.

☛ In most task-oriented groups, you should work for a culture in which each member can develop his or her full potential as a person of worth and dignity.

☛ When your group is in competition with other groups, it may develop tactics that are violent, rule-breaking, and out of tune with its goals.

☛ Do not allow your group to develop an "end justifies the means" rationale when it is in competition with other groups.

☛ Skill in public discussion continues to be a good way to further freedom of speech in society.

☛ The ideal model of small group communication is based on the value that all members can help run their groups.

☛ The ideal model of small group communication is based on the value that each member has an innate worth and dignity.

☛ The ideal model of small group communication is based on the value that members have the right and responsibility to make up their own minds.

☛ The ideal model of small group communication is based on the value that members ought to have the opportunity to develop their potential in the group.

☛ The ideal model of small group communication is based on the value that wisdom is prized above knowledge.

☛ If you deliberately choose to use your group or any of its members to attain your own ends, you are to be censored.

☞ You should choose to build cohesiveness, raise the status of others, volunteer to help the group, and release social tensions.

☞ When advising your group, be open about your sources and cooperate with the others in testing your statements.

☞ When you receive advice, you have a responsibility to test and evaluate it.

☞ Whatever the status arrangements of your group, you should communicate to reflect the values of trust, respect, and honesty.

☞ As you become more knowledgeable about group communication, you should develop a well-thought-out, professional code of ethics.

☞ As a professional, you should not use your knowledge to tease or to use groups for your own amusement.

☞ As a professional, you should work to develop better, healthier groups.

☞ As a professional, you should not pretend to have greater knowledge and understanding about groups than you possess.

☞ As a professional, you should not simplify the problems of working productively in groups in order to receive pay for your services.

QUESTIONS FOR STUDY

1. Do you believe that a good goal will justify almost any means that a group may use to achieve it effectively?

2. In what respect can it be said that a group member faces a two-step ethical problem?

3. What are some ways in which conformity to group norms can stifle individual integrity, freedom, and creativity?

4. To what extent do you think an individual should sacrifice personal desires for the good of a group?

5. Is a democratic group style preferable to an authoritarian one?

6. How important are free speech and freedom of dissent in the development of good groups and in individual fulfillment?

7. Is there a tension between specialization and the development of experts and the democratic value system?

8. What is your personal code of ethics for a group member?

9. Under what circumstances, if any, would you justify a member intentionally asserting a false statement of fact to be true to the other members of the group?

10. Do you agree that the use of group methods for persuasive intent without the knowledge of the group members is unethical? Why or why not?

EXERCISES

1. With a group of your classmates, develop a case study that poses a common ethical issue faced by a group member. Use the case study to stimulate a discussion of the issue in class.

2. With a group of your classmates, develop a role-playing exercise that places the role players in a situation of ethical tension. Use the role-playing exercise to stimulate discussion of the issue in class.

3. With a group of your classmates, set up a mock trial. Select members of the group to act as judge, prosecuting attorney, defense attorney, and defendant. Select one person to be a witness for the prosecution and another to be a witness for the defense. Accuse the defendant of some unethical group behavior. The prosecution makes the charge, the defense attorney answers, the prosecution examines the witness, the defense cross-examines. Then the defense presents its case, with each lawyer taking eight to ten minutes to sum up her or his side of the case. The rest of the class may serve as jurors.

REFERENCES AND SUGGESTED READINGS

For help with the original version of this chapter and for some of the basic ethical insights, I am indebted to the editorial advice and writings of the late Karl Wallace. See, for example:

Wallace, Karl R. "An Ethical Basis of Communication," *Communication Education*, 4 (1955), 1–9.

For group pressures regarding unethical conduct, see:

Janis, Irving L. *Victims of Groupthink.* 2nd ed. Boston: Houghton Mifflin, 1983.

The two Menninger books mentioned are:

Menninger, Karl. *Love Against Hate.* New York: Harcourt Brace, 1942.

Menninger, Karl. *Man Against Himself.* New York: Harcourt Brace, 1938.

For discussions of Long and McCarthy as demagogues, see:

Baskerville, Barnet. "Joe McCarthy: Brief-Case Demagogue," *Today's Speech*, 2 (1954), 8–15.

Bormann, Ernest G. "Huey Long: Analysis of a Demagogue," *Today's Speech*, 2 (1954), 16–19.

For other discussions of the ethics of communication, see:

Bormann, Ernest G. "Ethical Standards for Interpersonal/Small Group Communication," *Communication*, 6 (1981), 267–285.

Johannesen, Richard L. *Ethics in Human Communication.* 2nd ed. Prospect Heights, IL: Waveland, 1983.

Jaksa, James A., and Michael S. Pritchard. *Communication Ethics: Methods of Analysis.* Belmont, CA: Wadsworth, 1988.

Nilsen, Thomas R. *Ethics of Speech Communication.* Indianapolis: Bobbs-Merrill, 1966.

Appendix

The Minnesota Studies

The studies of the author and his associates in the Small Group Communication Seminar at the University of Minnesota furnish the empirical amplification as well as the key concepts of much of material in *Small Group Communication*. The Minnesota studies consist of the research of the author over the past 30 years and the work of his students as reported in seminar papers, master's theses, and doctoral dissertations. A number of the studies have been reported in convention papers and journal articles. This book, however, presents the only coherent and complete account of the research program in small groups over the years.

The seminar's basic approach has been the process analysis of the discourse of group meetings. The backbone of the program is the collection of exhaustive case studies of small task-oriented groups. Some of these were natural groups in the classroom and some were ongoing groups in nonclassroom settings. Many of the nonclass groups were parts of ongoing organizations. Since 1959, the author and his associates have made hundreds of case studies.

The controlling assumption of the Small Group Communication Seminar is that a group's role structure (including leadership), norms, and culture are to some extent idiosyncratic and that a given group's process can be completely explained only if one knows the history of the group. Thus, an intensive case study provides the best explanation of the group's communication.

To complement the group histories, the investigators have used a number of observational techniques to collect data. In the early years of the research program, investigators relied largely on rating blanks, attitude scales, and content analysis procedures. Among the techniques were the Bales system of content analysis of the interaction process, sociometric indexes, and whom-to-whom matrixes. As time went on, the investigators developed their own methods for studying groups. Among these were Berg's time-devoted-to-themes system, Fisher's content analysis procedure for studying decision emergence, and Putnam's comfort-with-procedural-order index.

Since 1970, a new line of investigation which is essentially a rhetorical analysis of the communication of the small group (sometimes called in organizational communication an *interpretative* approach) has provided another method for the study of group process and culture.

With the collection of more and more case studies, the investigators turned to syntheses of the findings, seeking patterns that would allow generalizations to cover small group communication in a larger context. Three major theoretical formulations were developed by the investigators. The first was the emergent model of how group communication processes resulted in the specialization of roles (including leadership) and how groups came to decisions. The second was the model of norm emergence. The third was the symbolic convergence theory of group acculturation.

The early case studies of natural groups in the classroom stressed intragroup communication. Since 1968, however, the author has taught an upper-division course in small group and organizational communication as a simulated organization called the Group Dynamics Institute. The author and his associates have made extensive studies of over 20 simulated organizations. Each of the simulations includes case studies of each of the component small groups. In addition to the basic divisions of the organization, the structure of the corporation includes management levels. These groups have been studied as well. The case studies of the organization include investigations of the informal communication networks, the communication flow and content from the management groups to the other divisions, the communication among all groups, and the nature and influence of symbolic convergence on the organization's emerging culture. For a publication reporting on aspects of one such organizational case study, see:

Bormann, Ernest G., Jerie McArthur Pratt, and Linda L. Putnam. "Power Authority and Sex: Male Response to Female Leadership," *Communication Monographs*, 45 (1978), 119–155.

Theses and Dissertations

The following theses have contributed to the Minnesota studies:

Baker, Debora. "A Rhetorical Analysis of Communication Style in Initial Meetings of Small Groups." Ph.D. dissertation, University of Minnesota, 1983.

Ball, Moya A. "A Descriptive and Interpretative Analysis of the Small Group Decision-Making Culture of the Kennedy and Johnson Administrations Regarding the Decisions Concerning the Expansion of the Vietnam War," Ph.D. dissertation, University of Minnesota, 1988.

Berg, David M. "A Descriptive Analysis of the Distribution and Duration of Themes Discussed by the Task-Oriented, Small Group." Ph.D. dissertation, University of Minnesota, 1963.

Faffler, Irene. "A Cross-Cultural Study of the Task-Oriented Small Group in the Middle East." Ph.D. dissertation, University of Minnesota, 1971.

Fisher, B. Aubrey. "Decision Emergence: A Process Model of Verbal Task Behavior for Decision-Making Groups." Ph.D. dissertation, University of Minnesota, 1968.

Forston, Robert. "The Decision-Making Process in the American Civil Jury: A Comparative Methodological Investigation." Ph.D. dissertation, University of Minnesota, 1968.

Gaetano, George. "The Joker and His Group." Master's thesis, University of Minnesota, 1979.

Geier, John. "A Descriptive Analysis of an Interaction Pattern Resulting in Leadership Emergence in Leaderless Group Discussion." Ph.D. dissertation, University of Minnesota, 1963.

Kee, Yong Tan. "Business Across Boundaries: A Laboratory Experiment to Analyze the Decision-Making Behavior of Groups from Different Cultures." Ph.D. dissertation, University of Minnesota, 1970.

Larson, Charles U. "Leadership Emergence and Attention Span: A Content Analysis of the Time Devoted to Themes in the Task-Oriented Small Group." Ph.D. dissertation, University of Minnesota, 1968.

Mortensen, Calvin David. "A Content Analysis of Leadership Communication in Small, Task-Oriented Discussion Groups." Master's thesis, University of Minnesota, 1964.

Olson, Clark. "A Case Study Analysis of Credentialing in Small Groups." Ph.D. dissertation, University of Minnesota, 1986.

Pratt, Jerie McArthur. "A Case Study Analysis of Male-Female Leadership Emergence in Small Groups." Ph.D. dissertation, University of Minnesota, 1979.

Putnam, Linda L. "Construction and Testing of a Questionnaire to Assess an Individual's Preference for Procedural Order in Small Groups." Ph.D. dissertation, University of Minnesota, 1976.

Runkel, Judy. "A Survey of the Small Group Techniques Used in College Beginning Speech Classes." Ph.D. dissertation, University of Minnesota, 1972.

Ryberg, Lillian A. "A Comparative Study of Small Group Discussion in the Native and Target Languages." Ph.D. dissertation, University of Minnesota, 1974.

Articles and Book Chapters

Some of the results of these studies have been published in the following articles:

Berg, David M. "A Descriptive Analysis of the Distribution and Duration of Themes Discussed by Task-Oriented Small Groups," *Communication Monographs*, 34 (1967), 172–175.

Berg, David M. "A Thematic Approach to the Analysis of the Task-Oriented Small Group," *Central States Speech Journal*, 18 (1967), 285–291.

Bormann, Ernest G. "The Paradox and Promise of Small Group Research," *Communication Monographs*, 37 (1970), 211–217.

Bormann, Ernest G. "The Paradox and Promise of Small Group Research Revisited," *Central States Speech Journal*, 31 (1980), 214–220.

Bormann, Ernest G. "The Symbolic Convergence Theory of Communication and the Creation, Raising, and Sustaining of Public Consciousness." In John Sisco, ed., *The Jensen Lectures: Contemporary Communication Studies*. Tampa: University of South Florida, 1983, pp. 71–90.

Bormann, Ernest G. "Symbolic Convergence: Organizational Communication and Culture." In Linda Putnam and Michael Pacanowsky, eds., *Communication and Organizations: An Interpretive Approach*. Beverly Hills, CA: Sage, 1983.

Bormann, Ernest G. "Symbolic Convergence Theory and Communication in Group Decision Making." In Randy Y. Hirokawa and Marshall Scott Poole, eds., *Communication and Group Decision Making.* Beverly Hills, CA: Sage, 1986, pp. 219–236.

Bormann, Ernest G, Jerie McArthur Pratt, and Linda L. Putnam. "Power Authority and Sex: Male Response to Female Leadership," *Communication Monographs.* 45 (1978), 119–155.

Chesebro, James W., John F. Cragan, and Patricia McCullough. "The Small Group Techniques of the Radical Revolutionary: A Synthesis of Consciousness Raising," *Communication Monographs,* 40 (1973), 136–146.

Fisher, B. Aubrey. "Decision Emergence: Phases in Group Decision Making," *Communication Monographs,* 37 (1970), 53–66.

Fisher, B. Aubrey. "The Process of Decision Modification in Small Discussion Groups," *Journal of Communication,* 20 (1970), 51–64.

Geier, John. "A Trait Approach in the Study of Leadership in Small Groups," *Journal of Communication,* 17 (1967), 316–323.

Larson, Charles U. "The Verbal Response of Groups to the Absence or Presence of Leadership," *Communication Monographs,* 38 (1971), 177–181.

Mortensen, Calvin. "Should the Discussion Group Have an Assigned Leader?" *Communication Education,* 15 (1966), 34–41.

Putnam, Linda L. "Preference for Procedural Order in Task-Oriented Small Groups, *Communication Monographs,* 46 (1979), 193–218.

Name Index

Subject Index